A TEXT BOOK OF

APPLIED THERMODYNAMICS

With Large Number of Multiple Choice Questions (MCQ's)

For

Semester - II

SECOND YEAR DEGREE COURSE IN MECHANICAL ENGINEERING AND
AUTOMOBILE ENGINEERING

As Per The New Revised Syllabus of University of Pune, June 2014

Dr. S. N. SAPALI
B.E. (Mech), M.E. (Mech) Ph.D. (IIT) Kharagpur
Professor & Head of Mechanical Engg. Dept.,
College of Engineering (COEP), Pune.
(An Autonomous Institute of Government of Maharashtra)

Dr. S. S. KORE
B.E. (Mech.), M.E. (Mech.), Ph.D.
Associate Professor,
Sinhgad Academy of Engineering,
Kondhwa (Bk.), Pune.

Prof. S. S. GHORPADE
B.E. (Mech.), M.E. (Mech.)
Assistant Professor,
Sinhgad Academy of Engineering
Kondhwa (Bk.), Pune.

NIRALI PRAKASHAN
Advancement of knowledge

APPLIED THERMODYNAMICS

First Edition : January 2014

© : Authors

ISBN 978-93-83750-94-8

The text of this publication, or any part thereof, should not be reproduced or transmitted in any form or stored in any computer storage system or device for distribution including photocopy, recording, taping or information retrieval system or reproduced on any disc, tape, perforated media or other information storage device etc., without the written permission of Authors with whom the rights are reserved. Breach of this condition is liable for legal action.

Every effort has been made to avoid errors or omissions in this publication. In spite of this, errors may have crept in. Any mistake, error or discrepancy so noted and shall be brought to our notice shall be taken care of in the next edition. It is notified that neither the publisher nor the authors or seller shall be responsible for any damage or loss of action to any one, of any kind, in any manner, therefrom.

Published By :
NIRALI PRAKASHAN
Abhyudaya Pragati, 1312, Shivaji Nagar,
Off J.M. Road, PUNE – 411005
Tel - (020) 25512336/37/39, Fax - (020) 25511379
Email : niralipune@pragationline.com

Printed By :
REPRO INDIA LTD.
50/2 T.T.C. MIDC,
Industrial Area, Mahape, Navi Mumbai
Tel - (022) 2778 2011

DISTRIBUTION CENTRES
PUNE

Nirali Prakashan
119, Budhwar Peth, Jogeshwari Mandir Lane
Pune 411002, Maharashtra
Tel : (020) 2445 2044, 66022708, Fax : (020) 2445 1538
Email : niralilocal@pragationline.com

Nirali Prakashan
S. No. 28/25, Dhyari,
Near Pari Company, Pune 411041
Tel : (020) 24690204Fax : (020) 24690316
Email : bookorder@pragationline.com

MUMBAI
Nirali Prakashan
385, S.V.P. Road, Rasdhara Co-op. Hsg. Society Ltd.,
Girgaum, Mumbai 400004, Maharashtra
Tel : (022) 2385 6339 / 2386 9976, Fax : (022) 2386 9976
Email : niralimumbai@pragationline.com

DISTRIBUTION BRANCHES

NAGPUR
Pratibha Book Distributors
Above Maratha Mandir, Shop No. 3, First Floor,
Rani Jhanshi Square, Sitabuldi, Nagpur 440012,
Maharashtra, Tel : (0712) 254 7129

BENGALURU
Pragati Book House
House No. 1, Sanjeevappa Lane, Avenue Road Cross,
Opp. Rice Church, Bengaluru – 560002.
Tel : (080) 64513344, 64513355,
Mob : 9880582331, 9845021552
Email:bharatsavla@yahoo.com

JALGAON
Nirali Prakashan
34, V. V. Golani Market, Navi Peth, Jalgaon 425001,
Maharashtra, Tel : (0257) 222 0395
Mob : 94234 91860

KOLHAPUR
Nirali Prakashan
New Mahadvar Road,
Kedar Plaza, 1st Floor Opp. IDBI Bank
Kolhapur 416 012, Maharashtra. Mob : 9850046155

CHENNAI
Pragati Books
9/1, Montieth Road, Behind Taas Mahal, Egmore,
Chennai 600008 Tamil Nadu, Tel : (044) 6518 3535,
Mob : 94440 01782 / 98450 21552 / 98805 82331, Email : bharatsavla@yahoo.com

---

RETAIL OUTLETS
PUNE

Pragati Book Centre
157, Budhwar Peth, Opp. Ratan Talkies,
Pune 411002, Maharashtra
Tel : (020) 2445 8887 / 6602 2707, Fax : (020) 2445 8887

Pragati Book Centre
Amber Chamber, 28/A, Budhwar Peth,
Appa Balwant Chowk, Pune : 411002, Maharashtra,
Tel : (020) 20240335 / 66281669
Email : pbcpune@pragationline.com

Pragati Book Centre
676/B, Budhwar Peth, Opp. Jogeshwari Mandir,
Pune 411002, Maharashtra
Tel : (020) 6601 7784 / 6602 0855

PBC Book Sellers & Stationers
152, Budhwar Peth, Pune 411002, Maharashtra
Tel : (020) 2445 2254 / 6609 2463

MUMBAI
Pragati Book Corner
Indira Niwas, 111 - A, Bhavani Shankar Road, Dadar (W), Mumbai 400028, Maharashtra
Tel : (022) 2422 3526 / 6662 5254, Email : pbcmumbai@pragationline.com

---

www.pragationline.com   info@pragationline.com

Preface...

It gives us an immense pleasure to present this Text Book of **"Applied Thermodynamics"** for under graduate students. Thermodynamics has been a part of the curricula of many disciplines like Mechanical, Automobile, and Chemical Engineering students. The object of this book is to present the subject matter in the most precise, compact and in a lucid manner.

As per the policy of University of Pune, Engineering Syllabi is revised every five years. Last revision was in the year 2009. New revision is coming little earlier, as university has introduced **online system of examination** from year 2012.

As per the new system, the **online examination** (separate Phase-I and Phase-II) will be conduced based on first, second and third and fourth units. The **Online examinations** will have objective types of questions with multiple choices. End semester examination will be based on all the six units and that will be conducted in traditional way.

Authors have tried to introduce the subject to the average students, with a large number of solved examples. The subject matter has been developed in a logical and coherent manner with neat illustrations along with a fairly large number of solved examples and exercises. Answers to many unsolved numerical problems are also given.

The main objectives of this text are :

- **To cover the basic principles of thermodynamics.**
- **To develop a very good understanding of the subject matter.**
- **To give practice to solve the numerical examples in thermodynamics.**
- **To give practice to solve the multiple choice questions in the subject.**

We take an opportunity to thank Nirali Prakashan Pune, for publishing this book. We are also thankful to the staff of "Nirali Prakashan Pune" and all others for the extra efforts they have made to make this book as good as it is. We are very much thankful to Shri. Dineshbhai Furia and Shri. Jignesh Furia of M/s Nirali Prakashan, Pune for giving a platform to provide good inputs the students community. We are grateful to Mr. Mallikarjun Munde, a Senior Manager for his endless efforts to make this book as best as it can be. We are also thankful to Mr. Malik Shaikh and Mrs. Anagha Kaware for their co-operation throughout the work.

Although every care has been taken to check mistakes, and errors, yet it is difficult to claim perfection. Any errors, mistakes and suggestions for the improvement of this book, brought to our notice will be thankfully acknowledged and incorporated in the next edition.

January 2014   **Authors**
Pune.

Syllabus ...

Unit I: Basics of IC Engines — 5 Hrs.
Heat Engine, IC and EC Engines, I.C. Engine Construction - Components and Materials, Engine Nomenclature, Valve Timing Diagram, Intake and Exhaust System, Engine Classification, Applications.

Fuel Air Cycle and Actual Cycle: — 5 Hrs.
Fuel Air Cycle, Assumptions, Comparison with Air Standard Cycle, Effect of Variables on Performance, Actual Cycle and Various Losses.

Unit II: SI Engines — 5 Hrs.
Theory of Carburetion, Types of Carburetors, Electronic Fuel Injection System, Combustion in Spark Ignition Engines, Stages of Combustion, Flame Propagation, Rate of Pressure Rise, Abnormal Combustion, Phenomenon of Detonation in SI engines, Effect of Engines Variables on Detonation. Combustion Chambers, Rating of Fuels in SI Engines, Additives.

Unit III: CI Engines — 5 Hrs.
Fuel Supply System, Types of Fuel Pump, Injector and Distribution System, Combustion in Compression Ignition Engines, Stages of Combustion, Factors Affecting Combustion, Phenomenon of Knocking in CI Engine. Effect of Knocking, Methods of Knock Control, Types of Combustion Chambers, Rating of Fuels in CI Engines, Dopes and Additives, Comparison of Knocking in SI and CI engines.

Unit IV: Testing of IC Engines — 5 Hrs.
Objective of Testing, Various Performance Parameters for I.C. Engine - Indicated Power, Brake Power, Friction Power, SFC, AF Ratio, etc. Methods to Determine Various Performance Parameters, Characteristic Curves, Heat Balance Sheet.

Supercharging: — 2 Hrs.
Supercharging and Turbo-charging Methods and their Limitations.

Unit V: I.C. Engine Systems — 6 Hrs.
Cooling System, Lubrication System, Ignition System, Governing System, Starting System.

I.C. Engine Emissions and Control — 4 Hrs.
Air Pollution due to IC Engine and its effect, Emissions from Petrol/Gas and Diesel Engines, Sources of Emissions, Euro Norms, Bharat Stage Norms, Emission Control Methods for SI and CI Engines.

Unit VI: Positive Displacement Compressors (Reciprocating and Rotary) — 10 Hrs.
Reciprocating Compressor - Single Stage Compressor - Computation of Work Done, Isothermal Efficiency, Effect of Clearance Volume, Volumetric Efficiency, Free Air Delivery, Theoretical and Actual Indicator Diagram, Multistaging of Compressor, Computation of Work Done, Volumetric Efficiency, Conditions for Maximum Efficiency, Inter-cooling and After-cooling, Capacity Control of Compressors.

Rotary Compressor - Introduction, Vane Compressors, Roots Blowers, Screw Compressor.

***

Contents ...

(A) HEAT ENGINES

1. Basics of IC Engines and Fuel Air Cycles and Actual Cycles
1.1 − 1.62

- 1.1 Heat Engines : Introduction 1.1
- 1.2 IC and EC Engines 1.1
- 1.3 IC Engine Construction, Components and Materials 1.2
  - 1.3.1 Cylinder and Cylinder Block 1.3
  - 1.3.2 Crank Case 1.3
  - 1.3.3 Cylinder Head 1.3
  - 1.3.4 Piston 1.3
  - 1.3.5 Piston Rings 1.4
  - 1.3.6 Connecting Rod 1.4
  - 1.3.7 Wrist Pin 1.4
  - 1.3.8 Crankshaft 1.4
  - 1.3.9 Camshaft and Cam 1.4
  - 1.3.10 Inlet and Exhaust Valves 1.4
  - 1.3.11 Inlet Manifold 1.5
  - 1.3.12 Exhaust Manifold 1.5
  - 1.3.13 Spark Plug 1.5
  - 1.3.14 Fuel Injector 1.5
- 1.4 Engine Nomenclature 1.5
  - 1.4.1 Cylinder Bore (d) 1.5
  - 1.4.2 Piston Area (A) 1.5
  - 1.4.3 Stroke (L) 1.6
  - 1.4.4 Dead Centre 1.6
  - 1.4.5 Top Dead Centre (TDC) 1.6
  - 1.4.6 Bottom Dead Centre 1.6
  - 1.4.7 Displacement or Swept Volume (V) 1.6
  - 1.4.8 Clearance Volume (V_c) 1.6
  - 1.4.9 Compression Ratio (r) 1.6
  - 1.4.10 Combustion Chamber 1.6
- 1.5 Engine Classification 1.7
  - 1.5.1 Engine Classification by Cylinder Arrangement 1.7
  - 1.5.2 SI Engine Classification By Valve Location 1.8
- 1.6 The Working Principle of IC Engines 1.9
  - 1.6.1 Four Stroke Spark Ignition Engine 1.9
  - 1.6.2 Four Stroke Compression Ignition (CI) Engine 1.11
  - 1.6.3 Comparison of SI and CI Engines 1.12
  - 1.6.4 Two Stroke Engine 1.12
  - 1.6.5 Comparison of Four-stroke and Two-stroke Engines 1.14
- 1.7 Actual Valve Timing of Four-Stroke Petrol Engine 1.15
- 1.8 Applications of IC Engines 1.18

(B) ANALYSIS OF ENGINE CYCLES

1.9 Introduction	1.19
1.10 Ideal or Air Standard Cycle	1.20
1.11 Limitations of Air Standard Cycles	1.21
1.12 Fuel-Air Cycle	1.21
1.13 Uses of Fuel-Air Cycle	1.22
1.14 Variation of Specific Heats	1.22
1.14.1 Loss Due to Variation of Specific Heat	1.23
1.15 Dissociation or Chemical Equilibrium Loss	1.25
1.16 Comparison of P-V Diagram of Air Standard and Fuel-Air Cycle for the SI Engine	1.28
1.16.1 Thermal Efficiency and Fuel Consumption	1.29
1.17 Effect of Variables	1.30
1.17.1 Compression Ratio	1.30
1.17.2 Effect of Fuel-Air Ratio	1.32
1.18 Properties of Constant Volume (Otto) Fuel-Air Cycle	1.35
1.19 Dual Combustion or Limited-Pressure Fuel-Air Cycle	1.36
1.20 Actual Cycles	1.36
1.21 Losses in Actual Engine Operation (Otto Cycle)	1.38
1.21.1 Time Losses	1.38
1.21.2 Incomplete Combustion Loss	1.41
1.21.3 Direct Heat Loss	1.42
1.21.4 Exhaust Blow-down Loss	1.43
1.21.5 Pumping Losses	1.44
1.21.6 Rubbing Friction Loss	1.44
1.22 Comparison of Actual and Fuel-Air Cycles in Diesel Engines	1.45
• Multiple Choice Questions (MCQ's)	1.46
• Exercise	1.61

2. Spark Ignition (SI) Engines   2.1 – 2.42

2.1 Theory of Carburetion	2.1
2.2 Factors Effecting Carburettors	2.2
2.3 Types of Air-Fuel Mixtures	2.2
2.4 Mixture Requirements	2.2
2.4.1 For Power and Economy	2.2
2.4.2 For Automotive Engines at Different Working Conditions	2.3
2.5 Carburettor Types	2.4
2.6 A Simple Carburettor	2.5
2.6.1 Limitations of Simple Carburettor	2.6
2.7 Solex Carburettor (modern carburettor)	2.6
2.8 Drawbacks of Carburettor	2.8
2.9 Gasoline Injection (GI) System	2.8
2.9.1 Classification	2.8

2.10 Multipoint Fuel Injection (MPFI) System	2.10
2.10.1 D-MPFI Systems	2.10
2.10.2 L-MPFI System	2.10
2.11 Electronic Fuel Injection Systems (EFI)	2.11
2.11.1 Advantages of EFI Systems	2.11
2.11.2 Disadvantages of EFI System	2.11
2.12 Combustion in Spark Ignition Engines	2.11
2.13 Combustion Phenomenon in S.I Engines	2.12
2.13.1 Ignition Delay/Ignition Lag	2.13
2.13.2 Second Phase (Spreading of Flame)	2.13
2.13.3 After Burning	2.14
2.14 Factor's Influencing Flame Speed	2.14
2.14.1 Turbulence	2.14
2.14.2 Fuel-Air Ratio	2.14
2.14.3 Intake Temperature and Pressure	2.14
2.14.4 Engine Load	2.15
2.14.5 Engine Size	2.15
2.14.6 Engine Speed	2.15
2.14.7 Compression Ratio	2.15
2.14.8 Residual Gases	2.15
2.15 Abnormal Combustion in S.I Engine	2.15
2.15.1 Pre Ignition	2.15
2.15.2 Detonation	2.16
2.16 Factors Affecting Detonation/Knocking	2.18
2.16.1 Temperature Factors	2.18
2.16.2 Time Factor	2.18
2.16.3 Density Factor	2.19
2.16.4 Composition Factor	2.19
2.17 Methods to Reduce Knocking	2.19
2.18 Rating of Fuels in S.I. Engine	2.20
2.18.1 Dopes and Additives for SI Engine and Performance Number	2.21
2.19 Combustion Chamber	2.22
2.20 Evolution of Chamber	2.23
2.21 Combustion Chambers in S.I. Engines	2.24
2.22 Different Types of Combustion Chambers	2.24
2.22.1 'L'-head Combustion Chamber	2.24
2.22.2 'T'-head Combustion Chamber	2.25
2.22.3 'I'-head Overhead Value Combustion Chamber	2.25
2.22.4 'F'-Head Combustion Chamber	2.27
2.22.5 Ricardo's Turbulent Combustion Chamber	2.27
• Multiple Choice Questions (MCQ's)	2.28
• Exercise	2.41

3. Compression Ignition (C.I.) Engines   3.1 – 3.30

    3.1   Fuel Supply System for CI Engines   3.1
    3.2   Types of Fuel Injection Systems   3.2
    3.3   Fuel Pump and Injector   3.4
    3.4   Types of Fuel Injectors   3.6
    3.5   Types of Nozzles   3.7
    3.6   Electronic Fuel Injection (EFI) System   3.8
    3.7   Multipoint Fuel Injection System (MPFI)   3.8
    3.8   Quantity of Fuel and Size of Nozzle Orifice   3.9

Combustion in C.I. Engine

    3.9   Introduction   3.10
    3.10   Combustion in C.I. Engine   3.11
    3.11   Stages of Combustion   3.12
    3.12   Variables Affecting Delay Period   3.13
    3.13   Knock in C.I. Engine   3.14
    3.14   Comparison of Diesel Knock and Detonation   3.15
    3.15   Factors Affecting Knock in C.I. Engines   3.15
    3.16   Cetane Rating of C.I. Engine Fuels   3.16
    3.17   Combustion Chambers in Diesel Engine   3.16
    3.18   Types of Diesel Combustion Systems   3.17
    3.19   Indirect Injection System (Divided Chamber Injection System)   3.18
    3.20   Dopes and Additives   3.19
    •   Multiple Choice Questions (MCQ's)   3.19
    •   Exercise   3.30

4. Testing of I.C. Engines and Supercharging   4.1 – 4.70

[A] TESTING AND PERFORMANCE

    4.1   Introduction   4.1
    4.2   Performance Parameter   4.1
    4.3   Basic Measurements   4.6
    4.4   Measurement of Speed   4.6
    4.5   Fuel Consumption Measurement   4.7
    4.6   Measurement of Air Consumption   4.7
    4.7   Measurement of Exhaust Smoke   4.7
    4.8   Measurement of Exhaust Emission   4.8
        4.8.1   Flame Ionization Detector (FID)   4.8
        4.8.2   Spectroscopic Analyzers   4.9
        4.8.3   Gas Chromatography   4.10
    4.9   Measurement of Brake Power   4.10
        4.9.1   Absorption Dynamometers   4.11
        4.9.2   Fan Dynamometer   4.14
        4.9.3   Transmission Dynamometers   4.15

4.10	Measurement of Friction Horse Power	4.15
4.11	Blowby Loss	4.19
4.12	Performance of SI Engines	4.19
4.13	Performance of CI Engines	4.23

(B) SUPERCHARGING

4.14	Introduction	4.50
4.15	Objects of Supercharging	4.50
4.16	Thermodynamic Cycle with Supercharging	4.51
4.17	Supercharging Power	4.52
4.18	Supercharging of Spark Ignition Engines	4.52
4.19	Supercharging of CI Engines	4.53
4.20	Effect of Supercharging on Performance of the Engine	4.54
	4.20.1 Power Output	4.54
	4.20.2 Mechanical Efficiency	4.55
	4.20.3 Fuel Consumption	4.55
4.21	Supercharging Limits	4.56
	4.21.1 Supercharging Limits of SI Engines	4.56
4.22	Supercharging Limits of CI Engines	4.57
4.23	Modification of an Engine for Supercharging	4.58
4.24	Methods of Supercharging	4.58
4.25	Superchargers	4.60
4.26	Turbochargers	4.61
•	Multiple Choice Questions (MCQ's)	4.62
•	Exercise	4.69

5. IC Engine Systems and IC Engine Emissions and Control

5.1 – 5.70

(A) IGNITION SYSTEMS OF S.I. ENGINE

5.1	Introduction	5.1
5.2	Ignition System Types	5.2
	5.2.1 Battery or Coil Ignition System	5.2
	5.2.2 Magneto Ignition System	5.3
5.3	Comparison between Battery and Magneto Ignition System	5.4
5.4	Drawbacks (Disadvantages) Of Conventional Ignition Systems	5.5
5.5	Advantages of Electronic Ignition System	5.5
5.6	Types of Electronic Ignition System	5.5
	5.6.1 Capacitance Discharge Ignition System	5.6
	5.6.2 Transistorised Assisted Contact (TAC) Ignition System	5.6
	5.6.3 Piezo-Electric Ignition System	5.7
	5.6.4 The Texaco Ignition System	5.7
5.7	Firing Order	5.7

(B) LUBRICATION SYSTEMS IN IC ENGINES

5.8	Introduction	5.9
5.9	Purpose and Functions of Lubrication	5.9
5.10	Properties of Good Lubricating Oil	5.9
5.11	Lubricating System	5.10
	5.11.1 Petrol or Mist System of Lubrication	5.10
	5.11.2 Wet Sump System	5.11
	5.11.3 Dry Sump System	5.12
5.12	Important Parts of Lubrication System	5.13

(C) STARTING SYSTEM

5.13	Introduction	5.16
5.14	Types of Starter Motors	5.17
5.15	Types of Starter Drive Mechanisms	5.17
5.16	Starting Drive – Standard Bendix Drive having Torsional Spring	5.17

(D) COOLING SYSTEMS IN IC ENGINE

5.17	Introduction	5.18
5.18	Methods of Cooling	5.18
5.19	Water Cooling System	5.19
5.20	Components of Water Cooling System	5.20
5.21	Advantages of Water Cooling System	5.23

(E) GOVERNING SYSTEM IN IC ENGINES

5.22	Introduction	5.24
5.23	Methods of Governing	5.24
5.24	Important Types of Centrifugal Governors used with the Engines	5.27
5.25	Application of Governors	5.29

(F) INTAKE AND EXHAUST SYSTEMS

5.26	Introduction	5.29
5.27	Various Parts and Functions of Intake System	5.31
5.28	Various Parts and Their Functions of Exhaust System	5.31

(G) DRIVE TRAIN (CAM SHAFT, VALVES ETC.)

5.29	Introduction	5.32

(H) EMISSIONS AND POLLUTION CONTROL

5.30	Introduction	5.35
5.31	Air Pollution	5.35
5.32	Sources of S.I. Engine Emissions	5.36
	5.32.1 Evaporate Emissions	5.37
	5.32.2 Crankcase Breather or Crankcase Emissions	5.37
	5.33.3 Exhaust Pipe Emissions	5.38

5.33	S.I. Engine Emissions	5.38
	5.33.1 Carbon Monoxide	5.38
	5.33.2 Unburned Hydrocarbons (HC)	5.39
	5.33.3 Oxides of Nitrogen	5.41
	5.33.4 Particulate Matter and Partial Oxidation Products	5.42
5.34	C.I. Engine Emissions	5.43
	5.34.1 Hydrocarbon Emissions	5.43
	5.34.2 Particulates	5.44
	5.34.3 Odour	5.44
5.35	Effect of Different Pollutants on Human Life	5.44
5.36	Diesel Smoke and Control	5.45
5.37	Exhaust Gas Treatment/Emission Control	5.46
	5.37.1 Thermal Reactor	5.46
	5.37.2 Catalytic Converters	5.47
	5.37.3 Oxidation Catalyst	5.48
	5.37.4 Particulate Traps	5.49
5.38	Exhaust Emission Standards and Norms	5.49
	5.38.1 Euro Norms	5.50
	5.38.2 Emission Norms in India	5.50
	5.38.3 Emissions from Tracks and Buses	5.51
	5.38.4 Emissions from Light Duty Diesel Vehicles	5.51
5.39	Light Duty Gasoline Vehicles	5.52
5.40	Three and Two-wheel vehicles	5.53
5.41	Control of Engine Emissions	5.54
	5.41.1 Engine Components and Fuel Modifications	5.55
	5.41.2 Evaporative Emission Control	5.55
5.42	Methods to control Oxides of Nitrogen	5.55
5.43	Hybrid Vehicles	5.57
	5.43.1 Hybrid Electric-Vehicle (HEVs)	5.58
	5.43.2 Components of the Hybrid Electric Vehicles	5.58
	5.43.3 Types of Configuration	5.59
	5.43.4 Benefits of Hybrid Vehicle	5.60
	5.43.5 The Future of Hybrid Vehicles	5.60
5.44	Engine Requirements for Automotive Applications	5.60
5.45	Selection of Engine for Automotive Applications	5.61
5.46	Specifications of Automotive Engines	5.63
5.47	Zero Emission Vehicles	5.64
5.48	Alternative Fuels for I.C. Engines	5.66
5.49	Definition of Carbon Credits	5.66
5.50	Global Warming Potential (GWP)	5.66
•	Exercise	5.69

6. Positive Displacement Compressor 6.1 – 6.50

A. RECIPROCATING COMPRESSORS

6.1	Introduction	6.1
6.2	Classification of Air Compressors	6.2
6.3	Difference between Reciprocating and Rotary Compressors	6.2
6.4	Difference between Compressor and Blower	6.3
6.5	Single-Stage Reciprocating Compressor	6.3
	6.5.1 Working of Single-stage Reciprocating Compressor	6.3
	6.5.2 Computation of Work Done (Neglecting Clearance)	6.5
6.6	Isothermal Efficiency	6.6
	6.6.1 Methods for Improving Isothermal Efficiency	6.7
6.7	Single-Stage Compressors with Clearance Volume	6.8
6.8	Volumetric Efficiency	6.9
6.9	Power of a Single-Stage Compressor	6.12
6.10	Mechanical Efficiency	6.12
6.11	Mean Effective Pressure	6.12
6.12	Free Air Delivery	6.13
6.13	Actual p-V (Indicator) Diagram for Single-Stage Compressor	6.13
6.14	Need of Multistage Compression	6.22
6.15	Two-Stage Reciprocating Air Compressor with Intercooler	6.23
6.16	Condition for Minimum Work of Compression or Maximum Efficiency (Perfect Intercooling)	6.25
	6.16.1 Work Done	6.26
6.17	Heat Rejected per kg of Air	6.27
6.18	Capacity Control of Compressors	6.28
6.19	Difference between Intercooler and Aftercooler	6.29
6.20	Theoretical and Actual p-V (Indicator) Diagram for Two-Stage Compressors	6.30
6.21	Cylinder Dimensions of Multistage Compressors for Perfect Intercooling	6.30
6.22	Advantages of Multistage Compressors	6.30
6.23	Roots Blower Compressors	6.41
6.24	Vane Blower Compressors	6.43
6.25	Rotary Screw Compressors	6.44
•	Exercise	6.48

***

UNIT I

BASICS OF IC ENGINES AND FUEL AIR CYCLES AND ACTUAL CYCLES

(A) HEAT ENGINES

1.1 HEAT ENGINES: INTRODUCTION

An engine is an energy conversion device which transforms one form energy into another form. While a heat engine is a device which transforms the chemical energy of fuel into thermal energy and uses this energy to produce mechanical work. Heat engines are divided into two broad classes:
- (a) External combustion engines, and
- (b) Internal combustion engines.

1.2 IC AND EC ENGINES

In an external combustion engine the products of combustion of air and fuel transfer heat to a second fluid which is the working fluid of the cycle. For example, in the steam turbine plant where the heat of combustion is employed to generate steam which is used in a turbine. Another example of an external combustion engine is closed cycle gas turbine plant in which heat of combustion in an external furnace is transferred to gas, usually air, which is used in a turbine. Stirling engine is also an external combustion engine.

In an internal combustion engine the products of combustion are directly the motive fluid. Petrol, gas, and diesel engines, Wankel engine, and open cycle gas turbines are examples of internal combustion engines.

Comparison of IC and EC Engines:

Table 1.1: Comparison of IC and EC Engines

IC Engines	EC Engines
1. Working fluid takes part in combustion process.	1. Working fluid does not take part in combustion process.
2. Heat of combustion is transferred to working fluid density.	2. Heat of combustion is transferred to a second fluid which acts as working fluid.
3. Move power to weight ratio.	3. Less power to weight ratio.
4. Absence of auxiliary apparatus like boiler or condenser.	4. Auxiliary apparatus are required.

IC Engines	EC Engines
5. Higher overall efficiency (upto 35 to 40%).	5. Overall efficiency is less (upto 20%).
6. Heat rejection is easier.	6. Separate device for heat rejection is must.
7. These are not self-starting.	7. These are self-starting.
8. Requires high starting torque.	8. Do not require starting torque.
9. Requires high grade fuels only.	9. Can use solid, liquid or gaseous fuels.
10. Application: Transport vehicles.	10. Application: Closed cycle, Gas turbine plant, steam power plant.

1.3 IC ENGINE CONSTRUCTION, COMPONENTS AND MATERIALS

(W-12)

A cross-section of a single cylinder spark-ignition engine with side valves is shown in **Fig. 1.1**. The major components of the engine and their functions are described below.

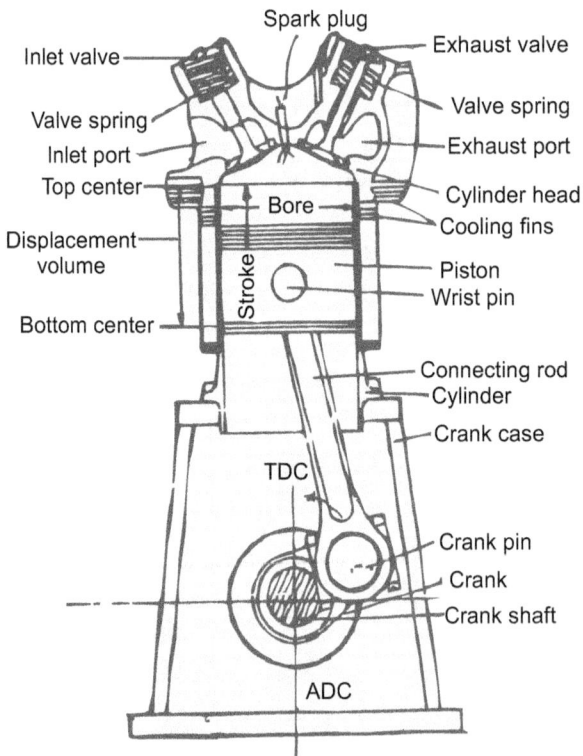

Fig. 1.1: Cross-section of a Spark Ignition Engine

1.3.1 Cylinder and Cylinder Block

- It forms basic framework of an IC engine.
- In the cylindrical vessel or space piston reciprocates.
- The working fluid undergoes various process inside cylinder.
- The cylinder is supported in cylinder block.
- The cylinder block carries lubrication oil to various components through drilled passages called oil galleries. These are made by casting. Diesel engines require heavier blocks than petrol engine.
  Material: Grey cast iron and aluminium alloys.
  Material requirements: Good casting properties, good thermal conductivity, corrosion resistance, creep resistance.

1.3.2 Crank Case

- It is casted separately or integral with cylinder block.
- It supports main journals and bearings of crankshaft and maintains alignment of their axes.
  Material: Cast iron and aluminium alloys.
  Material requirement: Rigidity.

1.3.3 Cylinder Head

- It is attached to deck that is top surface of cylinder block.
- It contains valves, seats, valve guides, potts, coolent jackets and has provision for spark plug or injectors.
- It forms combustion chamber above the cylinder.
  Material: Cast iron, aluminium alloy, and copper alloy for racing cars.
  Material requirement: High thermal conductivity.

1.3.4 Piston

- This cylindrical component fits perfectly into cylinder providing a gas tight space.
- It forms moving boundary of the combustion chamber.
- It transmits gas force to the crankshaft.
  Material: Cast iron was used in earlier days.
  Now-a-day, aluminium alloy containing silicon is used.
  Material requirement: Good wearing quality, light weight as to get less inertia, high thermal conductivity, high creep resistance.

1.3.5 Piston Rings

- They fit in the grooves which are cut towards the top of the piston.
- They prevent leakage of high pressure gases from combustion chamber into the crankcase.
- They also provide better heat dissipation and less cylinder wear.
  Materials: Fine grained alloy cast iron containing manganese and silicon.
  Material requirement: Wear resistance, thermal conductivity.
  For top ring chromium plated rings are used as they are subjected to high temperature and corrosive contact of combustion gases.

1.3.6 Connecting Rod

- It connects piston crankshaft.
- It transmits gas forces to the crankshaft moves linearly. When its small end connected to reciprocates piston big end connected to crankshaft moves in circular path.
  Materials: Steel, duralumin, malleable cast iron.
  Material requirement: High straight, light weight, high fatigue strength.

1.3.7 Wrist Pin

- It is also called as gudgeon pin or piston pin.
- It forms link between small end of connected rod and piston.
  Material: Low carbon case hardened steel.
  Material requirement: High hardness, fine surface finish.

1.3.8 Crankshaft

- It is the output shaft of the engine.
- The balance weights are provided for balancing of static and dynamic loads.
  Material: Chromium-Vanadium or Cr-Mo steels.
  Material requirement: High strength, toughness, hardness and fatigue strength.

1.3.9 Camshaft and Cam

- They control opening and closing of valves.
- Their associated parts include push rods, rocker arms, valve springs and trappets.
- Camshaft is driven by crankshaft.

1.3.10 Inlet and Exhaust Valves

- These valves are generally mushroom shaped type.
- These are provided either on cylinder head or on the side of cylinder.

1.3.11 Inlet Manifold
- It carries air-fuel mixture from carburetor to the cylinders.
- It is nothing but a pipe.

1.3.12 Exhaust Manifold
- It is a pipe which connects exhaust system to the exhaust valves of the engine.

1.3.13 Spark Plug
- It is used to initiate the combustion process in SI engines.
- It is normally located in the cylinder head.

1.3.14 Fuel Injector
- It is used in CI engines to inject the fuel into the cylinder.

1.4 ENGINE NOMENCLATURE

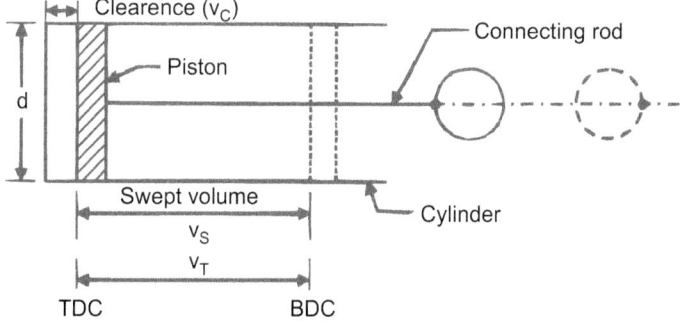

Fig. 1.2: Nomenclature

1.4.1 Cylinder Bore (d)
The inner diameter of the working cylinder is called as bore. It is denoted as d and expressed in mm. **Refer Fig. 1.2**.

1.4.2 Piston Area (A)
The area of a circle of diameter equal to the cylinder bore is called as piston area and is expressed in mm^2.

1.4.3 Stroke (L)

The nominal distance through which a piston moves from TDC (top dead centre) position to BDC (bottom dead centre) position is called as stroke. It is designated by the letter L and usually expressed in mm.

1.4.4 Dead Centre

The position of the working piston and the moving parts that are mechanically connected to it, at the moment when the direction of the piston is reversed at either end of the stroke is called the dead centre. There are two dead centres, namely TDC and BDC.

1.4.5 Top Dead Centre (TDC)

The position of the piston farthest from the crankshaft is called as TDC.

1.4.6 Bottom Dead Centre

The position of the piston nearest to the crankshaft is called as TDC.

1.4.7 Displacement or Swept Volume (V)

The volume swept by the working piston while travelling from one dead centre to the other is called the displacement volume. It is expressed in cubic centimeter (cc) and is given by,

$$V_s = A \times L = \frac{\pi}{4} d^2 L \qquad \ldots (1.1)$$

1.4.8 Clearance Volume (V_C)

The nominal volume of the combustion chamber above the piston when it is at the top dead centre is the clearance volume.

1.4.9 Compression Ratio (r)

It is the ratio of the total cylinder volume when the piston is at BDC position, V_T, to the clearance volume, V_C.

$$r = \frac{V_T}{V_C} = \frac{V_C + V_S}{V_C} = 1 + \frac{V_S}{V_C} \qquad \ldots (1.2)$$

1.4.10 Combustion Chamber

- It is the space enclosed in the upper part of engine cylinder by cylinder head, cylinder walls and piston top.
- This space is considered as thermodynamic system for engine analysis. In this system, cylinder head and walls provide fixed boundary whereas piston top provides moving boundary.

1.5 ENGINE CLASSIFICATION

The general classification of heat engines is given in Fig. 1.3.

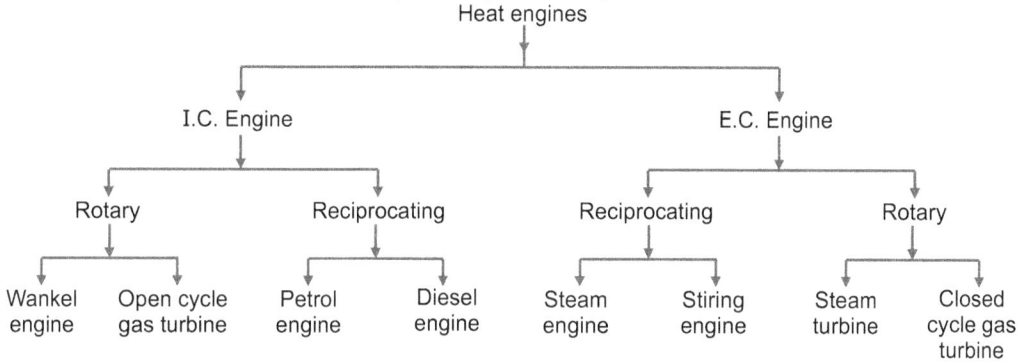

Fig. 1.3: Classification of Heat Engines

The IC engines are further classified according to cylinder arrangement, by valve location. The details is are as given in the following text.

1.5.1 Engine Classification by Cylinder Arrangement

One of the most common methods of classifying the reciprocating engines is by cylinder arrangements. A number of cylinder arrangements popular with designers are described below. Two terms used in connection with cylinder arrangements must first be defined.

Cylinder Row: An arrangement of cylinders in which the centre-line of the crankshaft journals is perpendicular to the plane containing the centre lines of the engine cylinders.

Cylinder Bank: An arrangement of cylinders in which the centre-line of the crankshaft journals so parallel to the plane containing the centre lines of the engine cylinders.

Basic Type of Cylinder Arrangements:
    (a) **In-line Engines:** In-line engine is an engine with one cylinder bank, i.e. all cylinders are arranged linearly, and transmit power to a single crankshaft. This type is very popular with automobiles where 4 and 6 cylinder in line engines is quite common.
    (b) **'V' Engines:** An engine with two cylinder banks (i.e., two in-line engines) inclined at an angle to each other and with one crankshaft. Most of the bigger automobiles use the 8-cylinder V-engine (4 cylinder in-line on each side of the V).
    (c) **Opposed Cylinder Engine:** An engine with two cylinder banks located in the same plane on opposite sides of the crankshaft. It can be visualized as two '*in-line*' arrangements 180 degree apart. It is inherently well-balanced and has the advantages of a single crankshaft. This design has been used in small aircrafts.

(d) **Opposed Piston Engine:** When a single cylinder houses two pistons, each of which drives a separate crankshaft, it is called an *'opposed piston'* type of engine. Opposed piston arrangement, like opposed-cylinder arrangement is inherently well balanced. Further, it has the advantage of requiring no cylinder head. In addition the relative piston velocity (rate of change of volume) is doubled for a given crank and piston speed. As shown, this arrangements lends itself to cylinder porting and straight flow-through of gases for scavenging, where the openings of the inlet and exhaust ports are controlled by the position of the pistons.

(e) **Radial Engine:** Radial engine is an engine with more than two cylinders in each row equally spaced Around the crankshaft. The radial engine is most commonly used in conventional air-cooled air craft engines where three, five, seven, or nine cylinders may be used in one bank and two or three banks may be used. The radial engine presents the problem of fastening 3, 5, 7 or 9 connecting rods to a single crank. A master rod is guided by the crank and articulated rods are attached to the master rod. It should be noted that the master rod executes the same motion as the connecting rod in other conventional engines, while an articulated rod follows a slightly different path since the point of attachment is not at the centre of the crankpin. Vertical shaft radial engines are used in large stationary power plants with vertical shaft generators mounted below. An odd number if cylinders per bank is necessary with alternate cylinders firing in successive revolutions for four-stroke cycle radial engines, but many number of cylinders can be used for two-stroke engines.

Besides the above important types of cylinder arrangements the other types are as follows:

(f) **'X' type:** This design is a variation of 'V' type. It has four banks of cylinders attached to a single crankshaft.

(g) **'H' type:** The `H' type is essentially two *'opposed cylinder'* types utilizing two separate, but interconnected, crankshafts.

(h) **'U' type:** The 'U' type is a variation of opposed piston arrangement.

(i) **Delta type:** The delta type is essentially three opposed piston with three crankshafts.

1.5.2 SI Engine Classification By Valve Location

The SI engines (as well as CI engines) may also classified by valve location.

The T-head design shown in now obsolete. The side valve, or L-head design was quite popular up to 1960. The most popular design today is the overhead valve design, which is also **called I-head** or valve-in-head engine. A combination of side valve design and overhead valve design is occasionally made to give a **F-head**. Here the intake valve so located in the head (overhead) while the exhaust valve is located in the block (under head).

In case of petrol (Gasoline) or diesel engines, fuel burnt in the atmosphere of air within the engine cylinder forms the working substance and hence these are called **IC engines**. In a steam engine or a steam turbine, the heat generated due to combustion of the fuel is employed to produce high pressure steam, which is used, as the working fluid is an example of EC engine.

Classification of heat engines is given in **Fig. 1.3**. IC engine is divided into two categories namely rotary and reciprocating type. Reciprocating engines appear to be simple in construction but they are highly complex units. These consist hundreds of components, which have to perform their functions satisfactorily to produce output power.

1.6 THE WORKING PRINCIPLE OF IC ENGINES

A heat engine works as per a thermodynamic cycle, which consists of a sequence of operations. The sequence of operations is quite rigid and cannot be changed. The working principles of both SI and CI engines are explained in the following subsection.

1.6.1 Four Stroke Spark Ignition Engine

In a four stroke engine, the cycle of operations is completed in four stroke of the piston or two revolutions of the crankshaft. During four stroke, the events such as suction, compression, combustion, expansion and exhaust are to be completed. For each stroke the crankshaft rotates through 180° revolution and hence a four-stroke cycle is completed through 720° of crank rotation. The cycle of operation for an ideal four-stroke SI engine consists of:

(1) Suction or intake stroke. (2) Compression stroke.
(3) Expansion or power stroke. (4) Exhaust stroke.

The series of operations for theoretical four-stroke S.I. engine is illustrated in **Fig. 1.4 (a)** while its P-V diagram is shown in **Fig. 1.4 (b)**.

(a) **Suction Stroke (0-1):** The piston is at TDC position and is about to move downwards. The suction valve is open and exhaust valve is closed. During the downward motion of piston, fresh charge (mixture of fuel and air) is sucked into the cylinder. At the end of this stroke, suction valves are closed.

(b) **Compression Stroke (1-2):** The fresh charge taken during the suction stroke is compressed and the piston moves from BDC to TDC position. Both inlet and exhaust valves remain closed. At the end of this stroke, the charge is ignited by the spark. Hence, combustion of fuel occurs instantly, releasing the chemical energy in the form of heat energy.

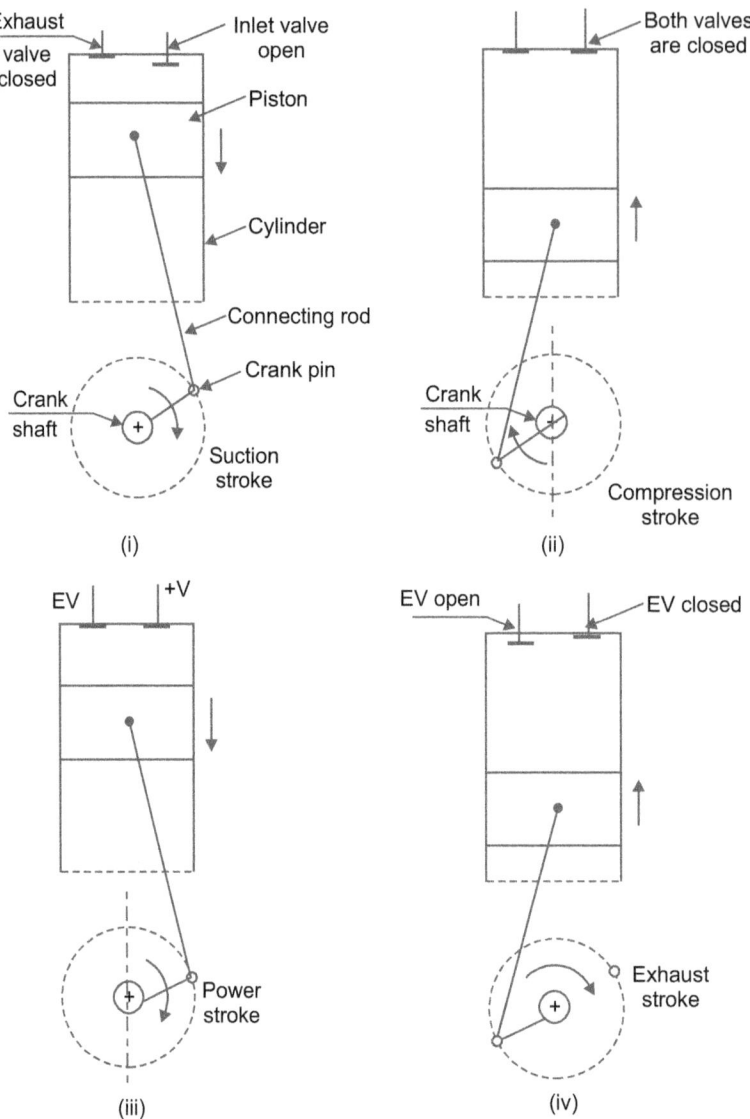

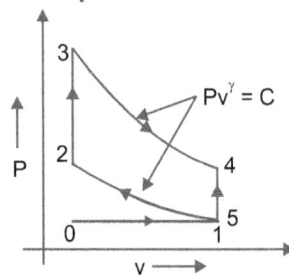

Fig. 1.4 (a): Series of Operations of Four Stroke S.I. Engine

Fig. 1.4 (b): P-V diagram for Theoretical Four Stroke S.I. Engine

(c) Expansion Stroke (3-4): It is also known as power stroke. Due to high pressure, the burnt gases force the piston towards BDC. Both inlet and exhaust valves remain in closed condition. The power is obtained during this stroke.

(d) Exhaust Stroke (5-0): At the end of power stroke, the exhaust valve opens, the inlet valve remains closed. The piston moves from BDC to TDC position pushing out the burnt gases.

1.6.2 Four Stroke Compression Ignition (CI) Engine

The working of four stroke CI engine is just similar to the four stroke SI engine but it operates at a much higher compression ratio. The compression ratio of an SI engine is in the range 6-10 while that of CI engine it is in the range 16-20. In the CI engine during the suction stroke, air is sucked into the cylinder instead of air-fuel mixture as in SI engine. Due to the high compression ratio employed, the temperature at the end of compression stroke is sufficiently high to self ignite the fuel which is injected into the combustion chamber at the end of compression stroke. In CI engines, a fuel pump and an injector are provided to inject the fuel into the combustion chamber. The carburettor and an ignition system is not necessary in CI engine. The ideal sequence of operations for the four stroke CI engine is as given below.

(a) Suction Stroke: During this stroke inlet valve is open and exhaust valve is closed **[Fig. 1.5 (a)]**. Air alone is sucked into the cylinder during this stroke. The piston moves from TDC position to BDC position.

(b) Compression Stroke: Air inducted in the cylinder is compressed into the clearance volume. Both valves remain closed during this stroke **[Fig. 1.5 (b)]**. The piston moves from BDC position to TDC position.

(c) Expansion Stroke: The fuel injection starts nearly at the end of compression stroke. The rate of injection is such that the combustion maintains the pressure constant in spite of the piston movement on its expansion. It means heat is assumed to be added at constant pressure. After the injection of fuel is complete (i.e. after cut-off), the products of combustion expand. Both the valves remain closed during this stroke. The piston moves from TDC position to BDC position. [Fig. 1.5 (c)].

(d) Exhaust stroke: The piston moving from BDC position to TDC position pushes the products of combustion. The exhaust valve is open and inlet valve is closed during this stroke **[Fig. 1.5 (d)]**.

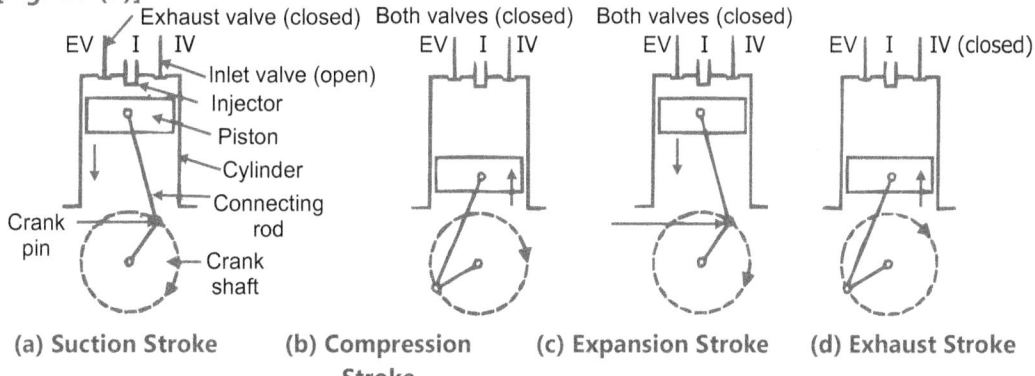

(a) Suction Stroke (b) Compression Stroke (c) Expansion Stroke (d) Exhaust Stroke

Fig. 1.5: Cycle of Operations of a Four-Stroke CI Engine

1.6.3 Comparison of SI and CI Engines

There are many things, which are in common; it is better to compare them based on important parameters like basic thermodynamic cycle, fuel supply, compression ratio etc. and are as given in the Table 1.2.

Table 1.2: Comparison of SI and CI engines

Description	SI engine	CI engine
Fuel	Gasoline (petrol) a highly volatile, self-ignition temperature high, is used as a fuel.	Diesel comparatively a low volatile and self-ignition temperature is also low.
Basic cycle	SI engine works on Otto or constant volume cycle.	CI engine works on diesel or constant pressure cycle.
Fuel supply	A mixture of fuel and air is supplied during suction stroke. A carburettor is required for the purpose.	Only air is inducted into the cylinder during suction stroke. Fuel is injected into the cylinder by fuel pump at the end of compression stroke. A carburettor is not required for the purpose.
Compression ratio	It is in the range 6-10. Upper limit is due to antiknock quality of the fuel.	It is in the range 16-22. Upper limit is due to increase in weight of the engine.
Speed	Due to light weight and homogeneous combustion of fuel, these are high speed engines.	Due to heavy weight and heterogeneous combustion of fuel, these are low speed engines.
Ignition	Requires an ignition system with spark plug in the combustion chamber.	Due to high compression ratio, self ignition temperature of fuel is reached. Therefore, no ignition system and spark plug is required.
Thermal efficiency	Due to low compression ratio, the maximum value of thermal efficiency achieved is lower.	Due to high compression ratio, the maximum value of thermal efficiency achieved is higher.
Weight	Lighter due to low peak pressure.	Heavier due to high peak pressure.

1.6.4 Two Stroke Engine

The main difference between two-stroke and four-stroke engine is the method of filling the cylinder with fresh charge and removing the burnt gases from it. In the four stroke engine, these operations are performed by the engine piston during suction and exhaust stroke separately. In two-stroke engine, the filling process is accomplished by the charge compressed in crankcase. The induction of the compressed charge pushes out the products of combustion through exhaust ports. Therefore, no piston strokes are required for these two operations. Two strokes are sufficient to complete the cycle, one for compressing the fresh charge and the other for expansion or power stroke.

Two stroke crankcase scavenged engine is shown in **Fig. 1.6** while its indicator diagram is shown in **Fig. 1.7**. The charge or air enters into the **crankcase** through spring loaded inlet valve when the pressure in the **crankcase** is reduced due to upward motion of the piston during compression stroke. After the compression and ignition, expansion takes place in the usual way. Charge is compressed in the **crankcase** during the expansion stroke. Just nearing the expansion stroke, the piston uncovers the exhaust ports and the cylinder pressure drops to atmospheric pressure as the combustion products leave the cylinder. Further movement of the piston uncovers the transfer ports, permitting the slightly compressed charge or air in the **crankcase** to enter the engine cylinder. The top of the piston has usually a projection to deflect the fresh charge towards the top of the cylinder before flowing to the exhaust ports. This process of driving out the fresh charge from the cylinder with the help of fresh charge is known as **scavenging**.

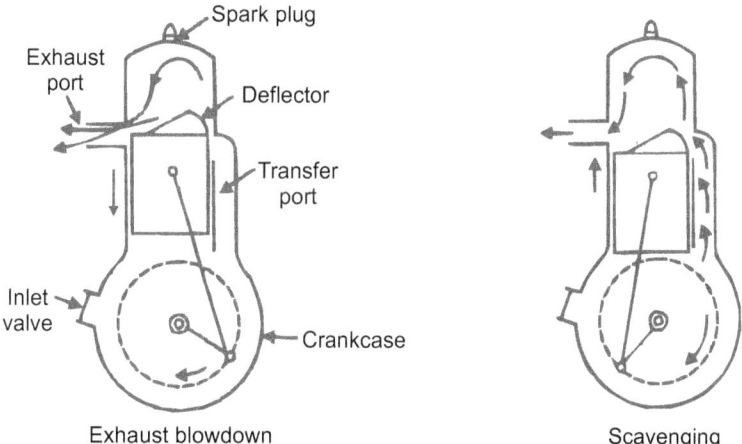

Fig. 1.6: Crankcase Scavenged Two-stroke Engine

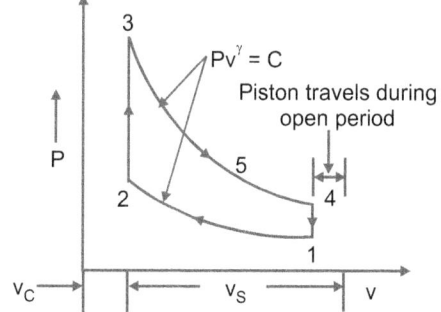

Fig. 1.7: Ideal Indicator Diagram of a Two-stroke SI Engine

1.6.5 Comparison of Four-stroke and Two-stroke Engines

Two-stroke engine was developed to obtain a greater output from the same size of the engine compared with four-stroke engine. It is simpler than four-stroke engine because it does not consist inlet and outlet valves. This simplicity of two-stroke engine makes it cheaper to produce and easy to maintain. There is one power stroke for every revolution of the crankshaft but there is one power stroke in two revolutions of the crankshaft in four- stroke engine. Theoretically speaking, it develops double the power that developed by four stroke engine but practically it is only 30% higher. This is because of reduced effective expansion stroke and increased heating caused by increased number of power strokes which limit the maximum speed.

In SI engine, the incoming charge consists of fuel and air. During scavenging, as both inlet and exhaust ports are open simultaneously for some time, there is a possibility that some of the fresh charge containing fuel escapes with the exhaust. This results in high fuel consumption and lower thermal efficiency. The two stroke engine operates with the same efficiency at all speeds. At part throttle operating condition, the amount of fresh mixture entering the cylinder is not enough to clear all the exhaust gases and a part of it remains in the cylinder to contaminate the charge. This results in irregular operation of the engine. Due to these disadvantages, the application of two-stroke SI engine is restricted to only small engines suitable for motor cycles, scooters, lawn movers etc.

The two-stroke diesel engines do not suffer from these drawbacks. There is no loss of fuel with exhaust gases as the intake charge in diesel engine is only air. The two stroke diesel engine is quite widely used. Two stroke petrol and diesel engine require greater cooling and lubricating oil due to one power stroke for every revolution of the crankshaft. The comparison of two stroke and four-stroke engines is given in Table 1.3.

Table 1.3: Comparison of Two-stroke and Four-stroke Cycle Engines

	Four-stroke Cycle Engine		Two-stroke Cycle Engine
1.	The thermodynamic cycle is completed in four strokes of the piston or in two revolutions of the crankshaft.	1.	The thermodynamic cycle is completed in two strokes of the piston or in one revolution of the crankshaft.
2.	Only one power stroke is there in every two revolutions of the crankshaft. Because of which, turning moment is not so uniform and hence a heavier flywheel is needed.	2.	One power stroke in each revolution of the crankshaft. Because of which, turning moment is more uniform and hence a lighter flywheel can be used.

Four-stroke Cycle Engine	Two-stroke Cycle Engine
3. Again, because of one power stroke for two revolutions, power produced for same size of engine is less, or for the same power the engine is heavier and bulkier.	3. Because of one power stroke for every revolution, power produced for same size of engine is more (theoretically twice; actually about 1.3 times), or for the same power, the engine is lighter and more compact.
4. Lesser cooling and lubrication is required due to one power stroke in two revolutions. Lower rate of wear and tear.	4. Because of one power stroke in one revolution, greater cooling and lubrication is required. Higher rate of wear and tear.
5. The four-stroke engine contains valves and valve actuating mechanisms to open and close the valves.	5. Two-stroke engines have only ports but no valves.
6. Initial cost of the engine is more because of the heavy weight and complicated valve mechanism.	6. Initial cost of the engine is less because of light weight and simplicity due to the absence of valve mechanism.
7. Volumetric efficiency is more due to more time for induction. Therefore, less cc per kW of power output.	7. Volumetric efficiency is low due to lesser time for induction. Therefore, more cc per kW of power output.
8. Thermal efficiency is higher, part load efficiency is better than two-stroke cycle engine.	8. Thermal efficiency is lower, part load efficiency is poor compared to a four-stroke cycle engine.
9. Used where efficiency is important, viz., in cars, buses, trucks, tractors, industrial engines, aero planes, power generation etc.	9. Used where low cost, compactness and light weight are important, viz., in mopeds, scooters, motorcycles, hand sprayers etc.

1.7 ACTUAL VALVE TIMING OF FOUR-STROKE PETROL ENGINE

Valve timing is the regulation of the points in the cycle at which the valves are set to open and close. In the ideal cycle inlet and exhaust valves open and close at dead centers, but in actual cycles they open or close before or after dead centers as explained below.

There are two factors, one mechanical and other dynamics, for the actual valve timing to be different from the theoretical valve timing.

(a) **Mechanical factor:** The poppet valves of the reciprocating engines are opened and closed by cam mechanisms. The clearance between cam, tappet and valve must be slowly taken up and valve slowly lifted, at first, if noise and wear is to be avoided. For the same reasons the valve cannot be closed abruptly, else it will *bounce* on its seat. (Also the cam contours should be so designed as to produce gradual and smooth changes in directional acceleration). Thus the valve opening and closing periods are spread over a considerable number of crankshaft degrees. As a result, the opening of the valve must commence ahead of the time at which it is fully opened (i.e., before dead centers). The same reasoning applies for the closing time and the valves must close after the dead centers. **Fig. 1.8** shows the actual valve timing diagram of a four-stroke engine in relation to its pressure - volume diagram.

   (b) Dynamic factor: Besides mechanical factor of opening and closing of valves, the actual valve timing is set taking into consideration the dynamic effects of gas-flow.

Intake valve timing: Intake valve timing has a bearing on the actual quantity of air sucked during the suction stroke i.e. it affects the volumetric efficiency. **Fig. 1.8** shows the intake valve timing diagram for both low speed and high speed SI engines. It is seen that for both low speed and high speed engine the intake valve opens 10° before the arrival of the piston at TDC on the exhaust stroke. This is to insure that the valve will be fully open and the fresh charge starting to flow into the cylinder as soon as possible after TDC.

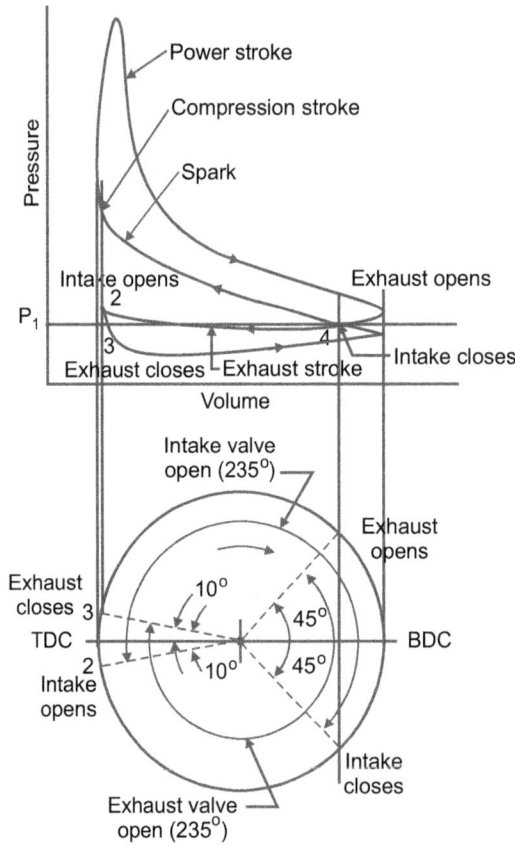

Fig. 1.8: Four-stroke Petrol Engine Value Timing Diagram in Relation to the Pressure Volume Diagram

As the piston moves out in the suction stroke, the fresh charge is drawn in through the intake port and valve. When the piston reaches the BDC and starts to move in the compression stroke, the inertia of the entering fresh charge tends to cause it to continue to move into the cylinder. To take advantage of this, the intake valve is closed after TDC so that maximum air is taken in. This is **called ram effect**. However, if the intake valve is to remain open for too long a time beyond BDC, the up-moving piston on the compression stroke would tend to force some of the charge, already in the cylinder, back into the intake manifold. The time the intake valve should remain open after TDC is decided by the speed of the engine. At low engine speed the charge speed is low and so the air inertia is low, and hence the intake valve should lose relatively early after BDC for a slow speed engine (say about 10° after BDC). In close high speed engines the charge speed is high and consequently the inertia is high and hence the induct maximum quantity of charge due to ram effect the intake valve should close relatively late after BDC (up to 60° after BDC). For a variable speed engine the chosen intake valve setting is a compromise between the best setting for low and high speeds.

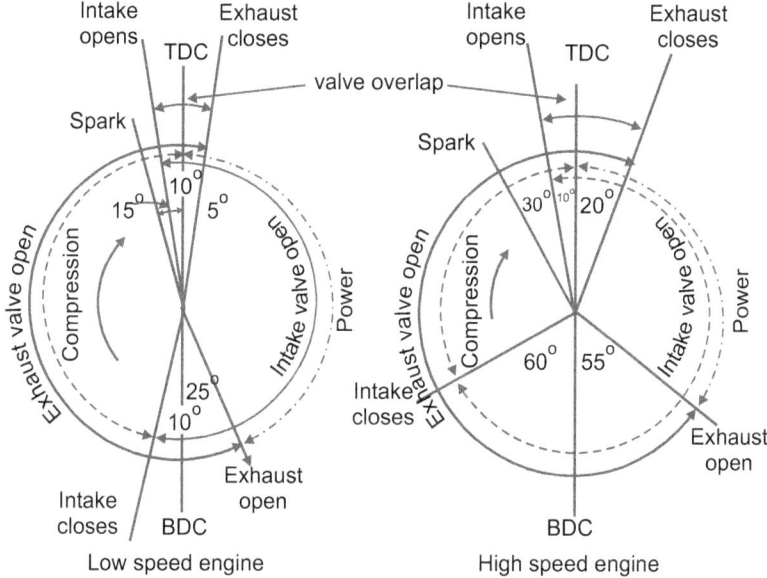

Fig. 1.9: Value Timing for Low and High Speed Four-stroke SI Engine

There is limit to the high speed for advantage of ram effect. At very high speeds the effect of fluid friction may be more than offset the advantage of ram effect and the charge for cylinder per I cycle falls off.

Exhaust valve timing: The exhaust valve is set to open before BDC (say about 25° before BDC in low speeds engines and 55 before BDC in high speed engines). If the exhaust valve did not start to open until BDC, the pressures in the cylinder would be considerably above atmospheric pressure during the first portion of the exhaust stroke, increasing the work required to expel the exhaust gases. But opening the exhaust valve earlier reduces the pressure near the end of the power stroke and thus causes some loss of useful work on this stroke. However, the overall effect of opening the valve prior to the time the piston reaches BDC results in overall gain in output.

The closing time of exhaust valve affects the volumetric efficiency. By closing the exhaust valve a few degree after TDC (about 150° in case of low speed engines and 20° in case of high speed engines) the inertia of the exhaust gases tends to scavenge the cylinder by carrying out a greater mass of the gas left in the clearance volume. This results in increased volumetric efficiency.

Note that there may be a period when both the intake and exhaust valves are open at the same time. This is called valve overlap (say about 15° in low speed engine and 30° in high speed engines). This overlap should not be excessive to allow the burned gases to be sucked into the intake manifold, or the fresh charge to escape through the exhaust valve.

1.8 APPLICATIONS OF IC ENGINES

The most important applications of internal combustion engines are in transport on land, sea and air. The other applications of IC engines include industrial applications and prime movers for electric generators.

(a) Small two-stroke petrol engines are used where simplicity and low cost of the prime mover are the main considerations. The smallest engines are used in mopeds (50 cc engine) and lawn movers. Scooters 100-150 cc capacity, produce 5 kW power at 5300 rpm. The motor cycle have generally 100-250 cc two-stroke or four-stroke petrol engine developing a maximum horse power of about 12 kW at 4500 rpm. The motor cycles with commercial names such as Hero Honda, Kawasaki Bajaj etc. have four stroke petrol engines. Suzuki motor cycle has a two stroke engine.

Two-stroke petrol engine may also be used in very small electric generating sets, pumping sets, and outboard engines.

(b) The most important application of small four-stroke petrol engine is in automobiles. The Fiat Car has a four-cylinder 1089 cc engine developing maximum power of about 30 kW at 5000 rpm. The American cars are much bigger and have 6 cylinder or 8 cylinder engines with maximum power upto 80 kW. However, the oil crisis and air pollution have reversed the trend towards smaller capacity cars.

The four-stroke petrol engines are also used for jeeps, buses, and trucks. They are generally 4000 cc six cylinder engines with maximum brake power of about 100 kW. However, in this application petrol engines have been practically superseded by diesel engines. Another application, of four-stroke petrol engines is in pumping sets and mobile electric generating sets, but even in these applications now-a-days diesel engines have taken over.

(c) Radial piston engine is used in small aircraft propulsion. The small aircrafts generally use radial four-stroke petrol engines. Engines having maximum power from 325 kW to 4000 kW have been used in aircrafts.

(d) Four-stroke diesel engines: The four-stroke diesel engine is one of the most versatile prime movers. It is manufactured in diameters from 5 cm to 60 cm with speeds ranging from 100 to 4400 rpm, while delivering from 1 kW to 1300 kW per cylinder.

Small diesel engines are used for pumping sets, construction machinery, air compressors and drilling rigs. Tractors use about 15 to 35 kW diesel engines, jeeps 60 kW engines, and buses and trucks about 100 kW diesel engines. Diesel engine is used both for mobile and stationary electric generating plants.

Research is going on for use of diesel engine in cars. Mercedes have already developed a diesel-powered car. Diesel engines are used in diesel-hydraulic and diesel-electric locomotives. Diesel engines are also used in boats and in ships.

(e) Two-stroke diesel engines: Very high power diesel engines for ship propulsion are generally two-stroke diesel engines. In fact all engines over 60 cm bore are two-stroke engines, uniflow with exhaust valves or loop scavenged. The horse power on one crankshaft can be upto 42,000 kW. Nordberg, 2-stroke, 12-cylinder 80 cm bore and 155 cm stroke, diesel engine develops 21,000 kW at 120 rpm. This speed allows the engine to be directly coupled to the propeller of a ship without the necessity of gear reducers.

(B) ANALYSIS OF ENGINE CYCLES

1.9 INTRODUCTION

Analysis of engine cycle is an important tool to design and study the internal combustion engines. A thermodynamic cycle consists of a series of processes through which the working fluid progresses (passes). In other words, a thermodynamic cycle implies a closed system with no exchange of matter with surroundings. Truly speaking internal combustion engine element operate on a thermodynamic cycle as it consists of an open system wherein a new fluid continuously enters the engine at one set of conditions and leaves at another condition. This is shown in Fig. 1.10.

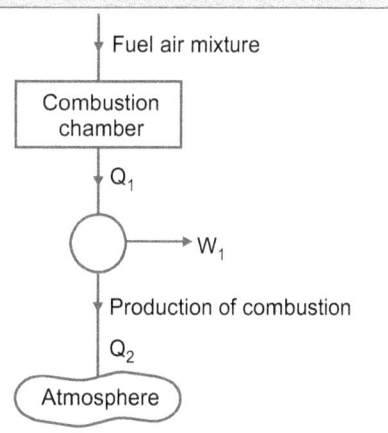

Fig. 1.10: Internal Combustion Engine: A Block Diagram

An accurate analysis of an internal combustion engine is very difficult due to the complex chemical reactions that take place when fuel burns. Not only it involves friction between piston and cylinder walls, but also heat transfer between the gases and cylinder walls. Hence, it is an usual practice to analyse the cycle making some simplifying assumptions.

The two commonly employed approximation of an actual engine in order of their increasing accuracy are:
- (i) Ideal or air standard cycle analysis.
- (ii) Fuel-air cycles analysis.

These two cycles are theoretical cycles.

Numerical result obtained by the above theoretical analysis are different from actual results due to above approximations. The results so obtained are not only for academic interests but have a great practical importance. The analysis of the theoretical cycle indicates the upper limit of the performance of an engine.

1.10 IDEAL OR AIR STANDARD CYCLE

Air standard cycles are defined as cycles using a perfect gas (ideal gas) as the working substance. Air is almost invariably used as the working fluid in internal combustion engines (I.C. engines). Air is assumed to behave as a perfect gas. The **following assumptions are made in the analysis of standard cycles**:

(1) The working substance is a *perfect* gas, i.e. it follows the characteristic gas equation, $pv = mRT$.

(2) The working substance (fluid) is a fixed mass of air contained in a closed system.

(3) The physical constants of the working medium (substance) such as c_p = 1.005 kJ/kg·K, c_v = 0.718 kJ/kg·K and γ = 1.4 are taken in the calculations, for air.

(4) The specific heats of working substance are assumed constant.

(5) The working medium does not undergo chemical changes.

(6) Heat is supplied and rejected in a reversible manner and if necessary, can be supplied and rejected instantaneously. (In actual engine, energy is supplied by combustion of fuel and rejected by exhaust gases).

(7) The compression and expansion processes are reversible adiabatic (isentropic).

(8) The operation of the engine is frictionless.

(9) Kinetic and potential energies are neglected.

(10) Inlet and exhaust takes place at atmospheric or constant pressure.

The work output, peak pressure, peak temperature and *thermal efficiency* based on ideal cycle are higher than those of actual engine.

Thermal efficiency is the ratio of work output to the heat supplied to the engine.

Mathematically, $$\eta_{th} = \frac{\text{Work output}}{\text{Heat supplied}}$$

Thermal efficiency is referred as **Air standard efficiency** for the cycle which uses air as the working substance.

1.11 LIMITATIONS OF AIR STANDARD CYCLES

Highly simplified approximations are involved in the theory of air standard cycle described in Part (B). In the air cycle approximation it was assumed that the working fluid is nothing but air (a perfect gas) and had constant specific heats. Therefore, air standard theory does not give actual performance of the engine. It gives an estimate of engine performance which is much greater than the actual performance.

For example: The actual indicated thermal efficiency of petrol engine of compression ratio 7 is of the order of 30% whereas the air standard efficiency is of the order of 54%. The main reason of divergence is the over-simplification in using the values of the properties of the working fluid for cycle analysis. In actual engine the working fluid is not air but a mixture of air, fuel and residual gases. Furthermore, the specific heats of the working fluid are not constant but increase as temperature rises, and finally, the products of combustion are subjected to dissociation at high temperatures.

1.12 FUEL-AIR CYCLE

Fuel-sir cycle is theoretical cycle based on the actual properties of the cylinder gases and represents a nearly attainable idea for comparison with actual performance. If the actual physical properties of the cylinder gases before and after burning are taken into account a much closer approach to actual performance figures is achieved.

The following points are taken into consideration for fuel-air cycle calculations:
1. The actual composition of the cylinder gases, i.e. (fuel + air + water vapour in air + residual gas). The fuel air ratio is changed during the operation of the engine which changes the relative amounts of CO_2, water vapour present in the exhaust emissions.
2. Specific heat increases with temperature except for monotamic gases. Therefore the value of 1 also changes with temperature and is considered.
3. The fact that the fuel-air mixture does not completely combine chemically at high temperatures (above 1600 K) and that CO_2 H_2, H and O_2 may be present at equilibrium condition.
4. The number of molecules present after combustion depend upon fuel-air ratio and upon the pressure and temperature after the combustion. For a given temperature, by the gas law PV = NRT, the pressure varies with the number of molecules present.

In addition to above factors into, consideration, the following assumptions are commonly made for fuel-air cycle analysis:
1. There is no chemical change in either fuel or air prior to combustion.
2. Subsequent to combustion, the charge is always in chemical equilibrium.
3. There is no heat exchange between the gases and the cylinder walls in any process i.e. they are adiabatic. Also the compression and expansion processes are frictionless.
4. In case of reciprocating engines the velocities are negligibly small.
5. Intake and exhaust take place at atmospheric pressure.

With particular reference to constant volume fuel-air cycle, it is assumed that (i) the fuel is completely vapourized and perfectly mixed with the air, and (ii) the burning takes place instantaneously at top dead centre (at constant volume).

1.13 USES OF FUEL-AIR CYCLE

The air standard cycle shows the general effect of only compression ratio on engine efficiency whereas the fuel-air cycle may be calculated for various fuel-air ratios, inlet pressures and temperatures. It is noted that compression ratio and fuel-air ratio are very important parameters of engine while inlet conditions are not so important.

The actual efficiency of a good engine is about 85 percent of the fuel-air cycle efficiency. Thus a very good estimate of the power to be expected from the actual engine can be made from fuel-air cycle analysis. Also, peak pressures and exhaust temperatures can be very closely approximated which affect the engine structure and design. Thus the effect of many engine variables can be understood by fuel-air cycle analysis.

1.14 VARIATION OF SPECIFIC HEATS

The specific heats of gases normally do not remain constant at all the temperatures. However the specific heat would increase with increase in temperature which is shown in **Fig. 1.11**. This not true for the monatomic gases.

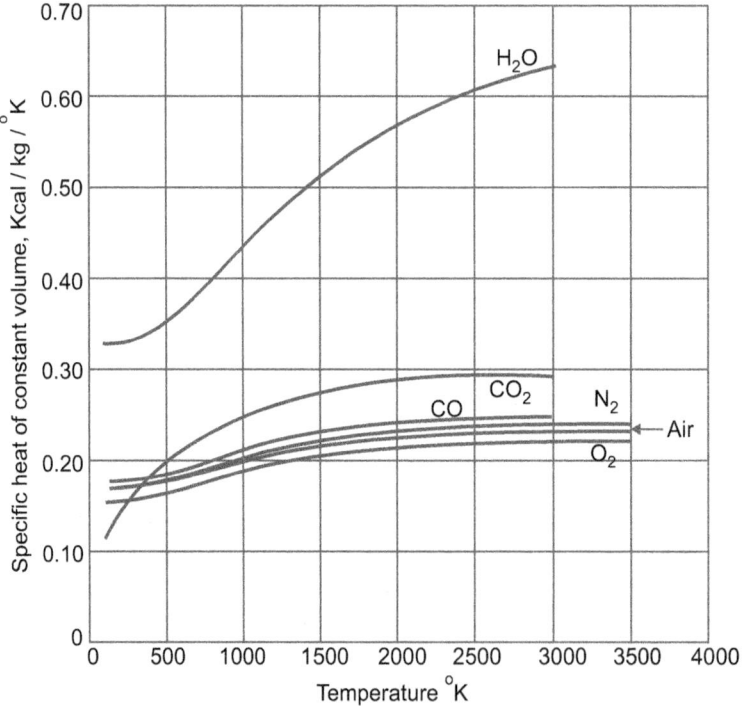

Fig. 1.11: Increase of Specific Heat with Temperature

The increase in specific heat does not follow any particular law. However, over the temperature range in general use for gases in heat engines (300 K to 1500 K) the specific heat curve is nearly a straight line as expressed in the form.

$$C_p = a + kT, \quad C_v = b + kT \qquad \ldots (i)$$

Where, a, b and k are constants.

Now,
$$R = C_p - C_v = a - b \qquad \ldots (ii)$$

Where, R is the characteristic gas constant.

Above 1500 K temperature the specific heat increases much more rapidly and may be approximated in the form

$$C_p = a + k_1 T + k_2 T^2, \quad C_v = b + k_1 T + k_2 T^2 \qquad \ldots (iii)$$

If one neglects the term T^2 in equation (equation (iii)) it becomes same as equation (i).

The reason of increase in specific heat is that as the temperature of the gas is increased then the molecules are set into motion with larger amplitude within the gas system. So as a whole the energy which goes into moving the atoms does not contribute to the temperature rise Hence more heat is required to raise the temperature of unit mass through one degree.

For air C_p = 1.005 kJ/kg·K at 0°C, and 01.26 at 2000°C.

1.14.1 Loss Due to Variation of Specific Heat

1. Since the difference between C_p and C_v is constant, the value of γ decreases as temperature increases.
2. Thus, if the variation of specific heats is taken into account during the compression stroke, the final temperature and pressure would be lower than if constant value of specific heats is used. This is shown in Fig. 1.12 (a).

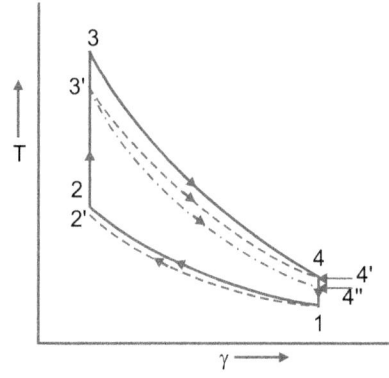

Cycle 1-2-3-4 – with constant specific heat
Cycle 1-2'-3'-4' – with variable specific heat.
Cycle 3'-4' – with constant specific heat point 3'.

Fig. 1.12 (a): Loss Due to Variation of Specific Heat

(a) With variable specific heat the point at the end of compression is slightly lower, 2', instead of 2.
(b) Also the pressure and temperature at the end of combustion will be lower, represented by 3' instead of 3. It is because the temperature rise due to a given heat release decreases as C_v increases and also because the temperature at 2' is lower than at 2.
(c) The isentropic expansion from 3' would be 3'-4' but the expansion taking variable specific heat into account is above 3'-4" and is represented by 3'-4". It is because the specific heats decrease as temperature decreases during expansion.

The process 3'-4" may be compared with the ideal expansion process 3-4, starting from the point 3. Thus with the above analysis the effect of variation in specific heat is to lower pressures and temperatures at point 2 and 3 and hence to deliver less work than the corresponding cycle with constant specific heats.

Derive the relation for the percentage variation in air standard efficiency of Diesel cycle with percentage variation of C_v.

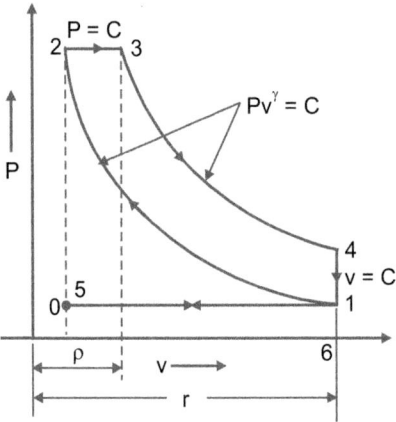

Fig. 1.12 (b): Diesel Cycle

∴ Efficiency of diesel engine is given by,

$$\eta_{air} = 1 - \frac{1}{R_c^{\gamma-1}}\left[\frac{\rho^\gamma - 1}{\gamma(\rho - 1)}\right]$$

where, R_c = Compression ratio = $\dfrac{V_1}{V_2}$

ρ = Cut-off ratio = $\dfrac{V_3}{V_2}$

γ = Adiabatic index

$$1 - \eta_{air} = \frac{1}{(r_c)^{\gamma-1}}\left[\frac{\rho^\gamma - 1}{\gamma(\rho - 1)}\right]$$

$$\log_e(1 - \eta_{air}) = -(\gamma - 1)\log_e(r_c) + \log_e(\rho^\gamma - 1) - \log_e(\gamma) - \log_e(\rho - 1)$$

But, $\gamma = \dfrac{R}{C_v} + 1 + \dfrac{R}{C_v} + 1$

$\therefore \quad \log_e(1 - \eta_{air}) = -\dfrac{R}{C_v}\log_e R_c + \log_e\left[(\rho)^{\frac{R}{C_v}+1} - 1\right] - \log_e\left(\dfrac{R}{C_v} + 1\right) - \log_e(\rho - 1)$

Differentiating above equation,

$$-\frac{d\eta_{air}}{\eta_{air}} = \frac{R}{C_v^2}\log_e(R_c)\cdot dC_v - \frac{-\dfrac{R}{C_v^2}\left\{(\rho)^{\frac{R}{C_v}+1} - 1\right\}\log_e(\rho)\cdot dC_v}{\left\{(\rho)^{\frac{R}{C_v}+1} - 1\right\}}$$

$$+ \frac{R}{C_v^2}\cdot\log_e(R_c)\, dC_v \quad \ldots (I)$$

Solving (I), we get,

$\therefore \quad \dfrac{d\eta_{air}}{\eta_{air}} = -\dfrac{dC_v}{C_v}\left(\dfrac{1 - \eta_{air}}{\eta_{air}}\right)\cdot(\gamma - 1)\left[\dfrac{1}{\gamma} + \log_e(R_c)\dfrac{\rho^\gamma \log_e \rho}{(\rho^\gamma - 1)}\right]$

where, C_v and γ are the average values in the given range of temperatures and $\dfrac{R}{C_v} = (\gamma - 1)$.

This equation gives variation in air standard efficiency of a diesel cycle on account of variation in C_v.

1.15 DISSOCIATION OR CHEMICAL EQUILIBRIUM LOSS (S-10, W-10)

Dissociation is the disintegration (splitting or breaking) of burnt gases at high temperatures. Dissociation is a reversible process. Dissociation increases with in temperature. During, dissociation a considerable amount of heat is absorbed. This heat will be liberated when the elements recombine as the temperature falls. Thus the general effect of dissociation is a suppression of a part of the heat during the combustion period and the liberation of it as expansion proceeds, a condition which is really identical with the effects produced by the change in specific heat. However, the effect of dissociation is much smaller than of change of specific heat.

The dissociation mainly is of CO_2 into CO and O_2.

$$2\,CO + O_2 \leftrightarrow 2\,CO_2 + \text{Heat}$$

The dissociation of CO_2 commences at about 1000°C and at 1500°C it amounts to one per cent.

There is very little dissociation of

$$2H_2O + O_2 \leftrightarrow 2H_2O + Heat$$

The arrow in the above equations is in both directions. The reaction has the same rate for either direction. The reaction is then said to be in equilibrium in either direction, that is, definite proportions of CO, O_2 and CO_2 are present in the equilibrium mixture at each temperature. At low temperature the proportion of CO_2 is high while at high temperature the proportion of CO is high in the mixture of gases. For this reason the fuel-air mixture temperature after combustion cannot go still higher because dissociation limits the release of chemical energy. Also, after the combustion the gases will contain CO_2, H_2O, H_2, N_2, CO, O_2, OH_2, H and O. The equilibrium composition of the products of combustion of octane (C_8H_8) and air for two different fuel-air ratios over the range from 600 to 3000 K is given in **Fig. 1.13**.

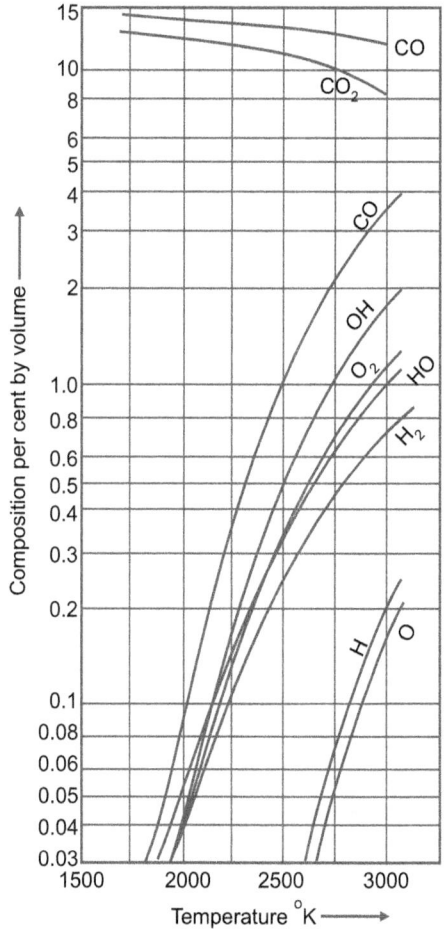

Fig. 1.13 shows the effect of dissociation of gases on the Otto engine is shown with the help of P-v diagram. During dissociation considerable amount of heat is absorbed which puts limit on the maximum temperature and pressure in the cycle.

Fig. 1.13: Equilibrium Composition of Products of Mixture of Octane and Air

(a) Therefore, lower maximum temperature subsequently lower the maximum pressure and state after combustion will be represented by 3' instead of 3.
(b) If there was no reassociation due to fall of temperature during expansion the expansion process would be represented by 3'-4' but due to reassociation the expansion follows the path 3'-4' (due to liberation of heat). The process 3'-4' should be compared with the ideal expansion 3-4.

(c) Thus, we see that the effect of dissociation is to lower the temperature and consequently the pressure at the beginning of the expansion stroke. This causes a loss of power and efficiency. Though during recombining the heat is given back but it is a too late and some of the heat given back is lost in the exhaust.

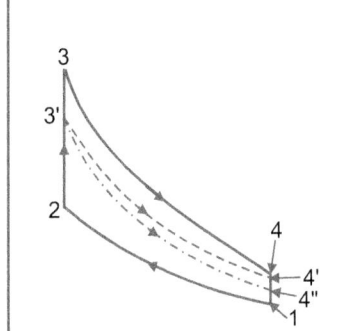

Fig. 1.14: Loss due to Dissociation or Chemical Equilibrium

The pressure of CO and O_2 in the gases tends to prevent dissociation. This is noticeable in a rich fuel mixture, which by producing more CO suppresses dissociation of CO_2. On the other hand there is no dissociation in the burnt gases of a weak fuel mixture as the temperature produced is too low for this phenomenon to occur. Hence, the maximum amount of dissociation occurs in the burnt gases of the chemically correct mixture, but decreases with the weaker and richer mixtures.

Fig 1.15 shows the loss in the temperature with air-fuel mixture strength. With no dissociation maximum temperature is attained with correct maximum strength. With dissociation maximum temperature is obtained when mixture is rich. Dissociation reduces the maximum temperature by about 300°C at the correct mixture strength.

The effect of dissociation, on power generated by the engine is shown in **Fig. 1.16**.

(a) If there is no dissociation, for a chemically correct mixture strength the brake power is maximum.

(b) The depth of the shaded area between the two brake power graphs shows the loss of power due to dissociation.

(c) When the mixture strength is chemically correct. The depth of the shaded area between the two bhp graphs shows the loss of power due to dissociation.

(d) When the mixture is lean there is no dissociation. As the air-fuel ratio decreases the maximum temperature rises and dissociation commences. The maximum dissociation occurs at correct mixture strength. As the mixture becomes rich dissociation effect commences to decline due to the increased quantity of CO.

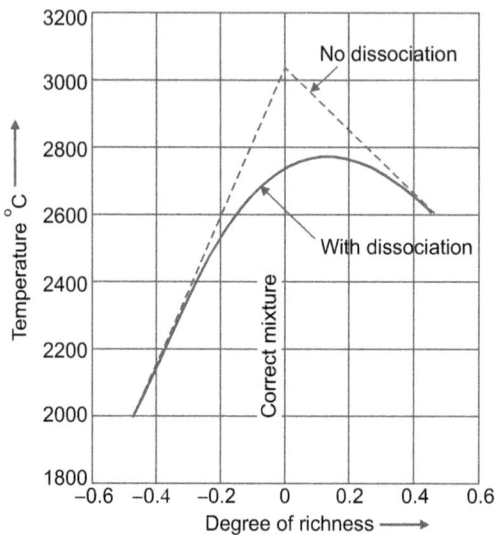

Fig. 1.15: Effect of Dissociation on Temperature at Different Mixture Strength

Dissociation effects are not as pronounced in the CI engine as in the SI engine. It is because of heterogeneous mixture and excess air in the CI engines, both of which reduce overall temperature of the exhaust gases.

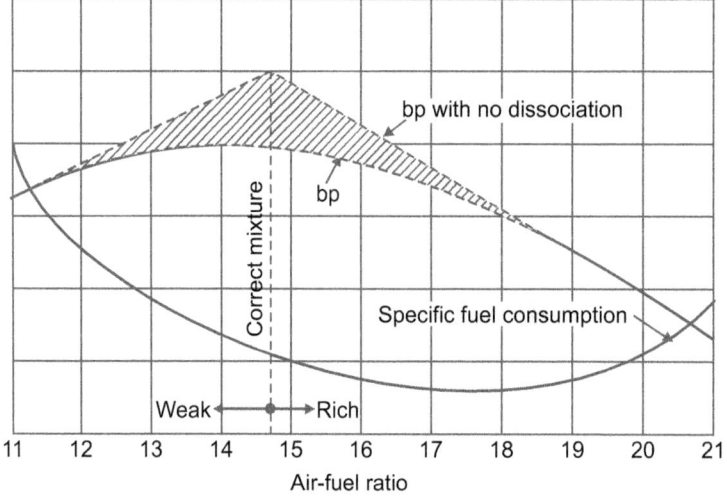

Fig. 1.16: Effect of Dissociation on Power

1.16 COMPARISON OF P-V DIAGRAM OF AIR STANDARD AND FUEL-AIR CYCLE FOR THE SI ENGINE

Fig. 1.17 shows the p-V diagram for a constant volume cycle. Three cycles are shown (i) air standard cycle, (ii) air standard cycle with allowance for variable specific heats, and (iii) fuel-air cycle, that is air cycle with allowance for variable specific heat and dissociation. In the

Table 1.4 above a comparison is made of maximum temperature maximum pressure, mean effective pressure and efficiency for the three approximations.

Table 1.4: Comparison of Three Approximate Cycles

Cycle	Maximum Temperature (T_3) °C	Maximum Pressure (P_3) bar	MEP bar	η%
1. Air standard cycle	5000	130	22.0	57.0
2. Air cycle with variable specific heat	3800	102	19.4	49.4
3. Fuel-air cycle	2600	81	14.5	35.5

The air standard efficiency decreases from 57% to 49.4% as one considers the effect of specific heats on the cycle performance. The efficiency is minimum for fuel-air cycle.

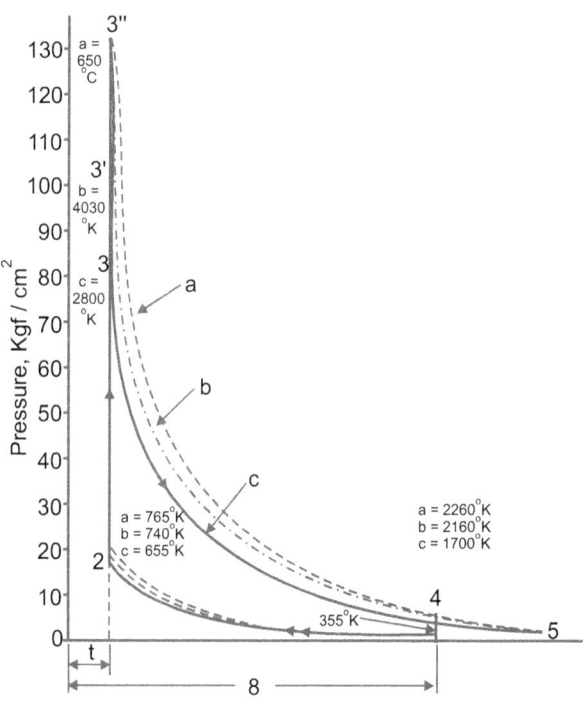

Fig. 1.17: Comparison of Air Cycle and Fuel-air Cycle for SI Engine

1.16.1 Thermal Efficiency and Fuel Consumption

(i) In the analysis of simple air standard cycle, air is the working media. So it does not predict variation of thermal efficiency with mixture strength.

(ii) However, fuel-air analysis suggests that the thermal efficiency will deteriorate as the mixture supplied to an engine is enriched.
(iii) This is explained by the increasing losses due to variable specific heats and dissociation as the engine temperatures are raised by enrichment towards the chemically correct ratio
(iv) Enrichment beyond the chemically correct ratio results in the supply of unusable excess fuel, and the thermal efficiency drops rapidly. It would, therefore, appear that the thermal efficiency would increase as the mixture is wreaked.
(v) Also, beyond a certain weakening the combustion becomes erratic with loss of efficiency. Thus the maximum efficiency is within the weak zone near chemically correct ratio.

The above points give rise to combustion loop, as shown in **Fig. 1.18** which can be plotted at different mixture strengths on an engine running at constant speed and constant throttle setting

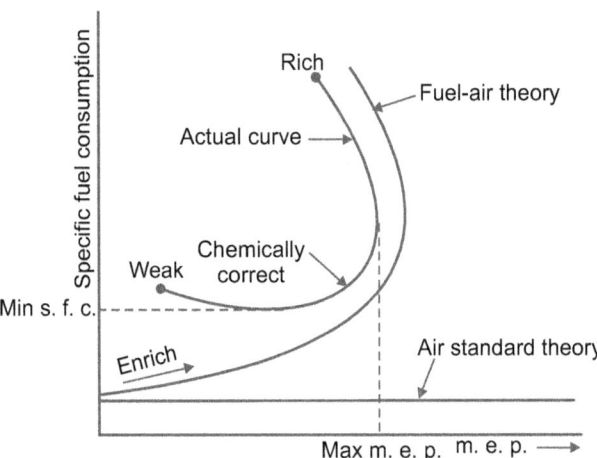

Fig. 1.18: Mean Effective Pressure Vs. Specific Fuel Consumption at Constant Speed and Constant Throttle Setting

1.17 EFFECT OF VARIABLES

The effect of the common engine variables on the pressure and temperature within the engine cylinder is better understood by fuel-air cycle analysis.

1.17.1 Compression Ratio

The effect of compression ratio on the thermal efficiency fuel-air cycle is shown in **Fig. 1.19** for different air-fuel mixture strengths. The fuel-air cycle efficiency increases With the compression ratio in the same manner as the air standard cycle efficiency, principally for the same reason.

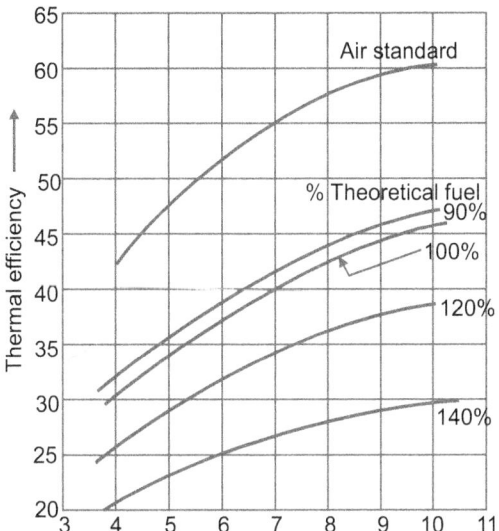

Fig. 1.19: Effect of Compression Ratio and Mixture Strength on Efficiency

Fig. 1.20 shows variation of efficiency with mixture strength. F_R is relative fuel-air ratio and is defined as ratio of actual fuel-air ratio to chemically correct fuel-air ratio on mass basis. The ratio of fuel-air cycle efficiency to air standard cycle efficiency is roughly constant for a given fuel-air ratio as shown in **Fig. 1.20**. The maximum pressure and maximum temperature increase with compression ratio because T_2 and P_2 are higher.

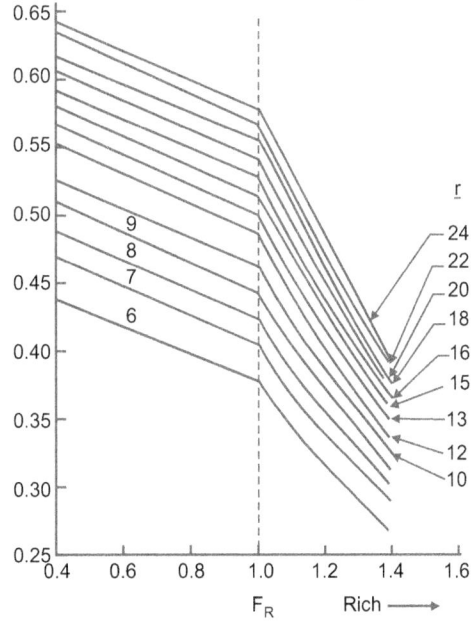

Fig. 1.20: Variation of the Efficiency with Mixture Strength for a Constant Fuel-Air Cycle with I-octane Fuel

Fig. 1.21 shows variation mixture strength with efficiency of fuel-air cycle relative to that of air cycle showing the gain in efficiency as eth mixture weakens. These gains are independent of compression ratio.

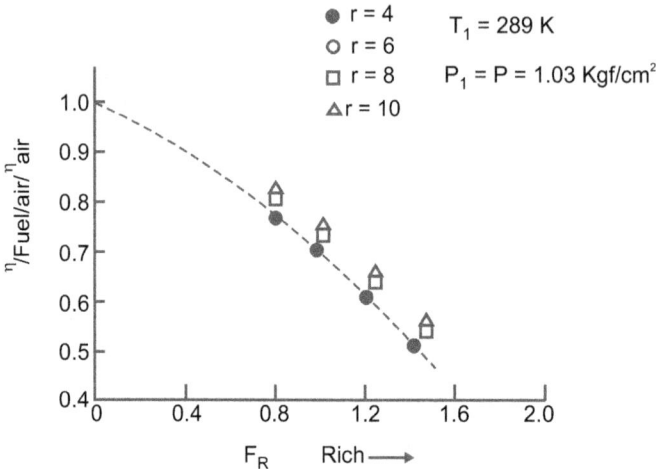

Fig. 1.21: Ratio of Fuel-air Cycle Efficiency and Air-cycle Efficiency with Mixture Strength (Independent of Compression Ratio)

1.17.2 Effect of Fuel-Air Ratio

(i) **Efficiency:** The effect of mixture strength on thermal efficiency at a given compression ratio is shown in **Fig. 1.22**. As the mixture is made lean (less fuel but more air) due to less energy input the temperature rise during the combustion will be less. The low temperature will result in lower specific heat. It will also mean lower chemical equilibrium losses (i.e. larger fraction of the fuel energy is in the form of sensible energy). The efficiency is, therefore, higher and, in fact, approaches the air-cycle efficiency as the fuel-air ratio is reduced.

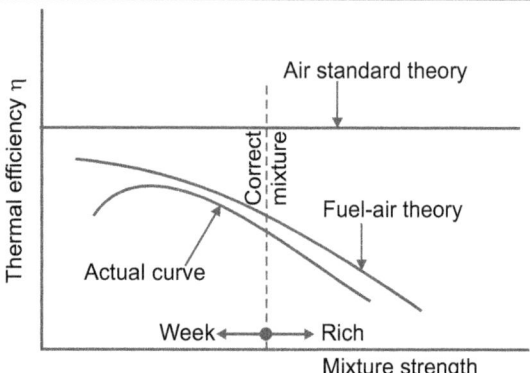

Fig. 1.22: Effect of Mixture Strength on Thermal Efficiency at a given Compression Ratio

(ii) **Maximum power:** Effect of mixture strength (fuel-air ratio) on maximum power produced at a given compression ratio is shown in **Fig. 1.23**. As the mixture becomes richer the efficiency falls rapidly. This is because in addition to higher specific heats and chemical equilibrium losses. There is insufficient air which will result in formation of CO and H_2 in combustibles, which represents a direct wastage of fuel.

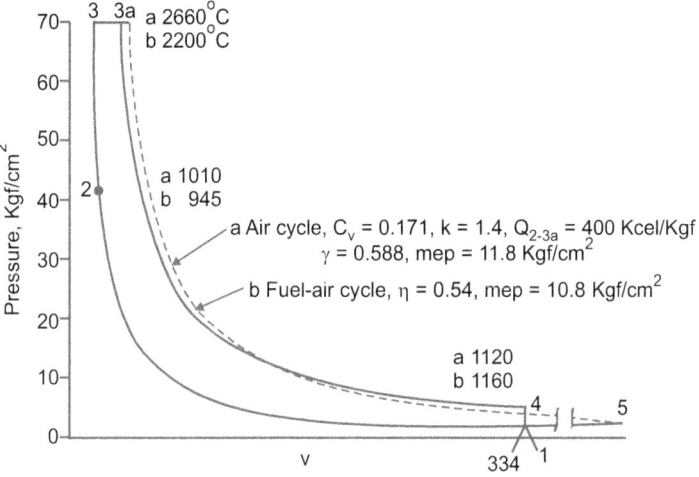

Fig. 1.23: Effect of Mixture Strength on Cycle Power

(iii) Maximum Temperature (T_3): Effect of mixture strength (fuel-air ratio) on maximum temperature in the engine at a given compression ratio is shown in **Fig. 1.24**. At a given compression ratio the maximum temperature is reached when the mixture is slightly rich, 6 per cent or so (F/A = 0.072 or A/F 14 : 1). At chemically correct ratio there is still some oxygen present at the point 3 because of chemical equilibrium effects and hence rich mixture will cause more fuel to combine with oxygen at the point 3, raising the temperature T_3. However, at richer mixtures more formation of CO overcomes the effect of more combustion and T_3 becomes less.

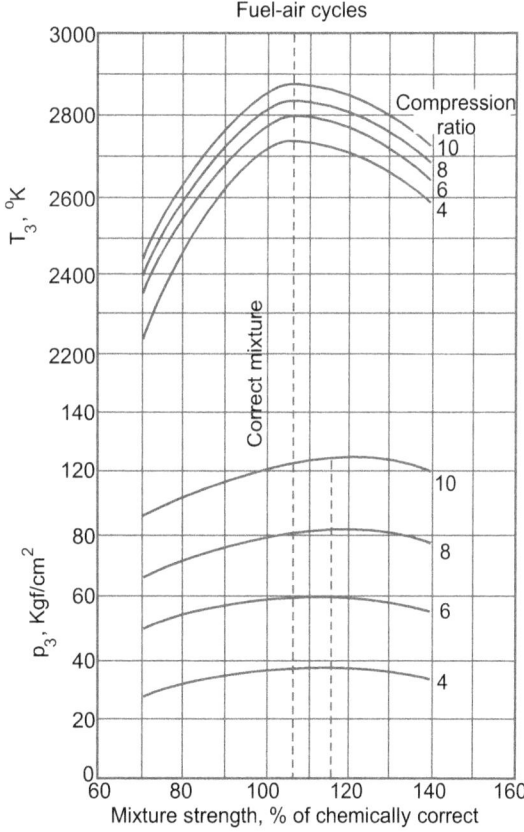

Fig. 1.24: Effect of Fuel-air Ratio on T_3 and P_3 at Different Compression Ratio

(iv) Maximum Pressure (P_3): The pressure of a gas in a given space, by the law $pV =$ NRT, depends upon its temperature and the number of molecules. The curve of maximum pressure P, therefore, follows T_3, but because of the increasing number of molecules P_3 does not start to decrease until the mixture is somewhat richer than that for maximum T_3 (at F/A = 0.083 or A/F 12: 1), i.e. about 20 percent rich.

(v) Exhaust Temperature (T_4): Effect of mixture strength (fuel-air ratio) on exhaust temperature in the engine at a given compression ratio is shown in Fig. 1.25. The exhaust temperature is maximum at the chemically correct mixture. At this point the fuel and oxygen are completely used up, as the effect of chemical equilibrium is not significant. At lean mixtures, because of less fuel, T_3 is less and hence exhaust temperature T_4 is less. At rich mixtures less sensible energy is developed and hence T_4 is less. That is, T_4 varies with fuel-air ratio in the same manner as T_3 except that maximum T_4 is at the correct fuel-air ratio in place of slightly rich fuel-air ratio (6 percent) as in case of T_3.

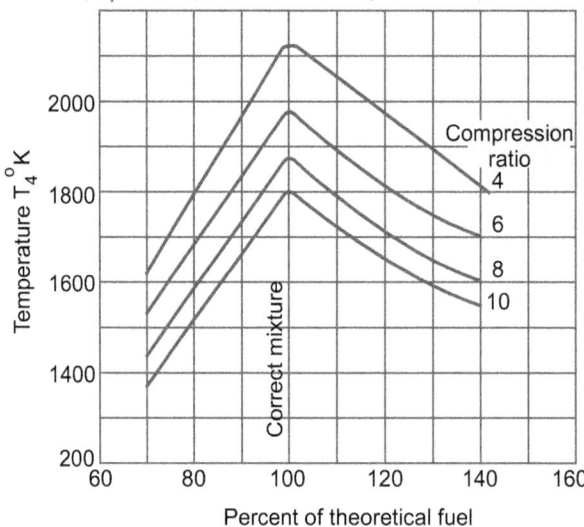

Fig. 1.25: Effect of Fuel-Air Ratio on T_3

The behaviour of T_4 with compression ratio is different from that of T_3 as shown in **Fig. 1.25**. Unlike T_3, T_4 is lower at high compression ratios, because the increased expansion causes the gas to do more work on the piston leaving less heat to be rejected at the end of the stroke. The same effect is present in the case of air-cycle approximation.

(vi) Mean Effective Pressure (MEP): The mean effective pressure increase with compression ratio as efficiency increases. It follows P_3 and P_4 and hence it is maximum at a fuel-air ratio slightly richer than the chemically correct ratio as shown in **Fig. 1.26**.

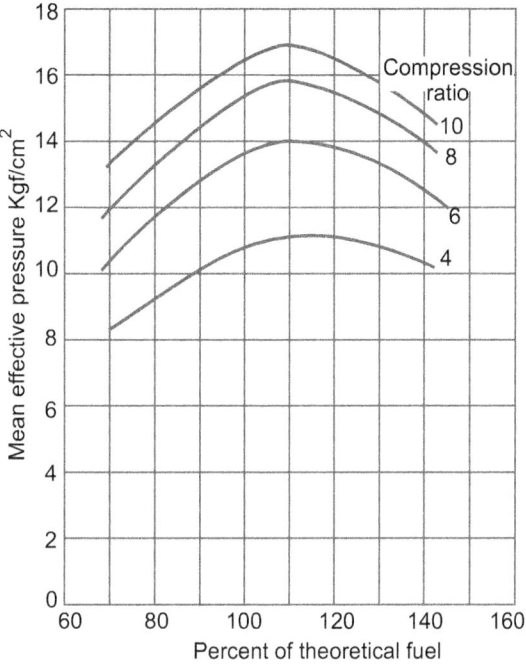

Fig. 1.26: Effect of Fuel-ratio on Mean Effective Pressure

1.18 PROPERTIES OF CONSTANT VOLUME (OTTO) FUEL-AIR CYCLE

The following are the characteristics of constant - volume fuel-air cycle:
  (a) The efficiency is mainly affected by the compression ratio and fuel-air ratio.
  (b) When fuel-air ratio is the variable, the efficiency decreases as fuel-air ratio increases. It is because of the increase in specific heat and dissociation at high temperature (maximum temperature at F_r = 1.1 approximately).
  (c) Above F_r = 1.1 approximately, expansion temperature decreases with increasing fuel-air ratio, but combustion is incomplete because mixture is rich and the net result is decrease in efficiency with increasing F_r.
  (d) The mean effective pressure is maximum at F_r = 1.05 to 1.10

$$p = \frac{m\,RT}{VM}$$

where, m is mass and M is molecular weight.

When fuel-air ratio is the only variable mR/V will be constant. Therefore, pressure depends on $\frac{T}{\text{mol. wt.}}$. Evidently as F_r increases, the decrease in the molecular weight offsets the decrease in temperature along the expansion line with the result that mep peaks in the region F_r = 1.05 to 1.10 and falls off more slowly than temperature.

1.19 DUAL COMBUSTION OR LIMITED-PRESSURE FUEL-AIR CYCLE

The difference between air cycle and fuel-air cycle of a diesel engine is shown in **Fig. 1.27**. The values are given for an engine having compression ratio of 16 and relative fuel-air ratio of 0.6. Note that the difference between air cycle and fuel-air cycle for diesel engine is much less than for Otto (petrol) engine.

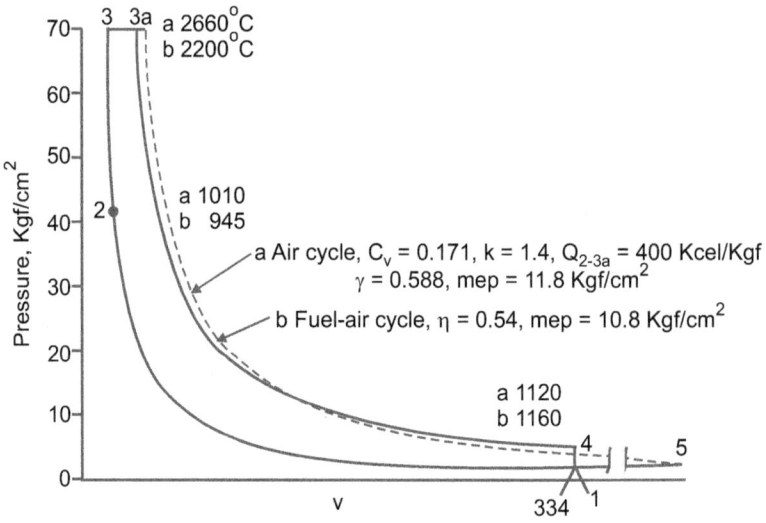

Fig. 1.27: Comparison of Air Cycle and Fuel-Air For Diesel Engine

1.20 ACTUAL CYCLES (S-09)

In air-standard cycle the working fluid is an ideal gas (air) while in Fuel-air cycle the working fluid is a mixture of fuel and air. The efficiency of fuel-air cycle is less than the air standard cycle efficiency. The actual cycles considers all the losses occurring while operating the engine. So actual cycle efficiency is much lower than the air standard efficiency due to various losses occurring in the actual engine operation. These are as follows:

1. Losses due to variation of specific heats with temperature.
2. Chemical equilibrium losses or dissociation losses.
3. Time losses.
4. Losses due to incomplete combustion.
5. Direct heat losses.
6. Exhaust blow-down loss.
7. Pumping losses.

An estimate of these losses can be made from past experience and some simple tests on the engines and these estimates are useful in evaluating an engine performance.

If we subtract losses due to variable specific heat and dissociation from the air-cycles we get fuel-air cycle analysis and if we further subtract other losses form fuel-air cycle analysis we can very closely approximate the actual cycle. This is shown diagrammatically in **Fig. 1.28**.

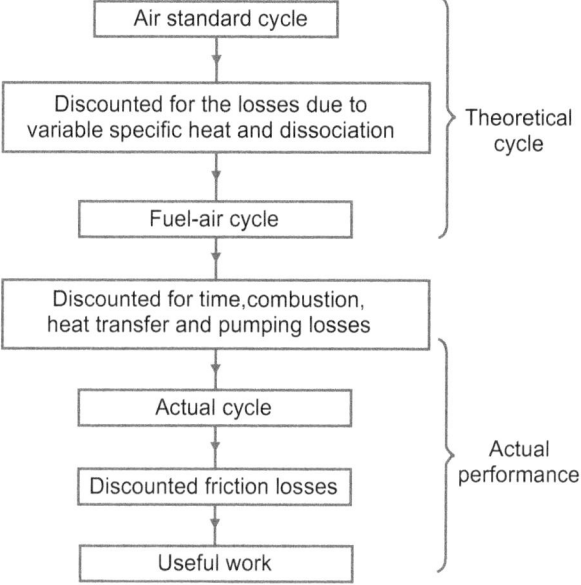

Fig. 1.28: Theoretical and Actual Cycle

Fig. 1.29 shows the difference between ideal Otto cycle and actual cycle. Fig. 1.30 shows the difference between the ideal cycle efficiency and actual cycle efficiency.

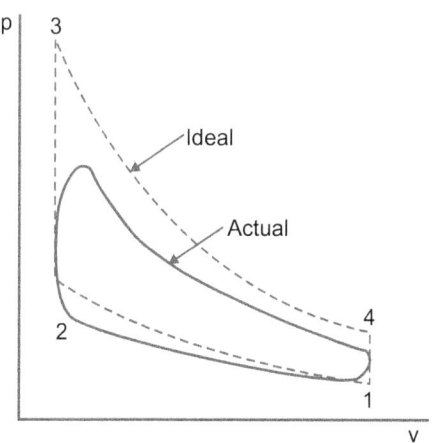

Fig. 1.29: Comparison of Ideal Cycle and Real Cycle for a Petrol Englue

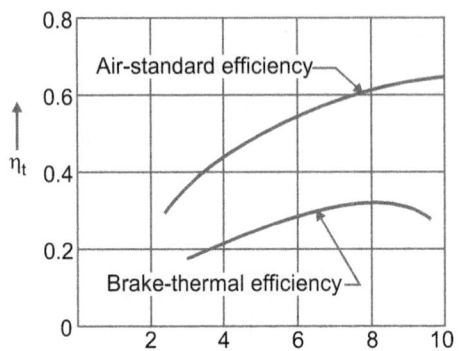
Fig. 1.30: Efficiency of Ideal and Actual Cycle

1.21 LOSSES IN ACTUAL ENGINE OPERATION (OTTO CYCLE)

We have discussed the (i) Losses due to Variation of Specific Heats and (ii) Chemical Equilibrium Losses (Dissociation) in chapter 3. Let us discuss the time loss.

1.21.1 Time Losses

In theoretical cycles (Otto cycle) the burning of fuel is assumed to be instantaneous whereas in an actual cycle the burning process is completed in a definite interval of time. The time required for combustion is such that under all circumstances some change in volume takes place while it is in progress. The crankshaft will usually turn about 40° between the time the spark occurs and the time the charge is completely burnt or when maximum pressure in the cycle is reached.

The effect of the finite time of combustion is that the maximum pressure will not be produced when the volume is minimum; but is produced some time after T.D.C. The pressure, therefore, rises in the first part of the working stroke from b to c as shown in **Fig. 1.31**.

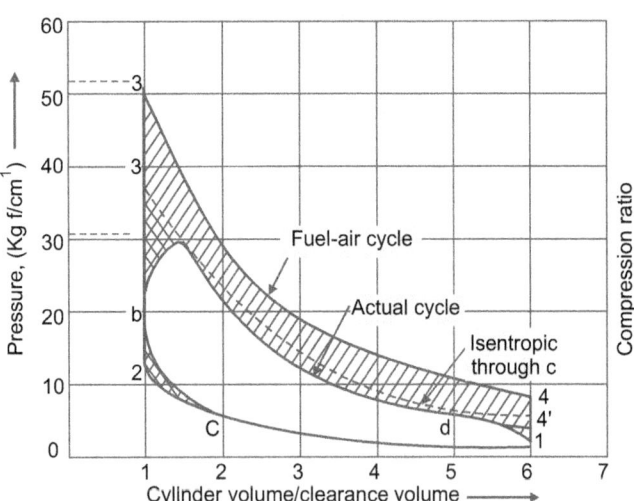

Fig. 1.31: The Effect of Time Losses on p-v Diagram

The point 3 represents the state of gases if the fuel combustion were instantaneous and an additional amount of work equal to the area shown hatched would have been done. This loss of work reduces the efficiency and is called **'burning time loss'** or merely **'time losses'**. The time taken for the burning depends upon the velocity of flame front and the distance from the point of ignition to the opposite side of the combustion space.

In order to that the maximum pressure is not reached too late in the expansion stroke, the time at which the burning starts is varied by varying the spark timing or spark advance. **Fig. 1.32** and **Fig. 1.33** show the effect of spark timing on p-v diagram. With spark at T.D.C. the pressure is low due to the expansion of gases. If the spark is advanced to achieve combustion at additional work is required to compress the burning gases.

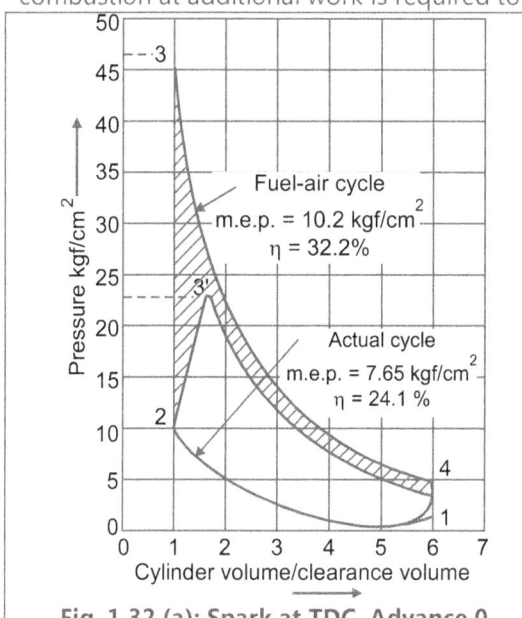

Fig. 1.32 (a): Spark at TDC, Advance 0

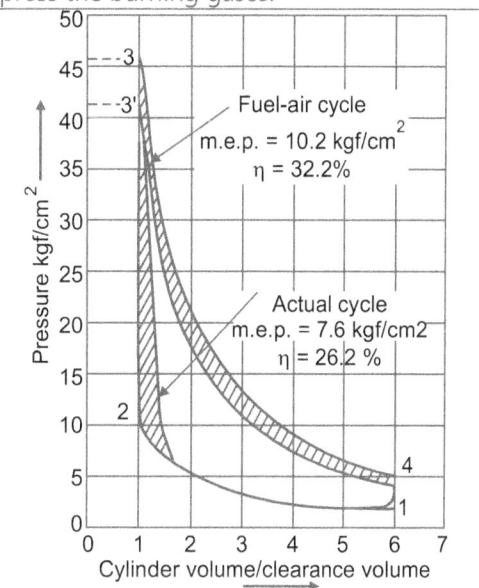

Fig. 1.32 (b): Combustion Completed at TDC, Advance 39°

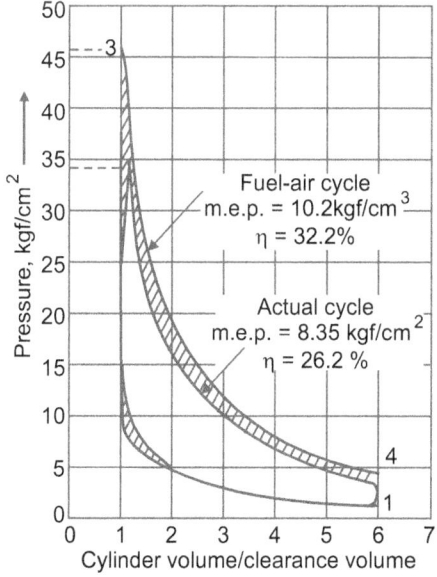

Fig. 1.32 (c): Optimum Advance 13°-26°

This represents a direct loss. In both the above cases the work area is less and the power and efficiency are lost. Therefore, a moderate spark advance is the best compromise, resulting in small losses on both the expansion stroke. Table 1.5 compares the performance for various ignition advance. **Fig 1.33** and **1.34** show the power loss by retarded ignition timing. A deliberate spark retard from optimum may be done in actual practice to avoid knocking and Co-reduce exhaust emissions of HC and CO.

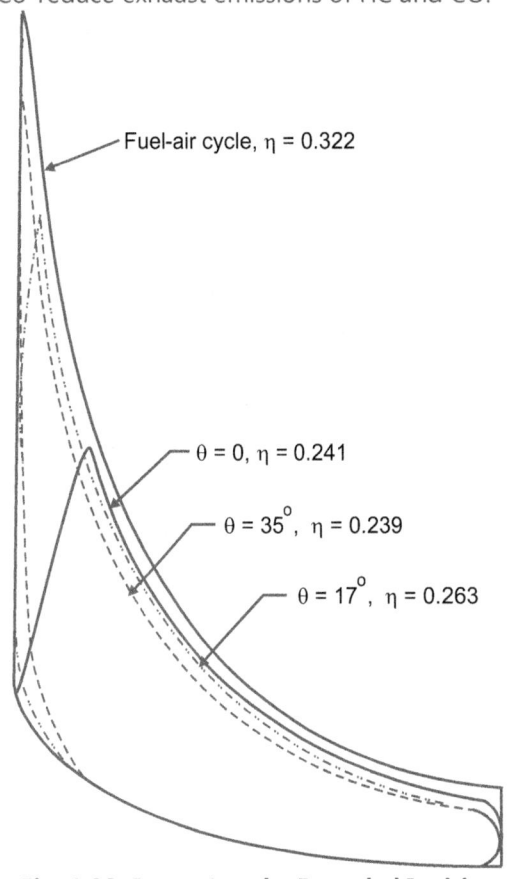

Fig. 1.33: Power Loss by Retarded Ignition Timing

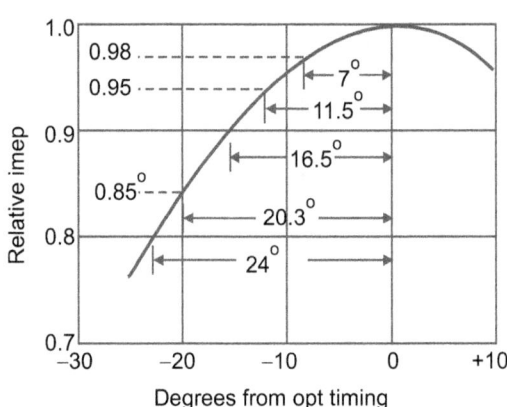

Fig. 1.34: Power Loss by Retarded Ignition Times

Table 1.5: Performance for Various Ignition Advance for Compression Ratio, r = 6

Cycle	Ignition advance	Max. Cycle pressure, kgf/cm²	mep kgf/cm²	Efficiency %	Actual η / Fuel-air η
Fuel air cycle	0°	44	10.2	32.2	0.1
Actual cycle	0°	23	7.5	24.1	0.75
Actual cycle	35°	41	7.6	23.9	0.74
Actual cycle	17°	34	8.35	26.2	0.81

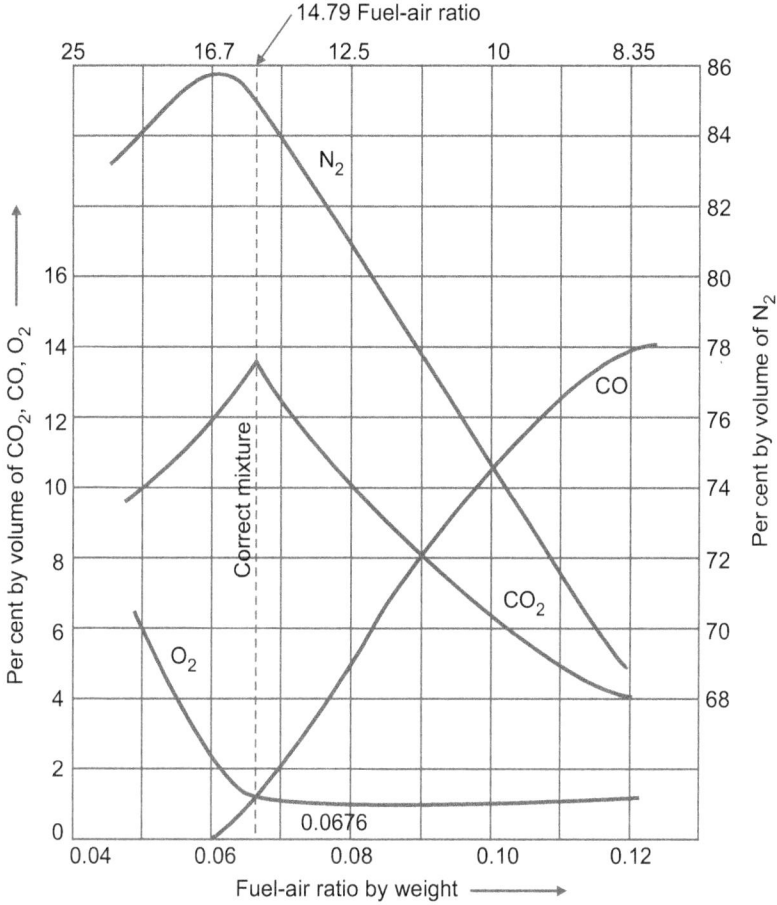

Fig. 1.35: The Composition of Exhaust Gases for Various Fuel-air Ratios

At full throttle with a 'best power' fuel-air ratio and optimum ignition advance the time losses may accounts for a loss in efficiency of about 5 percent (fuel-air cycle efficiency is reduced by about 2 percent). These losses will be large when the mixture is rich or lean, throttle is closed and ignition advance is not optimum.

1.21.2 Incomplete Combustion Loss

One can say it is not possible to achieve the 100% fuel combustion efficiency due to various practical reasons discussed. The engine designer always try to design the combustion chamber to get the homogeneous mixture and achieve the combustion efficiency. In spite of this is impossible to obtain perfect homogeneity in the mixture. Fuel vapour, air, and residual gas are present in the cylinder before ignition takes place. Under these circumstances it is possible to have excess oxygen in one part of the cylinder and excess fuel in another part. Therefore, some fuel does not burn or burns partially and hence CO and O_2 will appear in the exhaust as shown in **Fig. 1.35**. Energy release data show that only about 95 percent of the energy is released with fuel-air ratios near stoichiometric. Energy release in actual engine is about 90 to 93% of fuel energy input.

It should be noted that it is necessary to use a lean mixture to eliminate fuel waste, while a rich mixture is required to utilize all the oxygen. Slightly leaner mixture would give maximum efficiency but lean mixture will burn slowly, increasing the time losses or will not burn at all causing total waste. In the rich mixture some of the fuel will not get oxygen and will be completely wasted. Also the flame speed in the rich mixture is low, thereby, increasing the time losses and lowering the efficiency.

Even if fuel and oxygen eventually combine during the exhaust stroke, this energy, which is released later, cannot be utilized to force the piston and is a waste. Imperfect mixing may give different fuel-air ratios on succeeding suction strokes or certain cylinders may get continuously leaner mixture than others.

1.21.3 Direct Heat Loss

The temperature of the burnt gases is higher than cylinder walls. So during the combustion process and subsequent expansion stroke the heat flows from cylinder gases through the cylinder walls and cylinder head into the water jacket or cooling fins. Some heat enters the piston head and flows through the piston rings into the cylinder wall or is carried away by the engine oil which splashes on the underside of the piston. The heat loss is shown on the p-v diagram of Fig. 1.44.

(a) Heat loss during combustion will naturally have the maximum effect, while heat loss just before the end of the expansion stroke can have but every little effect, because its chance of doing useful work is very small.

(b) The heat lost during the combustion does not represent a complete loss because even under ideal conditions assumed for air standard cycle, only a part of this heat could be converted into work (equal to Q X $\eta_{thermal}$ and rest would be rejected at the end of the stroke.

(c) About 15 percent of the total heat is lost during combustion and expansion. If all heat loss is recovered, about 20% of it may appear as useful work. Fig. 1.70 shows percentage of time loss, heat loss, and exhaust loss in a CFR engine. Losses are given as percentage of fuel-air cycle work.

The effect of loss of heat during combustion is to reduce the maximum temperature. Thus this heat loss will result in more complete combustion and in a slight improvement in cycle efficiency to offset some, if only a small part of the loss.

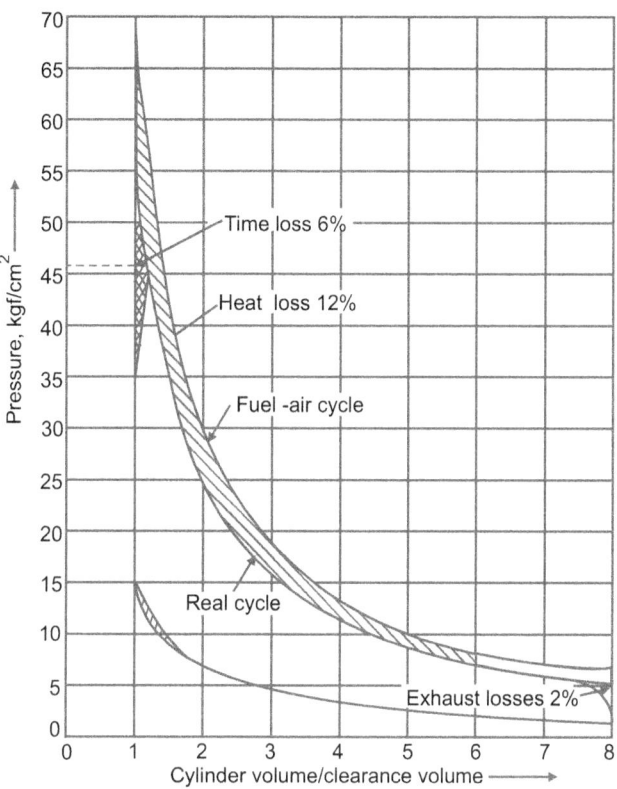

Fig. 1.36: Percentage of Time Loss, Heat Loss and Exhaust Loss in Petrol Engines

1.21.4 Exhaust Blow-down Loss

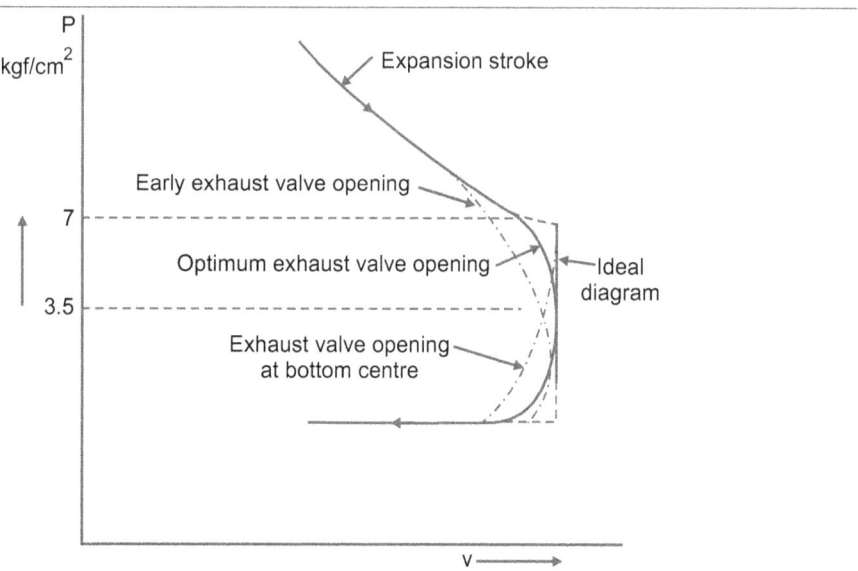

Fig. 1.37: Effect of Exhaust Valve Opening Time on Blowdown

The cylinder pressure at the end of exhaust stroke is about 7 kgf/cm².

(a) If the exhaust valve is opened at bottom dead centre, the piston has to do work against high cylinder pressures during part of the exhaust stroke.
(b) If the exhaust valve is opened too early, part of the expansion stroke is lost.
(c) The best compromise is to open the exhaust valve 40° to 70° before B.D.C., thereby, reducing the cylinder pressure to halfway to atmospheric before the exhaust stroke begins. This is shown in the **Fig. 1.37** by the roundness of the end of eth diagram.

1.21.5 Pumping Losses

The pressure of exhaust is higher than atmospheric pressure hence it has the potential to perform work Also during suction, the charge enters into the cylinder against the vacuum pressure, hence it has potential to perform work. *The difference of work done in expelling the exhaust gases and the work done by the fresh charge during suction stroke is called the pumping work.* In other words pumping loss is due to pumping gas from low inlet pressure point to higher exhaust pressure p_e. The pumping loss increases at part throttle because throttling reduces the suction pressure. Pumping loss also increases with speed.

1.21.6 Rubbing Friction Loss

These losses are due to
(i) Friction between piston and cylinder walls.
(ii) Friction in various bearings, and
(iii) Friction in the auxiliary equipment such as pumps and fans.

The piston friction increases rapidly with engine speed. It also increases to a small extent by increase in mean effective pressure. The bearing friction and auxiliary friction also increases with engine speed.

The efficiency of an engine is maximum at full load and reduces as load decreases. It is because the percentage of direct heat loss, pumping loss and rubbing friction loss increase at lower loads. The approximate losses for a petrol engine of high compression ratio, say 10 : 1 using chemically correct mixture is given in **Table 1.6**, a percentage of fuel energy input.

Table 1.6: Typical losses in a petrol engine

Item	Load	
	Full load	Half load
(a) Air standard cycle efficiency, %	60.0	60.0
1. Losses due to variation of specific heat and chemical equilibrium, %	13.3	13.3
2. Burning time loss, %	4.0	4.0
3. Incomplete combustion loss, %	2.5	2.5
4. Direct heat loss, %	3.5	5.0

Item	Load	
	Full load	Half load
5. Exhaust blow-down loss, %	0.5	0.5
6. Pumping loss, %	0.4	2.0
7. Rubbing friction loss, %	3.2	6.4
(b) Fuel air cycle efficiency = $\eta_{air\ standard}$ – (1)	46.7	46.7
(c) Gross indicated thermal efficiency		
= Fuel air cycle efficiency – (2 + 3 + 4 + 5)	36.2	3.7
(d) Actual brake thermal efficiency		
= Gross ihp – (6 + 7)	32.6	26.3

1.22 COMPARISON OF ACTUAL AND FUEL-AIR CYCLES IN DIESEL ENGINES

The main loss in diesel engine is due to incomplete combustion and is the cause of main difference between fuel-air cycle and actual cycle of the engine. This is shown in **Fig. 1.38**. In diesel engine the losses are less than that in the Otto engine. In fuel-air cycle the combustion is supposed to be completed at the end of constant pressure burning, whereas in actual practice after burning continues up to half of the expansion stroke. The ratio between actual and fuel-air cycle efficiency is about 0.85 in diesel engines.

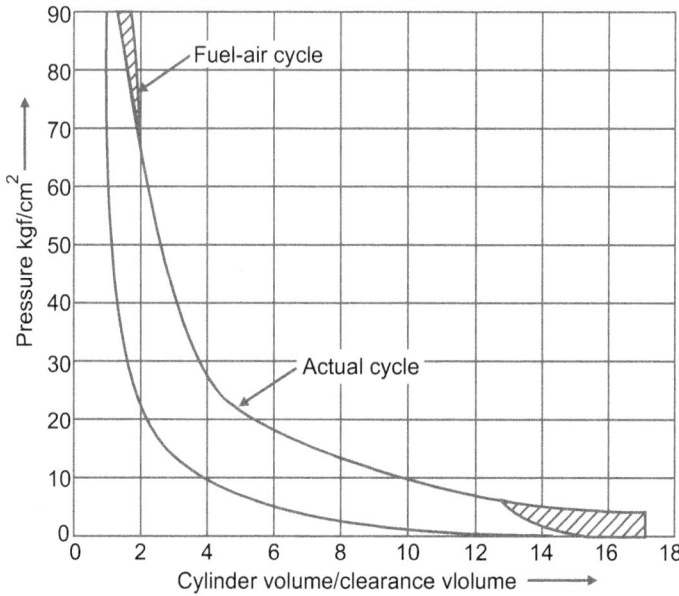

Fig. 1.38: Actual Diesel Cycle Vs. Equivalent Fuel Combustion Limited Pressure Cycle for Two Stroke Diesel Engine

Multiple Choice Questions (MCQ's)

1. Which of the following is incorrect?
   (a) Petrol engine works on Otto cycle
   (b) Carburetor is used in petrol engine
   (c) Diesel engine works on Otto cycle
   (d) Spark plug is used in petrol engine

2. A petrol engine is which diesel is used as a fuel will,
   (a) not run
   (b) increase knocking
   (c) Decrease knocking
   (d) run normally

3. If diesel is used in petrol engine, it will not run. What is the correct reason?
   (a) Low compression ratio
   (b) more density
   (c) less volatility
   (d) Low burning point

4. Stoichoimentric ratio means
   (a) Chemically correct air fuel ratio
   (b) Air fuel ratio which gives maximum efficiency
   (c) Air fuel ratio which gives maximum power
   (d) Air fuel ratio which gives maximum economy

5. Stoichoimetric ratio means
   (a) Chemically correct Air fuel ratio by volume
   (b) Chemically correct Air fuel ratio by mass
   (c) Air fuel ratio for maximum economy
   (d) Air fuel ratio for maximum power

6. Air fuel ratio is ratio of .... of air to .... of fuel.
   (a) mass, volume
   (b) volume, mass
   (c) volume, volume
   (d) mass, mass

7. Stroke engine produces more power then 4-stroke engine because
   (a) 2 stroke engine has 2 power strokes in one cycle whereas 4 stroke engine has 1 power strokes in one cycle.
   (b) 2 stroke engine has 1 expansion stroke in every 2 strokes whereas 4 stroke engine has 1 expansion strokes in every 4 strokes.
   (c) 2 stroke engine is bigger in size
   (d) 2 stroke engine has more compression ratio.

8. Which of the following is not true.
   (a) Efficiency of 2 stroke engine is more than 4 stroke engine.
   (b) Efficiency of 2 stroke engine is less than 4 stroke engine.
   (c) 2 stroke engines produce more power than 4 stroke engine.
   (d) Emissions from 4 stroke engine are less harmful than emissions from 2 stroke engine.

9. By suing fresh charge, the burn gases are removed from combustion chamber. This process is called as
   (a) Charging (b) Supercharging
   (c) Scavenging (d) Turbo charging
10. In Otto cycle, heat addition takes place during

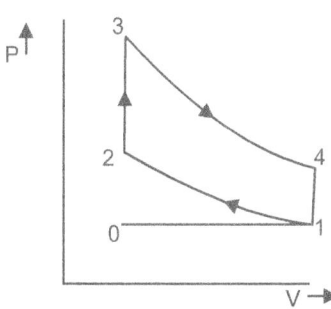

   (a) Process 1–2 (b) Process 2–3
   (c) Process 3–4 (d) Process 4–1
11. In Otto cycle, heat addition takes places at constant
    (a) volume (b) Enthalpy
    (c) pressure (d) Temperature
12. In Otto cycle heat rejection takes place at constant .... whereas in diesel cycle heat rejection takes place at constant ......
    (a) pressure, pressure (b) pressure, volume
    (c) volume, volume (d) volume, pressure
13. Which of the following is not true about EC engines?
    (a) less power to weight ratio **(b) No secondary working fluid**
    (c) these are self starting (d) can use solid, fuels
14. Which of the following is not true about IC engine?
    (a) More power to weight ratio (b) Not self starting
    (c) Higher efficiency **(d) Can use solid fuels**
15. Which of these is not on EC engine?
    (a) Wankel (b) Stirling
    (c) Steam (d) Close cycle gas turbine
16. Which of these is not an IC engine?
    (a) Wankle (b) Diesel
    (c) Open cycle gas turbine **(d) Closed cycle gas turbine**
17. Which of these is true about IC Engine as compared to
    (a) Higher overall efficiency
    (b) Does not require starting torque
    (c) Separate device for heat addition and rejection
    (d) Can use solid fuels

18. What is function of an engine cylinder?
    (a) To support crankshaft
    (b) To support camshaft
    (c) To provide space for piston reciprocate
    (d) To support journal
19. Oil galleries are ....
    (a) Place where oil is stored temporarily.
    (b) Drilled passages in cylinder block through which lubricating oil pass
    (c) The storage from where oil is splashed
    (d) None of the above
20. Which of these properties are not that much important while selecting material for an engine cylinder?
    (a) High thermal conductivity   (b) High castability
    (c) Good impact strength   (d) High corrosion resistance
21. The main function of crankcase is
    (a) To support journal and bearing of crankshaft and maintain alignment
    (b) To maintain air tight contact between piston and cylinder.
    (c) To guide rocker arm, push rods, etc.
    (d) To provide place for combustion
22. Rigidity is the most important consideration in selection of material for
    (a) Intake manifold   (b) Exhaust manifold
    (c) Piston rings   **(d) crankcase**
23. The cylinder block top surface to which cylinder head is attached is called as ....
    (a) Gallery   **(b) Deck**
    (c) Rocker   (d) Poppet
24. Which of these is having provisions for valve seats, valve guides, ports and coolent jackets?
    (a) Engine cylinder   **(b) Cylinder head**
    (c) Crankcase   (d) Fuel injectors
25. Material used for making of cylinder heads of racing cars is
    (a) Copper alloys   (b) Stainless steel
    (c) High speed streets   (d) Plain carbon steel
26. Which of the following parts does not take part in process of transmission of gas force to the output shaft?
    (a) Piston   (b) Gudgeon Pin
    (c) Crank   **(d) Cylinder**

27. Low intertia is the most desirable property for
    - **(a) Piston**
    - (b) Flywheel
    - (c) Crank
    - (d) Spark plug

28. Material for piston should not have ....
    - (a) Less specific gravity
    - (b) High thermal conductivity
    - **(c) More ductility**
    - (d) High wear resistance

29. For thermodynamic analysis, IC engines are .... system.
    - (a) Open
    - **(b) closed**
    - (c) Isolated
    - (d) Adiabatic

30. .... approach is used for thermodynamic analysis of an IC engine.
    - (a) Control mass
    - **(b) Control volume**
    - (c) Control enthalpy
    - (d) Stead flow

31. In a thermodynamic cycle, combustion chamber has
    - (a) Fixed volume
    - **(b) Fixed mass**
    - (c) Fixed temperature
    - (d) Fixed enthalpy

32. As compared to diesel engines, petrol engines are .... speed and have .... compression ratio.
    - (a) high, high
    - (b) low, high
    - **(c) high, low**
    - (d) low, low

33. Upper limit on compression ratio of petrol engine is due to ....
    - **(a) Knocking tendency**
    - (b) high volatility
    - (c) low ignition temperature
    - (d) High ignition temperature

34. Upper limit on compression ratio of diesel engine is due to ......
    - (a) Detonation tendency
    - (b) High ignition temperature
    - **(c) Increased size and weight**
    - (d) There is no upper limit for diesel engine

35. Thermodynamic cycle for a two-stroke engine has .... processes.
    - (a) Three
    - (b) One
    - (c) Two
    - **(d) Four**

36. In ideal Otto cycle, engine, inlet valve remains open for ...., and exhaust gass remains open for .... of crank rotation.
    - **(a) 180°, 180°**
    - (b) More than 180°, less than 180°
    - (c) less than 180°, less than 180°
    - (d) More than 180°, more than 180°

37. In actual IC engines, suction value and exhaust valve remain open respectively for .... and .... rotation of crank shaft
    - (a) 180°, 180°
    - **(b) More than 180°, more than 180°**
    - (c) More than 180°, less than 180°
    - (d) less than 180°, more than 180°

38. Main reason due to which valves are not opened or closed at dead centres is ......
    (a) Inertia effect					(b) Ram effect
    (c) Thermal loads				**(d) Non instantaneous processes**

39. For high speed engines valve overlap ......
    (a) Decreases					(b) remains same
    (c) Increases				(d) can't say anything

40. For high speed engines, valve overlap .... in degrees of crank rotation and .... in milliseconds.
    (a) Increases, increases			**(b) Increases, almost remains same**
    (c) Decreases, increases			(d) Decreases, almost remains same

41. For low speed and high speed engines, inlet valve opens at about .... and .... respectively.
    (a) 10° before, 10° after BDC.		**(b) 10° before, 10° before TDC**
    (c) 10° before, 35° before TDC		(d) 10° before, 35° before TDC

42. In low speed engines inlet valve opening and closing takes place at about .... and .... respectively.
    (a) 10° before TDC, 10° before BDC	(b) 10° before TDC, 10° after TDC
    (c) 10° after TDC, 10° before BDC	**(d) 10° before TDC, 10° after BDC**

43. In high speed engines, inlet valve opening and closing takes place at about .... and .... respectively.
    (a) 10° before TDC, 50° after BDC	(b) 50° before TDC, 10° after BDC
    (c) 10° before TDC, 10° after BDC	(d) 50° before TDC, 50° after BDC

44. In low speed engines exhaust valve opening and closing takes place at about .... and .... respectively.
    (a) 25° before BDC, 30° before TDC	(b) 25° before TDC, 10° after BDC
    (c) 25° before BDC, 10° after TDC	(d) 10° before BDC, 25° after BDC.

45. In high speed engines exhaust valve opening and closing takes place at about .... and .... respectively.
    (a) 55° before BDC, 20° before BDC	**(b) 55° before BDC, 20° after TDC**
    (c) 55° before TDC, 20° before TDC	(d) 55° after TDC, 20° before BDC

46. An valve overlap increases, volumetric efficiency tends to ....
    (a) Increase					**(b) Decrease**
    (c) Remain unaffected			(d) 50%

47. Which is not true for an air standard cycle analysis?
    (a) Values of specific heats and physical constants do not change.
    (b) All the processes are reversible
    (c) All the process are instantaneous
    (d) Working medium does not undergo chemical changes.

48. Which is not an assumption for an air standard cycle?
    (a) Working substance has a fixed mass
    (b) Due to combustion, chemical composition changes
    (c) Operation is frictionless
    (d) Working substance does not have Kinetic energy
49. Which is not an assumption for fuel-air cycle?
    (a) No heat exchange between the gases and cylinder walls.
    (b) Frictionless processes
    (c) No chemical change in either fuel or air prior to combustion.
    (d) Value of specific gas constant changes but of specific heat remains same
50. Which is true about air standard cycles?
    (a) Shows general effect of compression ratio on engine efficiency
    (b) Shows general effect of fuel-air ratio on engine efficiency
    (c) Shows general effect of variation in inlet temperature on engine efficiency
    (d) Show general effect of variation in inlet pressure on engine efficiency
51. Which assumption is not common for both air standard and fuel air cycles?
    (a) Intake and exhaust both take place at atmospheric pressure
    (b) Compression and expansion processes are isentropic.
    (c) Air fuel ratio is fixed.
    (d) Heat rejection is instantaneous process
52. Which is not true about fuel-air otto cycle?
    (a) Shows general effect of fuel-air ratio on engine efficiency.
    (b) Heat rejection is assumed to be instantaneous.
    (c) Heat addition is assumed to be instantaneous
    (d) During exhaust, pressure inside the cylinder is greater than atmospheric
53. A otto cycle works between temperatures 300k and 2000k. If higher limits is changed to 2200k, efficiency of cycle ....
    (a) **Increases**   (b) Decreases
    (c) Remains same   (d) Data insufficient
54. Dual cycle has 5 thermodynamic processes. These processes will take place in .... strokes.
    (a) 5   (b) 2
    (c) 4   (d) 5/2
55. For an otto cycle, the temperature ratio of after and before compression is 2.5, then compression ratio will be nearly ....
    (a) 8   (b) 9
    (c) 7   **(d) 10**

56. Consider the fig.

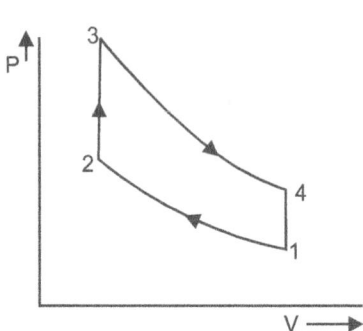

If $T_1 = \frac{2}{3} T_2$, $T_4 = 2T_1$ and $T_3 = 2.5\ T_2$ then thermal efficiency of cycle ....
   (a) 44% (b) **55%**
   (c) 66% (d) Data insufficient

57. If compression ratio of otto cycle is increased from 6 to 8, the % change in efficiency will be nearly ....
   (a) 5 (b) **10**
   (c) −5 (d) 10

58. Which of the following is not considered in fuel air cycle analysis?
   (a) Time required for heat addition and rejection
   (b) Change in air-fuel ratio.
   (c) Heat loss to the cylinder walls
   (d) Friction between moving parts.

59. What is the effect of increase in temperature on C_P and R ....
   (a) Both increase (b) C_p increases, R decreases
   (c) C_P increases, R remains same (d) C_P increases, R unpredictable

60. What is the effect of increase in temperature on C_V and r^L.
   (a) Both increases **(b) C_v increases, r^L decreases.**
   (c) V_v increases, r^L remains same. (d) C_V increases, r^L unpredictable

61. Consider following Fig.

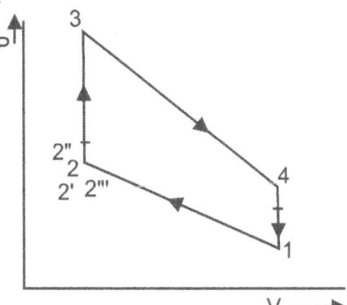

Due to variation in specific heat which will be new position of point 2.
   (a) 2 (b) 2′
   (c) 2″ (d) 2‴

62. Consider following Fig.

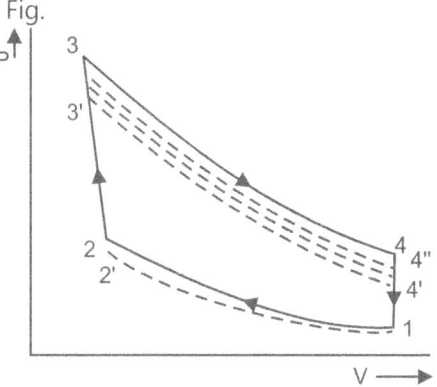

The process considering variation in specific heats is/are ....
(a) 1–2′,
(b) 1–2′ and 3′–4′
(c) 1–2′ and 3′–4″
(d) 1–2′ and 3–4′

63. In above fig. during process 3′–4′
(a) Constant C_P
(b) C_p decreases.
(c) C_P increases
(d) Can't predict what happens to C_P.

64. In above Fig. the process with constant C_P are ....
(a) 1–2, 3–4
(b) 1–2, 3–4, 3′–4′
(c) 1–2, 3–4, 3′–4″
(d) 1–2, 3–4, 3–4′

65. During adiabatic compression C_P
(a) Increases
(b) Decreases
(c) remains constant
(d) Unpredictable

66. In otto cycle, when variation of specific heats according to temperature is considered, what happens to slopes of compression and expansion curves?
(a) Both slopes increases
(b) Slope of compression curve increases, which slope of expansion curve decreases
(c) Slope of compression curve decreases while slope of expansion curve increases
(d) Both slopes decreases

67. Due to variation in specific heats due to temperature ....
(a) Peak pressure and temperature both reduce.
(b) Peak pressure reduces while peak temperature increases
(c) Peak pressure increases while peak temperature decreases
(d) Peak pressure and temperature both increases

68. In above fig. the work done will be maximum for which cycle?
(a) 1–2′–3′–4′
(b) 1–2–3–4
(c) 1–2′–3′–4″
(d) Can't compare

69. Dissociation effect is prominent for ....
    (a) Rich mixture, (b) lean mixture
    (c) Chemically correct mixture **(d) Both rich and lean mixture**
70. Dissociation effect is pronounced in ....
    (a) Petrol engine (b) Diesel engine
    (c) Both C1 and S1 engines. (d) Can't compare
71. Dissociation effects are pronounced in S1 engines. Which is not among the reasons for this?
    (a) Heterogeneous mixture (b) Higher compression ratio.
    (c) Higher temperature (d) Higher pressure.
72. What is the relation between thermal efficiency and specific fuel consumption?
    (a) directly proportional **(b) Inversely proportional**
    (c) Not related to each other (d) Both are the same
73. Relative fuel–air ratio is the ratio of
    (a) Actual fuel air ratio to chemically correct fuel air ratio on mass basis
    (b) Actual fuel air ratio to chemically correct fuel air ratio on volume basis
    (c) Chemically correct fuel-air ratio to actual fuel air ratio on mass basis
    (d) Chemically correct fuel-air ratio to actual fuel air ratio on volume basis.
74. Relative to efficiency air standard cycle the efficiency of fuel air cycle .... as the mixture weakens.
    (a) Decreases (b) does not affect
    (c) Increases (d) can't predict
75. The efficiency of fuel-air cycle relative to that of air standard cycle increases as the mixture weakens. The relation between this gain in efficiency and compression ratio is ....
    (a) Gain increases as compression ratio increases
    (b) Gain increases as compression ratio decreases
    (c) Gain increases as initially but decreases after certain value
    (d) The gain is independent of compression ratio.
76. Which of the following is not effect of lean mixtures?
    (a) Lower specific heat
    (b) Less chemical equilibrium losses
    (c) Higher efficiency
    (d) Efficiency equals to air standard efficiency
77. Which of the following is not effect of rich mixture?
    (a) High temperature (b) high chemical equilibrium losses
    (c) Higher specific fuel consumption **(d) Higher efficiency**

78. For given compression ratio, exhaust temperature is maximum for ....
    (a) lean mixture
    (b) rich mixture
    (c) chemically correct mixture
    (d) can't predict
79. If compression ratio is increased, what will happen to maximum cycle temperature (T_3) and exhaust temp (T_4)?
    (a) Both will increase
    (b) T_3 increases, T_4 decreases
    (c) T_3 decreases, T_4 increases
    (d) Both will decrease
80. Which of the following is considered in fuel air cycle?
    (a) Losses due to incomplete combustion
    (b) Time losses
    (c) Chemical equilibrium losses
    (d) Pumping losses
81. Consider following statements
    1. Air standard cycle is theoretical cycle
    2. Fuel air cycle is theoretical cycle.
    of these correct statement/s is/are
    (a) 1 and 2
    (b) Only 1
    (c) Only 2
    (d) neither 1 or 2
82. Consider following statements
    1. Air standard cycle is theoretical
    2. Fuel–air cycle is theoretical
    3. Actual cycle is practical
    of these correct statements are
    (a) 1 and 3
    (b) 1, 2 and 3
    (c) only 1
    (d) Only 3
83. The losses taking place due to non-instantaneous heat addition or rejection are termed as –
    (a) Direct losses
    (b) Pumping losses
    (c) Dissociation losses
    (d) Time losses
84. To reduce time losses, what is done?
    (a) Spark is introduced before TDC
    (b) Spark is introduced after TDC
    (c) Spark is introduced exactly at TDC
    (d) Time losses can't be reduced
85. What is the range of optimum spark advance for SI engines?
    (a) 13° to 26°
    (b) 0° to 5°
    (c) 30° to 40°
    (d) 40° to 50°

86. Which of the following factor will not affect time loss?
    (a) Mixture strength (b) throttle position
    (c) Ignition advance **(d) Intake pressure**
87. Blow down losses can be reduced by adjusting
    (a) Exhaust valve opening timing (b) Exhaust valve closing timing
    (c) Intake valve opening timing (d) Intake valve closing timing
88. Pumping loss .... at part throttle and .... as speed increases
    (a) Decreases, decreases (b) decreases, increases
    (c) increases, decreases **(d) increases, increases**
89. Which will not be logical choice for compression ratio of SI engines?
    (a) 6 (b) 8
    (c) 10 **(d) 14**
90. Exhaust valve opening and closing timing mainly depends upon ....
    (a) Engine power **(b) Speed**
    (c) Temperature (d) Efficiency
91. If V_C = clearance volume V_S = stroke volume, P_1 = inlet pressure, P_2 = exhaust pressure, then the pumping loss numerically equals to ....
    (a) $V_C (P_2 - P_1)$ (b) $(P_1 - P_2)(V_S - V_C)$
    (c) $V_S (P_2 - P_1)$ (d) $(P_2 - P_1)(V_S + V_C)$
92. For petrol engine arrange the various losses as percentage of total losses in ascending order.
    (a) Time loss, exhaust loss, heat loss **(b) exhaust loss, time loss, heat loss**
    (c) heat loss, time loss, exhaust loss (d) heat loss, exhaust loss, time loss
93.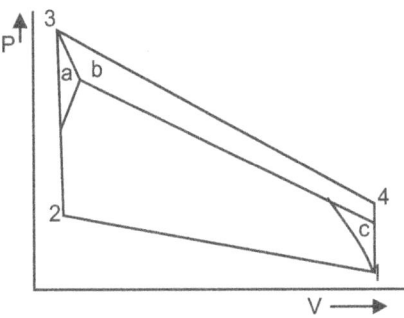
    In this fig. time losses are shown by area
    (a) a (b) b
    (c) c (d) Not shown in fig.
94. In above fig. Heat loss is shown by area
    (a) a **(b) b**
    (c) c (d) Not shown in fig.

95. In above fig. blow down loss is given by area
    (a) a   (b) b
    (c) c   (d) both b and c
96. At full load, the thermal efficiency of an IC engine is in the range.
    (a) 10 to 20%   **(b) 30 to 35%**
    (c) 60 to 70%   (d) 80 to 90%
97. Thermal efficiency of petrol engine as compared to diesel engine
    (a) higher   **(b) lower**
    (c) same for same speed   (d) same for same torque
98. Specific fuel consumption of diesel engine is compared to petrol engine is ……..
    (a) higher   **(b) lower**
    (c) same for same speed   (d) same for same output
99. For SI engine to have maximum thermal efficiency, fuel air mixture should be
    (a) lean   (b) rich
    (c) chemically correct   (d) does not depend on mixture strength
100. SI engine gives maximum power output when fuel-air mixture is
    (a) lean   (b) rich
    (c) chemically correct   (d) power is independent of strength
101. If dissociation is not considered peak temperature is obtained
    (a) at the chemically correct fuel air ratio
    (b) when the mixture is slightly rich
    (c) when the mixture is slightly lean
    (d) when the mixture is too rich
102. Due to dissociation, peak temperature is observed at ……..
    (a) chemically correct fuel-air ratio   **(b) slightly rich mixture**
    (c) slightly lean mixture   (d) too rich mixture
103. Due to dissociation exhaust gas temperature ……..
    (a) increases   **(b) Decreases**
    (c) remain unaffected   (d) firstly increases and then decreases
104. Dissociation is negligible when mixture is
    (a) chemically correct   (b) slightly rich
    (c) slightly lean   **(d) Too lean**
105. With dissociation maximum power is obtained at
    (a) chemically correct fuel-air ratio   **(b) slightly rich mixture**
    (c) slightly lean mixture   (d) Too rich mixture

106. M.E.P. is maximum when fuel-air mixture is
    (a) stoichiometric
    (b) slightly rich
    (c) slightly lean
    (d) Too lean

107. MEP is maximum when air fuel ratio is ....
    (a) slightly lower than stoichiometric
    (b) slightly higher than stoichiometric
    (c) Too much higher than stoichiometric
    d) stoichiometric

108. If mixture is made rich gradually and continuously, MEP will
    (a) increase continuously
    (b) Decrease continuously
    (c) remain constant
    (d) increase initially and then decrease

109. When mixture is rich ....
    (a) efficiency is high
    (b) power is less
    (c) maximum temperature is lower
    (d) maximum pressure is high

110. When mixture is lean
    (a) efficiency is less
    (b) power is high
    (c) maximum temperature is less
    (d) maximum pressure is lower

111. Time losses in engine cycle are due to
    (a) Heat transfer between gas and cylinder wall
    (b) gas leakage
    (c) progressive combustion
    (d) friction

112. Spark at TDC will result in
    (a) less wok done
    (b) Highest work done
    (c) zero work
    (d) work done is independent of spark time

113. The major loss in a SI engine is due to ....
    (a) pumping
    (b) incomplete combustion
    (c) variation in specific heat and chemical equilibrium
    (d) blow down

114. Major loss in Diesel engine is .... loss
    (a) incomplete combustion
    (b) Direct heat
    (c) friction
    (d) pumping

115. Difference in the efficiencies of fuel air cycle and air standard cycle is due to ....
    (a) Time loss
    (b) blow down loss
    (c) Chemical equilibrium loss
    (d) Friction loss

116. For CI engines actual efficiency is …….. percent of fuel air cycle efficiency
    (a) **60–80**
    (b) 100
    (c) 40–50
    (d) 30–35

117. Relative fuel air ratio can be defined as
    (a) Actual air : fuel ratio/chemically correct air fuel ratio
    (b) **Chemically correct air : fuel ratio/actual air : fuel ratio**
    (c) Chemically correct fuel : air ratio/actual fuel : air ratio
    (d) (Actual air – stoichiometric air)/actual fuel required.

118. As mixture strength varies, efficiency of fuel : air cycle varies. Relative change in efficiency with respect to air standard cycle. ……..
    (a) Increases with increase in compression ratio
    (b) Decreases with increase in compression ratio
    (c) **Independent of change in compression ratio**
    (d) Changes proportional to square of compression ratio.

119. Heat Engine converts ……..
    (a) Kinetic energy into mechanical energy
    (b) Potential energy into mechanical energy
    (c) **Heat energy of combustion of fuel into mechanical energy**
    (d) Mechanical energy into heat energy

120. Which of the following is an example of internal combustion engine?
    (a) Steam engine
    (b) Boiler
    (c) Closed cycle gas turbine
    (d) **Petrol Engine**

121. Which of the following is an example of internal combustion engine?
    (a) Open cycle gas turbine
    (b) Petrol engine
    (c) Diesel engine
    (d) **All of the above**

122. Disadvantage of reciprocating Internal combustion engines over External combustion engine is ……..
    (a) Overall efficiency is high
    (b) Low weight to power ratio
    (c) Lower initial cost
    (d) **None of the above**

123. Advantage of External combustion engines over reciprocating internal combustion engine is ……..
    (a) Overall efficiency is high
    (b) **Cheaper fuel can be used**
    (c) Lower initial cost
    (d) Low weight to power ratio

124. In a single cylinder, single spark plug SI engine working on two stroke cycle at 2000 rpm, the number of sparks produced by spark plug per minutes will be ……..
    (a) **2000**
    (b) 1000
    (c) 200
    (d) 4000

125. In a single cylinder, single spark plug SI engine working on four stroke cycle at 4000 rpm, the number of sparks produced by spark plug per minutes will be :
   (a) 400 (b) 4000
   (c) 2000 (d) 8000

126. In a single cylinder, single inlet valve and exhaust valve engine working on four stroke cycle at 4000 rpm the inlet valve will open for .... times per minutes.
   (a) 1000 (b) 2000
   (c) 4000 (d) 8000

127. In a single cylinder, single inlet valve and exhaust valve SI engine working on two stroke cycle at 4000 rpm the exhaust valve will open for .... times per minutes.
   (a) 400 (b) 2000
   (c) 4000 (d) 8000

128. Fuel is injected in SI engine ....
   (a) At the end of compression stroke   **(b) At the start of suction stroke**
   (c) At the start of compression stroke   (d) During combustion of fuel

129. Fuel is injected in CI engine ....
   (a) At the end of compression stroke   (b) At the start of suction stroke
   (c) At the start of compression stroke   (d) At the valve overlap

130. Which of the followings are not the parts of two stroke SI engine?
   (a) Spark plug and ignition coil   **(b) Inlet and exhaust valves**
   (c) Crank and connecting rod   (d) None of the above

131. Which of the followings are not the parts of two stroke SI engines?
   (a) Spark plug and ignition coil   **(b) Camshaft and rocker arm**
   (c) Crank and connecting rod   (d) None of the above

132. Which of the followings are not the parts of four stroke SI engines?
   (a) Spark plug and ignition coil   (b) Camshaft and rocker arm
   (c) Crank and connecting rod   **(d) Inlet and exhaust ports**

133. The time for which both inlet and exhaust valves remains open in reciprocating IC engine is called as ....
   (a) Valve sharing   (b) Scavenging
   (c) Valve overlap   (d) Valve combing

134. Cylinder block provides housing for ....
   (a) Inlet and exhaust valve   (b) Spark plug
   (c) Fuel injector   **(d) None of the above**

135. Cylinder head provides housing for ....
   (a) Inlet and exhaust valve   (b) Spark plug
   (c) Fuel injector   **(d) All of the above**

EXERCISE

1. What are the two general classes of combustion engines and how do they basically differ in principle?
2. Discuss the relative merits and demerits of internal combustion and external combustion engines.
3. State the various types of internal and external combustion engines and their principal uses. Which of them are modern developments?
4. What are the two basic types of internal combustion engines? What are the fundamental differences between the two?
5. List the important reciprocating engine parts and their materials?
6. How SI engines and CI engines are further sub-classified?
7. Define compression ratio. What is its range for (a) the SI engines, (b) the CI engine? What factors limit the compression ratio in each type of engine?
8. Discuss the differences between ideal and actual valve timing diagram of a petrol engine?
9. Compare the relative advantages and disadvantages of four-stroke and two-stroke cycle engines.
10. What will be the effect of variables on engine performance viz.
    (i) Compression ratio on thermal efficiency, (ii) Fuel: Air Ratio on thermal efficiency, (iii) Fuel-air ratio on maximum pressure and maximum temperature, (iv) Fuel-air ratio on exhaust gas temperature.
11. With the help of a neat sketch explain basic nomenclature used for I.C. engine.
12. Compare two-stroke and four-stroke cycle engines. Bring out clearly their relative merits and demerits.
13. Give limitations of air standard cycle. Explain with suitable graphs, the effect of dissociation on maximum temperature and brake power. How does the presence of CO affects dissociation?
14. Discuss the advantages and disadvantages of external combustion engine over internal combustion engine.
15. Derive the relation for the percentage variation in air standard efficiency of diesel cycle with percentage variation of C_v.
16. Explain with suitable sketches the working of a four-stroke S.I. engine.
17. Explain characteristic features of the fuel-air cycle.
18. What are the effects of operating variables on the performance of the fuel-air cycle?
19. List the differences between actual cycles and air-standard cycles.
20. What are the three principal factors that influence engine performance?

21. Why the actual cycle efficiency is much lower than the air standard cycle efficiency? List the major losses in an actual engine.
22. Explain the following:
    (i)   Heat loss   (ii) Time loss
    (iii) Exhaust blowdown factor
23. Compare the actual and fuel-air cycles of a gasoline engine.
24. Explain the pumping loss and its effect on the cycle performance.
25. How does the composition of exhaust gases vary for the various fuel-air ratios in a gasoline engine?
26. Define volumetric efficiency and discuss the effect of various factors affecting the volumetric efficiency.
27. Discuss the rubbing friction losses.
28. Explain the effect of time loss with the help of a p-v diagram of Otto-cycle.
29. Explain the power loss due to retarded ignition timing in Otto engine with p-v plot.
30. Explain how the composition of exhaust gases vary according to fuel-air ratios.
31. What is a thermodynamic cycle? Do internal combustion engines operate on a thermodynamic cycle? How IC engine cycles are analysed?
32. What are the assumptions made in air standard cycle analysis?
33. What is use of air standard cycle analysis?
34. Define mean effective pressure. What does this criterion indicate for reciprocating engines?
35. Obtain an expression for the air standard efficiency on a volume basis of an engine working on the Otto cycle.
    Hence show that the efficiency of the Otto cycle is lower than that of Carnot cycle.
36. Show by graphs how the efficiency of the Otto cycle varies with compression ratio and the ratio of specific heats of working medium.
37. Derive an expression for the mean effective pressure of the Otto cycle?
38. What is the difference between Otto and Diesel cycle? Derive the formula for the efficiency of the Diesel cycle. Hence show that the efficiency of Diesel Cycle is always lower than the efficiency of the Otto cycle for the same compression ratio.
39. Show by graph how the efficiency of Diesel cycle varies with compression ratio and cut-off ratio.
40. Explain why the higher efficiency of the Otto cycle compared to Diesel cycle for the same compression ratio is not a result of practical importance.
41. Derive an expression for the mean effective pressure of Diesel cycle.
42. Explain the dual combustion cycle? Why this cycle is also called limited pressure cycle? Derive an expression for the air standard efficiency of dual cycle.

✱✱✱

SPARK IGNITION (SI) ENGINES

2.1 THEORY OF CARBURETION

In SI engines, highly volatile fuels like petrol, alcohol, benzol are used. In this case air-fuel mixture is produced outside the engine cylinder. This air-fuel mixture is supplied to the engine cylinder during suction through the engine intake manifold. Then this air-fuel mixture is compressed by the upward moving piston and just before the end of compression, the mixture is ignited by means of spark, produced by spark plug.

Carburettor is a device, which atomises and vapourises the fuel and mixes it with air in varying proportions so as to suit the changing conditions (or changing loads) of SI engines.

The process of automisation-vapourisation and mixing with air is known as **carburretion**. The air-fuel mixture so produced is called **Combustible mixture**.

This combustible mixture (air-fuel mixture) is carried to the engine cylinder through intake manifold and quantity of air-fuel mixture is controlled by **throttle valve**.

Now, it is essential to know the correct meaning of following terms.

1. **Vapourisation:** Vapourisation means change of phase from liquid phase to vapour phase.
2. **Automisation:** It is the mechanical breaking up of the liquid fuel into small particles i.e. when the liquid fuel is sprayed into air, the fuel particles absorb heat of air and get vapourized instantly.

Fig. 2.1 shows the basic fuel supply system of a Petrol engine or Induction system.

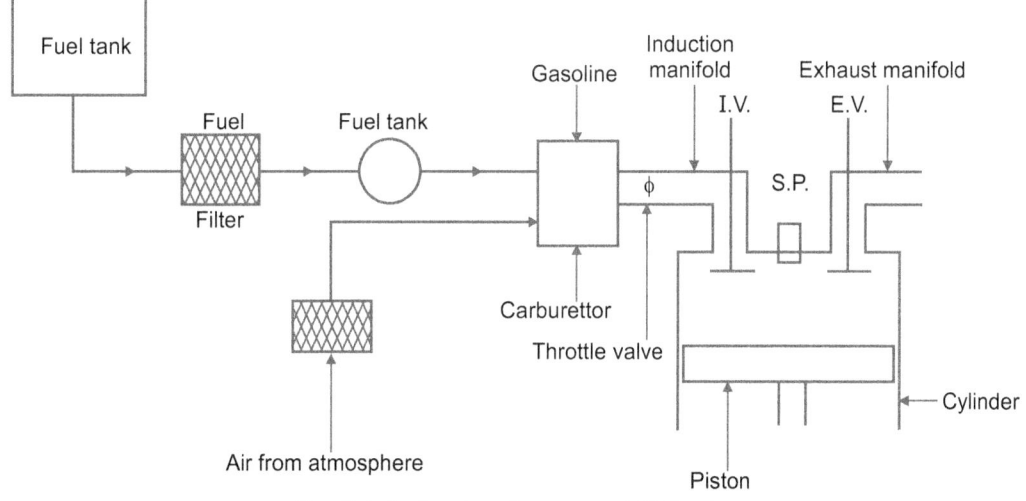

Fig. 2.1: Induction Systems of SI Engine

2.2 FACTORS EFFECTING CARBURETTORS

Following factors affect carburettion process:
1. **Engine Speed:** Directly affects the time available for preparation of mixture by the carburettor. When the engine speed increases, velocity of air must be increased by providing venturi in the carburettor.
2. **Temperature of Air at the Inlet:** When the temperature of atmosphere air increases, vapourisation increases, and decreases the density of air. Ultimately it results in decrease of efficiency and output power.
3. **The Vapourisation Characteristics of Fuel:** It is always desirable to use more volatile fuels, otherwise it is required to heat the fuels in the intake manifold to produce vapourisation. However this is expensive and reduce power output.
4. **Design of Intake Manifold:** In case of multicylinder engines, proper design of intake manifold is a must to ensure proper distribution of fuel to each cylinder.

2.3 TYPES OF AIR-FUEL MIXTURES

1. **Stoichiometric Air-Fuel Mixture or Chemically Correct Air-Fuel Mixture**
   (a) This mixture contains just sufficient air for the complete combustion of fuel.
   (b) Note after combustion all the fuel is burnt and all the air is consumed.
   (c) For 1 kg of Octane (C_8H_{18}) fuel, 15.14 kg of air is needed for complete combustion.
   Therefore, 15.14: 1 is called chemically correct air-fuel ratio.
2. **Rich Mix:** More fuel-less air.
   Therefore, 14, 13, 12, 10 or less: It is called **Rich Mix**.
3. **Lean Mix:** Less fuel-more air
   Therefore, 17, 18, 20, 22, or more: It is called **Lean Mix**.

The range of homogenous mixture which can be ignited in SI engine:
   7 : 1 Air-fuel by mass on Rich Side and @ 20 : 1 on Lean Side.

2.4 MIXTURE REQUIREMENTS

2.4.1 For Power and Economy

It is important to know the value of air-fuel at which max power and minimum fuel consumption is obtained.

Fig. 2.2 shows the graph of power output and bsfc against air-fuel ratio.

Maximum power is obtained at a considerably rich mixture with air-fuel ratio around 12 : 1. (This mixture is the best power mixture).

The minimum brake specific fuel consumption (bsfc) is obtained at a slightly leaner mixture with air-fuel ratio around 16:1. (This mixture is the best economy mixture).

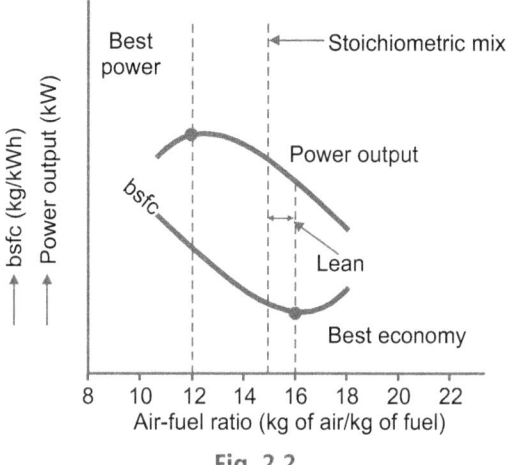

Fig. 2.2

2.4.2 For Automotive Engines at Different Working Conditions

Fig. 2.3 shows air-fuel ratio at different engine speeds.

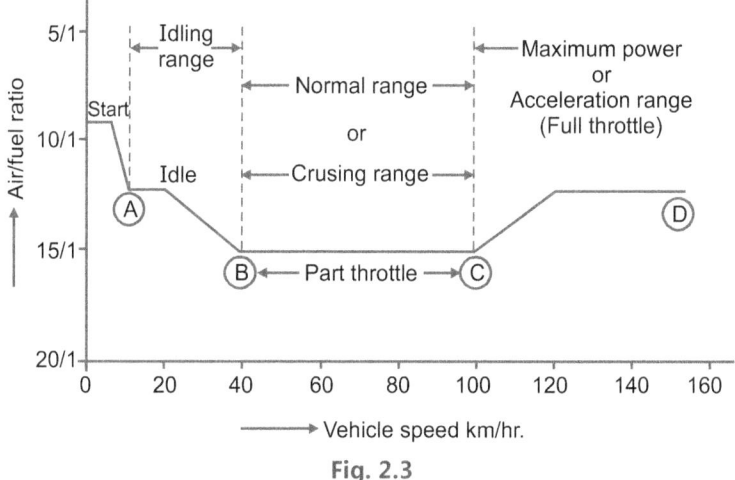

Fig. 2.3

- For the starting mixture required is very rich, because the engine is cold. Fuel does not vapourise properly. For idling air-fuel required is @ 12 : 1.
- Idling means engine running but there is no external load on engine. The engine has to overcome frictional load only.
- During starting and idling, suction created is very less, therefore less fuel is withdrawn from carburetor. Further walls of intake manifold are cold. This causes condensation of fuel vapours. Also there are residual gases present in the cylinder. These gases cause dilution of charge in the cylinder.
- Due to such conditions, at starting and idling a rich mixture is required.

Normal or Cruising Range (B-C). Throttle valve is gradually opened and load increases above 20%.
- Fuel economy is prime consideration.
- Air-fuel ratio required @ 16 or 17 : 1.

Maximum Power or Acceleration range (C-D). For max power rich mixture is required.
- Nearly full throttle.
- Air-fuel ratio required 12 to 14 : 1.

2.5 CARBURETTOR TYPES

1. **Constant Choke Carburettors:** Venturi is of fixed dimensions. Metering is affected by varying the pressure drop across it. Example, Solex, Zenith, Carter carburettors. (Venturi-fixed dimensions; pressure drop varied).

2. **Constant Vacuum Carburettors:** Area of air passage is varied, while pressure drop is kept constant. Example, S.U. carburettor.
(Venturi dimensions varied; pressure drop constant.)

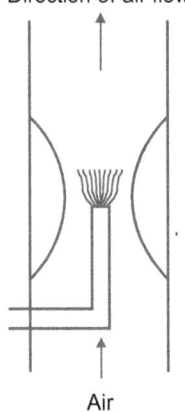

- The air has to lift fuel droplets against gravity
- Obsolete

Fig. 2.4: Up Draught

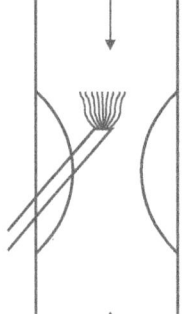

- Flow of air
- Mix flow is assisted by gravity

Fig. 2.5: Down Draught

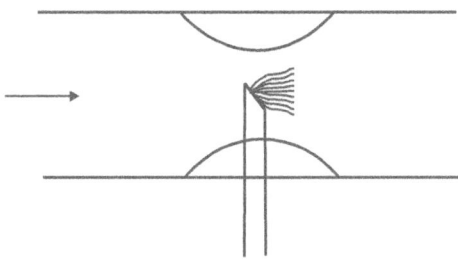

- Direction of flow of air or mix is horizontal
- Used where under bonnet space is limited

Fig. 2.6: Cross or Horizontal Draught

2.6 A SIMPLE CARBURETTOR

Fig. 2.7 shows a simple carburettor. It mainly consists of:
- A float chamber with hollow float, needle valve, air bleed hole.
- A cylindrical pipe called air-horn. Narrowest c/s of which is called venturi.
- A throttle valve.
- A choke valve.
- A main petrol jet.

Float with needle valve maintains constant level of petrol in the float chamber. As the petrol level goes downfloat move down-and needle valve opens-then petrol flows into the float chamber-level rises and comes to predecided level.

Through the air-bleed hole atmospheric pressure will be acting on the petrol surface.

During suction stroke, filtered air is drawn into the cylinder. This air passes through the **Venturi**. Venturi has a varying c/s, which first decreases to a minimum and then increases. Its narrowest c/s is called as the **throat**. As the air flows through the venturi, its velocity increases and pressure falls to a minimum at throat. The pressure differences between throat and float chamber exists and is called as **Intake Depression** or (Carburettor depression). Because of this intake depression, petrol will be sprayed through the nozzle into the throat. It is to be noted that the float chamber is connected to the venturi through nozzle as shown.

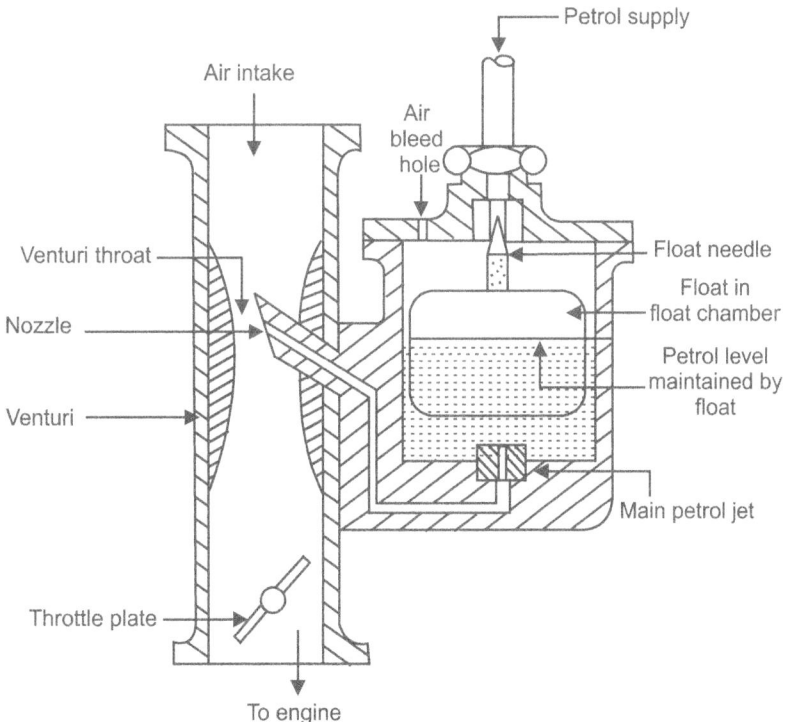

Fig. 2.7

When the petrol is sprayed in the high velocity air, petrol particles will absorb heat of air gets vapourised instantly. Then the combustible charge is produced and this charge admitted to engine cylinder. The amount of mixture is controlled by the throttle valve, which can be opened (or operated) by means of acceleration lever (or pedal) depending upon power requirements.

A choke valve is also provided, to start the engine from cold. When the choke lever is operated, it almost closes the air horn. The suction pressure will act on nozzle only. And more fuel less air (i.e. rich mixture) will go to engine and engine starts.

Note: Nozzle opening in the throat will be 1.5 to 2 mm above the petrol surface level. This is provided in order to avoid evapouration losses of petrol when the engine is not running. This difference in levels is called as nozzle lip.

2.6.1 Limitations of Simple Carburettor

- It provides correct air : fuel ratio only at one throttle position. As the throttle opening changes, mixture strength also changes.
  This is because, as the throttle position changes, air flow changes due to which pressure difference between venture throat and float chamber also changes.
- Also density of air at the throat changes as per pressure difference which is proportional to velocity at throat. But density of fuel remains same. Therefore, air : fuel ratio is less at high velocities and high at low velocities.
- Simple carburetor due to these factors:
  (a) Provides lean mixture at the starting warming up, idling range. Actually rich mixture is required.
  (b) At cruising provides increasingly rich mixture.
  (c) At acceleration provides lean mixture.

2.7 SOLEX CARBURETTOR (MODERN CARBURETTOR) (S-10)

This carburettor has all the four basic circuits viz.: Normal running; cold starting and warming up; Idling and slow running; Acceleration. It was used in Fiat cars, Ambassador cars, Gazal cars, Willys Jeeps etc. It is the basic carburetter – it is important to learn this carburetter so as to understand the working of any other newly developed carburettors.

(a) Normal Running: Fig. 2.8 shows the schematic diagram of Solex Carburettor. It consists of a float chamber. On the top of float needle valve is provided. Float chamber is connected to the air horn through main jet and emulsion tube. Emulsion tube has air jets, jets and orifices as shown and is provided in the venturi of air horn.

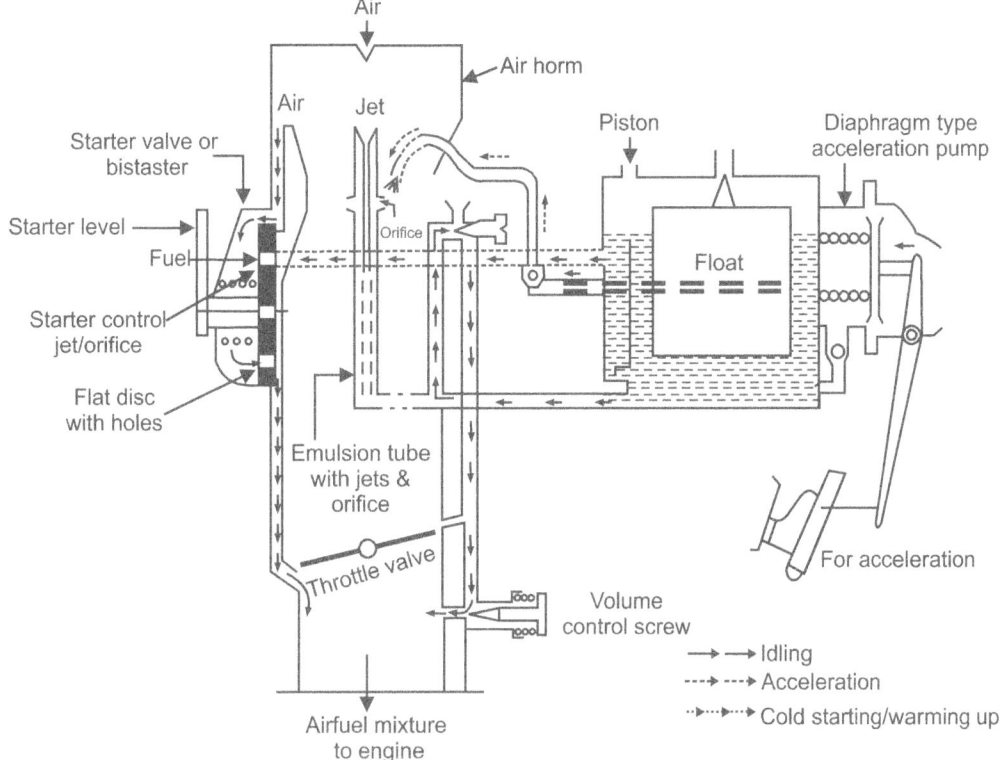

Fig. 2.8: Solex Carburettor

Similar to the working of simple carburettor, during suction stroke, filtered air enters the air horn and in the venturi mixing of high velocity air and fuel takes place and the charge produced goes to the engine for normal running.

(b) **Cold Starting and Warming Up:** For cold starting-turn the starter lever to start position. When the starter flat disc with holes rotates and orifices (A) comes in contact with the dotted passage. Because of the engine suction which acts through the passage shown by (→ ·· →) and air comes through the passage-mixing of air and fuel takes place - the charge goes to the engine cylinder and engine starts-then simultaneously acceleration is given to warm-up the engine. (It is to be noted that some operations are performed simultaneously).

(c) **Idling and Slow Running:** Once the engine starts and warm up-then for idle running the throttle valve will be almost closed (Not completely)-engine suction is applied through the passage shown by arrows (→)-Petrol from the main jet is sucked and air will enter from top at (14) − mixing of air and fuel takes place and charge goes to engine and engine will be just running at no load conditions.

(d) Acceleration Circuit: For acceleration i.e. when more power is required-then acceleration lever/foot pedal in pressed as shown. Because of lever and fulcrum-diaphragm of acceleration pump is pressed towards LHS direction and extra petrol is supplied through acceleration jet-through injector into venturi. This fuel will be in addition to the rich mixture which is created because of more opening of throttle valve. It is also to be noted that throttle valve is also connected through the links to acceleration pedal.

2.8 DRAWBACKS OF CARBURETTOR

Nowadays, carburetors are not used in SI engines because of their drawbacks. These problems are:

(i) Not providing air : fuel ratio as per need of engine.
(ii) Not maintaining air : fuel ratio at all throttle opening positions.
(iii) Not supplying economic mixture during idling and low load conditions.
(iv) Improper distribution of charge to various cylinders in case of multicylinder engines.
(v) Low volumetric efficiency because of restrictions provided to mixture flow by venturi.
(vi) Possibility of back firing at low speeds.
(vii) Lower thermal efficiency.
(viii) Higher emissions particularly during starting and idling.
(ix) Cold starting and ice formation.
(x) Vapour lock.

2.9 GASOLINE INJECTION (GI) SYSTEM (S-12)

Due to above drawbacks, carburetor are being replaced by Gasoline Injection Systems.

2.9.1 Classification

Gasoline injection systems are classified as:
- Port injection.
- Manifold injection.
- Direct injection into cylinder.

The injection may be continuous or timed. In timed system, the fuel is supplied in pulses.

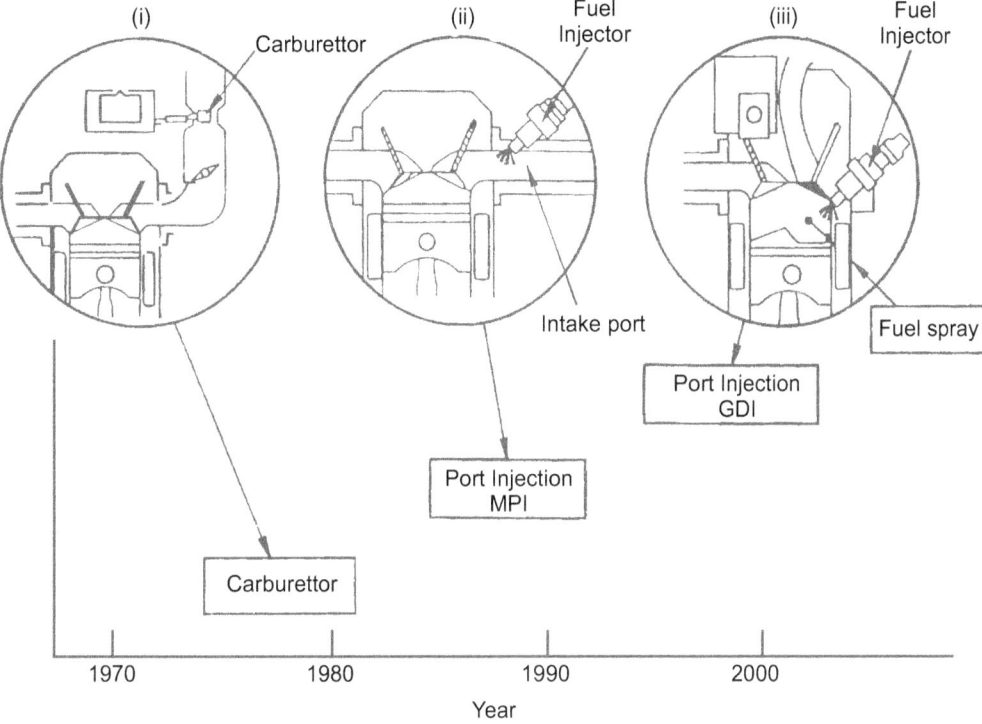

Fig. 2.9: Development of Various Fuel Supply Systems for SI Engines

In 1996, Dr. Ando and Dr. Akira developed Gasoline Direct Injection System. Mitsubishi was first to manufacture gasoline direct injection engine.

In Fig. 2.9 (i)   carburettor supplies air-fuel mix.
   Fig. 2.9 (ii)   injector is provided in the manifold.
   Fig. 2.9 (iii) injector is provided as shown it directly injects gasoline in the cylinder as shown.

The gasoline injection systems are also classified as:
   (i)   Single point or Throttle body injection.
   (ii) Multipoint fuel injection or port injection (MPFI).

In single point injection system, injector is placed inside the throttle body. Fuel injection is generally directed at one point which is generally the centre of intake manifold.

In MPFI system, there is separate injector for each cylinder.

2.10 MULTIPOINT FUEL INJECTION (MPFI) SYSTEM (S-12)

It is used to supply correct air fuel mixture to all the cylinders of a multicylinder engine.

The system consists of a separate injector for each of the cylinder. It has two types D and L systems.

2.10.1 D-MPFI Systems

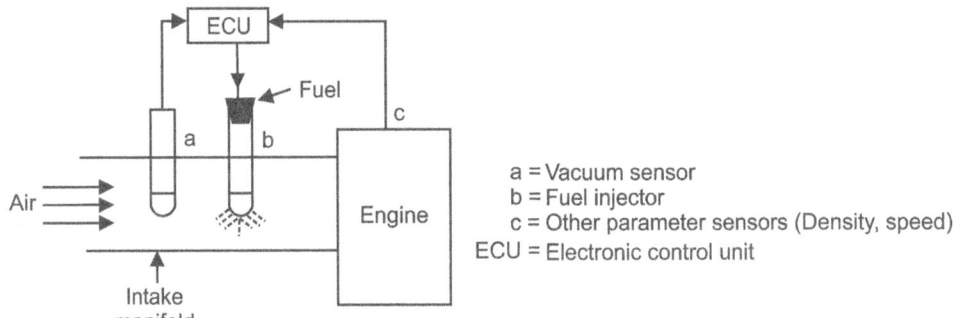

a = Vacuum sensor
b = Fuel injector
c = Other parameter sensors (Density, speed)
ECU = Electronic control unit

Fig. 2.10: D-MPFI System

It measures vacuum inside the intake manifold and controls time and quantity of fuel supply accordingly.

D is short form of Druck a German word meaning pressure.

It also senses volume of air from its density.

2.10.2 L-MPFI System

It measures amount of air entering in the manifold and controls time and quantity of fuel accordingly.

L is for Luft-a German word meaning air.

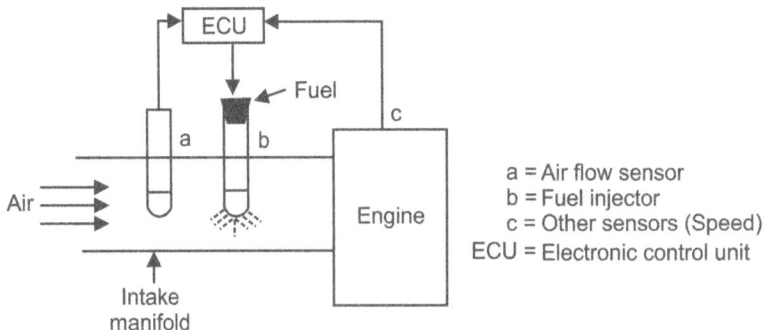

a = Air flow sensor
b = Fuel injector
c = Other sensors (Speed)
ECU = Electronic control unit

Fig. 2.11: L-MPFI System

2.11 ELECTRONIC FUEL INJECTION SYSTEMS (EFI)

These are used in modern engines.
A system consists of sensors, computer and injector.

  (i) **Sensors:** These are to sense engine operating conditions which include inlet temperature, air flow, exhaust gas or oxygen, engine temperature, manifold pressure etc.

  (ii) **Computer:** It receives signals from various sensors and by using stored data, it analyses the working conditions.

It then sends signals to operate injectors and other related devices of engine.

  (iii) **Injector:** It meters and injects correct quantity of fuel into the cylinder. It is nothing but a valve operated by solenoid which gets energized or de-energized as per signals from computer.

2.11.1 Advantages of EFI Systems

- Restrictions to air flow are removed. Therefore, volumetric efficiency increases.
- Better atomization of fuel resulting in better starting.
- No ice formation.
- Uniform distribution of fuel to all cylinders.
- Uniform supply while turning, moving or on slopes.
- Better space utilization.
- Engine height is reduced thereby increasing dynamic stability and better aerodynamic quality.

2.11.2 Disadvantages of EFI System

- High initial cost.
- High maintenance cost.

2.12 COMBUSTION IN SPARK IGNITION ENGINES

Introduction:

Combustion is defined as a relatively fast chemical reaction of carbon and hydrogen in the fuel with the oxygen present in the air producing energy in the form of heat. It is a very complicated phenomenon which requires a deep study for understanding. The energy produced by combustion is used for driving the I.C engine.

The basic conditions necessary for combustion in I.C engine are:

  (1) The presence of a combustible mixture.
  (2) Means of initiating combustion.
  (3) Stabilizing and propagation of flame in the combustion chamber.

For combustion in engine the above mentioned conditions must be fulfilled for which various parts are there in both S.I. and C.I engines. The combustible elements in fuels are generally carbon and hydrogen with small amount of sulphur and nitrogen. Liquid fuels are complex hydrocarbons and their combustion equation can be easily written as:

$$C_8H_{18} + 12.5\ O_2 = 8\ CO_2 + 9\ H_2O$$
(Iso-Octane)

In I.C. engine, combustion generally takes place when the fuel is in gaseous stable. It is necessary to have equipment in I.C. engine to achieve the gaseous state for example, in S.I. engine we have a carburettor.

2.13 COMBUSTION PHENOMENON IN S.I ENGINES

Combustion in the engine normally begins at the spark plug where the molecules in and around the spark plug starts burning, when an intense and high temperature spark is generated between the electrodes of spark plug. The molecules which are around the spark plug are a homogeneous mixture of vapourised fuel, air and residual gases. As the change near the spark burns a flame is formed whose speed of travelling is extremely low because, the reaction zone is yet to be established and heat loss is high since the spark plug is necessarily located on the cold walls of the chamber. The flame travels due to availability of homogeneous mixture adjacent to it. With the burning of adjacent layer's the flame travels the entire cylinder. The rate at which flame front would travel depends upon degree of turbulence, temperature of the flame front and the rate of chemical reaction in flame front.

Ricardo, the famous scientist has divided the combustion in S.I engine in basic two phases. The combustion diagram of the following is shown in Fig. 2.12 (a). The stages classified are:

(1) Ignition lag or preparation phase.
(2) Spreading of flame throughout the combustion chamber.
(3) After burning

The combustion diagram shown in Fig. 2.12 (b) is also known as indicator diagram.

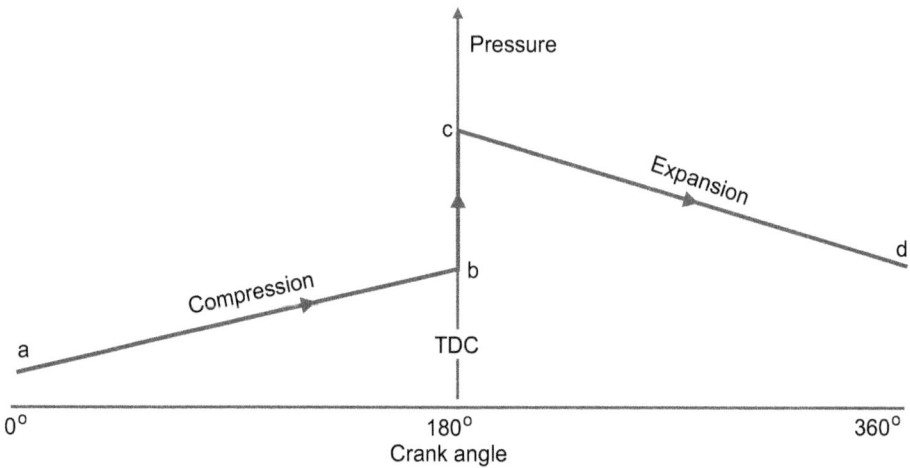

Fig. 2.12 (a): Theoretical P-θ Diagram

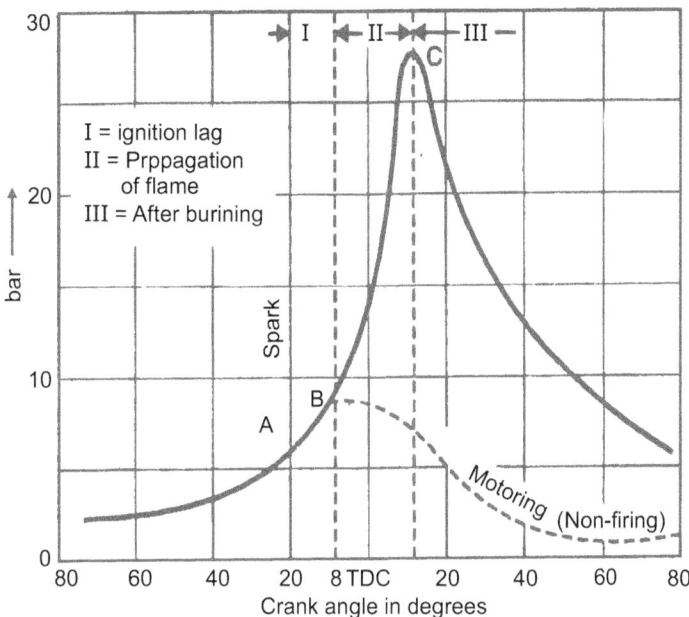

Fig. 2.12 (b): Stages of Combustion in SI Engine

2.13.1 Ignition Delay/Ignition Lag

It is purely chemical process and depends on various factors like nature of fuel, temperature, pressure and proportion of the exhaust gases. Ignition delay can be defined as the time between the formation of spark and appreciable pressure rise. When the spark is just produced, that is, the initial period, flame front spreads very slowly due to the very cause that the fraction of burnt mixture is very small and sufficient amount of energy is not produced due to this. There is hardly any pressure rise and indicator diagram shows no movement but once the flame front gets established it accelerates at a very high speed. The figure shows AB as region or stage I. It is some where around 20° crack angle rotation. In this region the pressure produced is around 1% of max combustion pressure and volume taken by burnt particle is about 5% of total volume of combustion chamber.

2.13.2 Second Phase (Spreading of Flame)

This stage starts from point B as shown in figure and ends at point C. In this stage the flame front travels with a maximum speed. This is the main stage of combustion in S.I engine due to the very fact that the maximum amount of combustion of fuel occur in this stage. This is a mechanical stage and is quite simple. The starting point of second stage is where first measurable rise of pressure can be seen on the indicator and its termination stage is point C where the maximum pressure is attained. As in this stage the flame front accelerates with a high velocity, keeps on continuously rising till it reaches point C in the chamber and therefore both the burned and unburned mixture are being compressed continually with accompanying temperature rise. In this stage the flame front travels in a spherical shape with its edges ragged. The main cause of high speed travel of flame is turbulence in the engine. In this zone the reaction rate plays only a small role. The determination of heat energy produced is done by turbulence rate in the cylinder. Turbulence is mainly created by the velocity of the mixture entering the cylinder on the intake stroke and also by the contours of the piston and cylinder head thus by improving the above factor turbulence can be increased and so would be flame speed which is to be maximised.

2.13.3 After Burning

The point C marks the completion of IInd stage and represents the end of flame travel but this does not indicate that at this point whole of the heat of the fuel has been liberated because even after the passage of flame the reaction of molecules take place which is known as AFTER BURNING. In after burning there is pressure rise due to expansion of gasses and it is assumed that around 10% to 12% of heat may be evolved in the process of after burning.

2.14 FACTOR'S INFLUENCING FLAME SPEED

Flame speed is very important in combustion of S.I engine because the flame velocity influences the rate of pressure rise in cylinder and also is the cause of some abnormal combustion in engine, the causes are as follows:

2.14.1 Turbulence

It plays a vital role in combustion, it is one of the major factor deciding flame speed. Generally the flame velocity, increases proportional to the turbulence velocity. Flame velocity is very low for non-turbulent fuel mixture and in this situation with low turbulence or "no" turbulence; time for each explosion would be so high that I.C. engine would become inpracticable.

2.14.2 Fuel-Air Ratio

The composition of the working mixture play an important role in deciding rate of combustion and the amount of heat evolved. When the mixture is too lean or too rich the flame speed decreases because too lean mixture produces less energy and too rich mixture results in incomplete combustion, therefore it has to be just correct.

2.14.3 Intake Temperature and Pressure

With increase in intake temperature and pressure the flame speed increases due to ease in combustion.

2.14.4 Engine Load
With increase in engine load the flame speed increases. Due to high load throttling is done and the working mixture becomes more suitable for combustion and hence smooth operation is obtained.

2.14.5 Engine Size
In small size the flame has to travel less distance and time is less if size is double then distance and so the time required is more however if the engine are similar then the time required would be same irrespective of size.

2.14.6 Engine Speed
Higher the engine speed, higher would be the turbulence and greater would be the flame speed. Flame speed increases almost linearly with engine speed.

2.14.7 Compression Ratio
A high compression ratio increases the pressure and temperature of the working mixture. These two conditions favour the flame speed hence it increases with increase in C.R.

2.14.8 Residual Gases
As the residual gases increase in the combustion chamber the flame speed reduces because of the simple reason, as it mixes with the fresh working mixture and diminishes it's capacity to produce energy.

2.15 ABNORMAL COMBUSTION IN S.I ENGINE
When we have a "normal" combustion, flame is initiated by a spark, flame travels across the combustion chamber in fairly distributed and even way. Due to certain condition there is a possibility that combustion in the cylinder is uneven and sudden this is known as Abnormal Combustion, Abnormal combustion is undesirable and it causes harm to the engine and its efficiency is reduced, for example, of Abnormal Combustion are 'detonation or knock', 'preignition', "rear" etc. From all of these preignition and detonation are most important and are discussed below.

2.15.1 Pre Ignition
Since the temperature at few places in the engine is very high like spark plug, exhaust value etc, there is a chance that at there places fuel mixture catches fire because of heat with out

the presence of spark. Due to this a turbulent flame gets developed at each point and starts to propagate across the chamber in the same manner as in which normal flame does. This process is known as "PRE IGNITION". That is production of flame front without the spark. The point which are over heated are known as "HOTSPOTS". Due to formation of number of flame front from "HOTSPOTS" and normal flame front is already present a net erratic flame front is produced which is erratic and sudden. Preignition is totally undesirable effect because it raises the temperature of the combustion chamber and this leads to production of more number of "HOTSPOTS" and the process multiplies thus causing severe damage to the parts of combustion chamber and producing uneven amount of energy. Preignition is also a cause for Detonation as a high amount of pressure and temperature is produced. Preignition is also harmfull as it reduces the efficiency of engine because if preignition occures during the compression stroke of the engine then the energy produced because of pre-ignition will oppose the compression stroke and thus reducing the efficiency of the engine. Another abnormal combustion in S.I engine is "Auto-ignition" for which "pre-ignition" plays a vital role both of these help each other in occurring.

2.15.2 Detonation (S-09, 12)

The normal combustion process hardly occur's without the presence of "Auto Ignition". A mixture of fuel and oxygen may spontaneously react without the presence of flame on the spark this is known as "Self Ignition" and its main cause is high temperature and the temperature at which the mixture self ignites is known as "SELF IGNITION" temperature. Consider a normal case in which the flame front is travelling across the chamber with its normal speed relating chemical energy and increasing the pressure and temperature of the mixture ahead it. Now, if suppose the "self ignition" temperature of the further fuel mixture is less than the temperature of the flame front then the mixture would ignite, this is known as "AUTO IGNITION", due to this a large amount of heat energy would be produced which is uncontrolled and erratic which leads to formation of "audible noise" which is known as "KNOCKING". This is produced due to the very fact that high release of energy produces a huge pressure difference which leads to vibrations of gaseous product in combustion chamber. Which leads to formation of "audible noise". This condition of engine is known as "Detonation", and generally occurs at the end stage of flame travel.

Abnormal combustion can be better understood with the help of P–θ diagram.

In Fig. 2.13 (a) it is seen that flame front is propagating at its normal speed of 15 to 30 m/s. As the flame front moves ahead the fuel mixture in this region BDB' gets compressed, due to compression and the reaction taking place in the flame front temperature of BDB' starts increasing. Now in case if the temperature of BDB' is less than "self igniting" temperature, then it won't auto ignite and flame front formed at BB' moves ahead in a normal manner to the rest of combustion chamber and reaches point D.

In Fig. 2.13 (b) the phenomenon of "Detonation or Knocking" is observed. Here to "auto-ignite", the unburnt fuel mixture attains the "CRITICAL TEMPERATURE" and remains at this point for some time. In this process some chemical reaction takes place which prepares mixture to auto ignite. This duration of preparation of mixture is known as "IGNITION DELAY". Now, if suppose the flame front BB' moves ahead and consumes the unburnt particle and reaches point D. There won't be any detonation but if the flame front BB' reaches to point CC' in the "ignition Delay" period there would be "Detonation or Knocking" and a huge variation in pressure would develop as shown in the figure. The pressure rise during detonation is very high and sometimes upto 3 to 4 times. Due to this high pressure generation detonation is needed to be removed or is undesirable. This phenomenon causes following damages:

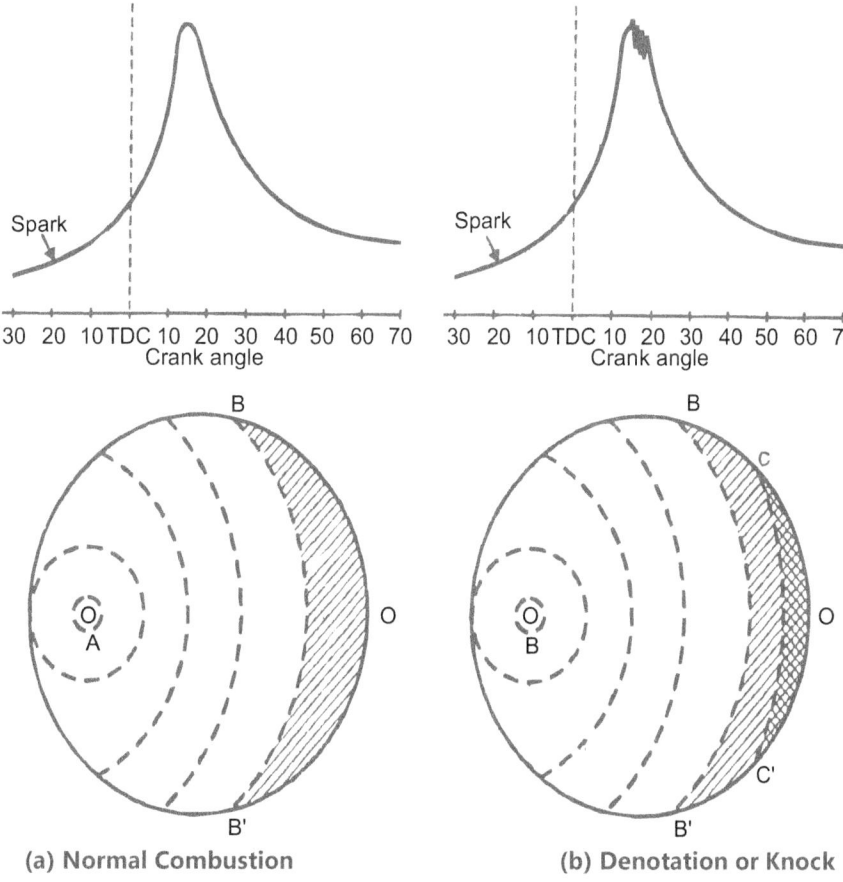

(a) Normal Combustion   (b) Denotation or Knock

Fig. 2.13: Combustion in the Spark-Ignition Engine

(a) Noise and roughness:

As knocking is produced in the engine which is not required and is unpleasant, also high vibration produced causes harm to crankshaft motion and this leads to rough operation of engine.

(b) Increase in heat transfer:
Due to detonation large amount of heat is produced which cause damage to engine parts, also it removes the lubricating film from the engine parts.

(c) Pre ignition:
Due to high production of heat detonation becomes major factor which causes preignition.

(d) Mechanical damage:
Due to high vibration and large heat generation there is damage caused to piston and other cylinder parts.

(e) Power output and efficiency:
With the formation of more heat energy. Power output and efficiency also decreases which is one of the major drawback.

2.16 FACTORS AFFECTING DETONATION/KNOCKING

There are various causes which affect Detonation from which temperature-and density are main causes.

2.16.1 Temperature Factors

Any of the process occuring in the cylinder which tend to increase the temperature of cylinder will lead to Detonation, following are the process:

(a) **Super Charging, Raising Compression Ratio:** Due to this both the temperature and density increases, more collision between the molecule occurs, this generates friction and heat.

(b) **Increasing the Load:** Due to this the cylinder temperature and combustion cylinder wall temperature increase. This lead to increment in end gas temperature carry detonation.

(c) If the intake of mixture is at high temperature it also causing detonation.

(d) The temperature of fuel mixture plays an important role. If it has low self igniting temperature possibility of detonation is more.

2.16.2 Time Factor

Any action which tend to increase the flame propagation speed and the increment of ignition delay period, will lead to avoiding of "detonation". By timing the various process and controlling the variable factor the temperature of mixture is brought down which lead to easy and normal movement of flame front in a uniform manner. Following are factors which cause detonation:

(a) Low turbulence, lead to less flame speed and more time is required to travel. In this time autoignition occurs, which can be removed by increasing speed.

(b) Distance travelled by the flame front is yet another cause. Larger the distance, more the time and more the probability hence this can be reduced by reducing the path travelled.
(c) Flame speed in sometime slow because of the fact that enough fuel is not present. Hence, this defect can be reduced by having rich Air-fuel mixture.

2.16.3 Density Factor

Due to increase in the density of the unburnt mixture (due to various causes) there is an increment in the probability of Detonation. Following are the causes:

(a) **Increasing the Load:** This lead to opening of throttle valve, more mixture enter's and causes detonation.
(b) **Super Charging the Engine:** By doing so, when the compression ratio is increased the mixture becomes highly dense, which leads to detonation.
(c) **Increasing the Inlet Pressure:** As the inlet pressure increases overall pressure in the engine increases which leads to less ignition delay, more dense change and high probability of detonation.
(d) **Advancing the Spark Timing:** This leads to burning of fuel in the dense form and causing detonation.

2.16.4 Composition Factor

We know that properties of fuel and the fuel-air ratio are the primary means for controlling knock. Once the compression ratio and engine size is decided, we can reduce knocking by having a change in composition which can be attained by:

(a) **Increasing Octane Rating of Fuel:** Adding Paraffins, Olefins in the fuel to have low carbon chain and increasing number of double bonds respectively. Which have less possibility of detonation.
(b) **Having Rich or Lean Mixture for Combustion:** This leads to longer delay period and low temperatures.

2.17 METHODS TO REDUCE KNOCKING

- Good combustion chamber design i.e. compact.
- Injecting water with the fuel to dissipiate heat.
- Increasing turbulence i.e. increasing flame speed.
- Increasing the number of spark plugs with proper placement.
- Use of lower compression ratio.
- Increasing the mixture ratio, making it too rich.
- Pressure at inlet manifold is reduced.
- Increasing engine speed (RPM).

There are other abnormal combustion but are not that particularly important.

Rumble:

A low pitch noise caused by multiple preignition raising the pressure greatly with consequent deflection of mechanical part.

Ping:

It is something similar to knocking and is superimposed with it present because "autoignition" produces different types of vibration which have different affect on the engine. It can also be known as knock which is sudden erratic, sharp and unpredictable.

2.18 RATING OF FUELS IN S.I. ENGINE

We know that the fuels which we used are the mixtures of hydrocarbon injected in the engine, knock. Hydrocarbons have a tendency to knock when the engine operating conditions become severe. Now this detonation is undesirable and resistance to this "detonation or knocking" is required to be present in the fuel and this measure of fuel resistance to knock is known as OCTANE RATING. This is a standard method which is used to determine the knocking capability of any S.I. engine fuel. In this rating technique, we have two compounds Iso-octane and normal heptane. Now Iso-octane being a very good anti knock fuel it is arbitrarily aligned a rating of 100 octane number, n-heptane on the other hand has a very poor resistance towards knocking and detonates very fast. Therefore, it is given a rating of 0-Octane number. Now, different engine fuels can be obtained by mixing these two compounds in different ratio. Now, suppose a S.I. engine fuel has Octane rating as 60 then, it has 60% of Iso-Octane and 40% of n-heptane hence greater the octane number greater would be the percentage of Iso-octane and larger would be resistance towards knocking. These two standard fuels are known as "PRIMARY REFERENCE FUELS" and the engine on which testing are done is called CO-OPERATING FUEL RESEARCH, variable compression ratio engine.

Octane rating is quite a standard method but we know that we have different engines, working under different conditions and thus a fuel can show different anti-knock quality under different circumstances depending upon engine condition of working. Thus a fuel is tested under more operating conditions to have Octane number in different situations, like Test and actual. Now, we generally calculate Octane number in two different conditions i.e. Research state there we have low engine speed and low temperature. Hence Octane number is known as Research Octane No (RON). The other one is motor octane number (MON), found out at motor test which is more severe and hard {High engine speed high and temperature. R.O. Rating is generally used with high loads whereas M.O. Rating is used for partial load.

Sensitivity: It is defined as difference between RON and MON.

Sensitivity = RON – MON

From RON and MON we can get the change that would occur under test condition and practical condition. Thus sensitivity can also be defined as the measure of the extent to which a gasoline is downgraded under severe conditions. Higher the sensitivity, poor will be its performance under severe conditions.

2.18.1 Dopes and Additives for SI Engine and Performance Number

Many applications are there in which we require a high anti-knocking condition like Aerospace engine where it is difficult to detect knocking. In such engines we require anti-knock property even higher then Iso-Octane. Also some times it is required to have a commercially viable product to have good anti-knock property which can be obtained by adding some other element in it and is also called as **dopes or additives.** The most commercially viable product invented by General Motors in 1923 it was TEL (TETRA ETHYL LEAD). If 3 ml of TEL is added to gasoline having Octane Rating as 75, the octane Rating got improved and became 87. Also TEL was added to have octane rating higher than 100. The effect of addition of TEL on Octane Number is shown in figure. It can be seen with the increase in quantity of T.E.L proportional increase in O.N. is less. Increase in O.N, is maximum for first 2 ml, after that, increase in O.N. is relatively less. The units of the scale drawn is known as PERFORMANCE NUMBER. Now Iso-Octane has a performance Number of 100. Performance Number can also be defined as ratio of knock limited Indicated mean effective pressure of test fuel to knock limited indicated M.E.P of Iso Octane.

$$PN = \frac{\text{KLIMEP of test fuel}}{\text{KLIMEP of Iso Octane}}$$

To find out Octane Number above, 100 we have to make use of P.N hence.

$$\text{O.N. (above 100)} = 100 + \frac{PN - 100}{3}$$

PN can also be used for measuring O.N, less than 100 as shown in Fig. 2.14 but it is generally used for greater values only. PN can also be expressed in terms of ml. of T.E.L. present in some fixed quantity of Gasoline.

There are other method's for S.I engine rating. Like Ricardo's toluene number in which toluene and heptane are reference fuels and scale is drawn.

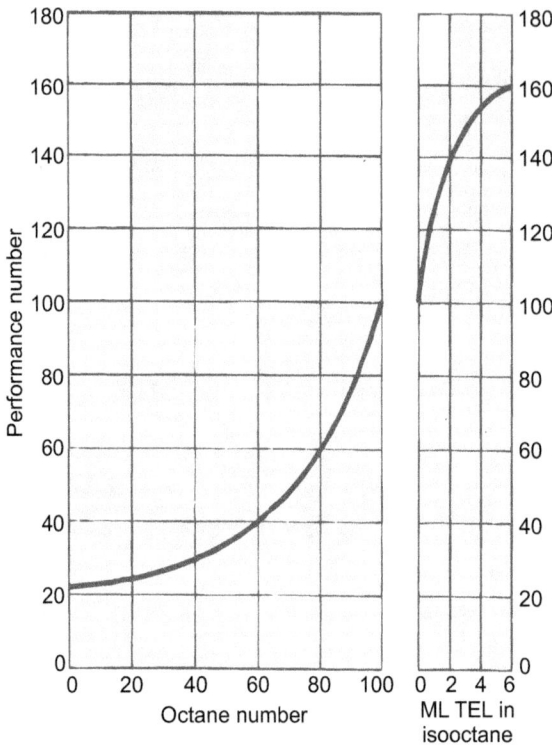

Fig. 2.14: Performance Number Equivalents for Octane Numbers and Tetraethyl Lead in Iso-octane

2.19 COMBUSTION CHAMBER (S-09, 13)

The type of Combustion chamber plays a vital role in deciding the efficiency of engine. Thus a combustion chamber must fulfill following conditions:
- There should be sufficient power produced.
- The operation should be as smooth as possible.
- Pressure rise should be uniform and smooth.
- Maximum Resistance to Knocking/Detonation.

To fulfill the above conditions. The chamber must be designed considering following factors:

(1) **High Compression Ratio:** Higher the compression ratio higher would be the output and efficiency. Hence, combustion chamber should withstand high compression Ratio.

(2) There should be minimum excess air i.e. there should be complete utilization of the available air.

(3) Turbulence should be adequate to have high speed flame propagation.

(4) Flame travel should be minimum hence engine should be compact, also compactness gives small surface volume ratio which leads to less heat loss during combustion.

(5) There should be no presence of any kind of exhaust gases.
(6) Spark plugs should be properly located to have a good flame start and travel. Also its operation should be good.
(7) Also there should be absence of "HOT SPOTS" i.e. presence of good cooling arrangement.
(8) Pressure rise in the combustion chamber should be uniform and a moderate. Sudden pressure rise should be avoided.
(9) Valve head, should have right size and right cooling arrangement.
(10) Time taken for the Combustion Process should be as minimum as possible.

2.20 EVOLUTION OF CHAMBER

Earlier the engine types were "T-head" engine which were utilised in as early as 1908 by ford company for its automobiles. The figure of the engine is shown in Fig. 2.15 (i). The main disadvantage was presence of two camshafts, there was a large probability of detonation. After the invention of T type, "I head" also known as side valve engine was invented. Here the valves are placed side by side in the block. It is mainly used in Petrol engines. Figure 2.15 (ii) shows a I-head combustion chamber. This type of construction was good from manufacturing and maintenance a point of view. It lacked in providing good turbulence and also probability of detonation was large due to presence of low combustion process.

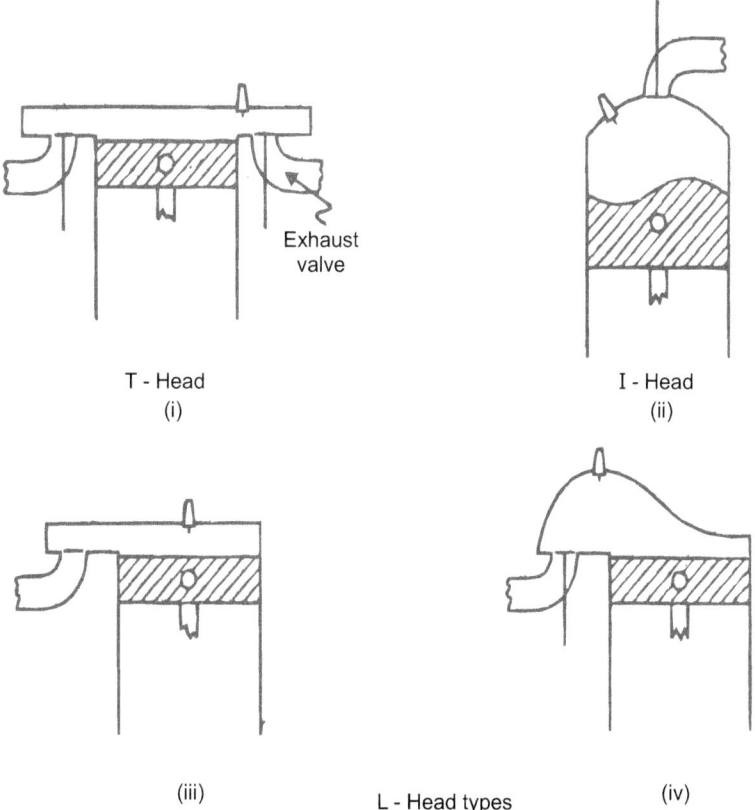

T - Head
(i)

I - Head
(ii)

(iii)

(iv)

L - Head types

Fig. 2.15: Examples of Typical Combustion Chambers (not to scale)

Ricardo turbulent combustion chamber was designed to obtain fast flame speed fess knocking. This designed also reduced effective flame travel by reducing distance between piston crown and head. It was designed to dissipate heat at a much faster rate and thus was improvement to T head and I-head chambers.

2.21 COMBUSTION CHAMBERS IN S.I. ENGINES

As discussed earlier the design of S.I. engines plays a crucial role in deciding the performance and efficiency of the engine. The various conditions that a combustion chamber must fulfill to give good efficiency are:
- It should have the required power output.
- Tendency to knock should be minimum.
- Thermal efficiency should be high for proper heat transfer.
- Operation should be smooth continuous.
- Pressure rise should be uniform and maximum limit of temperature should not be very high.

2.22 DIFFERENT TYPES OF COMBUSTION CHAMBERS

2.22.1 'L'-head Combustion Chamber

In this type of chamber, inlet and outlet values are on the same side as shown in Fig. 2.16. We can remove cylinder head without disturbing valve assembly. This chamber has slow rate of combustion and has tendency to detonate because it has long air flow path and due to tendency to detonate, the compression ratio used is small. The major advantage of this type of chamber is that it has less; maintenance which help using in those applications where regular checking is not feasible.

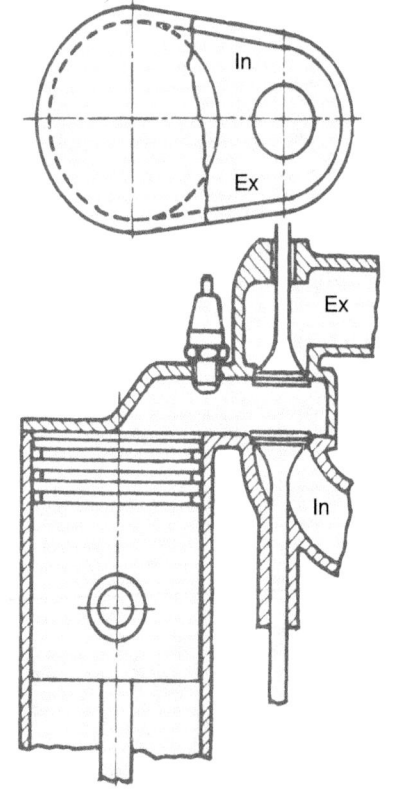

Fig. 2.16: L-head Combustion Chamber

2.22.2 'T'-head Combustion Chamber

Unlike L type this type of chamber has valves on the opposite side as shown in the Fig. 2.17. This combustion chamber is not in much use as compression ratio cannot exceed a specified limit due to fact that this chamber facilitates large flame travel. This type of combustion chamber was first time used by Ford Company.

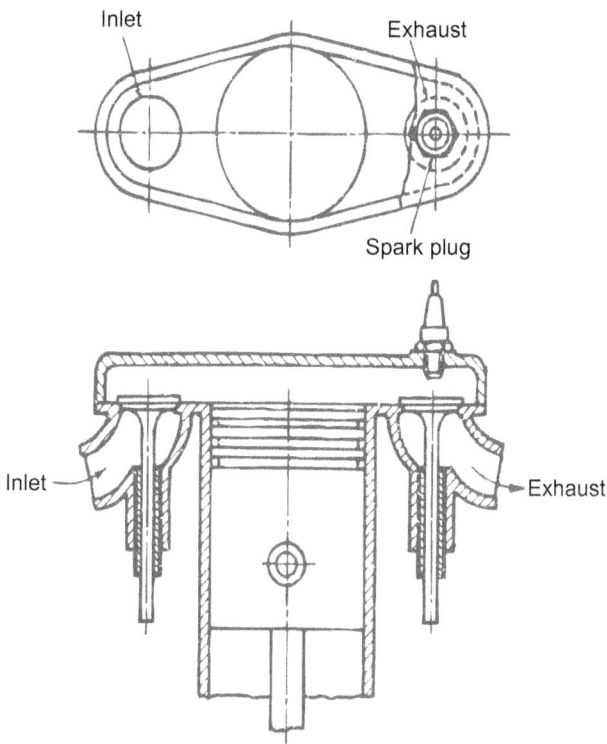

Fig. 2.17: T-Head Combustion Chamber

2.22.3 'I'-head Overhead Value Combustion Chamber (S-13)

Different type of 'I' head combustion chambers are available as shown in Fig. 2.18; designs like "bath tub design" "wedge design" etc. are available. These type of chambers have a peculiar characteristic of having both valves on the cylinder head. The spark plug in these chambers are fitted on the top on side of chamber. These type of chambers have higher volumetric efficiency and pressure rise is also smooth and uniform. Therefore, these are operated on high compression ratio. These type of chambers also have a very less tendency to detonate due to cause of absence of long flame travel as the chambers are made compact by utilising all the available space. Thus these are used in most of Indian cars.

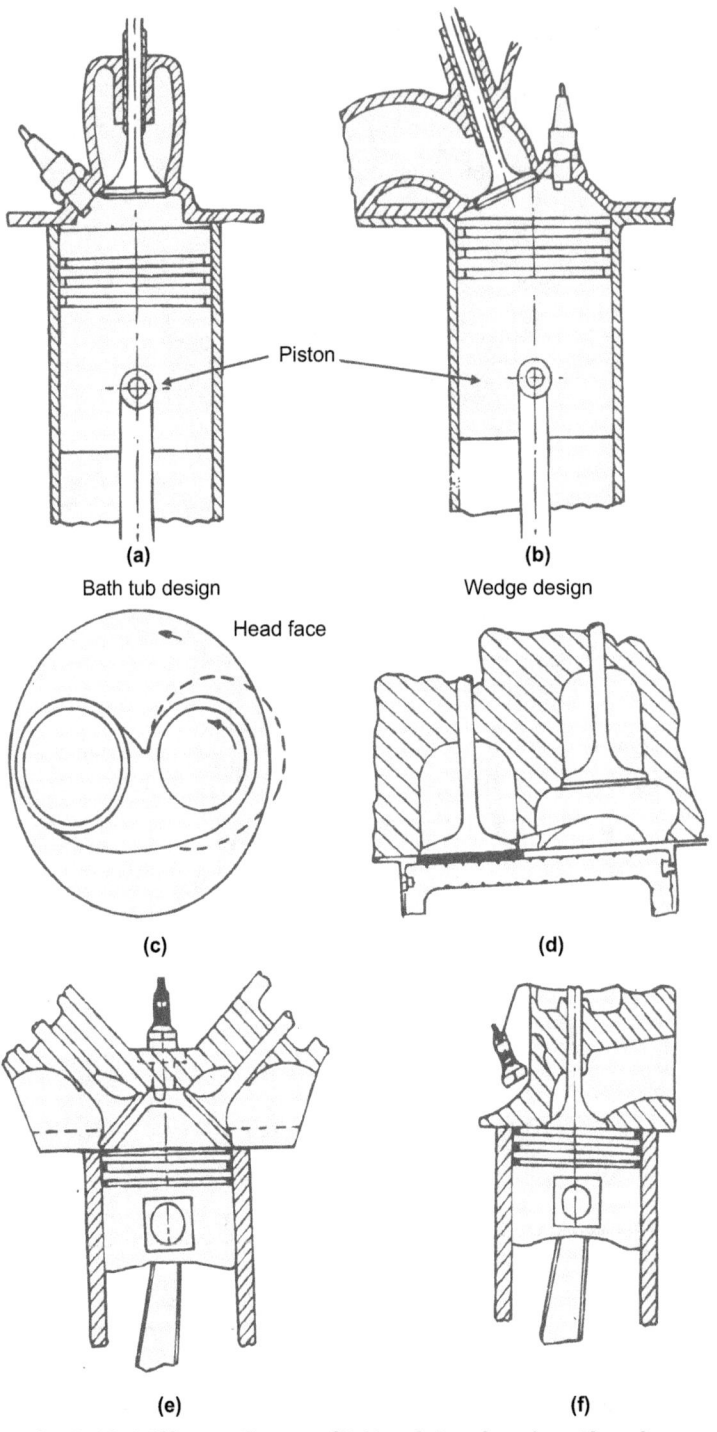

Fig. 2.18: Different Types of I-Head Combustion Chambers

2.22.4 'F'-Head Combustion Chamber

This type of chamber has a complicated design. In this the inlet valve is placed on top and the exhaust valve is located at the bottom of the combustion chamber as shown in the Fig. 2.19.

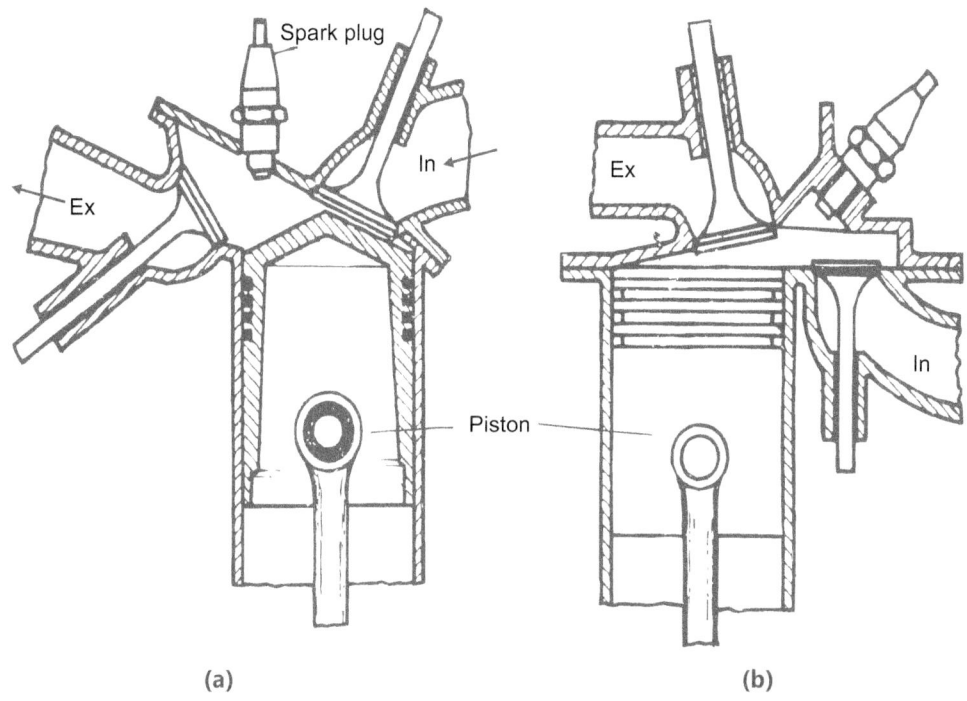

Fig. 2.19: F-Head Combustion Chamber

These type of chambers are quite compact. In these spark plugs are generally placed on the top of chamber. Due to good positioning of spark plug and compactness of the chamber these have high efficiency, work on higher pressure and they have knocking tendency almost nil. The biggest limitation that is faced with these kind of chambers is difficulty in large scale production as the chamber's are quite complicated which leads to increase in cost and efforts.

2.22.5 Ricardo's Turbulent Combustion Chamber

This type is similar to 'L' type chamber but some improvements have been incorporated in this due to which its efficiency and application have increased. In this type of chamber position of valve is similar to that of 'L' type but there is a change in the shape of combustion chamber, due to variation in shape that is "Hemispherical One", the flame speed is increased and more "turbulence" is induced and therefore the name. In this type, due to peculiar shape of combustion chamber, more better is mixing of air and fuel which results in homogeneous and distributed fuel. This is used in many cars. This kind of chamber also has less tendency to detonate because of presence of higher flame speed and homogeneous mixture.

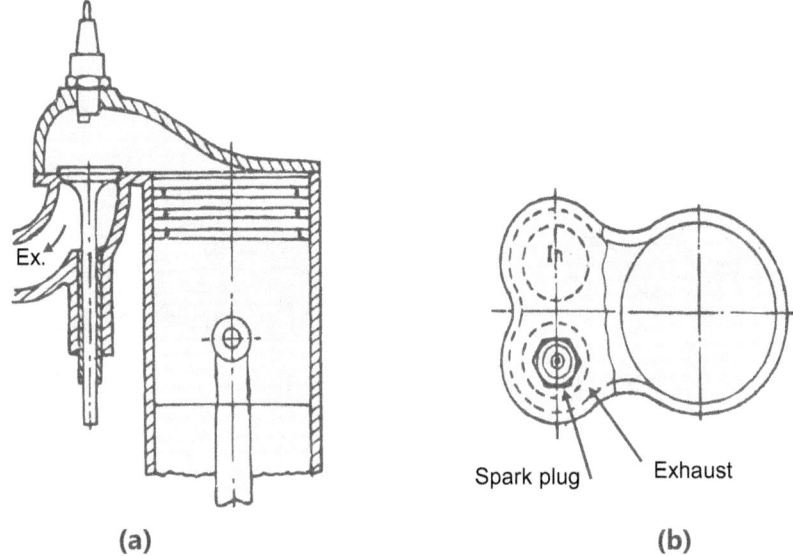

Fig. 2.20: Ricardo Turbulent Design

MULTIPLE CHOICE QUESTIONS (MCQ'S)

1. Stoichometric air fuel ratio for petrol is approximately
   (a) 10 : 1
   (b) 12 : 1
   (c) 15 : 1
   (d) 18 : 1

2. Equivalence ratio means ………
   (a) $\dfrac{\text{actual fuel air : ratio}}{\text{Stoichimetric fuel : air ratio}}$
   (b) $\dfrac{\text{Stoichometric fuel : air ratio}}{\text{actual fuel : air ratio}}$
   (c) $\dfrac{\text{mass of fuel}}{\text{mass of air}}$
   (d) $\dfrac{\text{mass of air}}{\text{mass of fuel}}$

3. If equivalence ratio is greater than one, then mixture is ………
   (a) lean
   (b) Chemical Correct
   (c) rich
   (d) Perfectly mixed

4. If air fuel ratio is greater than 16 : 1 then mixture is ....
   (a) lean   (b) chemical correct
   (c) rich   (d) perfect
5. The function of venture in the carburettor is ....
   (a) To decrease fuel flow   (b) To increase fuel flow
   (c) To decrease air velocity   **(d) To increase air velocity**
6. To get maximum power, aim is ....
   (a) To use all fuel present inside the combustion chamber.
   (b) To use all oxygen present inside the combustion chamber.
   (c) To get more economy
   (d) To get less fuel consumption
7. If bonnet space is limited, the carburettor used is ....
   (a) Updraught   (b) down draught
   (c) horizontal draught   (d) slant draught
8. In constant choke carburettor .... is/are kept constant
   (a) air flow area   (b) fuel flow area
   (c) Both air and fuel flow areas (d) pressure drop
9. A venturi of fixed dimension is used in
   (a) Constant choke carburettor   (b) Constant vacuum carburettor
   (c) Multiple venturi carburettor   (d) Multijet carburettor
10. In .... carburettors, pressure drop is kept constant.
    (a) Constant venturi   **(b) Constant vaccum**
    (c) Multiple venturi   (d) Multijet
11. Fuel flow rate as per demand is varied by varying pressure difference in .... carburettor.
    (a) S.U.   (b) Carter
    (c) Solex   (d) Alpha
12. Fuel flow area is varied in .... carburettor.
    (a) Solex   (b) Zennith
    (c) Alpha   **(d) Carter**
13. In these carburettors, air lifts the fuel droplets against gravity.
    (a) Up drought   (b) Down draught
    (c) Cross draught   (d) Horizontal draught
14. If inlet temperature of air increases ....
    (a) Efficiency of IC Engine increases but power output decreases
    (b) Efficiency of IC Engine decreases but power output increases
    (c) Both efficiency and power output decrease
    (d) Both efficiency and power output increase

15. The chemically correct air fuel ratio for octane is ....
    (a) 13.14 : 1 (b) **15.14 : 1**
    (c) 17.14 : 1 (d) 1.17 : 14
16. Which air : fuel mixture will give maximum power for SI engine ?
    (a) 15 : 1 (b) 18 : 1
    (c) 8 : 1 **(d) 12 : 1**
17. Which air : fuel mixture will give minimum brake specific fuel consumption ?
    (a) 15 : 1 **(b) 16 : 1**
    (c) 19 : 1 (d) 12 : 1
18. Rich mixture is required during ....
    (a) idling and cruising (b) cruising and acceleration
    (c) idling, cruising and acceleration **(d) idling and acceleration**
19. The choke is closed when engine is ....
    (a) cold (b) hot
    (c) accelerating (d) idling
20. SI engines use mixtures having air fuel ratio between ....
    (a) 4 : 1 to 24 : 1 **(b) 9 : 1 to 18 : 1**
    (c) 15 : 1 to 80 : 1 (d) 1 : 1 to 5 : 1
21. In SI engines for maximum power, the relative fuel air ratio should be
    (a) 0.6 (b) 0.8
    (c) 1 **(d) 1.2**
22. Leane mixture is required during ....
    (a) Idling and cruising (b) Cruising and starting
    (c) Cruising only (d) Cruising, starting and idling
23. For maximum thermal efficiency, the aim is to ....
    (a) Use all the oxygen present in combustion chamber.
    (b) Use all the fuel present in combustion chamber.
    (c) To get maximum pressure in the cylinder.
    (d) To get maximum temperature in the cylinder.
24. The mixture requirements during starting and idling are respecting
    (a) rich and rich (b) rich and lean
    (c) lean and rich (d) lean and lean
25. For maximum fuel economy the mixture should be
    (a) rich **(b) lean**
    (c) stoichometric (d) inert
26. The pressure difference between throat and the float chamber is ....
    (a) Nozzle nip (b) Nozzle dip
    (c) Intake depression (d) Potential difference

27. When choke is cold, suction pressure is applied on ....
    (a) Air intake   **(b) nozzle**
    (c) Both air and nozzle (d) everywhere

28. Ecomoniser comes into action during ....
    (a) cruising   (b) idling
    (c) starting   **(d) full throttle operation**

29. During cruising mixture provided by simple carburettor is ....
    (a) Increasingly rich (b) Increasingly lean
    (c) constantly chemically correct   (d) sometimes rich sometimes lean

30. During acceleration mixture provided by simple carburettor is ....
    (a) Increasing rich   **(b) lean**
    (c) chemically correct   (d) sometimes rich

31. During idling, mixture provided by simple carburettor is ....
    (a) chemically correct   **(b) lean**
    (c) rich   (d) fluctuating

32. The function of choke is to provide ....
    (a) lean mixture   (b) some mixture
    (c) rich mixture   (d) stoichiometric mixture

33. Simple carburettor provides correct quality of mixture
    (a) at all operating conditions   (b) During acceleration only
    (c) During cruising only   **(d) Only at one throttle position**

34. The correct expression for nozzle and nip is ....
    (a) tip height - fuel surface height
    (b) tip height - throat height
    (c) throat height - float chamber height
    (d) fuel surface height

35. The tip of nozzle is kept
    (a) at the same level as that of fuel in float chamber.
    (b) at level above the fuel level on float chamber.
    (c) at level below the fuel level in float chamber
    (d) sometime above sometimes below the fuel level

36. The drawbacks of carburettor include ....
    (a) non-uniform distribution for multi cylinder engines
    (b) less breathing capacity
    (c) supply varies as per road contoors
    (d) All of these

37. MPFI means
    (a) Metal point fuel injection
    (b) Multipoint fuel injection
    (c) Metal power fuel injection
    (d) Multiple pin fuel injection
38. In port injection system location of injector is ....
    (a) Inside cylinder near intake port
    (b) Near carburettor
    (c) On side of intake manifold near intake port.
    (d) Inside cylinder near exhaust port.
39. L–MPFI system uses
    (a) port injection
    (b) manifold injection
    (c) direct injection
    (d) throttle injection
40. D-MPFI system uses .... injection
    (a) port
    (b) direct
    (c) manifold
    (d) throttle
41. The cold start injector provides ....
    (a) stoichometric mixture
    (b) rich mixture
    (c) lean mixture
    (d) heating of fuel
42. Ignition lag, spreading of flame and after burning are the states observed during combustion in
    (a) SI engines
    (b) CI engine
    (c) PI engines
    (d) Turbocharged engines
43. The phase of combustion starting immediately after spark plug.
    (a) Flame propagation
    (b) Afterburning
    (c) Ignition lag
    (d) Motoring
44. The time interval between formation of spark and beginina of appreciable pressure rise is called as ....
    (a) spark lag
    (b) Ignition lag
    (c) Propagation lag
    (d) Burning lag
45.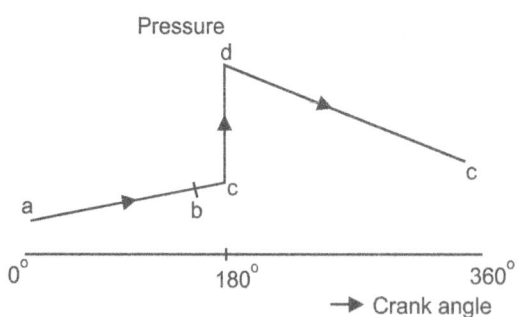

In above diagram, the point at which spark is given is shown by
(a) Point a (b) Point b
(c) Point c (d) Point d

46. A motoring curve is plotted when
    (a) when the vehicle is not running
    (b) when vehicle is running at no load condition
    (c) The cycle is taking place due to combustion of fuel
    (d) The cycle is not fired

47. Which of the following is not necessary condition for starting of combustion process in SI engines ?
    (a) Compression of charge (b) Presence of fuel
    (c) Presence of oxygen (d) Formation of spark

48. Effect of spark in SI engines is ....
    (a) Ionisation of gases (b) Rise in volume
    (c) Rise in pressure **(d) Rise in temperature**

49. In SI engines maximum amount of fuel is burnt during the stage ......
    (a) pre-burning (b) Ignition lag
    (c) Flame propagation (d) After burning

50. In SI engines the flame travels in ....
    (a) spherical shape (b) circular shape
    (c) linear direction (d) sinusoidal pattern

51. In D-MPFI system the quantity sensed is ......
    (a) pressure (b) volume
    (c) Temperature (d) Mixture flow rate

52. The D-MPFI system responds to vacuum sensed
    (a) carburettor **(b) Intake manifold**
    (c) Exhaust manifold (d) Piston

53. L-MPFI system responds to ....
    (a) pressure (b) volume
    (c) Temperature **(d) flow rate**

54. Arrange the phases of combustion in ascending order according to amount heat evolved in each phase.
    (a) Ignition lag, after burning, flame propagation
    (b) Ignition lag, flame propagation, after burning.
    (c) After burning flame propagation, ignition lag
    (d) After burning ignition lag, flame propagation

55. In SI engines flame speed decreases with increase in
    (a) Intake temperature (b) peak temperature
    (c) compression ratio **(d) residual gases**
56. In SI engines, maximum flame speed is obtained when equivalence ratio is ......
    (a) less than 1 (b) between 1 to 1.1
    (c) between 1.1 to 1.2 (d) Greater than 1.2
57. With increase in compression ratio, flame travels
    (a) faster (b) slower
    (c) with same speed (d) with fluctuations
58. In SI engines flame speed always increases with ....
    (a) turbulence (b) air-fuel ratio
    (c) residual gases **(d) compression ratio**
59. With increase in speed, the crank angle required for flame propagation ....
    (a) increases (b) decreases
    (c) remains same (d) can't determine
60. If cooling water temperature is decreased flame speed ....
    (a) increases **(b) decreases**
    (c) remains same (d) can't predict
61. Increasing cooling water temperature in SI engines, knocking tendency ....
    (a) increases (b) decreases
    (c) remains same (d) can't predict
62. To reduce knocking, the fuel in SI engine should have .... self ignition temperature.
    (a) low **(b) high**
    (c) any (d) automatic
63. Detonation in SI engine means
    (a) Sudden ignition of charge before the spark
    (b) Pre ignition of charge before the spark
    (c) Auto ignition of charge before the spark
    (d) Auto ignition of charge after the spark
64. Knocking in SI engine occurs when ......
    (a) Flame reaches the unburnt charge before delay period is over
    (b) Flame reaches after the delay period is over.
    (c) Spark is produced before charge coming in
    (d) Spark is produced several times
65. Preingnition takes place when ....
    (a) Flame reaches the unburnt charge before delay period is over
    (b) Ignition takes place after spark.
    (c) Ignition starts before spark
    (d) Flame travels very first

66. Larger combustion chambers
    - **(a) Increase detonation**
    - (b) Decrease detonation
    - (c) do not affect detonation
    - (d) can't say
67. To prevent knocking flame propagation should be
    - **(a) retarded**
    - (b) accelerated
    - (c) sinusoidal
    - (d) upfront
68. To reduce knocking in SI engines, self ignition temperature of fuel should be ......
    - **(a) high**
    - (b) low
    - (c) varying
    - (d) constant
69. Which of the following is not an effect of increased intake temperature ?
    - (a) Less delay period
    - (b) higher flame speed
    - (c) more knocking tendency
    - **(d) does not affect anything**
70. As load increases, the knocking tendancy of SI engines -
    - **(a) increases**
    - (b) decreases
    - (c) can't predict
    - (d) remains same
71. As the speed of flame travel increases detonation
    - (a) increases
    - **(b) decreases**
    - (c) remain same
    - (d) can't predict
72. As distance of flame travel increases, detonation ......
    - **(a) increases**
    - (b) decreases
    - (c) remains same
    - (d) can't predict
73. Denotation tendency is maximum for air : fuel ratio ......
    - (a) 8 : 1 to 10 : 1
    - (b) 10 : 1 to 12 : 1
    - **(c) 12 : 1 to 14 : 1**
    - (d) 16 : 1 to 18 : 1
74. To reduce denonation, the spark plug should be located
    - (a) near to intake valve
    - (b) at the corner
    - **(c) centrally**
    - (d) neat piston
75. Which is not a probable location of preigntion ?
    - (a) spark plug tip
    - (b) exhaust value
    - (c) remote corner of chamber
    - **(d) Intake value**
76. Knocking in SI engines will be less if
    - (a) Delay period is less and flame speed is high.
    - (b) Delay period is less and flame speed is less
    - **(c) Delay period is high and flame speed is high**
    - (d) Delay period is high and flame speed is less

77. In SI engines, to avoid knock, combustion chamber should have ....
    (a) small bore
    (b) large bore
    (c) large flame path
    (d) large ratio of flame path to bore
78. Due to supercharging, the detonation tendency of SI engines.
    (a) increases
    (b) decreases
    (c) remains same
    (d) can't predict
79. Octane rating is ....
    (a) measure of fuel resistance to knock in SI engines
    (b) measure of fuel resistance to knock in CI engines
    (c) measure of fuel assistance to knock in SI engines
    (d) measure of fuel assistance to knock in CI engines
80. For octane rating a standard reference fuel consists of
    (a) Iso-octane only
    (b) n-heptane only
    (c) Combination of 2,2,4 trimethyl pentane and n-heptane
    (d) Combination of iso heptane and n-octane
81. 2, 2, 4 trimethyl pentane has octane number equal to
    (a) 1
    (b) 0
    (c) 100
    (d) 120
82. n-heptane has octane number equal to
    (a) 0
    (b) 1
    (c) 100
    (d) 120
83. Octane number 60 means, the fuel has antiknock proper equal to fuel from by
    (a) 60% of n-octane 40% of petrol.
    (b) 60% of iso octane and 40% n-heptane
    (c) 60% of iso octane and 40% of petrol
    (d) 60% of iso octane and 40% of TEL
84. Dopes are ....
    (a) chemical which will increase knocking tendency of fuel
    (b) chemical which will decrease knocking tendency of fuel
    (c) chemical which will decrease exhaust from engine
    (d) chemical which will increase exhaust from engine
85. RON means ....
    (a) Radical oxygen number
    (b) Research oxygen number
    (c) Radical octane number
    (d) Research Octane number
86. MON means ....
    (a) Metal oxygen number
    (b) Motor oxygen number
    (c) Metal octane number
    (d) Motor octane number

87. RON is calculated at ....
    (a) low speed and low temperature (b) high speed and low temperature
    (c) low speed and high temperature (d) high speed and high temperature
88. Which is correct expression ?
    (a) RON = sensitivity – MON (b) Sensitivity = RON/MON
    (c) Sensitivity – RON – MON (d) Sensitivity = MON/RON
89. Sensitivity shows
    (a) change in performance of fuel under test condition and practical condition
    (b) change in octane number
    (c) ratio of octane number of ideal fuel and actual fuel
    (d) ratio of octane number of actual fuel to ideal fuel.
90. Higher sensitivity of fuel shows ......
    (a) better performance under serve conditions.
    (b) poor performance under serve conditions.
    (c) better emissions under serve conditions
    (d) less emissions under serve conditions
91. Performance number gives rating of fuel with
    (a) Octane number less than 1 (b) Octane number more than 1
    (c) Octane number less than 100 **(d) Octane number more than 100**
92. Performance number = ...
    (a) KLimep of test fuel – KLimep of iso octane
    (b) KLimep of LSO octane – KLimep of test fuel.
    (c) KLimep of iso octane/KLimep of test fuel.
    (d) KLimep of test fuel/KLiemp of iso octane.
93. Toluene and heptane are reference fuels used in ....
    (a) octane rating (b) heptane rating
    (c) toluene rating (d) D.N. rating
94. Performance number of iso-octane is
    (a) 1 **(b) 100**
    (c) zero (d) 50
95. The maximum compression ratio which can be used without knocking is ....
    (a) HCR **(b) HUCR**
    (c) PN (d) ON
96. Ideal fuel for SI engine should have
    (a) low SIT **(b) high SIT**
    (c) low CV (d) less volatility

97. Which is not true about L-head combustion chamber?
    (a) **High rate of combustion** (b) More tendency to detonate
    (c) permits low compression ratio (d) requires less maintenance
98. Main drawback of T-hear combustion chamber is ....
    (a) More maintenance (b) Permits more compression ratio
    (c) More flame travel **(d) Permits less compression ratio**
99. In T-head combustion chamber, spark plug is located ......
    (a) near intake valve (b) centrally
    (c) near exhaust valve (d) near injector
100. Which is not true about I-head combustion chamber?
    (a) Higher volumetric efficiency **(b) Non-uniform pressure rise**
    (c) Permits higher compression ratio (d) Less flame travel
101. Main drawback of F-Head combustion chamber is ....
    (a) Improper positioning of spark plug
    (b) More knocking tendency
    (c) Less efficiency
    (d) Difficult manufacturing
102. For petrol engine the method of governing is ....
    (a) Hit and miss governing (b) Quality governing
    (c) Quantity governing (d) None of the above
103. Economizer is used to provide enriched mixture during ....
    (a) Starting (b) Idling
    (c) Cruising **(d) Full throttle opening**
104. When the throttle is suddenly opened, the mixture from the simple carburettor tends to become ....
    (a) Rich **(b) Lean**
    (c) Stoichiometric (d) Not affected
105. The choke in automobile carburettor system is meant for supplying ....
    (a) Lean mixture **(b) Rich mixture**
    (c) Stoichiometric mixture (d) Weak mixture
106. Modern carburettor provide the correct quality of air-fuel mixture during ....
    (a) Starting (b) Idling
    (c) Cruising **(d) All conditions**
107. The essential conditions for combustion are ....
    i) The presence of combustible mixture
    ii) Initiation by any means like spark plug is not required
    iii) Stabilization and propagation of flame in the combustion chamber
    Out of these following is correct
    (a) All correct **(b) I and III**
    (c) II and III (d) I and II

108. In the rich mixtures used for automobile applications ....
    (a) Fuel quantity is more than stoichiometric quantity
    (b) Air quantity is more than stoichiometric quantity
    (c) Both the quantities are same
    (d) Fuel quantity is more than the air quantity

109. In the Lean mixtures used for automobile applications ....
    (a) Fuel quantity is more than stoichiometric quantity
    (b) Air quantity is more than stoichiometric quantity
    (c) Both quantities are same
    (d) Fuel quantity is more than the air quantity.

110. Stoichiometric air fuel ratio suggests ....
    (a) Correct quantity of fuel-air ratio which gives more economy
    (b) Correct quantity of fuel-air ratio which gives more power
    (c) Correct quantity of fuel-air ratio which gives complete combustion
    (d) All of the above

111. Practical limits of fuel air ratio for combution in SI engines is ....
    (a) 0.11 to 0.05   (b) 0.2 to 0.1
    (c) 0.05 to 0.033   (d) 0.2 to 0.033

112. Practical limits for air fuel ratio in SI engines provides ....
    (a) Range of air fuel ratio which gives comfortable working of SI engine
    (b) Range of air fuel ratio to get combustion close to stochiometric conditions in SI engine
    (c) Range of air fuel ratio for obtaining maximum power in SI engine
    (d) All of the above

113. Ignition limits in the SI engine depends upon ....
    (a) Mixture ratio and temperature
    (b) Volumetric efficiency and temperature
    (c) Engine size and volumetric efficiency
    (d) Mixture ratio and engine size

114. Maximum pressure obtained in normal SI engine during motoring is about ....
    (a) 2 bar   (b) 15 bar
    (c) 8 bar   (d) 40 bar

115. Pressure during motoring in SI engine compared to CI engine is ....
    (a) Less   (b) more
    (c) same   (d) None of the above

116. Maximum pressure in SI engine is about ....
    (a) 10 bar   (b) 70 bar
    (c) 50 bar   **(d) 30 bar**

117. Approximate temperature produced by spark plug is ....
   (a) 5,000 deg. celsius
   (b) 20,000 deg. celsius
   (c) 2,000 deg. celsius
   (d) 10,000 deg. celsius

118. The preparation phase in SI engine will last for about ....
   (a) 20 deg. of crank rotation
   (b) 40 deg. of crank rotation
   (c) 30 deg. of crank rotation
   (d) 10 deg. of crank rotation

119. The peak pressure in SI engine will be observed when crank position is ....
   (a) About 10 deg. Before TDC
   (b) About 10 deg. after TDC
   (c) At TDC
   (d) At BDC

120. The peak temperature in SI engine will be observed when crank position is ....
   (a) About 10 deg. Before TDC
   (b) About 10 deg. after TDC
   (c) At TDC
   (d) At BDC

121. On P.θ. diagram, start of second phase in the combustion of SI engine is indicated by ....
   (a) Separation of velocity line from compression line
   (b) Constant pressure
   (c) Fall of pressure
   (d) Separation of combustion curve from motoring curve

122. On P.θ. diagram, separation of combustion curve from motoring curve in SI engine takes place ....
   (a) When crank angle is about 10 deg. before TDC
   (b) When crank angle is about 10 deg. after TDC
   (c) When crank angle is about 10 deg. before BDC
   (d) When crank angle is about 10 deg. after BDC

123. On P.θ. diagram, first measurable rise of pressure in SI engine takes place approximately ....
   (a) When crank angle is about 10 deg. before TDC
   (b) When crank angle is about 10 deg. after TDC
   (c) When crank angle is about 10 deg. before BDC
   (d) When crank angle is about 10 deg. after BDC

124. Which phase of combustion takes place during expansion stroke ....
   (a) Ignition lag
   (b) Preparation phase
   (c) Propagation of flame
   (d) After burning

125. During propagation of flame in SI engine crank rotates by about ....
   (a) 20 deg.
   (b) 40 deg.
   (c) 30 deg.
   (d) 10 deg.

126. During afterburning phase in SI engine crank rotates by about ....
    (a) 20 deg. (b) 190 deg.
    (c) 170 deg. (d) 10 deg.
127. Gap size in spark plug electrodes in about ....
    (a) 10 to 20 mm **(b) 1 to 2 mm**
    (c) 0.01 mm to 0.1 mm (d) None of the above
128. As compared to level of fuel in float chamber, the carburettor nozzle opening is at .... level
    (a) same **(b) higher**
    (c) lower (d) fluctuating
129. SI engine in which diesel is used as a fuel will ....
    (a) not run at all (b) run with detonation
    (c) run normally (d) run with less efficiency
130. If diesel is used in SI engine, it will not run. What is the correct reason?
    (a) low compression ratio (b) more density
    (c) less volatility (d) low burning point

EXERCISE

1. Define and explain the following:
    (i) Carburetion
    (ii) Carburettor
    (iii) Vapourisation
    (iv) Automisation
2. Explain with a neat sketch S.I. engine induction system.
3. What do you mean by stoichiometric air-fuel mixture, rich mixture, lean mixture?
4. Discuss mixture requirements:
    (i) For power and economy
    (ii) For automotive engines
5. What are the different type of carburettors?
6. Explain the following with neat sketches:
    (i) Simple carburettor
    (ii) Solex carburetor
    (iii) Carter carburetor

7. Explain in brief gasoline direct injection system with a neat sketch.
8. Explain combustion phenomenon in SI engines.
9. What are the factors influencing flame speed?
10. What is abnormal combustion?
11. What are the different type of combustion chambers for SI engines?
12. Explain with neat sketch Ricardo's turbulent combustion chamber.

UNIT III

COMPRESSION IGNITION (C.I.) ENGINES

3.1 FUEL SUPPLY SYSTEM FOR CI ENGINES

The fuel supply system of a diesel engine can be called as the heart of the engine, since the engine performance directly depends upon the proper functioning of this system-which must supply, meter, inject and atomize the fuel.

Fuel injection systems are manufactured with great accuracy, hence they are costlier.

General Arrangement of Fuel Supply System of a CI Engine:

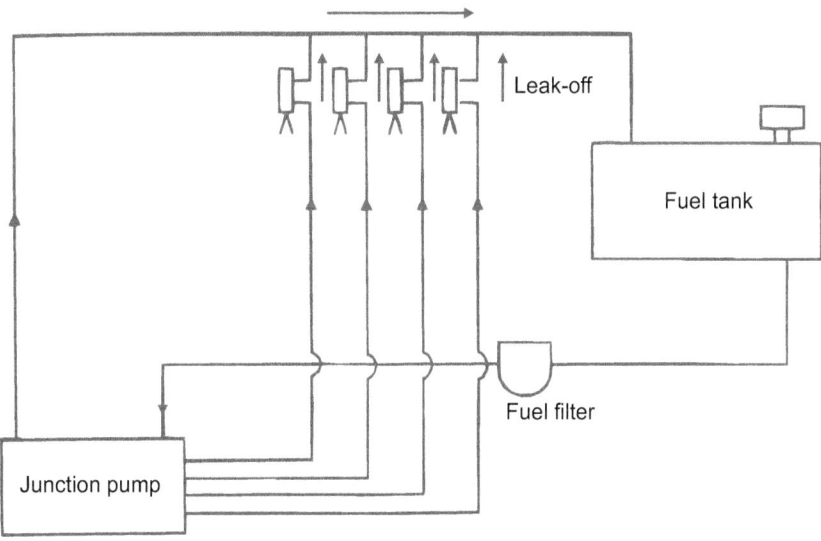

Fig. 3.1

Fuel will flow either because of gravity or fuel feed pump, which is provided to supply fuel through the filter to the injection pump. Which pumps the fuel to the injectors which are provided in the cylinder heads.

3.2 TYPES OF FUEL INJECTION SYSTEMS (S-09, 13)

The fuel injection systems are of 2 types:

1. Air Injection System (S-11): In this case fuel is injected under the pressure of air. For supplying high pressure air multistage air compressors are required, which are very much costly and hence this system is not in use.

2. Solid Injection System (S-11): In this case diesel fuel is directly injected by fuel pump (Bosch Pump). Further these are of 3 types of solid injection systems.

A) Individual Pump System (S-12): (Figs. 3.2-3.4 are self explanatory)

As shown fuel will flow from the storage tank to filters to low pressure pumps. This low pressure pump pumps the fuel to 4 separate metering and pressure pumps.

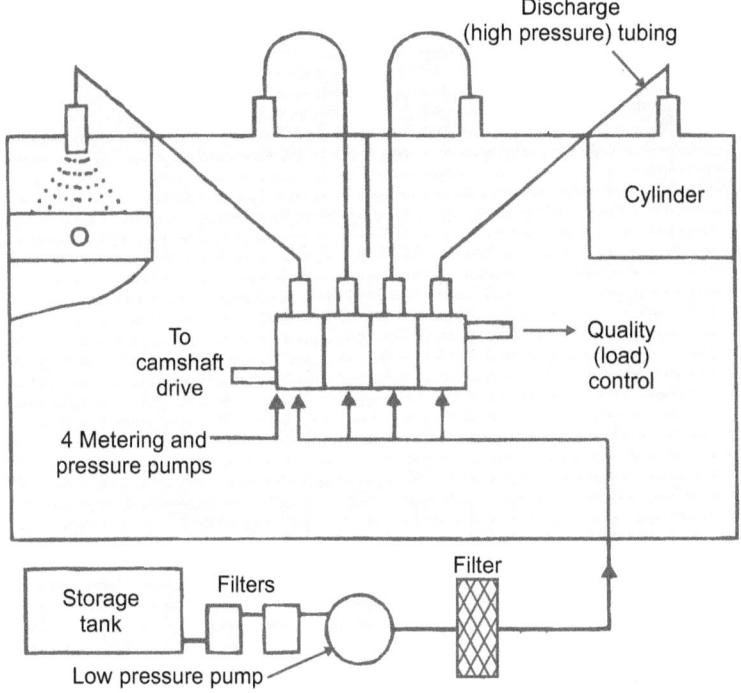

Fig. 3.2: Individual Pump System

These separate metering and pressure pumps will pump the fuel to individual injectors which are provided in the cylinder heads. These are used in large slow speed engines.

B) Distributor System (S-10, 13): Fuel will flow from storage tank to low pressure pump through filters, then to metering and pressure pumps. This metering and pressure pump pumps the fuels to distributor unit which distributes and sends required quantity of fuel to each injectors/each cylinders. Used in small and medium size engines.

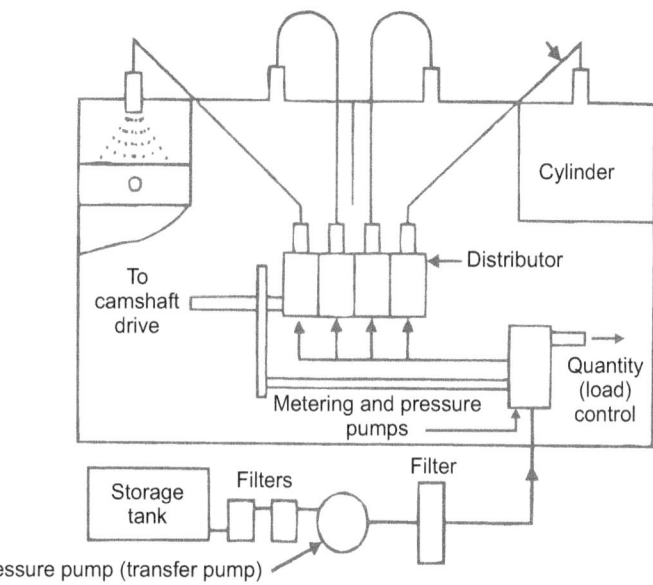

Fig. 3.3: Distributor System

C) Common Rail System (S-09): In this case fuel flow's from storage tank to low pressure pump through filters. Low pressure pump, pumps the fuel to high pressure pump, which pumps the fuel to high pressure pump, which pumps the fuel to common rail. Thus high pressure fuel is collected in common rail and from here, through the metering devices required quantity of fuel goes to injectors/cylinders. Generally Cummins and multicylinder engines use this system.

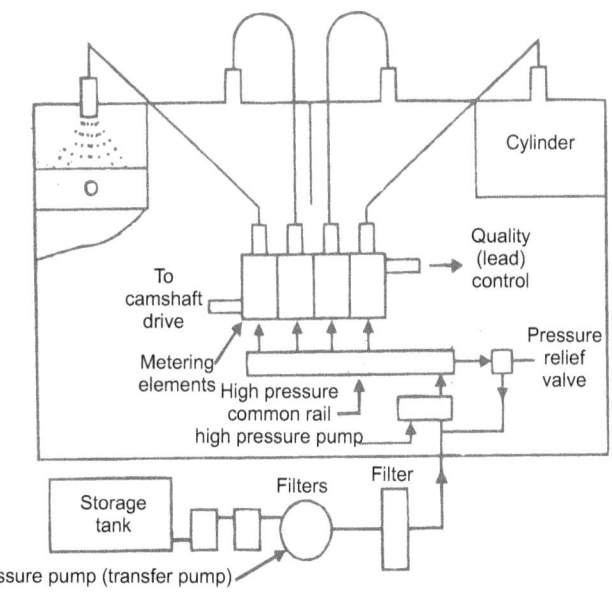

Fig. 3.4: Common Rail System

3.3 FUEL PUMP AND INJECTOR

Rack (1) is connected to the accelerator pedal or governor, which moves in and out when the accelerator pedal is operated.

Rack is in contact with the Quadrant gear (2) (a part of gear), which has cylindrical bottom part (Skirting cylinder). This skirting cylinder has cross slot. In this cross slot, cross bottom part of the plunger (3) is held. As the rack moves in and out-quadrant gear rotates-in turn plunger with helical groove moves in the cylinder (4).

The cylinder has inlet and overflow ports. This fuel pump and injector operates under primed conditions. Valve (5) is resting on the valve seat by the spring (6).

Injector and pump are connected by the delivery pipe (7).

In the injector (8) is the nozzle body, (9) is the nozzle valve and (10) is valve cap nut, (11) is the spindle-held in position by spring (12).

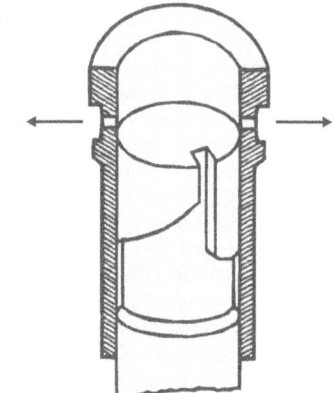

Fig. 3.5

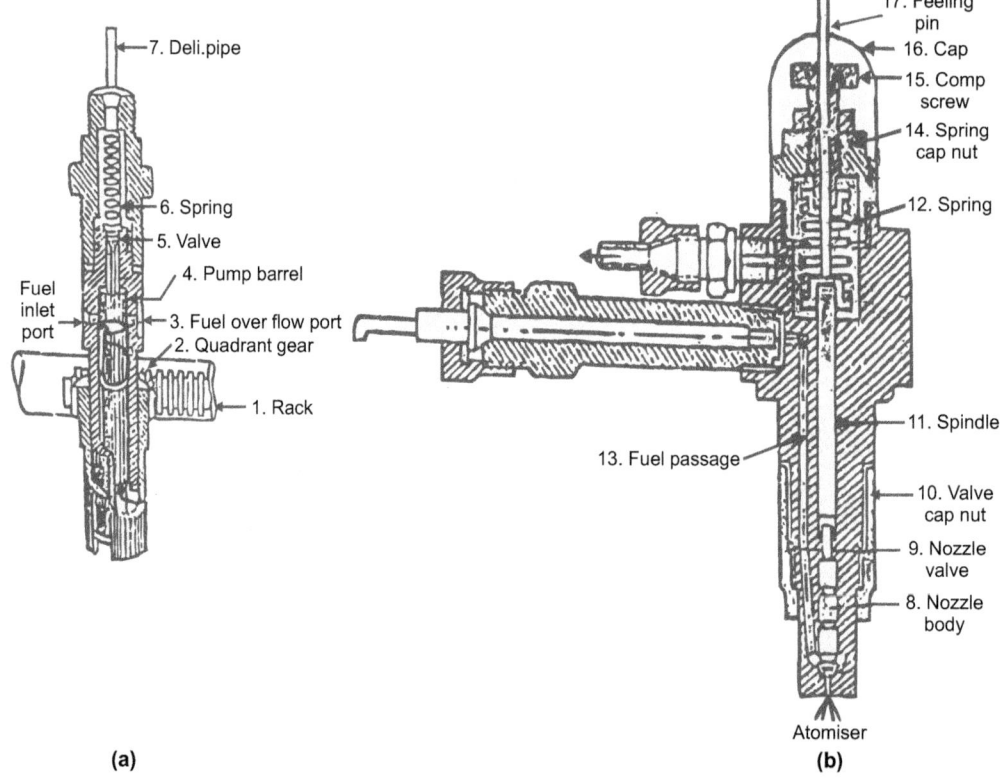

Fig. 3.6: Fuel Pump and Injector

It is to be noted that the plunger has up and down reciprocating motion-which is obtained by the camshaft below it and has rotary motion because of rack. When the rack moves in and out depending upon the power requirement, quadrant gear moves-in turn plunger rotates-plunger has helical grooves-height of groove with respect to ports varies-so amount of fuel to be injected will vary. During the upward motion of plunger-once the ports are closed-valve is lifted from its seat because of fuel pressure and fuel flows through the delivery pipe-through the fuel passage (13) to nozzle valve (9). Because of fuel pressure-nozzle valve (9) is lifted against the compression of spring (12) and fuel is injected till the edge of helical groove comes in contact with port-when pressures of fuel is released and injection stops.

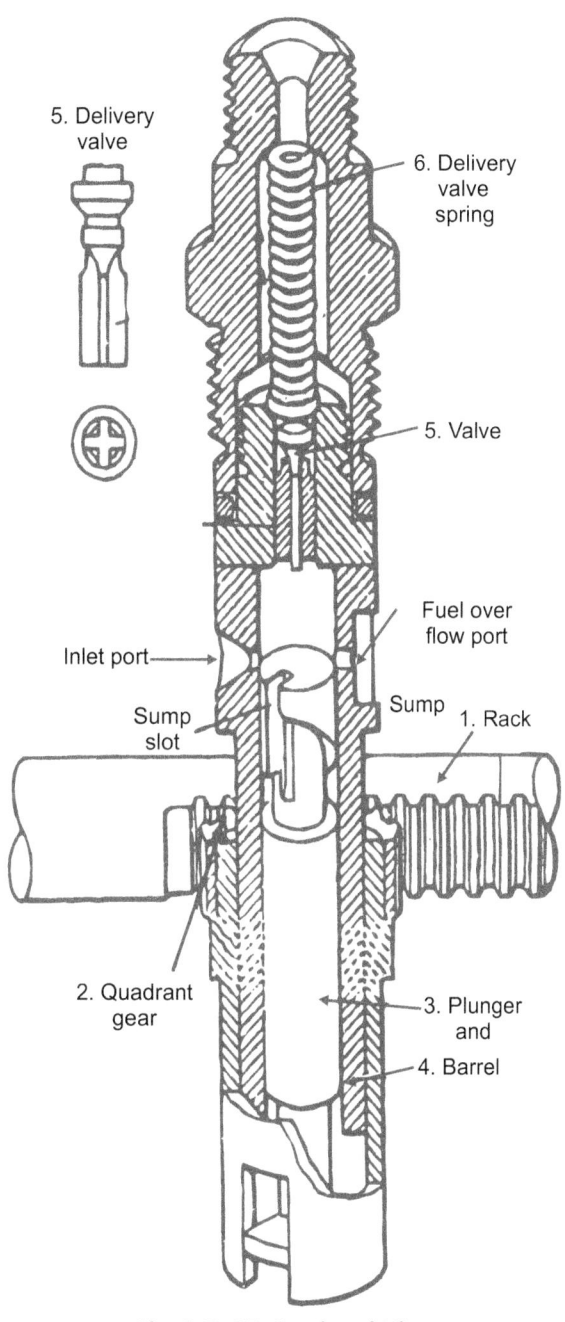

Fig. 3.7: 3D-Sectional View of Bosch Pump Element

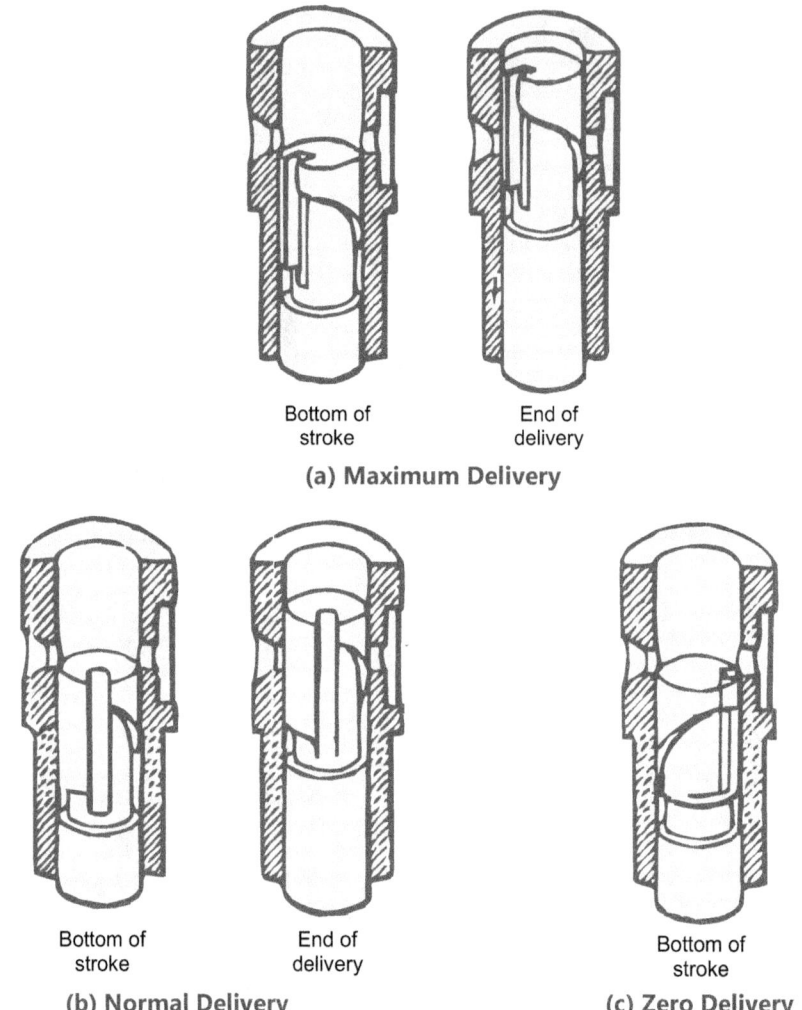

Fig. 3.8: Position of the Helix for Various Load Condition

3.4 TYPES OF FUEL INJECTORS

1. **Air Blast Injectors:** These are used in air injection systems. Now-a-days air injection systems are not in use as they require multistage compressors. And hence these injectors are no more used.
2. **Mechanically Operated Injectors:** These injectors are operated by a mechanism similar to that used to operate. IC engine valves i.e. it uses camshaft, push rods, rocker arms etc. Cam operates the plunger.
3. **Automatic Fuel Injector:** All automobile CI engines use these Automatic Fuel Injectors. They comprise needle valve, which is lifted up by fuel pressure. This fuel pressure is created by fuel pump.

3.5 TYPES OF NOZZLES

Following types of nozzles are normally used with diesel engines.

1. Single Hole Type
2. Multiple Hole type
3. Pintle Type

1. Single Hole Type: At the centre of nozzle body a hole of 0.2 mm diameter is provided. Spray cone angle is 15°.

Used in open combustion chambers.

High pressure is required to get same velocity. No good mixing with air. It has a tendency to dribble.

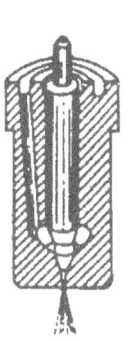 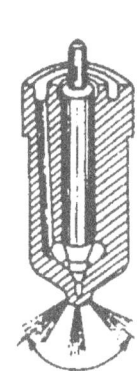 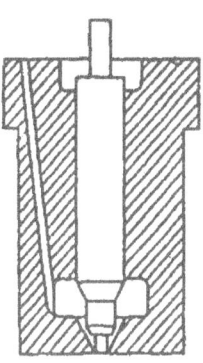 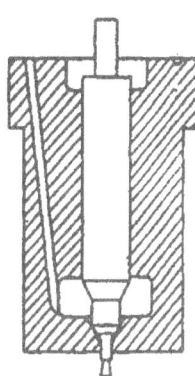

(a) Single and Multiple Hole Type   (b) Pintle Type

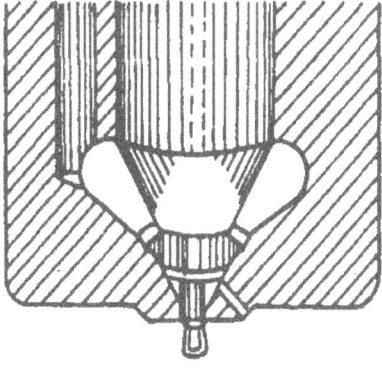

(c) Pintaux Nozzle

Fig. 3.9

2. Multiple Hole Type (S-11): Proper mixing with air. 4 to 18 holes. Size of the holes will be 0.35 to 1.5 mm. Ref. Fig. 3.9 (a).

3. Pintle Type (S-11): To avoid weak injection and dribbling, the spindle is provided with projection called **Pintle**.

It protrudes through the mouth of nozzle body. It may be cylindrical or conical in shape. Dribbling is avoided. Used in precombustion chambers, air cells, swirl chambers. Refer Fig. 3.9 (b).

4. Pintaux: Good for cold starting. It is a development of pinter nozzle. It has an auxiliary hole in the nozzle body Refer Fig. 3.9 (c). It results in good cold starting.

Disadvantage: Side hole may be choked-better filter needed.

3.6 ELECTRONIC FUEL INJECTION (EFI) SYSTEM

Electronics is introduced in automobiles in 1965. About 30-40% of cost of vehicles is for electronic items. Max power and best economy are attained by using electronics and computers in automobiles.

EFI systems was various sensors to sense various parameters like temperature, pressure of gases, position of throttle valve, air flow rate etc.

Sensors feed this data to Electronic Control Unit (ECU)-which is basically a computer.

This ECU-processes the data and operates injectors and other devices to have maximum power, with best economy, and low emissions.

3.7 MULTIPOINT FUEL INJECTION SYSTEM (MPFI)

MultiPoint Fuel injection system is used to supply air-fuel mixture of proper strength and in required quantify to each cylinder of a multicylinder engine, at all engine speeds loads.

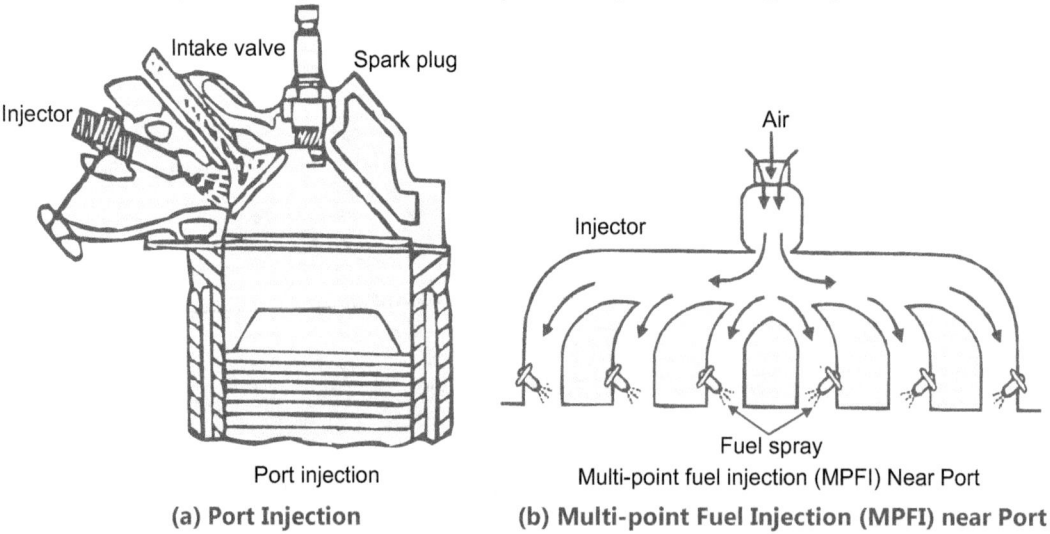

(a) Port Injection (b) Multi-point Fuel Injection (MPFI) near Port

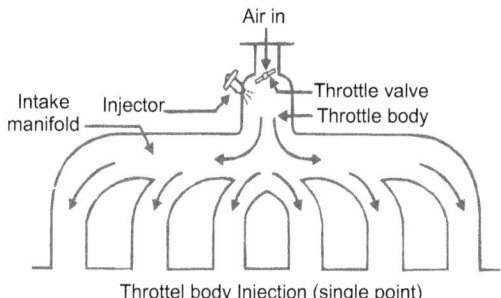

(c) Throttle Body Injection (Single Point)
Fig. 3.10

MPFI-Systems functions under 2-basic arrangements.

    1. Port Injection: In this case injector is placed in the intake manifold, near the inlet valve. The injector sprays petrol into air flowing through the intake manifold. Homogenous air-fuel mixture produced enters cylinder. Note that each cylinder has a separate injector placed in its intake manifold. [Refer Fig. 3.10 (a) and (b)].

Advantages:
1. Uniform fuel distribution. 2. Increase in power output.
3. More precise control of air-fuel ratio.

    2. Throttle Body Injection: In this case injector is provided at a single point in the throttle body. Throttle valve controls the amount of air entering intake manifold. [Refer Fig. 3.10 (c)].

3.8 QUANTITY OF FUEL AND SIZE OF NOZZLE ORIFICE

1. Velocity of fuel $C_f = C_{d_f} \cdot \sqrt{\dfrac{2\Delta P}{\rho_f}}$

$$C_f = C_{d_f} \cdot \sqrt{\dfrac{2(P_i - P_c)}{\rho_f}}$$

where, C_{d_f} = Coefficient of discharge for fuel orifice
P_i = Fuel pressure at the inlet to injector N/m^2
P_c = Cylinder pressure N/m^2
ΔP = Change of pressure
ρ_f = Density of fuel

2. Also, C_f in terms of h

$$C_f = C_{d_f} \cdot \sqrt{2gh}$$

where, h = Pressure different between injection pressure in m of fuel

3. Volume of fuel injected/sec, Q

$$Q = \left(\dfrac{\pi}{4}d^2 \cdot n\right) \times C_f \times \left[\dfrac{\theta}{360} \times \dfrac{60}{N}\right] \times \dfrac{N_i}{60}$$

where, n = Number of orifices
N = Speed in r.p.m.

$$N_i = \frac{N}{2} \text{ for 4-stroke}$$

$$N_i = N \text{ for 2-stroke}$$

$$\theta = \text{Duration of fuel injection in crank angle degree}$$

$$N_i = \text{Number of injections/min.}$$

4. $\quad$ Fuel consumed/cycle $= \dfrac{\text{bsfc} \times \text{Power}}{\text{Cycles/hr.}}$

$$\text{Cycles/hr.} = \frac{N}{2} \times 60 \text{ (4-stroke engine)}$$

$$= N \times 60 \text{ (2-stroke engine)}$$

5. $\quad$ Time of injection $= \left(\dfrac{Q}{360} \times \dfrac{60}{N}\right)$ sec.

Example 3.1:

In a solid fuel injection system find the velocity of fuel injection, when the difference in fuel pressure and cylinder pressure is 90 bar. Assuming S = 0.905 and Cd for orifice = 0.86.

Solution:

Data:
$$\Delta P = 90 \times 10^5 \text{ N/m}^2$$
$$S = 0.905$$
$$\rho = 0.905 \times 10^3 \text{ kg/m}^3$$
$$Cd_f = 0.86$$

We know that,

$$C_f = Cd_f \times \sqrt{\frac{2\Delta P}{\rho_f}}$$

$$= 0.86 \times \sqrt{\frac{2 \times 90 \times 105}{905}}$$

$$\boxed{C_f = 121.285 \text{ m/sec.}}$$

COMBUSTION IN C.I. ENGINE

3.9 INTRODUCTION $\quad$ (S-09, 10, 11, 12, W-11, 12)

Compression Ignition engine is also known as Diesel engine. The very cause of it was that the engine was invented and developed by Dr. Rudolf Diesel. C.I. engines are highly preferred where we require:

(1) High thermal efficiency.
(2) Cost constraint is there as C.I engine fuel is cheap.

Because of the above two reasons it was preferred in industries like buses, travelers, locomotives, tractors, pumping sets, stationary Industrial application, power generation and machine application but because of its large weight, smoke and odour it was not able to take the passenger car market. The varied application of C.I engine resulted in production of large variety of C.I engine it varies from around 2 to 40,000 bhp in power.

3.10 COMBUSTION IN C.I. ENGINE (S-09, 10, 11, W-11, 12)

Working of C.I engine is different from S.I. engine. In C.I. engine, air is compressed to a very large extent. Compression ratio is of the order of (12 : 1 to 22 : 1) because of such a high compression the air temperature and pressure rises to a very extreme point. At this point fuel injector injects the fuel in the form of jet at a high pressure. As the fuel enters the combustion chamber containing hot gases it vapourises and after some time because of heat it ingnites and combustion occurs.

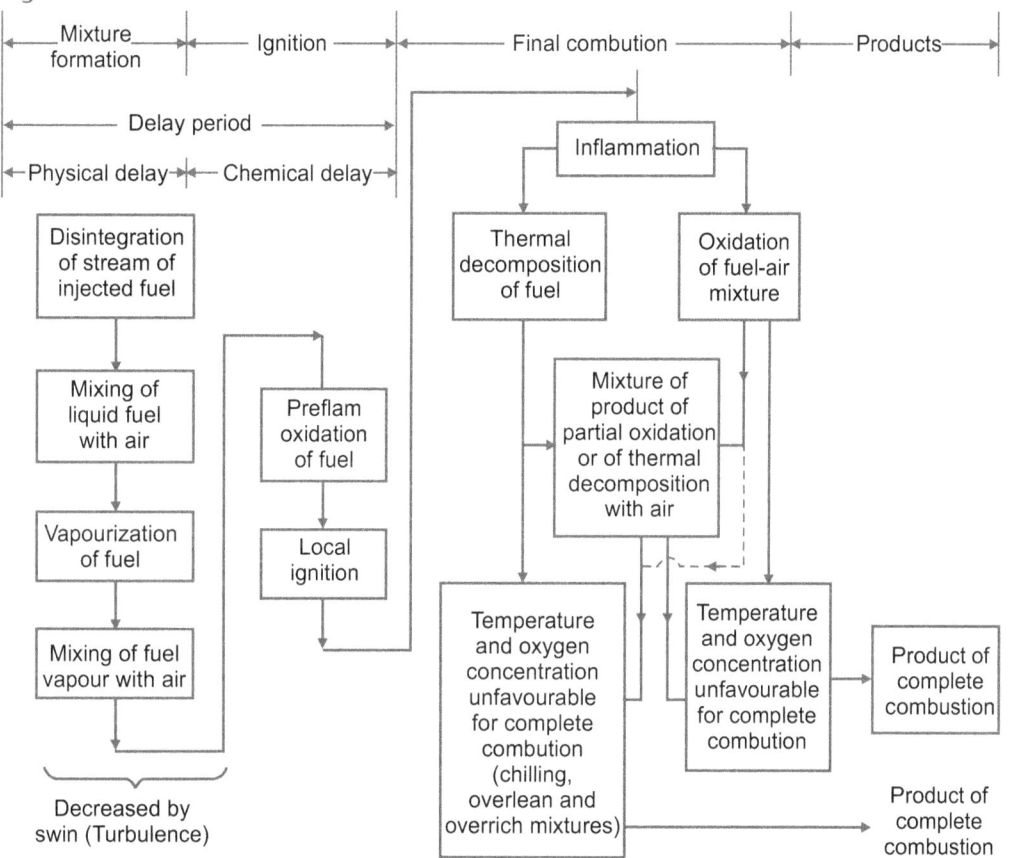

Fig. 3.11: Combustion in the CI Engine

For vapourisation, fuel takes the heat from the air, therefore the point from which it takes heat becomes cold and this point has to take heat from the nearby air because the combustion cannot occur till the full mixture reaches a particular temperature. This delay period is known as PHYSICAL DELAY. After the physical delay we have CHEMICAL DELAY in which reaction starts slowly and then accelerates until ignition takes place. The Sum of both the delay is known as IGNITION DELAY.

It should be noted that in C.I. engine we don't have a homogeneous mixture like what we had in S.I. engine. Here we have a heterogeneous mixture i.e. there can be only fuel at a point, or can be only air or the mixture of both. Thus the reaction is unpredictable, it can be slow or steady or can be explosive, this is the root cause of chemical delay. The detailed study of ignition delay is done at the later part of this chapter. .

3.11 STAGES OF COMBUSTION

The great scientist "Ricardo" has given the following stages in C.I combustion process.

   (1) First Stage (Ignition Delay): It is preparatory phase, as shown in Fig. 3.12. It is the stage in which fuel has been injected in the combustion chamber but has not been ignited. Designer wants this stage to be as small as possible but it can neither be removed nor minimised after a certain extent for the proper working of engine.

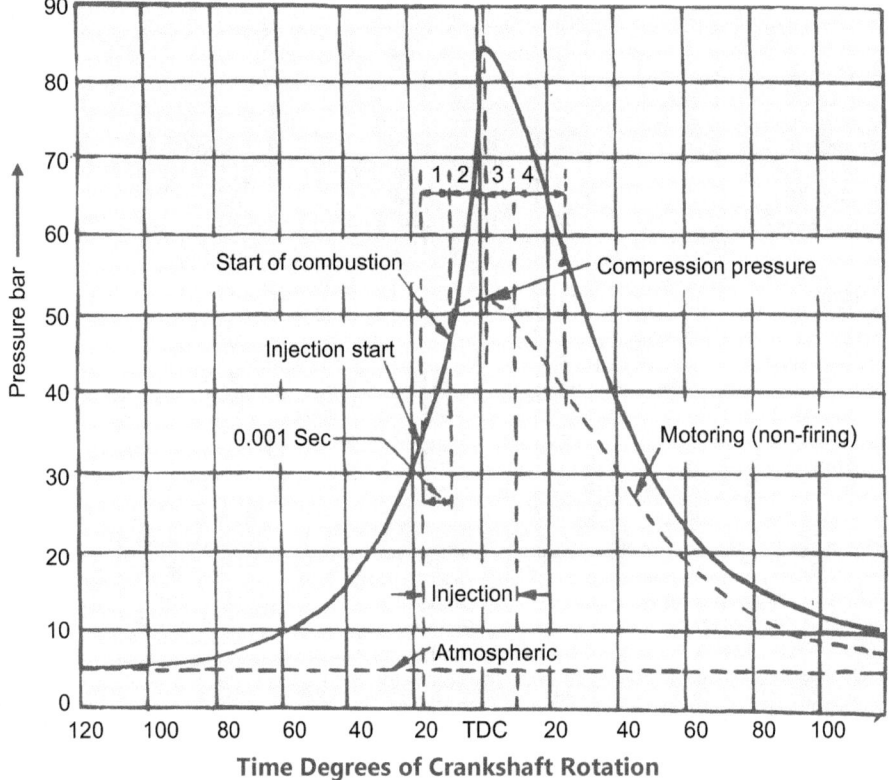

Fig. 3.12: Stages of Combustion in the CI Engine

   (2) Second Stage (Rapid on Uncontrolled Combustion): This is the stage which starts from end of ignition delay and terminated when maximum pressure is shown on the indication diagram. In this phase pressure rise is rapid because fuel burns at a great speed. In this situation during the Ignition Delay period, the fuel get's fully distributed mixed in the chamber and burns at a very high rate. Due to production of such a high pressure a-violent pounding noise in produced known as "Diesel knock".

(3) Third Stage (Controlled Combustion): It starts at end of attainment of maximum pressure and ends at attainment of maximum temperature by the end of this stage about 70% to 80% of total heat gets generated whereas by the end of 2nd stage about 30% to 35% of heat gets generated. This is known as controlled stage as the fuel gets burned as soon as it enters the chamber in this stage because of high temperature and pressure, thus by controlling the timing and state of the fuel entering, the phenomenon is controlled.

(4) Fourth Stage (After Burning): This is not a necessary stage in all process. Theoretically combustion should end after 3rd stage but this does not happen in actual, because we have a heterogeneous mixture of air-fuel due to which the combustion still continues, it produces around 5% to 10% of total energy.

3.12 VARIABLES AFFECTING DELAY PERIOD (S-09)

To tell the exact division of physical and chemical delay is very difficult hence only an idea can be made about them which tells that generally chemical delay is larger than physical delay. Ignition delay plays a very important role in both design and performance of the engine. It affects the pressure rise in the engine and thus is responsible for knocking. Figure shows the exact points where ignition delay starts and ends. Following are the factor's affecting ignition delay.

(1) **Fuel:** Type of fuel plays a very important role in deciding ignition delay as self ignition temp is a property of fuel. A lower self ignition temperature means a wider margin between the compressed air temperature and fuel temperature. A short ignition delay results in smooth operation of engine in the presence of good fuel. Cetane number measures the ignition delay.

(2) **Injection Advance-Angle:** The delay period increases with increase in injection advance angle in high speed diesel engine.

(3) **Injection Pressure (W-10):** With the increase in inlet pressure ignition delay would decrease.

(4) **Compression Ratio (W-10, S-13):** Due to increase in temperature and density with increase in compression ratio, delay period gets reduced.

(5) **Intake Temperature:** Increasing the, intake temperature would result in increase in compressed air temperature which reduces the delay period.

(6) **Jacket Water Temperature:** Ignition delay reduces with increases in jacket water temperature.

(7) **Speed:** With the engine speed increment, temperature and pressure of air rises thus reducing the delay period.

(8) **Air-fuel Mixture:** Fuel air ratio increases with load, thus decrease in the ratio will reduce the cylinder wall temperature and hence delay period increases.

(9) **Engine Size:** Large engine operate on slow speed because of size limitation. Because of slow speed, the period increases.

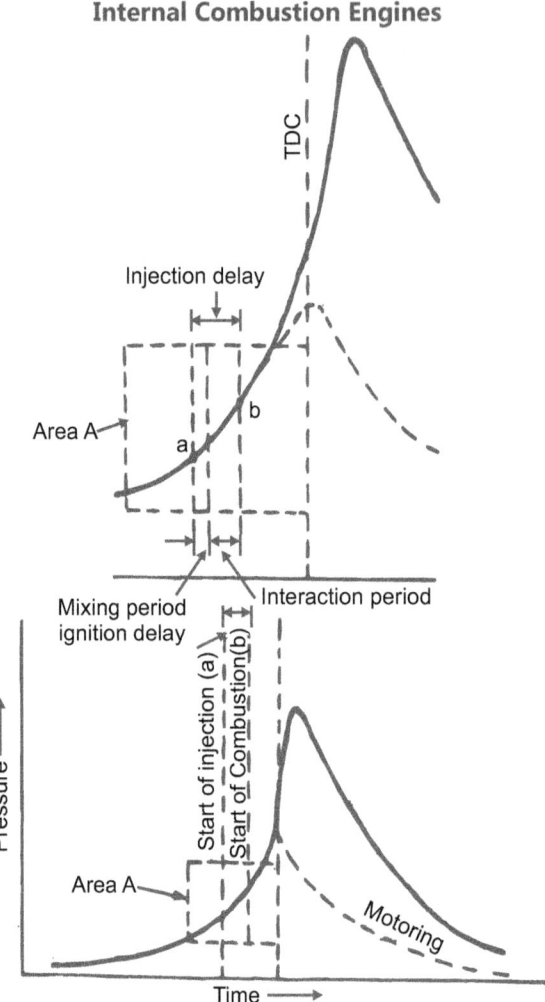

Fig. 3.13: Pressure-Time Diagram showing Delay Period

3.13 KNOCK IN C.I. ENGINE (S-10, W-10, 11, 12)

In C.I. engines knocking start with the ignition only, as we know there is a heterogeneous mixture in chamber and in IInd stage there is very large pressure rise also. Combustion begins with autoignition as self ignition temperature is attained. It is very difficult to distinguish or separate knocking in C.I. engine but it does not mean that it always occurs. There are methods to reduce or minimise it. Thus in C.I. engine knocking occurs in the initial phase only, whereas in S.I. engine it occurs in last phase but though the phenomenon sounds same there is a difference as follows.

3.14 COMPARISON OF DIESEL KNOCK AND DETONATION

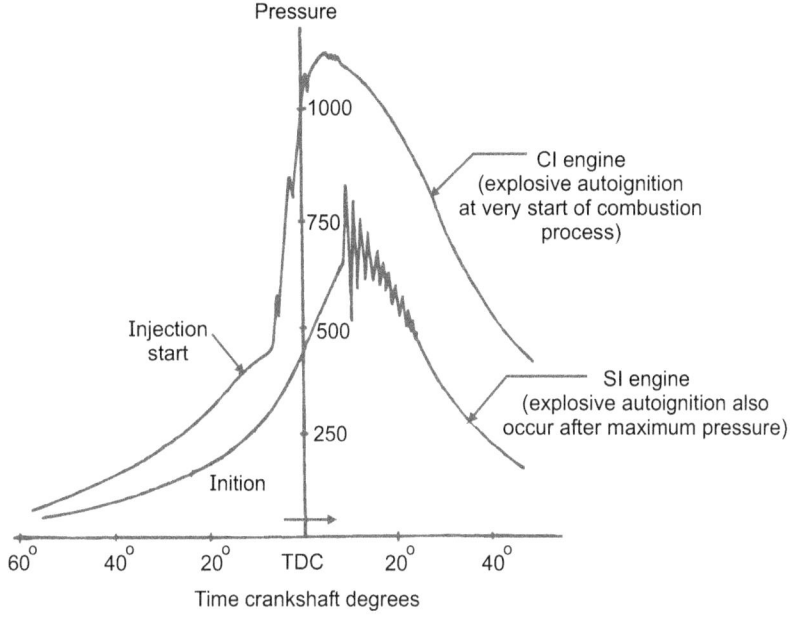

Fig. 3.14: Comparison of Time of Knock in the SI and CI Engine

Detonation in S-I	Knocking in C.I.
(1) Here detonation occurs at the end of combustion.	(1) Detonation occur's at the starting of combustion.
(2) Here the rate of pressure is very high as mixture is homogeneous also maximum pressure is high.	(2) Here the rate and maximum pressure both are low because of the fact that heterogeneous mixture is present.
(3) There are chances of Pre-ignition.	(3) Pre-Ignition cannot occur as fuel is injected after compression.
(4) The S.I. engine we can distinguish easily between knocking and non-knocking engine as it is audible by human ear.	(4) In C.I engine it is difficult because the normal combustion process itself starts with autoignition and hence they have sufficient rate of Pressure-rise and already a high audible noise is there. Hence here a personal judgment experience is required.

3.15 FACTORS AFFECTING KNOCK IN C.I. ENGINES

For having less tendency to knock the fuel air mixture should have:
(a) High temperature (b) High density
(c) Short delay (d) Reactive mixture.

Also tendency of knock would increase if:
(1) Compression ratio is lowered.
(2) Inlet air temperature is lowered.
(3) Coolant temperature is reduced.
(4) Load is reduced.
(5) Decreasing the injection pressure.
(6) Decreasing the speed.
(7) Decreasing the turbulence.

3.16 CETANE RATING OF C.I. ENGINE FUELS

It is a similar method as in S.I, engine where we had octane no where it was measure of resistance to knock. Here we have a Cetane no which measures the ignition lag. Cetane ($C_{16}H_{34}$) has a good ignition quality and assigned arbitrarily a rting of 100 cetane number (CN) also Alpha Methyl Napthalene ($C_{11}H_{10}$) which has got poor ignition quality has been assigned a zero cetane number. Thus, a cetane number for blend is calculated by

$$\text{Cetane number} = (\% \text{ of n-cetane}) + 0.15\ (\% \text{ heptamethyl nonane})$$
$$= (\% \text{ of n-cetane}) + (\% \ (x\text{-methyl-napthalene})$$

It is defined as the % by volume of cetane in a mixture of cetane and α-methyl napthalene that produceoss the same ignition delay as the fuel being tested in the same standard engine under the same standard operating condition.

For example: A cetane rating of 60 indicates that fuel has the same ignition delay in a standard engine under definite operating conditions as a mixture by volume of 60 points n-cetane and 40 parts of hepthamethyl nonane if hepta methyl nonane is considered instead of (x-methyl napthalene. Thus this proves that "knock" in the engine is directly related to the "ignition delay" of fuel.

Additives: Certain additives can be added in the diesel to reduce its tendency to knock, such additives serve to reduce the self ignition temperature of fuel by acting as local ignition points. Thus they improve the ignition quality of fuel by reducing ignition delay. These are given in following table.

Additives	Cetane Rating	Change
Isopropylnitrate	39	+ 15
Amyl nitrate	39	+ 15
Heptylyl Peroxide	77	+ 16
Butyl Peroxide	39	+ 2
Methyl Acetate	26	+ 16

3.17 COMBUSTION CHAMBERS IN DIESEL ENGINE

The design of combustion chamber in diesel engine is very important because in C.I. engine mixing is done in combustion chamber, also more oxygen is provided to other part of fuel by proper design only. We know that fuel droplet in combustion chamber can be injected in such a manner that they get equally distributed hence heterogeneous mixture is formed and thus only a few parts of the mixture would find right amount of oxygen thus it is essential to impart an orderly and controlled movement to air and fuel so that a continuous supply of fresh air is brought to each burning droplets and the combustion products are taken away. This effect is known as "Air Swirl". "Air swirl" in the C.I, engine varies from the "turbulence" in S.I engine in the basic manner that "air swirl" has to be systematic and a particular direction whereas turbulence is in general.

As discussed, production or presence of "swirl" is of extreme importance in C.I engine. There are various methods to do so. Following are a few of them:

(1) Induction SWIRL: In this air flow is directed in a particular path during it's entering in the cylinder. This method is generally employed for open combustion chamber.

(2) Compression SWIRL: Here the swirl is produced during the compression stroke, air is forced through a passage into swirl chamber made separately during the compression stroke, as shown in figure.

(3) Combustion Induced SWIRL: This swirl is produced by using the phenomenon of high initial pressure rise due to partial combustion.

Mainly the above three methods are used for production of "swirl" in C.I engine without which the efficiency of engine gets restricted.

3.18 TYPES OF DIESEL COMBUSTION SYSTEMS

Diesel engines can be broadly categorised as:
(1) Direct Injection Engines (DI).
(2) Indirect Injection Engines (IDI).

DI Engines:

These are non-turbulent chambers. These engines are also known as engine with open combustion chambers. By open combustion chamber we mean, that we have combustion space which is in the form of a single cavity and pressure throughout the chamber is uniform. In these type of engines the above mentioned cavity is formed between the piston K cylinder head. In these type of engines fuel enters in a highly atomised form and multipoint injections are used to distribute fuel evenly in the chamber. There are many designs of this type of engine. Fig. 3.15 shows an example which is adopted for large engines running at slow speeds. In this "squish" is negligible. "Squish" can be defined as radially inward flow of air towards the combustion recess by squaring it out from between the piston and cylinder head during the end of compression stroke. It is a required as much as possible but is generally weak in open type combustion chamber.

Fig. 3.15 II shows a hemispherical shape of chamber. This also has a low squish. Generally a cylindrical chamber is better for "squish".

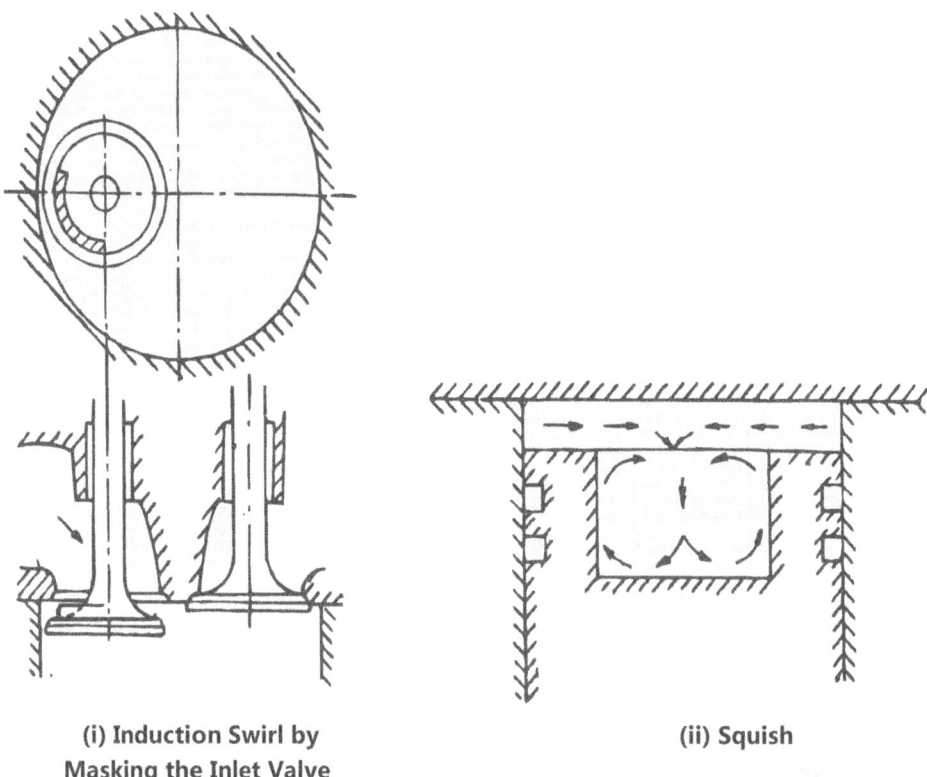

(i) Induction Swirl by Masking the Inlet Valve

(ii) Squish

Fig. 3.15

3.19 INDIRECT INJECTION SYSTEM (DIVIDED CHAMBER INJECTION SYSTEM)

In this type of injection system combustion space is divided between two compartments connected by a small passage. The two compartments are:

(1) Auxillary chamber

(2) Piston and cylinder head chamber.

Two broad category of these type of chambers are:

(1) Swirl Chamber system

(2) Pre-combustion chamber system

An example of swirl chamber is Ricardo Comet Mark II. In this type of engine swirl chamber is of spherical shape in which maximum amount of air enters during compression. This swirl chamber is made separate from combustion chamber as shown in figure.

The air entering the swirl chamber experiences a strong rotary movement because of design of passage way which is made in such a manner that air enter's tangential. Thus this results in good swirl production. Fuel is injected in the swirl chamber and because of high swirl proper mixing and uniform distribution occurs.

The second type that is pre combustion chamber works on the principle of combustion induced swirl. These are turbulent chambers and are not recommended these days. In this type we have pre-combustion chamber connected to main chamber through very small holes. Small amount of fuel is admitted in pre-combustion chamber and the combustion is initiated in it which results in pressure rise because of which air and combustion products rushes out of the hole. Thus creating turbulence and distributing evenly the fuel and air mixture in main combustion chamber.

3.20 DOPES AND ADDITIVES

Dopes are the some chemical substances added to diesel fuel to decrease the delay period. Following are the dopes which are commonly added to the diesel fuel.
1. Annyl Nitrate [$CH_3 (CH_2)_4 ONO$].
2. Ether ($CH_3CH_2OCH_2CH_3$).
3. Ethyl Nitrate ($CH_3CH_2ONO_2$).

Dopes are added to a maximum amount of 0.01 cc – 2 cc per litre of diesel fuel.

Additives: Additives serve to reduce the self-ignition temperature of fuel by the way of acting as locals ignition points. Additives can be added or mixed with diesel to reduce the tendency to knock. Thus, they improve the ignition quality of fuel by reducing ignition delay. Following table gives some of additives.

	Additives	Cetane Rating	Change
1.	Amyl Nitrate	39	+ 15
2.	Butyl Peroxide	39	+ 2
3.	Heptyl Peroxide	77	+ 2
4.	Isopropyl Nitrate	39	+ 18
5.	Methyl Acetate	26	+ 16

MULTIPLE CHOICE QUESTIONS (MCQ'S)

1. In C.I. engines with increase in compression ratio the delay period ....
   (a) decreases   (b) increases
   (c) first increase and then decreases ....
2. Knocking in C.I. engine takes place
   (a) During the combustion process   **(b) at the start of combustion**
   (c) at the end of combustion   (d) all of the above
3. Knocking tendency in C.I. engines increases with ....
   (a) increase in compression ratio
   (b) increasing coolant water temperature
   (c) increase in inlet temperature of air
   (d) decrease in compression ratio

4. In C.I. engines by increasing inlet air pressure the knocking tendency ....
   (a) decreases (b) increases
   (c) not affected (d) first increase and then decreases
5. Open combustion chambers in C.I. engines require ....
   (a) accurate metering of fuel (b) high injection pressures
   (c) both (a) and (b) (d) none of the above
6. Advantages of indirect injection combustion chambers are ....
   (a) low injection pressure (b) direction of spray is not critical
   (c) good cold starting performance (d)
7. In C.I. engines the delay period is affected by ....
   (a) engine speed (b) compression ratio
   (c) output **(d) all of above**
8. In the following Fig. ....

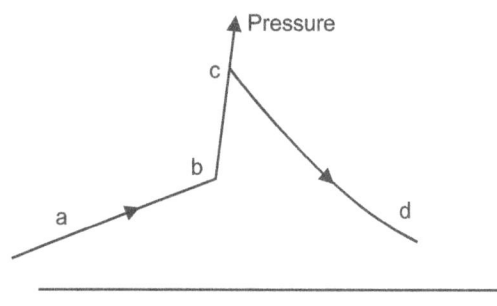

i) Process a–b represent
   (a) compression (b) combustion
   (c) expansion (d) None of above
ii) In Fig. Process b–c represents
   (a) compression **(b) combustion**
   (c) expansion (d) None of above
iii) In Fig. Process c–d represents
   (a) compression (b) combustion
   (c) expansion (d) None of above
9. In C.I. engines in the combustion chamber ....
   (a) Homogeneous mixture is supplied
   (b) Heterogeneous mixture is supplied
   (c) both Homogenous and heterogeneous mixture is supplied
   (d) None of above

10. In C.I. engines combustion is initiated by ……….
    (a) spark plug   **(b) Auto Ignition**
    (c) external combustion (d) All of the above
11. In C.I. engines combustion takes place at ……….
    (a) constant pressure
    (b) constant volume
    (c) at constant pressure and constant volume
    (d) None of the above
12. The turbulence in combustion chamber ……….
    (a) Reduces combustion duration
    (b) minimizes tendency of abnormal combustion
    (c) Accelerates the mixing of fuel and oxygen
    (d) All of the above
13. Flame speed in C.I. engine combustion chamber ……….
    (a) Increases with increase in intake temperature
    (b) Increases with increase in pressure
    (c) decreases with increase in intake temperature
    (d) a and b
14. High compression ratio in C.I. Engine combustion chamber ……….
    (a) increases pressure in the combustion chamber
    (b) increases temperature in the combustion chamber
    (c) Reduces ignition delay
    (d) all of the above
15. When cycle pressure increases the output of the engine ……….
    (a) increases   (b) decreases
    (c) remains same   (d) None of the above
16. If C.I. engine speed increases ……….
    (a) turbulence inside the combustion chamber increases
    (b) The time required for flame travel decreases
    (c) flame speed increases
    (d) All of the above
17. The air swirl in C.I. engine combustion chamber ……….
    (a) required for orderly movement of air
    (b) not required for movement of air
    (c) required for braking of fuel jet
    (d) a and c

18. During ignition delay period ....
    (a) Air is only admitted combustion chamber
    (b) Air and fuel is already admitted but not ignited
    (c) Air and fuel is already admitted and ignition is going on
    (d) None of the above
19. Delay period in the C.I. engine combustion chamber ....
    (a) affects combustion rate
    (b) affects knocking tendency
    (c) affects presence of smoke in exhaust
    (d) All of the above
20. The physical delay period can be reduced by ....
    (a) high injection press   (b) low turbulence
    (c) low combustion temperature   (d) highly viscous fuel
21. As engine speed increases in C.I. engines ....
    (a) Ignition delay decreases
    (b) Ignition delay increases
    (c) Ignition delay is not affected by engine speed
    (d) Ignition delay initially increases and then decreases
22. With increase in C.I. engine output ....
    (a) Operating temperature increase and delay period decreases
    (b) Operating temp. remains constant and delay period decreases
    (c) Operating temp. decreases and delay period decreases
    (d) Operating temperature and delay period both increases
23. Increasing the degree of atomization in C.I. engines ....
    (a) Reduces delay period   **(b) Increases delay period**
    (c) there is no effect on delay period (d) none of above
24. In C.I. engines self ignition temperature is lower ....
    (a) Delay period is higher
    (b) delay period is lower
    (c) self ignition temperature has no effect on delay period
    (d) None of above
25. Increased intake temperature of air in C.I. engines ....
    (a) increases delay period   **(b) reduces delay period**
    (c) has no effect on delay period   (d) delay period remains constant

26. Increase in cetin number of fuel ....
    (a) Increases delay period
    (b) decreases delay period
    (c) having no effect on delay period
    (d) None of above
27. Increase in C.I. engine injection pressure ....
    (a) Reduces physical delay
    (b) increases physical delay
    (c) first increases then decreases
    (d) None of the above
28. Increase compression ratio of C.I. engine ....
    (a) reduces air temperature and pressure and reduces auto ignition temperature
    (b) reduces air temperature and pressure and increases auto ignition temperature
    (c) increases air temperature and pressure and reduces auto ignition temperature
    (d) increases air temperature and pressure and increases auto ignition temperature
29. Increase in cooling water temperature in C.I. engines ....
    (a) Reduces delay period
    (b) Increases delay period
    (c) There is no effect on delay period
    (d) None of the above
30. Supercharging in C.I. engines ....
    (a) increases density of air and increases auto ignition temperature
    (b) decreases density of air and increases auto ignition temperature
    (c) decreases density of air and decreases auto ignition temperature
    (d) increase density and also reduces auto ignition temperature
31. Knocking in C.I. engines is due to ....
    (a) auto ignition of charge at the start of combustion
    (b) auto ignition of charge at the end of combustion
    (c) auto ignition of charge at the mid way of combustion chamber
    (d) none of above
32. In knocking or detonation ....
    (a) pressure rise at auto ignition is more in SI engine.
    (b) pressure rise at auto ignition is less in CI engine
    (c) pressure rise at auto ignition is less in SI engine
    (d) pressure rise at auto ignition is more in CI engine
33. Which of the following statement is true?
    (a) Fuel injector is used in SI engine.
    (b) Inlet and outlet valves are used in 2 stroke engine
    (c) Compression ratio in diesel is higher than petrol engine
    (d) None of above

34. If diesel is used in petrol engine, it will ....
    (a) not run
    (b) increase knocking
    (c) decrease knocking
    (d) none of above
35. Compression ratio of CI engine varies from ....
    (a) 6 to 10
    (b) 10 to 15
    (c) 15 to 20
    (d) 20 to 40
36. Which of the following is not true for C.I. engine?
    (a) C.I. engines are more bulky than SI engines
    (b) C.I. engines are more efficient than S.I. engines
    (c) Lighter flywheels are required in C.I. engines
    (d) Starting of diesel engines are more difficult due to cracking efforts.
37. For diesel engines, the method of governing employed is ....
    (a) quantity governing
    (b) quality governing
    (c) hit and miss governing
    (d) none of the above
38. Cetane number of the fuel used commercially for diesel engine in India is in the range ....
    (a) 80 to 90
    (b) 60 to 80
    (c) 60 to 70
    (d) 40 to 45
39. The knocking tendency in C.I. engines increases with ....
    (a) decrease in compression ratio
    (b) increase in compression ratio
    (c) increasing the temperature of inlet air
    (d) increasing cooling water temperature
40. A diesel engine is generally more efficient than a petrol engine because of ....
    (a) proper air fuel mixing and combustion
    (b) high calorific value of diesel fuel
    (c) knock-free operation
    (d) high compression ratio
41. To injection pressure in diesel engine is of the order of ....
    (a) 20-40 bar
    (b) 100-150 bar
    (c) 160-220 bar
    (d) 400-500 bar
42. The ignition temperature of diesel fuel is about ....
    (a) 250°C
    (b) 400°C
    (c) 500°C
    (d) 750°C
43. Which of the following fuel has a Cetane number of 100?
    (a) Normal heptane
    (b) Centane
    (c) Ethyl fluid
    (d) $\propto$-methyl napthalene

44. Due to following reasons diesel engines are preferred for road transport?
    (a) Complete combustion of charge
    (b) Low operating cost
    (c) Low specific fuel consumption over a large range of load
    (d) Easy starting
45. In a diesel engine if one of the cylinders receives more fuel than the others than which of the following will happen for that cylinder?
    (a) Exhaust temperature will be high
    (b) Exhaust will be smoky
    (c) Piston rings would stick into piston grooves
    (d) All of the above
46. Compression ratio in diesel engine is .... in comparison to expansion ratio.
    (a) less (b) same
    (c) more (d) variable
47. Due to following the tendency of a diesel engine to knock increases?
    (a) increase in compression ratio (b) increase in engine speed
    (c) increase in octane value of fuel **(d) increase in engine power**
48. Cetane number is the measure of ....
    (a) calorific value of fuel (b) viscosity of fuel
    (c) ignition quality (d) auto ignition temperature
49. In order to obtain higher output from diesel engine, it is required to use ....
    (a) High excess air (b) High compression ratio
    (c) High fuel-air ratio (d) fine atomisation of fuel
50. Highest useful compression ratio is the compression ratio at which ....
    (a) the engine can operate without detonation
    (b) the engine consumes minimum fuel for a particular power output
    (c) the engine gives maximum power output
    (d) the engine maintains operating pressures and temperatures within prescribed limits
51. .... regulates the pressure strokes in the fuel injector pump of a diesel engine.
    (a) Needle valve (b) Lift of plunger
    (c) Control rack (d) pump shaft
52. Which of the following could be the probable reasons of power loss in a diesel engine?
    (a) ineffective cooling **(b) low injection pressure**
    (c) restricted exhaust (d) clogging of aircleaner

53. Which of the following is the anti-knock quality of diesel fuel
    (a) Octane number
    (b) Cetane number
    (c) either of the above
    (d) none of the above
54. In a C.I. engine high combustion chamber wall temperature will ....
    (a) reduce knocking tendency
    (b) reduce exhaust temperature
    (c) increase knocking tendency
    (d) have no effect
55. .... acts as ignition accelerator for C.I. engines fuel.
    (a) Hydrogen peroxide
    (b) Acetone peroxide
    (c) n-heptane
    (d) none of the above
56. In C.I. engine, the fuel ignition accelerators are added to ....
    (a) increase delay period
    (b) reduce combustion knock
    (c) accelerates combustion knock
    (d) reduce combustion chamber temperature.
57. Highest useful compression ratio is the compression ratio at which ....
    (a) an engine can be safety operated
    (b) an engine operates smoothly
    (c) detonation first becomes audible
    (d) an engine gives maximum thermal efficiency
58. A diesel engine as compared to petrol engine is ....
    (a) less efficient
    (b) more efficient
    (c) equally efficient
    (d) none of the above
59. What is swirl in C.I. engines?
    (a) directional movement of fuel spray
    (b) circular motion imparted to suction air
    (c) radial motion imparted to fuel-air mixture
    (d) circular motion imparted to gases after combustion
60. In a C.I. engine squish is created ....
    (a) at the end of suction stroke
    (b) at the beginning of suction stroke
    (c) during combustion
    (d) towards the end of compression stroke
61. An increase in the mean effective pressure of a diesel engine with fixed compression ratio can be obtained with increase in ....
    (a) engine speed
    (b) back pressure
    (c) cut off ratio
    (d) charge density
62. Due to which of the following injection lag in diesel engine is caused?
    (a) leakage past the fuel-oil plunger
    (b) compressibility of fuel
    (c) expansion of fuel-oil discharge lines under high pressure
    (d) All of the above

63. Due to which of the following reasons a diesel engine gives a smoky exhaust?
    (a) fuel injection is late
    (b) water in the fuel
    (c) exhaust valve receives too much tube oil
    (d) all of the above
64. Free acids in diesel oil for diesel engine lead to which of the following?
    (a) deposition of engine parts
    (b) excessive fuel consumption
    (c) damaging of both the storage tank and the engine
    (d) excessive engine near
65. By which of the following methods diesel smoke can be reduced?
    (a) A adherence to proper fuel specification
    (b) Using additives in the fuel
    (c) Avoidance of overloading
    (d) Reducing maximum flow of fuel
    (e) All of the above
66. The rating of a diesel engine will ……….. with increase in air inlet temperature.
    (a) Increase linearly   (b) increase parabolically
    (c) decrease parabolically   **(d) decrease linearly**
67. Which of the following statement is correct for the same compression ratio?
    (a) Otto cycle is more efficient than diesel cycle
    (b) Diesel cycle is more efficient than Otto cycle
    (c) Both diesel and otto cycles are equally efficient
    (d) Compression ratio has no relation with efficiency
68. The pressure at the end of compression in the case of diesel engine is of the order of ……….
    (a) 6 bar   (b) 12 bar
    (c) 40 bar   (d) 100 bar
69. The thermal efficiency of a diesel cycle having fixed compression ratio, with increase in cut-off ratio will ………..
    (a) increase   **(b) decrease**
    (c) be independent   (d) may increase or decrease on other factors
70. The output of a diesel engine can be increased without increasing the engine revolution or size by ………..
    (a) scavenging   (b) increasing flywheel size
    (c) supercharging   (d) feeding more fuel
71. Which of the following medium is compressed in a diesel engine cylinder?
    (a) Air alone   (b) Air and lube oil
    (c) Fuel alone   (d) Air and fuel

72. In a typical medium speed, 4-stroke cycle diesel engine ....
    (a) fuel injection starts at 10° before to dead center and ends at 20° after top dead center
    (b) fuel injection starts at top dead center and ends at 20° after top dead center
    (c) fuel injection starts at just before top dead center and ends just after to dead center
    (d) may start and end anywhere

73. In a typical medium, speed 4-stroke cycle diesel engine ....
    (a) exhaust valve opens at 35° before bottom dead center and closes at 20° after top dead center
    (b) exhaust valve opens at bottom dead center and closes at top dead center
    (c) exhaust valve opens just after bottom dead center and closes just before top dead
    (d) may open and close anywhere

74. Scavenging is usually done to increase ....
    (a) pressure   (b) speed
    (c) power output   (d) fuel consumption

75. The knock in diesel engine occurs due to ....
    (a) instantaneous and rapid burning of the first part of the change
    (b) instantaneous auto ignition of last part of charge
    (c) delayed burning of the first part of the charge
    (d) reduction of delay period

76. The practical maximum limit on compression ratio of diesel engine is due to ....
    (a) increasing knock   (b) decreasing efficiency
    (c) increasing weight and size (d) increasing fuel consumption

77. Thermal efficiency of a diesel engine is .... to/than SI engine.
    (a) equal   **(b) higher**
    (c) lower   (d) equal or lower

78. Thermal efficiency of a diesel cycle as compared to Otto cycle is having same compression ratio is ....
    (a) more   **(b) less**
    (c) same   (d) double

79. The delay period in CI engines is reduced by the ....
    (a) high charge temperature   (b) high fuel temperature
    (c) a fuel with short induction period **(d) all above**

80. The diesel knock can be reduced by ....
    (a) reducing delay period   (b) increasing delay period
    (c) reducing compression ratio   (d) reducing inlet temperature

81. In a four stroke cycle, the minimum temperature inside the engine cylinder occurs at the ....
    (a) beginning of suction stroke
    (b) end of suction stroke
    (c) beginning of exhaust stroke
    (d) end of exhaust stroke

82. The brake power of a diesel engine, keeping other parameters constant, can be increased by ....
    (a) decreasing the density of intake air
    (b) increasing the temperature of intake air
    (c) increasing the pressure of intake air
    (d) decreasing the pressure of intake air

83. Pre-ignition is caused by the spontantaneous combustion of the mixture before the end of the compression stroke, and is due to ....
    (a) cylinder walls being too hot
    (b) overheated spark plug points
    (c) red hot carbon deposits on cylinder walls
    (d) any one of these

84. L-MPFI system uses ....
    (a) port injection
    (b) manifold injection
    (c) direct injection
    (d) throttle body injection

85. M-MPFI system uses ....
    (a) port injection
    (b) manifold injection
    (c) direct injection
    (d) throttle body injection

86. Advantage of pintaux nozzle is ....
    (a) better cold starting performance
    (b) ability to distribute the fuel
    (c) good penetration
    (d) good atomization

87. Ignition quality of diesel fuel is indicated by its ....
    (a) octane number
    (b) cetane number
    (c) flash point
    (d) fire point

88. A good fuel for diesel engine should have ....
    (a) high SIT
    (b) low SIT
    (c) high delay period
    (d) high latent heat

EXERCISE

1. Explain with a neat sketch the general arrangement of fuel supply system for C.I. engines.
2. Explain different types of fuel injection systems with neat sketches.
3. Explain fuel pump and injector with a neat sketch.
4. What are the different types of fuel injectors?
5. What are the different types of nozzles? Explain with neat sketches.
6. Explain electronic fuel injection system.
7. Explain MPFI with neat sketch.
8. Discuss combustion in CI engine.
9. Discuss stages of combustion in CI engines.
10. What is knocking in CI engine?
11. Compare detonation in S.I. engine and knocking in CI engine.
12. What do you mean by cetane rating of CI engine fuels?
13. What are the different types of combustion chambers in CI engines?

Unit IV

TESTING OF I.C. ENGINES AND SUPERCHARGING

[A] TESTING AND PERFORMANCE

4.1 INTRODUCTION

At a design and development stage an engineer would design an engine with certain aims in his mind. The aims may include the variables like indicated power, brake power, brake specific fuel consumption, exhaust emissions, cooling of engine, maintenance free operation etc. The other task of the development engineer is to reduce the cost and improve power output and reliability of an engine. In trying to achieve these goals he has to try various design concepts. After the design the parts of the engine are manufactured for the dimensions and surface finish and may be with certain tolerances. In order verify the designed and developed engine one has to go for testing and performance evaluation of the engines.

Thus, in general, a development engineer will have to conduct a wide variety of engine tests starting from simple fuel and air-flow measurements to taking of complicated injector needle lift diagrams, swirl patterns and photographs of the burning process in the combustion chamber. The nature and the type of the tests to be conducted depend upon various factors, some of which are: the degree of development of the particular design, the accuracy required, the funds available, the nature of the manufacturing company, and its design strategy. In this chapter, only certain basic tests and measurements will be considered.

4.2 PERFORMANCE PARAMETER

Engine performance is an indication of the degree of success of the engine performs its assigned task i.e. the conversion of the chemical energy contained in the fuel into the useful mechanical work. The performance of an engine is evaluated on the basis of the following:

    (i)   Specific Fuel Consumption.

    (ii)   Brake Mean Effective Pressure.

    (iii) Specific Power Output.

    (iv) Specific Weight.

    (v)   Exhaust Smoke and Other Emissions.

The particular application of the engine decides the relative importance of these performance parameters.

For example: For an aircraft engine specific weight is more important whereas for an industrial engine specific fuel consumption is more important.

For the evaluation of an engine performance few more parameters are chosen and the effect of various operating conditions, design concepts and modifications on these parameters are studied. **The basic performance parameters are the following:**

1. Power and Mechanical Efficiency.
2. Mean Effective Pressure and Torque.
3. Specific Output.
4. Volumetric Efficiency.
5. Fuel-air Ratio.
6. Specific Fuel Consumption.
7. Thermal Efficiency and Heat Balance.
8. Exhaust Smoke and Other Emissions.
9. Specific Weight.

1. Power and Mechanical Efficiency: The main purpose of running an engine is to obtain mechanical power.

- Power is defined as the rate of doing work and is equal to the product of force and linear velocity or the product of torque and angular velocity.
- Thus, the measurement of power involves the measurement of force (or torque) as well as speed. The force or torque is measured with the help of a dynamometer and the speed by a tachometer.

The power developed by an engine and measured at the output shaft is called the brake power (bp) and is given by,

$$bp = \frac{2\pi NT}{60} \text{ Watt} \qquad \ldots (4.1)$$

Where, T is torque in N-m and N is the rotational speed in revolutions per minute.

The total power developed by combustion of fuel in the combustion chamber is, however, more than the bp and is called indicated power (ip). Of the power developed by the engine i.e., ip, some power is consumed in overcoming the friction between moving parts, some in the process of inducting the air and removing the products of combustion from the engine combustion chamber.

Indicated power: It is the power developed in the cylinder and thus, forms the basis of evaluation of combustion efficiency or the heat release in the cylinder.

$$IP = \frac{p_{im} \, LANk}{60} \text{ Watt}$$

where, p_m = Mean effective pressure, N/m²
L = Length of the stroke, m
A = Area of the piston, m²
N = Rotational speed of the engine, rpm (It is N/2 for four stroke engine)
k = Number of cylinders

Thus, we see that for a given engine the power output can be measured in terms of mean effective pressure.

The difference between the ip and bp is the indication of the power lost in the mechanical components of the engine (due to friction) and forms the basis of mechanical efficiency; which is defined as follows:

$$\text{Mechanical efficiency} = \frac{bp}{ip} \qquad \ldots(4.2)$$

The difference between ip and bp is called friction power (fp).

$$fp = ip - bp \qquad \ldots(4.3)$$

$$\therefore \quad \text{Mechanical efficiency} = \frac{bp}{(bp + fp)} \qquad \ldots(4.4)$$

2. Mean Effective Pressure and Torque: Mean effective pressure is defined as a hypothetical/average pressure which is assumed to be acting on the piston throughout the power stroke. Therefore,

$$P_m = \frac{ip \times 60}{LANK} \text{ N/m}^2 \qquad \ldots(4.5)$$

where, P_m = Mean effective pressure, N/m²
I_p = Indicated power, Watt
L = Length of the stroke, m
A = Area of the piston, m²
N = Rotational speed of the engine, rpm (It is N/2 for four stroke engine)
k = Number of cylinders

If the mean effective pressure is based on bp it is called the brake mean effective pressure (bmep P_{mb} replace ip by bp in equation 4.5), and if based on ihp it is called indicated mean effective pressure (imep). Similarly, the friction mean effective pressure (fmep) can be defined as,

$$fmep = imep - bmep \qquad \ldots(4.6)$$

The torque is related to mean effective pressure by the relation

$$bp = \frac{2\pi NT}{60} \qquad \ldots(4.7)$$

$$iP = \frac{p_{im} LANk}{60}$$

By equation (4.5),

$$\frac{2\pi NT}{60} = (bemp \cdot A \cdot L \cdot Nk/60)$$

or $\quad T = (bemp \cdot A \cdot L \cdot k)/2\pi \quad$ ... (4.8)

Thus, the torque and the mean effective pressure are related by the engine size. A large engine produces more torque for the same mean effective pressure. For this reason, torque is not the measure of the ability of an engine to utilize its displacement for producing power from fuel. It is the mean effective pressure which gives an indication of engine displacement utilization for this conversion. Higher the mean effective pressure, higher will be the power developed by the engine for a given displacement.

Again we see that the power of an engine is dependent on its size and speed. Therefore, it is not possible to compare engines on the basis of either power or torque. Mean effective pressure is the true indication of the relative performance of different engines.

3. **Specific Output:** Specific output of an engine is defined as the brake power (output) per unit of piston displacement and is given by,

$$\text{Specific output} = \frac{bp}{A \times L}$$

$$= \text{Constant} \times bmep \times rpm \quad ...(4.9)$$

- The specific output consists of two elements - the bmep (force) available to work and the speed with which it is working.
- Therefore, for the same piston displacement and bmep an engine operating at higher speed will give more output.
- It is clear that the output of an engine can be increased by increasing either speed or bmep. Increasing speed involves increase in the mechanical stress of various engine parts whereas increasing bmep requires better heat release and more load on engine cylinder.

4. **Volumetric Efficiency:** Volumetric efficiency of an engine is an indication of the measure of the degree to which the engine fills its swept volume. It is defined as the ratio of the mass of air inducted into the engine cylinder during the suction stroke to the mass of the air corresponding to the swept volume of the engine at atmospheric pressure and temperature. Alternatively, it can be defined as the ratio of the actual volume inhaled during suction stroke measured at intake conditions to the swept volume of the piston.

Volumetric efficiency, η_v

$$= \frac{\text{Mass of charge actually sucked in}}{\text{Mass of charge corresponding to the cylinder intake P and T conditions}} \quad ...(4.10)$$

The amount of air taken inside the cylinder is dependent on the volumetric efficiency of an engine and hence puts a limit on the amount of fuel which can be efficiently burned and the power output.

For supercharged engine the volumetric efficiency has no meaning as it comes out to be more than unity.

5. Fuel-Air Ratio (F/A): Fuel-air ratio (F/A) is the ratio of the mass of fuel to the mass of air in the fuel-air mixture. ***Air-fuel ratio (A/F) is reciprocal of fuel-air ratio***. Fuel-air ratio of the mixture affects the combustion phenomenon in that it determines the flame propagation velocity, the heat release in the combustion chamber, the maximum temperature and the completeness of combustion.

Relative fuel-air ratio is defined as the ratio of the actual fuel-air ratio to that of the stoichiometric fuel-air ratio required to burn the fuel supplied. Stoichiometric fuel-air ratio is the ratio of fuel to air is one in which case fuel is completely burned due to minimum quantity of air supplied.

$$\text{Relative fuel-air ratio, } F_R = \frac{\text{Actual fuel - Air ratio}}{\text{Stoichiometric fuel-Air ratio}} \quad \ldots (4.11)$$

6. Brake Specific Fuel Consumption: Specific fuel consumption is defined as the amount of fuel consumed for each unit of brake power developed per hour. It is a clear indication of the efficiency with which the engine develops power from fuel.

$$\text{Brake specific fuel consumption (bsfc)} = \frac{\text{Fuel consumed in gms/hr.}}{\text{Brake power developed}} \quad \ldots (4.12)$$

This parameter is widely used to compare the performance of different engines.

7. Thermal Efficiency and Heat Balance: Thermal efficiency of an engine is defined as the ratio of the output to that of the chemical energy input in the form of fuel supply. It may be based on brake or indicated output. It is the true indication of the efficiency with which the chemical energy of fuel (input) is converted into mechanical work. Thermal efficiency also accounts for combustion efficiency, i.e., for the fact that whole of the chemical energy of the fuel is not converted into heat energy during combustion.

$$\text{Brake thermal efficiency} = \frac{bp}{m_f * C_v} \quad \ldots (4.13)$$

where, C_v = Calorific value of fuel, kJ/kg
m_f = Mass of fuel supplied, kg/sec.

- The energy input to the engine goes out in various forms - a part is in the form of brake output, a part into exhaust, and the rest is taken by cooling water and the lubricating oil.
- The break-up of the total energy input into these different parts is called the heat balance.
- The main components in a heat balance are brake output, coolant losses, heat going to exhaust, radiation and other losses.
- Preparation of heat balance sheet gives us an idea about the amount of energy wasted in various parts and allows us to think of methods to reduce the losses so incurred.

8. Exhaust Smoke and Other Emissions: Smoke and other exhaust emissions such as oxides of nitrogen, unburned hydrocarbons etc., are nuisance for the public environment. With increasing emphasis on air pollution control all efforts are being made to keep them as minimum as it could be.

Smoke is an indication of incomplete combustion. It limits the output of an engine if air pollution control is the consideration.

Exhaust emissions have of late become a matter of grave concern and with the enforcement of legislation on air pollution in many countries; it has become necessary to view them as performance parameters.

9. **Specific Weight:** Specific weight is defined as the weight of the engine in kilogram for each brake power developed and is an indication of the engine bulk. Specific weight plays an important role in applications such as power plants for aircrafts.

4.3 BASIC MEASUREMENTS

The basic measurements to be undertaken to evaluate the performance of an engine on almost all tests are the following:

1. Speed.
2. Fuel consumption.
3. Air consumption.
4. Smoke density.
5. Brake horse-power
6. Indicated horse power and friction horse power.
7. Heat going to cooling water.
8. Heat going to exhaust.
9. Exhaust gas analysis.

In addition to above a large number of other measurements may be necessary depending upon the aim of the test.

4.4 MEASUREMENT OF SPEED

One of the basic measurements is that of speed. A wide variety of speed measuring devices are available in the market. They range from a mechanical tachometer to digital and triggered electrical tachometers.

The best method of measuring speed is to count the number of revolutions in a given time. This gives an accurate measurement of speed. Many engines are fitted with such revolution counters.

A mechanical tachometer or an electrical tachometer can also be used for measuring the speed.

The electrical tachometer has a three-phases permanent-magnet alternator to which a voltmeter is attached. The output of the alternator is a linear function of the speed and is directly indicated on the voltmeter dial.

Both electrical and mechanical types of tachometers are affected by the temperature variations and are not very accurate. For accurate and continuous measurement of speed a magnetic pick-up placed near a toothed wheel coupled to the engine shaft can be used. The magnetic pick-up will produce a pulse for every revolution and a pulse counter will accurately measure the speed.

4.5 FUEL CONSUMPTION MEASUREMENT

Fuel consumption is measured in two ways:
- (a) The fuel consumption of an engine is measured by determining the volume flow in a given time interval and multiplying it by the specific gravity of the fuel which should be measured occasionally to get an accurate value.
- (b) Another method is to measure the time required for consumption of a given mass of fuel.

Accurate measurement of fuel consumption is very important in engine testing work.
As already mentioned two basic types of fuel measurement methods are:
- Volumetric type
- Gravimetric type.

Volumetric type flowmeter includes Burette method, Automatic Burrette flowmeter and Turbine flowmeter.

Gravimetric Fuel Flow Measurement: The efficiency of an engine is related to the kilograms of fuel which are consumed and not the number of litres. The method of measuring volume flow and then correcting it for specific gravity variations is quite inconvenient and inherently limited in accuracy. Instead if the weight of the fuel consumed is directly measured a great improvement in accuracy and cost can be obtained.

There are three types of gravimetric type systems which are commercially available include *Actual weighing of fuel consumed, Four Orifice Flowmeter* etc.

4.6 MEASUREMENT OF AIR CONSUMPTION

One can say the mixture of air and fuel is the food for an engine. For finding out the performance of the engine accurate measurement of both is essential.

In IC engines, the satisfactory measurement of air consumption is quite difficult because the flow is pulsating, due to the cyclic nature of the engine and because the air a compressible fluid. Therefore, the simple method of using an orifice in the induction pipe is not satisfactory since the reading will be pulsating and unreliable.

All kinetic flow-inferring systems such as nozzles, orifices and venturies have a square law relationship between flow rate and differential pressure which gives rise to severe errors on unsteady flow. Pulsation produced errors are roughly inversely proportional to the pressure across the orifice for a given set of flow conditions. The various methods and meters used for air flow measurement include (1) Air box method and (ii) Viscous-flow air meter.

4.7 MEASUREMENT OF EXHAUST SMOKE

All the three widely used smokemeters, namely, Bosch, Hartridge, and PHS are basically soot density (g/m^3) measuring devices, that is, the meter readings are a function of the mass of carbon in a given volume of exhaust gas.

Hartridge smokemeter works on the light extinction principle.

The basic principles of the Bosch smokemeter is one in which a fixed quantity of exhaust gas is passed through a fixed filter paper and the density of the smoke stains on the paper are evaluated optically. In a recent modification of this type of smokemeter units are used for the measurement of the intensity of smoke stain on filter paper.

In Von Brand smokemeter which can give a continuous reading a filter tape is continuously moved at a uniform rate to which the exhaust from the engine is fed. The smoke stains developed on the filter paper are sensed by a recording head. The single obtained from the recording head is calibrated to give smoke density.

4.8 MEASUREMENT OF EXHAUST EMISSION

Substances which are emitted to the atmosphere from any opening of the exhaust port of the engine are termed as exhaust emissions. If combustion is complete and the mixture is stoichiometric the products of combustion would consist of carbon dioxide (CO_2) and water vapour only.

However, there is no complete combustion of fuel and hence the exhaust gas consists of variety of components, the most important of them are carbon monoxide (CO), unburned hydrocarbons (UBHC) and oxides of nitrogen (NO_x). Some oxygen and other inert gases would also be present in the exhaust gas.

Over the decade numerous devices have been developed for measuring these various exhaust components. A brief discussion of some of the more commonly used instruments is given below:

4.8.1 Flame Ionization Detector (FID)

The schematic diagram of a flame ionization detector burner is shown in Fig. 4.1 (a) and (b) shows burner.

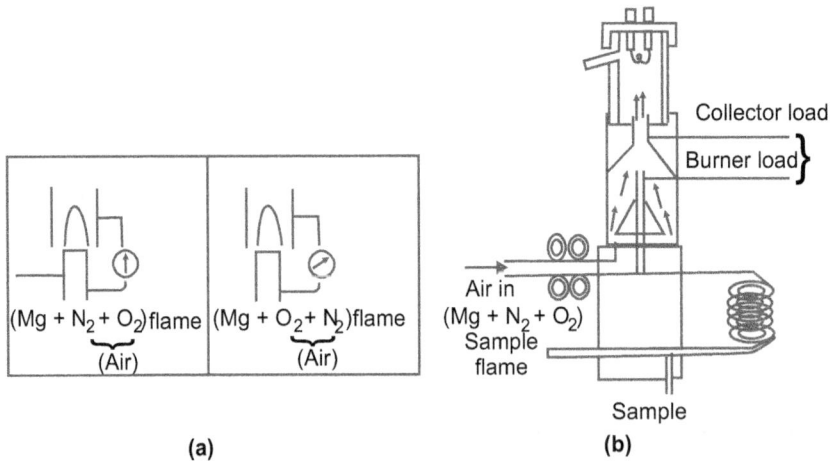

Fig. 4.1: Flame Ionisation Detector Burner

The working principle of this burner is as follows: A hydrogen-air flame contains a negligible amount of ions. However, if even trace amounts of an organic compound such as HC are introduced into the flame, a large number of ions are produced. If a polarized voltage is applied across the burner jet and an adjacent collector, an ion migration will produce a current proportional to the number of ions and thus to the HC concentration present in the flame.

The output of the FID depends on the number of carbon atoms passing through the flame in a unit time. Doubling the flow velocity would also double the output. Hexane (C_6H_{14}) would give double the output of propane (C_3H_8). Therefore, FID output is usually referred to a standard hydrocarbon, usually as ppm of normal hexane.

Presence of CO, CO_2, NO_x, water and nitrogen in the exhaust have to effect on the FID reading. Oxygen slightly affects the reading of FID.

FID analyzer is a rapid, continuous and accurate method of measuring HC in the exhaust gas. Concentration as low as 1 ppb can be measured.

4.8.2 Spectroscopic Analyzers

- A spectrum shows the light absorbed as a function of wavelength (or frequency).
- Each compound shows a different spectrum for the light absorbed.
- All the spectroscopic analyzers work on the principle that the quantity of energy absorbed by a compound in a sample cell is proportional to the concentration of the compound in the cell. There are two types of spectroscopic analyzers.

(i) **Dispersive analyzers:** These analyzers use only a narrow dispersed frequency of light spectrum to analyze a compound. These are usually not use for exhaust emission measurements.

(ii) **Non-Dispersive Infra-red (NDIR) Analyzers:** In the NDIR analyzer the exhaust gas species being measuring is used to detect itself. This is done by selective absorption. The infrared energy of a particular wavelength or frequency is peculiar to a certain gas in that the gas will absorb the infracted energy of this wavelength and transmit and infrared energy of other wavelengths. For example, the absorption band for carbon monoxide is between 4.5 and 5 microns. So the energy absorbed at this wavelength is an indication of the concentration of CO in the exhaust gas.

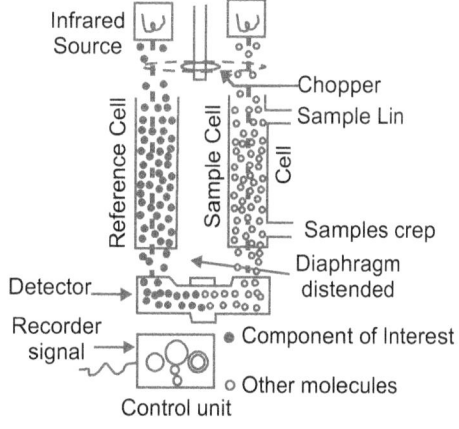

Fig. 4.2: Schematic of Non-dispersive Infrared Analyzer (NDIR)

The NDIR analyzer as shown in **Fig. 4.2** consists of two infrared sources, interrupted simultaneously by an optical chopper. Radiation from these sources pass in parallel paths through a reference cell and a sample cell to opposite side of a common detector. The sample cell contains the compounds to be analyzed, whereas this compound is not present in the reference cell. The latter is usually filled with an inert gas, usually nitrogen, which does not absorb the infrared energy for the wavelength corresponding to the compound being measured. A closed container filled with only the compound to be measured works as a detector.

The detector is divided into two equal volumes by a thin metallic diaphragm. When the chopper blocks the radiation, the pressure in both parts of the detector is same and the diagram remains in the neutral position. As the chopper blocks and unblocks the radiation, the radiant energy from one source passes through the reference cell unchanged whereas the sample cell absorbs the infrared energy at the wavelength of the compound in cell. The absorption is proportional to the concentration of the compound to be measured in the sample cell. Thus unequal amounts of energy are transmitted to the two volumes of the detector and the pressure differential so generated causes movement of the diaphragm and a fixed probe, thereby generating an a.c., displayed on a meter. The signal is a function of the concentration of the compound to be measured.

The NDIR can accurately measure CO, CO_2 and those hydrocarbons which have clear infrared absorption peaks. However, usually the exhaust sample to be analyzed contains other species which also absorb infrared energy at the same frequency. For example, an NDIR analyzer sensitized to n-hexane for detection of HC responds equally well to other paraffin HC but not to olefins, acetylenes or aromatics. Therefore, the reading given by such analyzer is multiplied by 1.8 to correct it to the total UBHC as measured by an FID analyzer in the same exhaust stream.

4.8.3 Gas Chromatography

Gas chromatography is first a method of separating the individual constituents of a mixture and then a method of assured their concentration. After separation, each compound can be separately analyzed for concentration. This is the only method by which each component existing in an exhaust sample can be identified and analyzed. However, it is very time consuming and the samples can be taken only in batches. Gas chromatograph is primarily a laboratory tool.

In addition to the above methods such as mass spectroscopy, chemiluminescent analyzers, and electrochemical analyzer are also used for measuring exhaust emissions.

4.9 MEASUREMENT OF BRAKE POWER

The brake power measurement involves the determination of the torque and the angular speed of the engine output shaft. The torque measuring device is called a dynamometer.

Dynamometers can be broadly classified into two main types, power absorption dynamometers and transmission dynamometer.

Fig. 4.3 shows the basic principle of a dynamometer. A rotor driven by the engine under test is electrically, hydraulically or magnetically coupled to a stator. For every revolution of the shaft, the rotor periphery moves through a distance $2\pi r$ against the coupling force F. Hence, the work done per revolution is .

$$W = 2\pi RF$$

The external moment or torque is equal to $S \times L$ where, S is the scale reading and L is the arm. This moment balances the turning moment $R \times F$, i.e.

$$S \times L = R \times F$$

∴ Work done/revolution = 2π SL

Work done/minute = 2πSLN

where, N is rpm. Hence, power is given by

Brake power P = 2πNT Watt

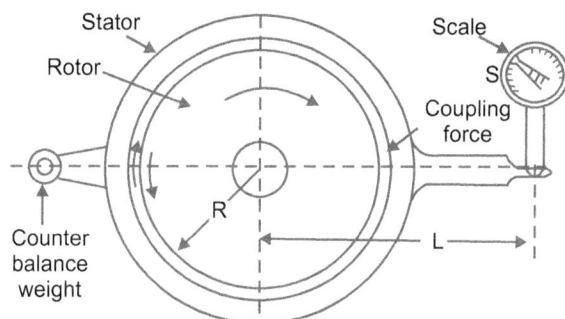

Fig. 4.3: Principle of a Dynamometer

(a) **Absorption Dynamometers:** These dynamometers measure and absorb the power output of the engine to which they are coupled. The power absorbed is usually dissipated as heat by some means. Example of such dynamometers is prony brake, rope brake, hydraulic dynamometer, etc.

(b) **Transmission Dynamometers:** In transmission dynamometers, the power is transmitted to the load coupled to the engine after it is indicated on some type of scale. These are also called torque-meters.

4.9.1 Absorption Dynamometers

These include Prony brake type, Rope brake type, Hydraulic type.

1. **Prony Brake:** One of the simplest methods of measuring brake power (output) is to attempt to stop the engine by means of a brake on the flywheel and measure the weight which an arm attached to the brake will support, as it tries to rotate with the flywheel. This system is known as the prony brake and forms its use; the expression brake power has come.

The Prony brake shown in Fig. 4.4 works on the principle of converting power into heat by dry friction. It consists of wooden block mounted on a flexible rope or band the wooden block when pressed into contact with the rotating drum takes the engine torque and the power is dissipated in frictional resistance. Spring-loaded bolts are provided to tighten the wooden block and hence increase the friction. The whole of the power absorbed is converted into heat and hence this type of dynamometer must the cooled. The brake horsepower is given by

$$BP = 2\pi NT$$

where, $T = W \times l$

W being the weight applied at a radius l.

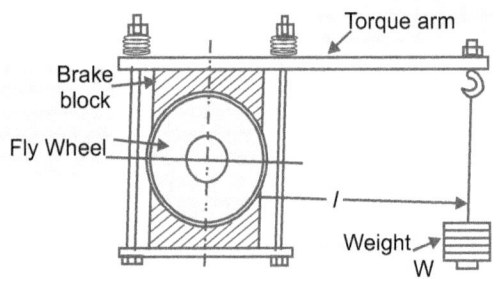

Fig. 4.4: Prony Brake

2. **Rope Brake:** The rope brake as shown in Fig. 4.5 is another simple device for measuring bp of an engine. It consists of a number of turns of rope wound around the rotating drum attached to the output shaft. One side of the rope is connected to a spring balance and the other to a loading device. The power is absorbed in friction between the rope and the drum. The drum therefore requires cooling.

Rope brake is cheap and easily constructed but not a very accurate method because of changes in the friction coefficient of the rope with temperature.

The bp is given by

$$bhp = \pi DN(W - S)$$

Where, D is the brake drum diameter, W is the weight in Newton and S is the spring scale reading.

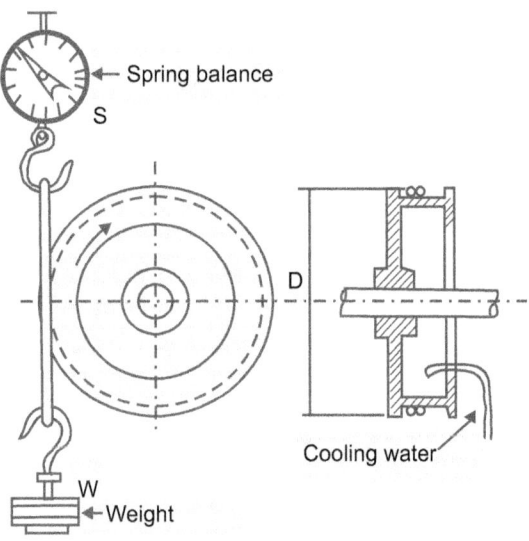

Fig. 4.5: Rope Brake

3. Hydraulic Dynamometer: Hydraulic dynamometer shown in Fig. 4.6 works on the principle of dissipating the power in fluid friction rather than in dry friction.
- In principle its construction is similar to that of a fluid flywheel.
- It consists of an inner rotating member or impeller coupled to the output shaft of the engine.
- This impeller rotates in a casing filled with fluid.
- This outer casing, due to the centrifugal force developed, tends to revolve with the impeller, but is resisted by a torque arm supporting the balance weight.
- The frictional forces between the impeller and the fluid is measured by the spring-balance fitted on the casing.
- The heat developed due to dissipation of power is carried away by a continuous supply of the working fluid, usually water.
- The output can be controlled by regulating the sluice gates which can be moved in and out to partially or wholly obstruct the flow of water between impeller, and the casing.

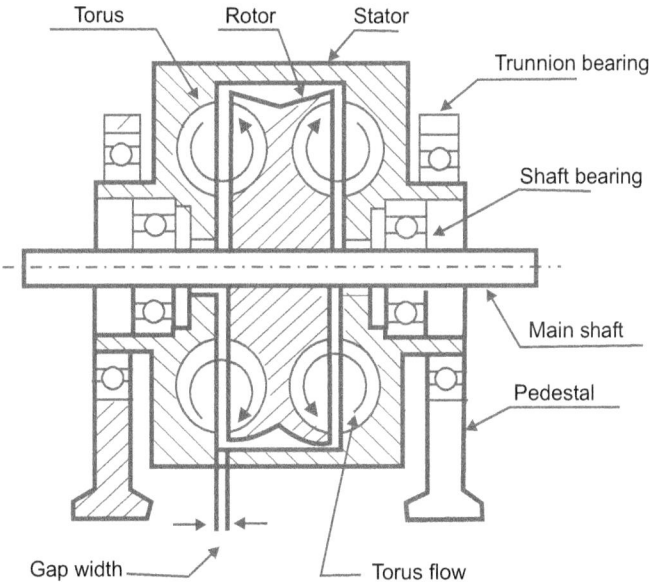

Fig. 4.6: Hydraulic Dyanmometer

4. Eddy Current Dynamometer: The working principle of eddy current dynamometer is shown in **Fig. 4.7**. It consists of a stator on which are fitted a number of electromagnets and a rotor disc made of copper or steel and coupled to the output shaft of the engine. When the rotor rotates eddy currents are produced in the stator due to magnetic flux set up by the passage of field current in the electromagnets. These eddy currents are dissipated in producing heat so that this type of dynamometer also requires some cooling arrangement. The torque is measured exactly as in other types of absorption dynamometers, i.e., with the help of a moment arm. The load is controlled by regulating the current in the electromagnets.

The following are the main advantages of eddy current dynamometers:
1. High brake power per unit weight of dynamometer.
2. They offer the highest ratio of constant power speed range (upto 5 : 1).
3. Level of field excitation is below 1% of total power being handled by dynamometer, thus, easy to control and programme.
4. Development of eddy current is smooth hence the torque is also smooth and continuous under all conditions.
5. Relatively higher torque under low speed conditions.
6. It has no intricate rotating parts except shaft bearing.
7. No natural limit to size-either small or large.

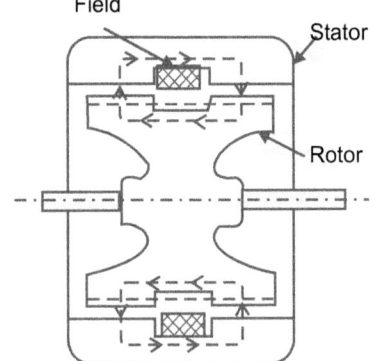

Fig. 4.7: Eddy Current Dynamometer

5. **Swinging Field d.c. Dynamometer:** Basically, a swinging field d.c. dynamometer is a d.c. shunt motor so supported on trunnion bearings to measure there action torque that the outer case and filed coils tend to rotate with the magnetic drag. Hence, the name swinging field. The torque is measured with an arm and weighing equipment in the usual manner.

Many dynamometers are provided with suitable electric connections to run as motor also. Then the dynamometer is reversible, i.e., works as motoring as well as power absorbing device.
- When used as an absorption dynamometer it works as a d.c. generator and converts mechanical energy into electric energy which is dissipated in an external resistor or fed back to the mains.
- When used as a motoring device an external source of d.c. voltage is needed to drive the motor.

The load is controlled by changing the field current.

4.9.2 Fan Dynamometer

It is also an absorption type of dynamometer in that when driven by the engine it absorbs the engine power. Such dynamometers are useful mainly for rough testing and running-in. The accuracy of the fan dynamometer is very poor. The power absorbed is determined by using previous calibration of the fan brake.

4.9.3 Transmission Dynamometers

Transmission dynamometers, also called torque meters, mostly consist of a set of strain-gauges fixed on the rotating shaft and the torque is measured by the angular deformation of the shaft which is indicated as strain of the strain gauge. Usually, a four arm bridge is used to reduce the effect of temperature to minimum and the gauges are arranged in pairs such that the effect of axial or transverse load on the strain gauges is avoided.

Fig. 4.8 shows a transmission dynamometer which employs beams and straingauges for a sensing torque.

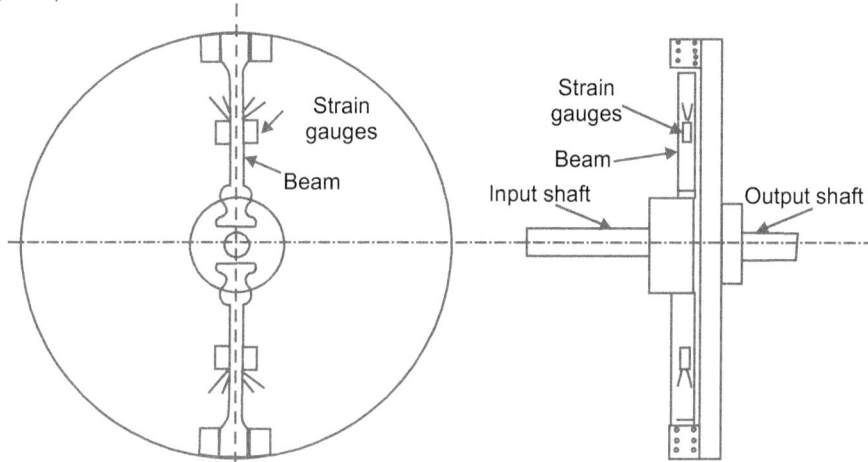

Fig. 4.8: Transmission Dynamometer

Transmission dynamometers are very accurate and are used where continuous transmission of load is necessary. These are used mainly in automatic units.

Fig. 4.8 shows a transmission dynamometer which employs beams and strain-gauges for a sensing torque.

Transmission dynamometers are very accurate and are used where continuous transmission of load is necessary.

4.10 MEASUREMENT OF FRICTION HORSE POWER

- The difference between indicated power and the brake power output of an engine is the friction power.
- Almost invariably, the difference between a good engine and a bad engine is due to difference between their frictional losses.
- The frictional losses are ultimately dissipated to the cooling system (and exhaust) as they appear in the form of frictional heat and this influences the cooling capacity required. Moreover, lower friction means availability of more brake power, hence brake specific fuel consumption is lower.

- The bsfc rises with an increase in speed and at some speed it renders the sue of engine prohibitive. Thus, the level of friction decides the maximum output of the engine which can be obtained economically.

In the design and testing of an engine; measurement of friction power is important for getting an insight into the methods by which the output of an engine can be increased. In the evaluation of ip and mechanical efficiency measured friction power is also used.

The friction force power of an engine is determined by the following methods:
1. Willan's line method.
2. Morse test.
3. Motoring test.
4. Difference between ip and bp.

1. Willan's Line Method or Fuel Rate Extrapolation: In this method, gross fuel consumption vs. bp at a constant speed is plotted and the graph is extrapolated back to zero fuel consumption as illustrated in Fig. 4.9.

The point where this graph cuts the bp axis in an indication of the friction power of the engine at that speed. This negative work represents the combined loss due to mechanical friction, pumping and blowby.

The test is applicable only to compression ignition engines.

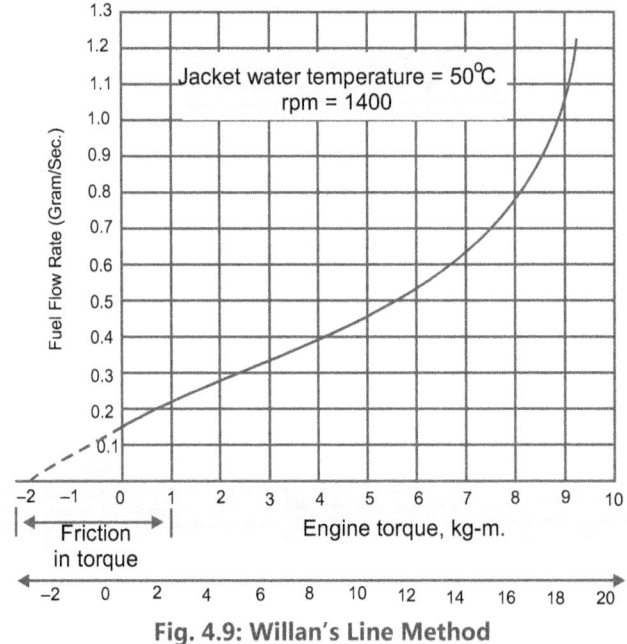

Fig. 4.9: Willan's Line Method

- The main drawback of this method is the long distance to be extrapolated from data measured between 5 and 40% load towards the zero line of fuel in put.
- The directional margin of error is rather wide because of the graph which may not be a straight line many times.
- The changing slope along the curve indicates part efficiencies of increments of fuel. The pronounced change in the slope of this line near full load reflects the limiting influence of the air-fuel ratio and of the quality of combustion.
- Similarly, there is a slight curvature at light loads. This is perhaps due to difficulty in injecting accurately and consistently very small quantities of fuel per cycle.
- Therefore, it is essential that great care should be taken at light loads to establish the true nature of the curve.
- The Willan's line for a swirl-chamber CI engine is more straight than that for a direct injection type engine.
- The accuracy obtained in this method is good and compares favourably with other methods if extrapolation is carefully done.

2. **Morse Test:** The Morse test is applicable only to multicylinder engines.
- In this test, the engine is first run at the required speed and the output is measured.
- Then, one cylinder is cut out by short circuiting the spark plug or by disconnecting the injector as the case may be.
- Under this condition all other cylinders 'motor' this cut-out cylinder. The output is measured by keeping the speed constant at its original value.
- The difference in the outputs is a measure of the indicated horse power of the cut-out cylinder.
- Thus, for each cylinder the ip is obtained and is added together to find the total ip of the engine.

The ip of n cylinder is given by

$$ip_n = bp_n + fp \quad \ldots (4.14)$$

ip for (n – 1) cylinders is given by

$$ip_{n-1} = bp_{n-1} + fp \quad \ldots (4.15)$$

Since, the engine is running at the same speed it is quite reasonable to assume that fhp remains constant.

From equations (4.17) and (4.18), we see that the ihp of the nth cylinder is given by

$$(ip) n^{th} = bp_n - bp_{n-1} \quad \ldots (4.16)$$

And the total ip of the engine is,

$$hp_n = \Sigma (ihp) n^{th} \quad \ldots (4.17)$$

By subtracting bpn from this the fp of the engine can be obtained.

This method though gives reasonably accurate results and is liable to errors due to changes in mixture distribution and other conditions by cutting-out one cylinder. In gasoline engines, where there is a common manifold for two or more cylinders the mixture distribution as well as the volumetric efficiency both change. Again, almost all engines have a common exhaust manifold for all cylinders and cutting-out of one cylinder may greatly affect the pulsations in exhaust system which may significantly change the engine performance by imposing different back pressures.

3. **Motoring Test:**
   - In the motoring test, the engine is first run upto the desired speed by its own power and allowed to remain at the given speed and load conditions for some time so that oil, water, and engine component temperatures reach stable conditions.
   - The power of the engine during this period is absorbed by a swinging field type electric dynamometer, which is most suitable for this test.
   - The fuel supply is then cut-off and by suitable electric-switching devices the dynamometer is converted to run as a motor to drive for 'motor' the engine at the same speed at which it was previously running.
   - The power supply to the motor is measured which is a measure of the fhp of the engine. During the motoring test the water supply is also cut-off so that the actual operating temperatures are maintained.
   - This method, though determines the fp at temperature conditions very near to the actual operating temperatures at the test speed and load, does, not give the true losses occurring under firing conditions due to the following reasons.
     (i) The temperatures in the motored engine are different from those in a firing engine because even if water circulation is stopped the incoming air cools the cylinder. This reduces the lubricating oil temperature and increases friction increasing the oil viscosity. This problem is much more sever in air-cooled engines.
     (ii) The pressure on the bearings and piston rings is lower than the firing pressure. Load on main and connecting road bearings are lower.
     (iii) The clearance between piston and cylinder wall is more (due to cooling). This reduces the piston friction.
     (iv) The air is drawn at a temperature less than when the engine is firing because it does not get heat from the cylinder (rather loses heat to the cylinder). This makes the expansion line to be lower than the compression line on the p-v diagram. This loss is however counted in the indicator diagram.
     (v) During exhaust the back pressure is more because under motoring conditions sufficient pressure difference is not available to impart gases the kinetic energy is necessary to expel them from exhaust.

Motoring method, however, gives reasonably good results and is very suitable for finding the losses due to various engine components. This insight into the losses caused by various components and other parameters is obtained by progressive stripping-off of the under progressive dismantling conditions keeping water and oil circulation intact. Then the cylinder head can be removed to evaluate, by difference, the compression loss. In this manner piston rings, piston etc., can be removed and evaluated for their effect on overall friction.

4. **Difference between ip and bp:**
    (a) The method of finding the fp by computing the difference between ip, as obtained from an indicator diagram, and bp, as obtained by a dynamometer, is the ideal method. However, due to difficulties
    (b) In obtaining accurate indicator diagrams, especially at high engine speeds, this method is usually only used in research laboratories. Its use at commercial level is very limited.

Comments on Methods of Measuring fp:
- The Willan's line method and Morse tests are very cheap and easy to conduct.
- However, both these tests give only an overall idea of the losses whereas motoring test gives a very good insight into the various causes of losses and is a much more powerful tool.
- As far as accuracy is concerned the ip-bp method is the most accurate if carefully done.
- Motoring method usually gives a higher value for fhp as compared to that given by the Willan's line method.

4.11 BLOWBY LOSS

Blowby is the escape of unburned air-fuel mixture and burned gases from the combustion chamber, past the piston rings, and into the crank-case. High blowby is quite harmful in that it results in higher ring temperatures and contamination of lubricating oil.

4.12 PERFORMANCE OF SI ENGINES

The performance of an engine is usually studied by heat balance-sheet. The main components of the heat balance are:
- heat equivalent to the effective (brake) work of the engine,
- heat rejected to the cooling medium,
- heat carried away from the engine with the exhaust gases, and
- unaccounted losses.

The unaccounted losses include the radiation losses from the various parts of the engine and heat lost due to incomplete combustion. The friction loss is not shown as a separate item to the heat balance-sheet as the friction loss ultimately reappears as heat in cooling water, exhaust and radiation.

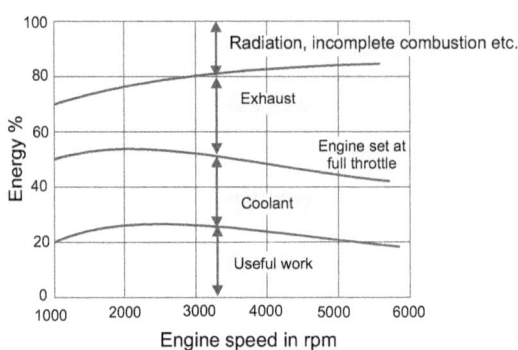

Fig. 4.10: Heat Balance Vs. Speed for a Petrol Engine at Full Throttle

The following Table 4.1 gives the approximate percentage values of various losses in SI and CI engines.

Table 4.1: Components of Heat Balance in Percent at Full Load

Engine Type	Brake Load Efficiency %	Heat rejected to cooling water %	Heat rejected through exhaust gases %	Unaccounted heat %
SI	21-28	12-27	30-55	3-55 (including incomplete combustion loss 0-45)
CI	29-42	15-35	25-45	21-0 (including incomplete combustion loss 0-5)

Fig. 4.10 shows the heat balance for a petrol engine run at full throttle over its speed range. In SI engines, the loss due to incomplete combustion included on unaccounted form can be rather high. For a rich mixture (A/F ratio = 12.5 to 13) it could be 20%. Fig. 4.11 shows the heat balance of uncontrolled Otto engine at different loads.

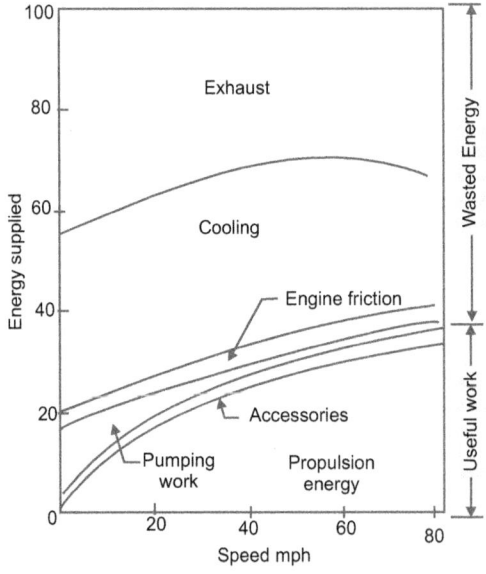

Fig. 4.11: Uncontrolled Otto Engine

Fig. 4.12 shows the brake thermal efficiency, indicated thermal efficiency, mechanical efficiency and specific fuel consumption for the above SI engine.

Fig. 4.13 shows the ip, bp, fp (by difference) brake torque, brake mean effective pressure and brake specific fuel consumption of a high compression ratio (9) automotive SI engine at full or Wide Open Throttle (W.O.T.).

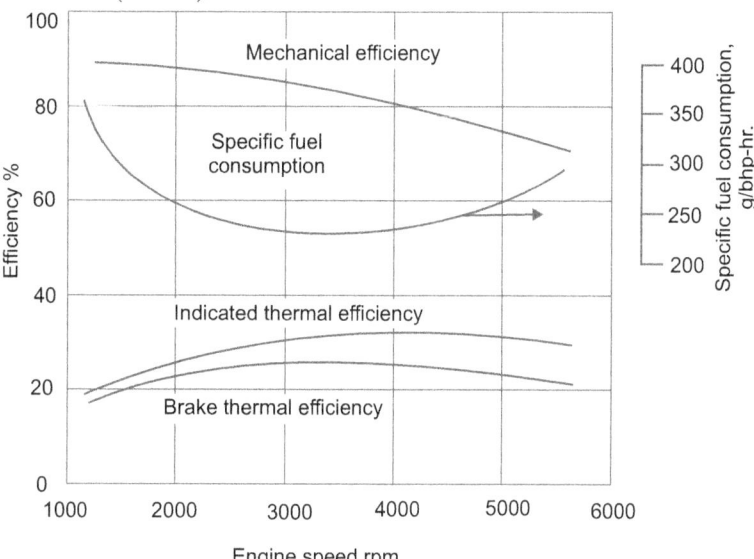

Fig. 4.12: Efficiency and Specific Fuel Consumption Vs. Speed for a Petrol Engine at Full Throttle

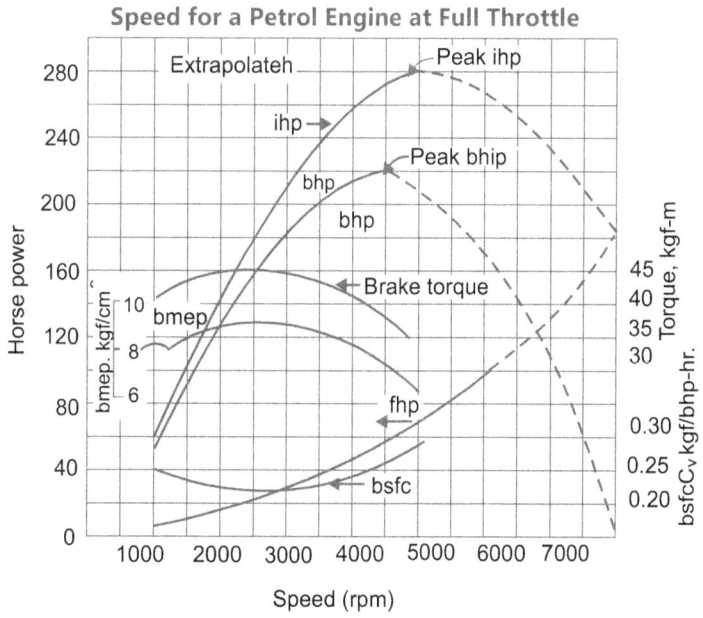

Fig. 4.13: Variable Speed Test of Automotive SI Engine at Full Throttle (CR = 9)

Referring to the Fig. 4.10 through 4.13 the following conclusions can be drawn:

(1) At full throttle the brake thermal efficiency at various speeds varies from 20 to 27 percent, maximum efficiency being at the middle speed range.

(2) The percentage heat rejected to coolant is more at lower speed (≈ 35 percent) and reduces at higher speeds (≈ 25 percent). Considerably more heat is carried by exhaust at higher speeds.

(3) Torque and mean effective pressure do not strongly depend on the speed of the engine, but depend on the volumetric efficiency and friction losses. Maximum torque position corresponds with the maximum air charge or minimum volumetric efficiency position.

Torque and mep curves peak at about half that of the brake-power.

Note: If size (displacement) of the engine were to be doubled, torque would also double, but mean effective pressure (mep) is a 'specific' torque, a variable independent of the size of the engine.

(4) High power arises from the high speed. In the speed range before the maximum power is obtained, doubling the speed doubles the power.

(5) At low engine speed the friction power is relatively low and bhp is nearly as large as ip (Fig. 4.13). As engine speed increases, however, fp increases at continuously greater rate and therefore bp reaches a peak and starts reducing even though ip is rising. At engine speeds above the usual operating range, fp increases very rapidly. Also, at these higher speeds ip will reach a maximum and then fall off. At some point, ip and fp will be equal, and bp will then drop to zero.

Performance of SI engine at constant speed and variable load: The performance of SI engine at constant speed and variable loads is different from the performance at full throttle and variable speed. Fig. 4.14 shows the heat balance of SI engine at constant speed and Fig. 4.14 variable load. The load is varied by altering the throttle and the speed is kept constant by resetting the dynamometer.

Closing the throttle reduces the pressure inside the cylinders but the temperature is affected very little because the air/fuel ratio is substantially constant, and the gas temperatures throughout the cycle are high. This results in high loss to coolant at low engine load. This is reason of poor part load thermal efficiency of the SI engine compared with the CI engine.

- At low loads the efficiency is about 10 percent, rising to about 25 percent at full load.
- The loss to coolant is about 60 percent at low loads and 30 percent at full load.
- The exhaust temperature rises very slowly with load and as mass flow rate of exhaust gas is reduced because the mass flow rate of fuel into the engine is reduced, the percentage loss to exhaust remains nearly constant (about 21% at low loads to 24% at full load).
- Percentage loss to radiation increases from about 7% at loads or 20% at full load.

4.13 PERFORMANCE OF CI ENGINES

The performance of a CI engine at constant speed variable load is shown in Fig. 4.15.
- As the efficiency of eth CI engine is more than the SI engine the total losses are less. The coolant loss is more at low loads and radiation, etc. losses are more at high loads.
- The bmep, bp and torque directly increase with load, as shown in Fig. 4.16. Unlike the SI engine bhp and bmep are continuously rising curves and are limited only by the load. The lowest brake specific fuel consumption and hence the maximum efficiency occurs at about 80 percent of the full load.

Fig. 4.17 shows the performance curves of variable speed GM 7850 cc. four cycle V-6 Toroflow diesel engine. The maximum torque value is at about 70 percent of maximum speed compared to about 50 percent in the SI engine. Also, the bsfc is low through most of the speed range for the diesel engine and is better than the SI engine.

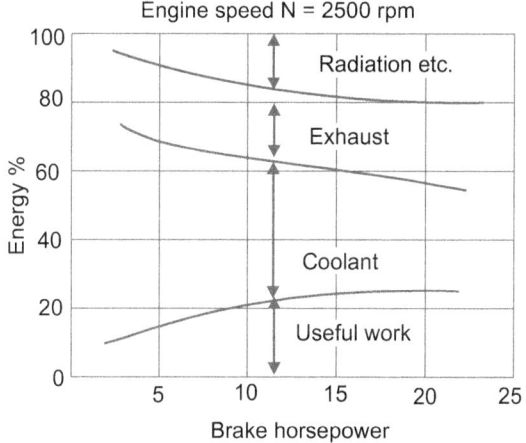

Fig. 4.14: Heat Balance Vs. Load for a Petrol Engine

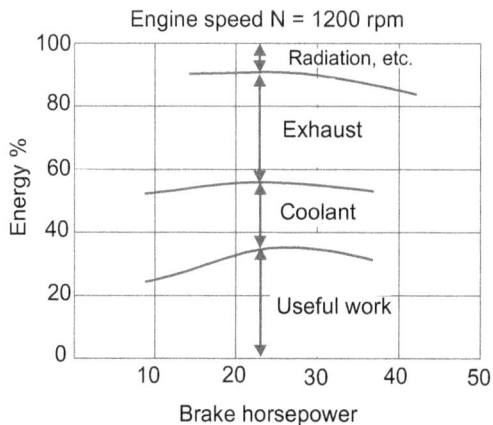

Fig. 4.15: Heat Balance Vs. Load for a CI Engine

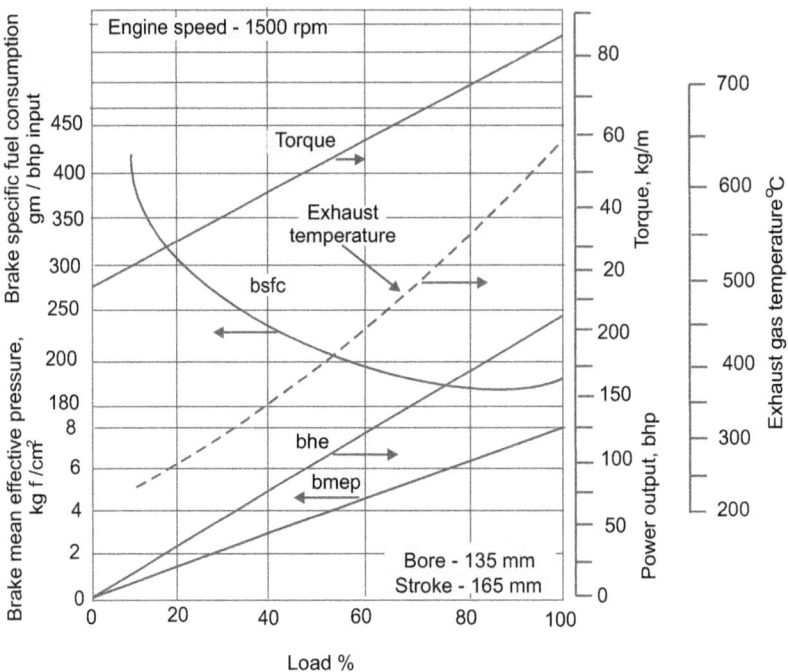

Fig. 4.16: Performance Curves of a Six Cylinder Four-stroke Cycle Automotive Type CI Engine at Constant Speed

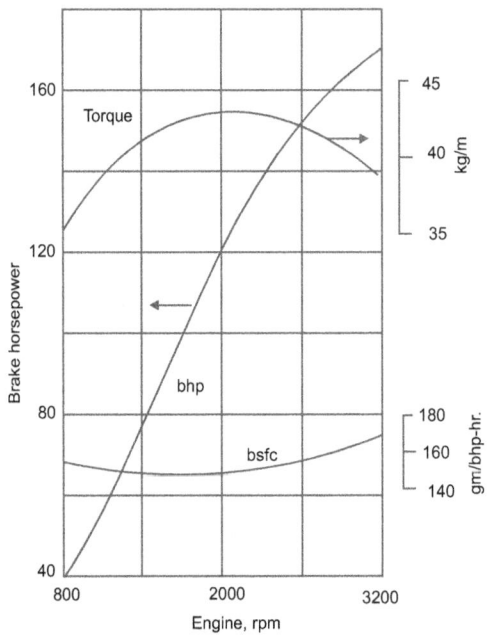

Fig. 4.17: Performance Curves of GM-four Cycle Toro-flow Diesel Engine

SOLVED EXAMPLES

Example 4.1: A gasoline engine works on Otto cycle. It consumes 8 litres of gasoline per hour and develops power at the rate of 25 kW. The specific gravity of gasoline is 0.8 and its calorific value is 44000 kJ/kg. Find the indicated thermal efficiency of the engine.

Solution: Heat liberated at the input

$$= mC_v$$

$$= 8 \times \frac{0.8}{60 \times 60} = \frac{6.4}{3600}$$

Power at the input $= \frac{6.4}{3600} \times 44000$ kW

$$\eta_{ith} = \frac{\text{Output power}}{\text{Input power}}$$

$$= \frac{25 \text{ kW}}{\frac{6.4 \times 44000}{3600}} \text{ kW} = \frac{25 \times 3600}{6.4 \times 44000}$$

$$= \mathbf{0.3196}$$

$$\%\eta = 0.3196 \times 100$$

$$\%\eta = \mathbf{31.96\%}$$

Example 4.2: A single cylinder engine operating at 2000 rpm develops a torque of 8 N-m. The indicated power of the engine is 2.0 kW. Find loss due to friction as the percentage of brake power.

Solution:

$$\text{Brake power} = \frac{2\pi NT}{60000} = \frac{2 \times \pi \times 2000 \times 8}{60000} \text{ Nm/sec.}$$

$$= 1.6746 \text{ kW}$$

$$\text{Friction power} = 2.0 - 1.6746 = 0.3253$$

$$\% \text{ loss} = \frac{0.3253}{2} \times 100$$

$$\% \text{ loss} = \mathbf{16.2667\%}$$

Example 4.3: A vertical single cylinder four stroke diesel engine has a bore = 80 mm and stroke = 100 mm respectively. It is water cooled and develops a torque of 3.5 N-m. Calculate the mean effective of the engine.

Solution:

$$P = \frac{2\pi NT}{60000} = \frac{P_{bm} LA_n}{60000}$$

$$P_{bm} = \frac{2\pi NT}{LA_n} = \frac{2\pi NT}{L \times \frac{\pi}{4} \times D^2 \frac{N}{2}} = \frac{16\,T}{D^2 L}$$

$$= \frac{16 \times 23.5}{(0.08)^2 \times 0.1} = 5.875 \times 10^5 \text{ Pa}$$

$$= 5.875 \text{ bar}$$

APPLIED THERMODYNAMICS — TESTING OF I.C. ENGINES AND SUPERCHARGING

$$P_{bm} = \frac{P \times 6 \times 10^4}{\frac{\pi}{4} D^2 L \frac{N}{2}} \times 10^{-5} \text{ bar}$$

$$= \frac{4 \times 60000}{\frac{\pi}{4} \times (0.08)^2 \times 0.1 \times \frac{1500}{2}} \times 10^{-5} = \frac{24 \times 10^4 \times 4 \times 2 \times 10^{-5}}{\pi \times (0.08)^2 \times 0.1 \times 1500}$$

$$= 6.369 \text{ bar}$$

$$T = \frac{P \times 60000}{2\pi N} = \frac{4 \times 6 \times 10^4}{2 \times 3.14 \times 1500}$$

$$= \mathbf{25.477 \text{ Nm}}$$

Example 4.4: A diesel engine consumes 5 grams fuel per second and develops a brake power 75 kW. It has a mechanical efficiency of 85%. Find (a) Brake specific fuel consumption in kg/hWhr., (b) Indicated specific fuel consumption.

Solution:
$$\text{bsfc} = \frac{m_f}{bp} = \frac{5}{75} = 0.066 \text{ g/kWs}$$

$$= \frac{0.066}{1000} \text{ g} \times 3600$$

$$= 0.24 \text{ kg/kWh}$$

$$\text{isfc} = \text{bsfc} \times \eta_m$$

$$= 0.24 \times 0.85$$

$$= \mathbf{0.204 \text{ kg/kWh}}$$

Example 4.5: A four stroke gas engine has a bore of 20 cm and stroke of 35 cm and runs at 400 rpm firing every cycle. The air-fuel ratio is 4: 1 by volume. Its volumetric efficiency at NTP conditions is 80%, determine the volume of gas used per minute. If the calorific value of the gas is 8 MJ/m³ at NTP and the brake thermal efficiency is 25%. Determine brake power of engine.

Solution: Swept volume, $V_s = \frac{\pi}{4} D^2 L$

$$= \frac{\pi}{4} \times 20^2 \times 25$$

$$= 7853.93 \text{ cc}$$

Total charge taken in per cycle
$$V_c = 0.8 \times 7853.98$$
$$= 6.2832 \times 10^{-3} \text{ m}^3$$

Volume of gas used per minute
$$V_g = \frac{6.2832 \times 10^{-3}}{4 + 1} \times \frac{400}{2}$$
$$= 0.25133 \text{ m}^3 \text{ at NTP/min.}$$

$$\text{Heat input} = 8000 \times 0.25133 = 2010.64 \text{ kJ/min}$$
$$\text{bp} = \eta_{th} \times \text{Heat input}$$
$$= \frac{0.25 \times 2010.64}{60}$$
$$\text{bp} = \mathbf{8.377 \text{ kW}}$$

Example 4.6: The following readings are taken during a test of a four-cylinder, two stroke gasoline engine. Diameter = 10 cm, Stroke = 15 cm, Speed = 1700 rpm, Area of positive loop of the indicator diagram = 5.75 sq.cm; Area of the negative loop of the indicator diagram = 0.25 cm^2; Length of indicator diagram = 5.5 cm, Spring constant = 4.0 bar/cm. Find the indicated power of the engine.

Solution: Net area of diagram = 5.75 − 0.25
$$= 5.5 \text{ cm}^2$$

Average height of the diagram
$$= \frac{5.5}{5.5} = 1 \text{ cm}$$

P_{im} = Average height of the diagram × Spring constant
$$= 1 \times 4 = 4 \text{ bar}$$

$$\text{ip} = \frac{P_{im} \, L \, A_n K}{60000}$$

$$= \frac{4 \times 10^5 \times 0.15 \times \frac{\pi}{4} \times 0.1^2 \times 1700 \times 4}{60000}$$

$$i_p = \mathbf{53.38 \text{ kW}}$$

Example 4.7: A four cylinder engine running at 1250 rpm delivers 21 kW power. The average torque when one cylinder was cut is 110 N-m. The calorific value of the fuel is 43 MJ/hr. The engine uses 360 gms of gasoline per kWh. Find indicated thermal efficiency.

Solution:
$$\text{Average bp for 3 cylinders} = \frac{2\pi NT}{60000}$$
$$= \frac{2\pi \times 1250 \times 110}{60000}$$
$$= 14.39 \text{ kW}$$

Average ip with 1 cylinder = 21 − 14.39
$$= 6.608 \text{ kW}$$

Total input = 4 × 6.608 = 26.433 kW

$$\text{isfc} = \text{bsfc} \times \frac{\text{bp}}{\text{ip}} = 360 \times \frac{21}{26.433}$$

$$= 286.006 \approx 286 \text{ g/kWh}$$

$$\text{Fuel combustion} = \frac{\text{isfc} \times \text{ip}}{3600 \times 1000}$$

$$= \frac{286 \times 26.433}{3600 \times 1000}$$

$$= 2.099 \times 10^{-3} \text{ kg/sec.}$$

$$\eta_{ith} = \frac{\text{ip}}{m_f \times C_v}$$

$$= \frac{26.433}{2.099 \times 10^{-3} \times 43000} \times 100$$

$$\eta_{ith} = \mathbf{29.29\%}$$

Example 4.8: A diesel engine consumes fuel at the rate of 5.5 gm/sec. and develops a power of 75 kW. If the mechanical efficiency is 85%. Calculate bsfc and isfc. The lower heating value of the fuel is 44 MJ/Kg.

Solution:
$$\text{bsec} = \frac{\text{kW heat input}}{\text{kW heat output}}$$

$$= \frac{C_v \times m_f}{P} = C_v \times \text{bsfc}$$

$$\text{bsfc} = \frac{5.55}{75} = 0.074 \text{ g/kWs}$$

$$= 0.074 \times 10^{-3} \text{ kg/kWs}$$

$$C_v = 44 \text{ MJ/kg} = 44 \times 10^3 \text{ kJ/kg}$$

$$\text{bsec} = \text{bsfc} \times C_v = 44 \times 10^3 \times 0.074 \times 10^{-3}$$

$$= 3.256$$

$$\text{isec} = \text{bsec} \times \eta_n = 3.256 \times 0.85$$

$$\text{isec} = \mathbf{2.7676}$$

Example 4.9: Find the air-fuel ratio of a 4-stroke, 1 cylinder, air cooled engine with fuel consumption time for 10 cc as 20.0 sec. and air consumption time for 0.1 m³ as 16.3 sec. The load is 16 kg at speed of 3000 rpm. Also find brake specific fuel consumption in g/kWh and thermal brake efficiency. Assume the density of air as 1.175 kg/m³ and specific gravity of fuel to be 0.7. The lower heating value of fuel is 44 MJ/kg and the dynamometer constant is 5000.

Solution:
$$\text{Air consumption} = \frac{0.1}{16.3} \times 1.175 = 7.21 \times 10^{-3} \text{ kg/s}$$

$$\text{Fuel consumption} = \frac{10}{20} \times 0.7 \times \frac{1}{1000}$$

$$= 0.35 \times 10^{-3} \text{ kg/s}$$

$$\text{Air-fuel ratio} = \frac{7.21 \times 10^{-3}}{0.35 \times 10^{-3}}$$

$$= 20.6$$

$$\text{Power output (P)} = \frac{WN}{\text{Dynamometer constant}}$$

$$= \frac{16 \times 3000}{5000} = 9.6 \text{ kW}$$

$$\text{bsfc} = \frac{\text{Fuel consumption (g/hr)}}{\text{Power output}}$$

$$= \frac{0.35 \times 10^{-3} \times 3600 \times 1000}{9.6}$$

$$\text{bsfc} = \textbf{131.25 g/kWh}$$

$$\eta_{bth} = \frac{9.6}{0.35 \times 10^{-3} \times 44000} \times 100$$

$$\eta_{bth} = \textbf{62.3377}$$

Example 4.10: A six-cylinder, gasoline engine operates on the four-stroke cycle. The bore of each cylinder is 80 mm and the stroke is 100 mm. The clearance volume per cylinder is 70 cc. At the speed of 4100 rpm, the fuel consumption is 5.5 gm/sec. [or 19.8 kg/hr.) and the torque developed is 160 Nm.

Calculate: (i) Brake power, (ii) The brake mean effective pressure, (iii) Brake thermal efficiency if the calorific value of the fuel is 44000 kJ/kg and (iv) The relative efficiency on a brake power basis assuming the engine works on the constant volume cycle r = 1.4 for air.

Solution:
$$bp = \frac{2\pi NT}{60000} = \frac{2 \times \pi \times 4100 \times 160}{60000} = \textbf{68.66}$$

$$P_{bm} = \frac{bp \times 6000}{LAnK}$$

$$= \frac{68.66 \times 60000}{0.1 \times \frac{\pi}{4} \times (0.08)^2 \times \frac{4100}{2} \times 6}$$

$$= 6.66 \times 10^5 \text{ P}_a$$

$$Pb_m = \textbf{6.66 bar}$$

$$\eta_{bth} = \frac{bp}{m_f \times C_v} = \frac{68.66 \times 3600}{19.8 \times 43000} \times 100$$

$$= 29.03\%$$

$$\text{Compression ratio, } r = \frac{V_s + V_{cl}}{V_{cl}}$$

$$V_s = \frac{\pi}{4}D^2L = \frac{\pi}{4} \times 8^2 \times 10$$

$$= 502.65 \text{ cc}$$

$$r = \frac{502.65 + 70}{70}$$

$$r = \mathbf{8.18}$$

Air-standard efficiency, $\eta_{otto} = 1 - \dfrac{1}{(8.18)^{0.4}} = 1 - \dfrac{1}{2.3179}$

$$= 0.56858$$

Relative efficiency, $\eta_{rel} = \dfrac{0.2903}{0.568} \times 100$

$$= \mathbf{51.109\%}$$

$$\eta_{bth} = \frac{bp}{m_f \times c_v}$$

$$= \frac{119.82 \times 60}{\frac{4.4}{10} \times 44000} \times 100$$

$$\eta_{bth} = \mathbf{37.134\%}$$

Volume flow rate of air at intake condition.

$$\dot{V}_a = \frac{\dot{m}_a RT}{P} = \frac{6 \times 287 \times 300}{1 \times 10^5}$$

$$= \mathbf{5.17 \text{ m}^3/\text{min.}}$$

Swept volume per minute,

$$V_s = \frac{\pi}{4}D^2LnK$$

$$= \frac{\pi}{4} \times (0.1)^2 \times 0.9 \times \frac{4500}{2} \times 8$$

$$= \mathbf{127.17 \text{ m}^3/\text{min.}}$$

Volumetric efficiency, $\eta_v = \dfrac{5.17}{127.17} \times 100$

$$\eta_v = \mathbf{4.654\%}$$

Air-fuel ratio, A/F $= \dfrac{6.0}{0.44}$

$$A/F = \mathbf{13.64} \qquad \ldots \textbf{Ans.}$$

Example 4.11: An 8-cylinder, four stroke engine of bore 10 cm and 9 cm stroke has a compression ratio of 7 is 4500 rpm on a dynamometer which has 54 cm arm. During a 10 minutes test the dynamometer scale beam reading was 48 kg and the engine consumed 4.4 kg of gasoline having a calorific value of 44000 kJ/kg. Air at 27°C temperature and 1 bar pressure was supplied to the carburetor at the rate of 6 kg/min. Find (i) The brake power delivered. (ii) The brake mean effective pressure, (iii) The brake specific fuel consumption, (iv) The brake specific air consumption, (v) The brake thermal efficiency, (vi) The volumetric efficiency, (vii) The air-fuel ratio.

Solution:

$$bp = \frac{2\pi NT}{60000}$$

$$= \frac{2\pi \times 4500 \times 48 \times 0.54 \times 9.81}{60000}$$

$$bp = 119.82 \text{ kW}$$

$$bmep = \frac{bp \times 60000}{LAnK}$$

$$= \frac{119.82 \times 60000}{0.09 \times \frac{\pi}{4} \times (0.1)^2 \times \frac{4500}{2} \times 8}$$

$$= 5.653 \times 10^5 \text{ P}_a$$

$$bmep = 5.653 \text{ bar}$$

$$bsfc = \frac{\frac{4.4}{10} \times 60}{119.82}$$

$$bfsc = 0.2203 \text{ kg/kWh}$$

$$bsac = \frac{6 \times 60}{119.82}$$

$$bsac = \textbf{3.004 kg/kWh} \qquad \text{... Ans.}$$

Example 4.12: In a test for a four-cylinders, four-stroke engine has a diameter of 100 mm, stroke = 120 mm, speed of engine = 1800 rpm, fuel consumption of 0.2 kg/min, calorific value of fuel is 44000 kJ/kg. Difference in tension on either side of brake pulley = 40 kg, Brake circumference is 300 cm. If the mechanical efficiency is 90%. Calculate (i) Brake-thermal efficiency, (ii) Indicated thermal efficiency, (iii) Indicated mean effective pressure and (iv) Brake specific fuel consumption.

Solution:

$$bp = \frac{2\pi NT}{60000} = \frac{2\pi NWR}{60000} = \frac{WN2\pi R}{60000}$$

$$= \frac{40 \times 9.81 \times 1800 \times 3}{60000} = 35.316 \text{ kW}$$

$$\eta_{bth} = \frac{bp}{m_f \times C_v} \times 100 = \frac{35.316 \times 60}{0.2 \times 44000} \times 100$$

$$\eta_{bth} = 24.079\%$$

$$\eta_{ith} = \frac{\eta_{bth}}{\eta_m} \times 100 = \frac{24.079}{0.9} \times 100$$

$$\eta_{ith} = 26.75\%$$

$$imep = \frac{\frac{bp}{\eta_m} \times 60000}{LAnK}$$

$$= \frac{\frac{35.316}{0.8} \times 60000}{0.12 \times \frac{\pi}{4} \times (0.1)^2 \times \frac{1800}{2} \times 4} = 6.94 \times 10^5 \, P_a$$

$$imep = 6.94 \, \text{bar}$$

$$b_{sfc} = \frac{\dot{m}_f}{bp} = \frac{0.2 \times 60}{35.316}$$

$$b_{sfc} = \mathbf{0.339 \, kg/kWh} \quad \ldots \text{Ans.}$$

Example 4.13: A 4-stroke cycle gas engine has a bore of 20 cm and a stroke of 35 cm. The compression ratio is given to be 8. In a test on the engine the indicated mean effective pressure is 5 bar, the air to gas ratio is 6: 1 and the calorific value of the gas is 12 MJ/m³ at NTP. At the beginning of the compression stroke the temperature is 77°C and pressure is 0.98 bar. Neglecting residual gases, determine the indicated power, the thermal efficiency and the relative efficiency of the engine at 250 rpm.

Solution: Swept volume, $V_s = \frac{\pi}{4} D^2 L = \frac{\pi}{4} \times 20^3 \times 35 = 10990 \, cc$

Volume of gas in cylinder $= \frac{1}{1 + A/F} \times V_1$

$$V_1 = V_s + \frac{V_s}{r-1} = V_s \frac{8}{5} = \frac{1}{8+1} \times 10990 \times \frac{8}{5}$$

Since, the residual gases are to be neglected, one can assume a volumetric efficiency of 100%.

Normal pressure = 1 bar

$$\left(\frac{PV}{T}\right)_{NTP} = \left(\frac{P_1 V_1}{T_1}\right)_{Working}$$

Volume of gas at NTP condition

$$= 1953.7 \times 0.98 \times \frac{273}{350}$$

$$= 1493.4 \text{ cc}$$

Heat added $= 1493.4 \times 10^{-6} \times 12 \times 10^3$

$$= \mathbf{17.92 \text{ kJ/cycle}}$$

$$ip = \frac{P_{im} \times V_s \eta}{60000} = \frac{5 \times 10^5 \times 10990 \times 10^{-6} \times \frac{250}{2}}{60000}$$

$$ip = \mathbf{11.44 \text{ kW}}$$

$$\eta_{ith} = \frac{ip}{\text{Heat added (in kW)}} \times 100$$

$$= \frac{11.44}{17.92 \times \frac{250}{2 \times 60}} \times 100$$

$$= 30.66\%$$

Air-standard efficiency $= 1 - \frac{1}{8^{0.4}} = 0.5647$

Relative efficiency $= \frac{0.3066}{0.5647} \times 100$

Relative efficiency $= \mathbf{54.29\%}$ ... Ans.

Example 4.14: A gasoline engine is specified to be 4-stroke and four-cylinder. It has a bore of 80 mm and a stroke of 100 mm. On test it develops a torque of 75 Nm when running at 3000 rpm. If the clearance volume in each cylinder is 60 cc the relative efficiency with respect to brake thermal efficiency is 0.5 and the calorific value of the fuel is 42 MJ/kg; determine the fuel consumption in kg/hr. and the brake mean effective pressure.

Solution: Swept volume, $V_s = \frac{\pi}{4} = 0.08^2 \times 0.1$

$$= 5.024 \times 10^{-4} \text{ m}^3/\text{cylinder}$$
$$= 502.4 \text{ cc/cylinder}$$

Compression ratio $= \frac{502.4 + 60}{60} = \mathbf{9.373}$

Air-standard efficiency $= 1 - \frac{1}{(9.373)^{0.4}} = 0.5914$

η_{bth} = Relative $\eta \times$ Air-standard η

$$= 0.5 \times 0.5914$$

$\eta_{bth} = \mathbf{0.2954}$ ... Ans.

$$bp = \frac{2 \times \pi \times 3000 \times 75}{60000} = 23.55 \text{ kW}$$

$$\text{Heat supplied} = \frac{23.55}{0.2957} = 79.64 \text{ kJ/s}$$

$$\text{Fuel consumption} = \frac{79.64 \times 3600}{42000}$$

$$= \mathbf{6.8264 \text{ kg/hr}}$$

$$P_{bm} = \frac{P \times 60000}{V_s n K}$$

$$= \frac{23.55 \times 60000}{5.024 \times 10^{-4} \times \frac{3000}{2} \times 4} = 4.6875 \times 10^5 \text{ N/m}^2$$

$$P_{bm} = \mathbf{4.6875 \text{ bar}} \qquad \ldots \text{ Ans.}$$

Example 4.15: An indicator diagram taken from a single-cylinder, four-stroke CI engine has a length of 100 mm and an area 2000 mm². The indicator pointer deflects a distance of 10 mm for pressure increment of 2 bar in the cylinder. If the bore and stroke of the engine cylinder are both 100 mm and the engine speed is 1200 rpm. Calculate the mean effective pressure and the indicated power. If the mechanical efficiency is 85%. What is the brake power developed?

Solution: Mean height of the indicator diagram

$$= \frac{2000}{100} = 20 \text{ mm}$$

$$\text{Mean effective pressure} = \frac{20}{10} \times 2 = \mathbf{4 \text{ bar}}$$

$$\text{Indicated power, ip} = \frac{P_{im} L A n}{60000}$$

$$= \frac{4 \times 10^5 \times 0.1 \times \frac{\pi}{4} \times 0.1^2 \times \frac{1200}{2}}{60000}$$

$$= 3.14 \text{ kW}$$

$$bp = ip \times \eta_m = 3.14 \times 0.85$$

$$bp = \mathbf{2.669 \text{ kW}} \qquad \ldots \text{ Ans.}$$

Example 4.16: A six-cylinder, four-stroke engine gasoline engine having a bore of 90 mm and stroke of 100 mm has a compression ratio 8. The relative efficiency is 60%. When the indicated specific fuel consumption is 3009 g/kWh. Estimate (i) The calorific value of the fuel and (ii) Corresponding fuel consumption given that imep is 8.5 bar and speed is 2500 rpm.

Solution: Air-standard efficiency = $1 - \dfrac{1}{r^{\gamma-1}} = 1 - \dfrac{1}{8^{0.4}} = 0.5647$

$$\text{Relative efficiency} = \dfrac{\text{Thermal efficiency}}{\text{Air-standard efficiency}}$$

Indicated thermal efficiency = 0.6×0.5647
= 0.3388

$$\eta_{ith} = \dfrac{1}{i_{sfc} \times C_v}$$

$$C_v = \dfrac{1}{\eta_{ith} \times i_{sfc}} = \dfrac{3600}{0.3 \times 0.3388}$$

C_v = **35417.035 kJ/kg**

$$ip = \dfrac{P_{im} LAnK}{60000}$$

$$= \dfrac{8.5 \times 10^5 \times 0.1 \times \dfrac{\pi}{4} \times 0.09^2 \times \dfrac{2500}{2} \times 6}{60000}$$

ip = **67.6 kW**

Fuel consumption = isfc × ip = 0.3 × 67.6

ip = **20.28 kg/h**

Example 4.17: A gasoline engine working on 4-stroke develops a brake power of 22 kW. A Morse test was conducted on this engine and the brake power (kW) obtained when each cylinder was made inoperative by short circuiting. The spark plugs are 14.9, 14.3, 14.8 and 14.5 respectively. The test was conducted at constant speed. Find the indicated power, mechanical efficiency and bmep when all the cylinders are firing. The bore of engine is 80 mm and stroke is 90 mm. The engine is running at 3000 rpm.

Solution:

$ip_1 = bp_{1234} - bp_{234}$
= 22 − 14.9
= **7.1 kW**

$ip_2 = bp_{1224} - bp_{134}$
= 22 − 14.3 = **7.7 kW**

$ip_3 = bp_{1234} - bp_{124}$
= 22 − 14.8 = **7.2 kW**

$ip_4 = bp_{1234} - bp_{123}$
= 22 − 14.5
= **7.5 kW**

$ip_1 + ip_2 + ip_3 + ip_4 = ip_{1234} = 7.1 + 7.7 + 7.2 + 7.5$

= **29.5 kW**

$$\eta_w = \frac{22}{29.5} \times 100$$

$$\eta_w = 74.57$$

$$P_{bm} = \frac{bp \times 60000}{\angle AnK}$$

$$= \frac{22 \times 60000}{0.09 \times \frac{\pi}{4} \times (0.08)^2 \times \frac{3000}{2} \times 4}$$

$$= 4.8655 \times 10^5 \, P_a$$

$$P_{bm} = 4.8655 \text{ bar}$$

Example 4.18: The observations recorded after the conduct of a retardation test on a single-cylinder diesel engine are as follows:

Rated power = 10 kW
Rated speed = 500 rpm

Sr. No.	Drip in Speed	Time for fall of speed at no load, $t_2(s)$	Time for fall of speed at 50% load, $t_3(s)$
1.	500-400	7	2.2
2.	500-350	10.6	3.7
3.	500-325	12.5	4.8
4.	500-300	15.0	5.4
5.	500-275	16.6	6.5
6.	500-250	18.9	7.2

Solution:

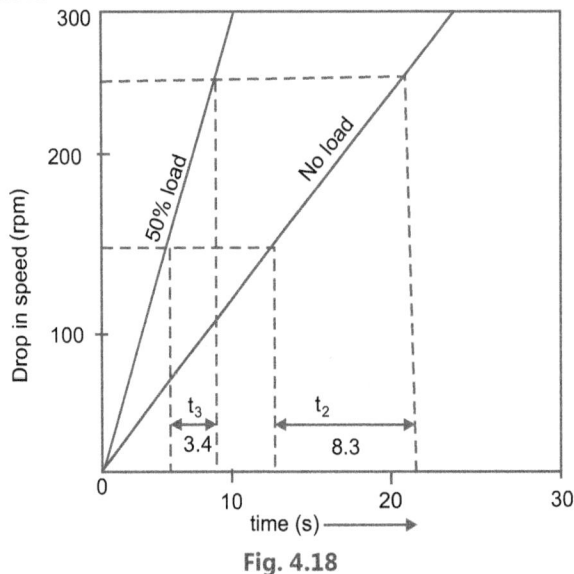

First we draw a graph of drop in speed versus time taken for the drop.

Fig. 4.18

$$P = \frac{2\pi NT}{60000} \text{ kW}$$

$$\text{Full load torque, } T = \frac{P \times 60000}{2\pi N}$$

$$= \frac{10 \times 60000}{2 \times \pi \times 500} = 191.083 \text{ Nm}$$

Torque at half load, $T_{1/2} = 95.5415$ Nm

From graph:

Time for the fall of 100 rpm at no load, $t_2 = 8.3$ sec.

Time for the fall of same 100 rpm at half load, $t_3 = 3.4$ sec.

$$T_f = \frac{t_3}{t_2 - t_3} \times \text{Torque at 50\% load}$$

$$= \frac{t_3}{t_2 - t_3} \times T_{1/2}$$

$$= \frac{3.4}{(8.3 - 3.4)} \times 95.5415$$

$$= 66.294 \text{ Nm}$$

$$\text{Friction power} = \frac{2\pi N T_f}{60000} = \frac{2\pi \times 500 \times 66.294}{60000}$$

$$= \textbf{3.469 kW}$$

$$\eta_m = \frac{bp}{bp + fp} = \frac{10}{10 + 3.469} \times 100 = \textbf{74.24\%}$$

Example 4.19: A two stroke diesel engine was subjected to motoring test. The wattmeter reading was 1.6 kW. The engine was then tested for one hour and following observations were noted.

Observations:
- (i) Net brake torque = 125 Nm
- (ii) Engine rpm = 610
- (iii) Fuel consumption = 2.7 kg
- (iv) Calorific value of the fuel = 41000 kJ/kg
- (v) Cooling water used = 825 kg
- (vi) Temperature rise of cooling water = 8°C
- (vii) Exhaust gas temperature = 350°C
- (viii) Room temperature = 30°C
- (ix) Air fuel ratio = 32: 1
- (x) Specific heat of exhaust gas = 1.05 kJ/kgK.

Calculate:
- (a) Brake power
- (b) Indicated power
- (c) Mechanical efficiency
- (d) Indicated thermal efficiency and
- (e) Heat balance on minute and percentage basis.

Solution: Given Data:

Two stroke diesel engine
Tested for one hour
Wattmeter reading = 1.6 kW
Net brake torque = T = 125 Nm
Speed of engine = N = 61 rpm

Fuel consumption = $\dot{m}_f$ = 2.7 kg/hr.
C.V. of fuel C_v = 41000 kJ/kg
Flow of cooling water = m_W = 825 kg/hr.
Temperature rise of cooling water = DT_w = 8°C
Exhaust gas temperature = T_g = 350°C
Room temperature = T_a = 30°C.
A/F ratio = 32 : 1
Specific heat OR Exhaust gas = Cp_g = 1.05 kJ/kg·K

(a) Brake power = B.P. = $\dfrac{2\pi NT}{60}$

$= \dfrac{2\pi \times 610 \times 125}{60}$

= 7984.88 W
= **7.985 kW**

(b) Indicated power = I.P. = B.P. + Wattmeter reading
= 7.985 + 1.6
= **9.585 kW**

(c) Mechanical efficiency = $\eta_m = \dfrac{B.P.}{I.P.} = \dfrac{7.985}{9.585} \times 100$

= **83.31%**

(d) Indicated thermal efficiency

$\eta_{ith} = \dfrac{I.P.}{m_f \times C_v}$

$= \dfrac{9.585}{\dfrac{2.7}{3600} \times 41000} \times 100$

= **31.17%**

(e) Heat Balance:

Total heat supplied = $\dfrac{2.7}{60} \times 41000$ = 1845 kJ/min.

(i) Heat to B.P. = 7.985 kW
= 479.1 kJ/min.
= **25.96%**

(ii) Heat to cooling water

$$= m_w \cdot \Delta T_w \cdot Cp_w$$
$$= \frac{825}{60} \times 8 \times 4.18$$
$$= 459.8 \text{ kJ/min.}$$
$$= \mathbf{24.92\%}$$

(iii) Heat to exhaust gases

$$= m_g \cdot Cp_g \cdot (T_g - T_a)$$
$$= m_f (32 + 1) \times 1.05 \times (350 - 30)$$
$$= \frac{2.7}{60} (33) \times 1.05 \times 320$$
$$= 498.96 \text{ kJ/min.}$$
$$= \mathbf{27\%}$$

(iv) Heat to radiation or unaccounted

$$= 1845 - (479.1 + 459.8 + 498.96)$$
$$= 1845 - 1437.86$$
$$= 407.14 \text{ kJ/min } 0 = \mathbf{22.07\%}$$

Heat balance sheet on % and minute basis

Total Heat kJ/min.	%	Heat Distribution		kJ/min.	%
1845	100%	(i)	Heat to B.P.	479.1	25.96
		(ii)	Heat to cooling water	459.8	24.92
		(iii)	Heat to exhaust gases	498.96	27.01
		(iv)	Heat to radiation or unaccounted	407.14	22.07
Total 1845	100%			1845	100%

Example 4.20: A 4-cylinder, 4-stroke cycle engine having cylinder diameter 100 mm and stroke 120 mm was tested at 1600 rpm and the following readings were obtained:
Fuel consumption = 0.27 litres/minute, Specific gravity fuel = 0.74, B.P. = 31.4 kW, Mechanical efficiency = 80%, Calorific value of fuel = 44000 kJ/kg.
Determine: (i) bsfc, (ii) imep, (iii) Brake thermal efficiency.

Solution:
$$D = 100 \text{ mm} = 0.1 \text{ m}$$
$$L = 120 \text{ mm} = 0.12 \text{ m}$$
$$\eta_m = 80\% = 0.8$$

(i) Brake Specific Fuel Consumption (bsfc):

$$= \frac{\dot{m}_f}{B.P.}$$
$$= \frac{0.27 \times 0.74 \times 60}{31.4}$$
$$= \mathbf{0.38174 \text{ kg/kW·hr.}}$$

(ii) Indicated Power:

$$I.P. = \frac{n \times P_{imep} \times L \times A \times N}{2 \times 60}$$

$$\frac{B.P.}{\eta_m} = \frac{n \times P_{imep} \times 0.12 \times \frac{\pi}{4} \times (0.1)^2 \times 1600}{2 \times 60}$$

$$\therefore \frac{31.4}{0.8} = 4 \times P_{imep} \times 0.01256637$$

$$\therefore P_{imep} = \textbf{780.85 kN/m}^2$$

(iii) Brake Thermal Efficiency:

$$\eta_{bth} = \frac{\text{Brake power}}{\text{Heat supplied}}$$

$$= \frac{31.4}{\dot{m}_f \times C_v}$$

$$= \frac{31.4}{\frac{0.27 \times 0.74}{60} \times 44000} \times 100$$

$$\eta_{bth} = \textbf{21.43\%} \qquad \text{... Ans.}$$

Example 4.21: A single cylinder and stroke cycle I.C. engine when tested, the following observations available:
Area of indicator diagram = 3 sq.cm, Length of indicator diagram = 4 cm, Spring constant = 10 bar/cm, Speed of engine = 400 rpm, Brake drum diameter = 120 cm, Dead weight on brake = 380 N, Spring balance reading = 50 N, Fuel consumption = 2.8 kg/hr., C_v = 42000 kJ/kg, Cylinder diameter = 16 cm, Piston stroke = 20 cm.
Find: (i) F.P., (ii) Mechanical efficiency, (iii) bsfc, (iv) Brake thermal efficiency.

Solution: Indicated mean effective pressure,

$$P_{imep} = \frac{\text{Area of indicated diameter}}{\text{Length of indicated diameter}} \times \text{Spring constant}$$

$$= \frac{A_i}{L_i} \times K_i$$

$$= \frac{3}{4} \times 10$$

$$P_{imep} = \textbf{7.5 bar} \qquad \text{... (1)}$$

Indicated power = I.P. = $\dfrac{P_{imep} \times L \times A \times N}{60}$

$$= \frac{7.5 \times 10^5 \times 0.2 \times \frac{\pi}{4}(0.16)^2 \times 400}{60 \times 2}$$

$$= \textbf{10.05 kW} \qquad \text{... (2)}$$

$$\text{Brake Power} = \text{B.P.} = \frac{2\pi NT}{60} = \frac{2\pi N (W-S)\frac{b}{2}}{60}$$

∴
$$\text{B.P.} = \frac{2\pi \times 400\,(380 - 50)}{60} \times \frac{1.2}{2}$$

$$= 8.294 \text{ W}$$

$$\text{B.P.} = 8.294 \text{ kW} \qquad \ldots (3)$$

(i) Frictional Power = F.P. = I.P. − B.P.

$$= 10.05 - 8.294$$

$$= \mathbf{1.756 \text{ kW}}$$

(ii) Mechanical Efficiency $= \eta_m = \dfrac{\text{B.P.}}{\text{I.P.}}$

$$= \frac{8.294}{10.05} \times 100$$

$$= \mathbf{82.53\%}$$

(iii) Brake Specific Fuel Consumption (bsfc):

$$= \frac{\dot{m}_f}{\text{B.P.}}$$

$$= \frac{2.8}{8.294}$$

$$= \mathbf{0.3376 \text{ kg/kW·hr.}}$$

(iv) Brake Thermal Efficiency (η_{bth})

$$= \frac{\text{B.P.}}{\text{Heat supplied}}$$

$$= \frac{8.294}{\dfrac{2.8}{3600} \times 42000} \times 100$$

$$= \mathbf{25.39\%}$$

Example 4.22: A six-cylinder 4-stroke petrol engine having a bore of 90 mm and stroke of 100 mm has a compression ratio of 7. The relative efficiency with reference to indicated thermal efficiency is 55% when indicated mean specific fuel consumption is 0.3 kg/kWh. Estimate the calorific value of the fuel and fuel consumption in kg/hr. Given that indicated mean effective pressure is 8.5 bar and speed is 2500 r.p.m.

Solution: Number of cylinders = n_1 = 6, L = 100 mm = 0.1 m

$$d = 90 \text{ mm} = 0.09 \text{ m}, r = 7 \qquad \textbf{(P.U. May 2006)}$$

η_r = 55% = 0.55 [based on indicated thermal efficiency]
isfc = 0.3 kg/kWh
P_{mi} = 8.5 bar
N = 2500 rpm

$$\text{I.P.} = \frac{P_{mi} \times A \times L \times N}{60000} \times n_1$$

where,
$$n = \frac{N}{2} = \frac{2500}{2} = 1250 \text{ strokes/mm [for 4 stroke engine]}$$

$$A = \frac{\pi}{4} d^2$$

From equation (1), we have,

$$\text{I.P.} = (8.5 \times 10^5) \times \frac{\pi}{4} \times (0.09)^2 \times 0.1 \times 1250 \times 6 \times \frac{1}{60000}$$

$$= 67.593 \text{ kW}$$

1. **Fuel consumption, $\dot{m}_f$:**

$$\text{isfc} = \frac{\dot{m}_f}{\text{I.P.}} = \text{i.e. } 0.3 = \frac{\dot{m}_f}{67.593}$$

$$\dot{m}_f = \mathbf{20.278 \text{ kg/hr}}$$

2. **Calorific Value (C_v) of fuel:**

Air standard efficiency, $\eta_a = 1 - \frac{1}{(r)^{(\gamma-1)}} = 1 - \frac{1}{(7)^{(1.4-1)}} = 0.42647$

Relative efficiency, $\eta_r = \dfrac{\text{Indicated thermal efficiency, } \eta_i}{\text{Air standard efficiency, } \eta_a}$

$\eta_i = \eta_r \times \eta_a = 0.55 \times 0.42647 = 0.2346$

But,
$$\eta_i = \frac{\text{I.P.}}{\dot{m}_f \times C_v}$$

$$0.2346 = \frac{67.593}{\left(\frac{20.278}{3600}\right) \times C_v}$$

∴ C_v = **51150.6 kJ/kg** ... Ans.

Example 4.23: The following particulars were obtained in a trial on a 4-stroke, single-cylinder engine:

Duration of trial = 1 hour   Revolutions = 14000
Number of missed cycles = 500   Net brake load = 1470 N
Indicated mean effective pressure = 7.5 bar   Gas consumption = 20000 litres
LCV of gas at supply condition = 21 kJ/litre   Cylinder diameter = 250 mm
Stroke = 400 mm   Effective brake circumference = 4 m
Compression ratio = 6.5 : 1

Calculate: (i) Indicated power, (ii) Brake power, (iii) Mechanical efficiency, (iv) Indicated thermal efficiency, (v) Relative efficiency. **(P.U. May 2006)**

Solution: Given: Time, t = 1 hr. = 60 min, Revolutions = 14000

i.e. N = $\dfrac{14000}{60}$ r.p.m.

Number of strokes missed = 500/hr.; Net brake load,

W_b = 1470 N, P_{mi} = 7.5 bar, V_g = 20000 litres

C_v of gas = 21 kJ/litre; d = 250 mm = 0.25 m

L = 400 mm = 0.4 m;

Brake circumference, πD_b = 4 m = $2\pi R_b$, r = 6.5

(i) Indicated Power (I.P.):

Actual number of stroke/min.

n = Theoretical strokes/min. − Missed stroke/min.

$= \dfrac{1}{60}\left[\dfrac{4000}{2} - 500\right] = \dfrac{6500}{60}$

I.P. $= \dfrac{P_{mi} \times A \times Ln}{60000} = \dfrac{(7.5 \times 10^5) \times \dfrac{\pi}{5}(0.25)^2 \times 0.4 \times \dfrac{6500}{60}}{60000}$

= **26.589 kW**

(ii) Brake Power (B.P.):

B.P. $= \dfrac{\text{(Brake load) } R_b \times 2\pi N}{60 \times 1000}$ kW

$= \dfrac{W_b \times R_b \times 2\pi N}{60 \times 1000} = \dfrac{1470 \times 4}{60 \times 1000} \times \dfrac{14000}{60}$

= **22.867 kW**

(iii) Mechanical Efficiency (η_m) = $\dfrac{B.P.}{I.P.}$

∴ $\eta_m = \dfrac{22.867}{26.589}$ = 0.86 or 86%

(iv) Indicated Thermal Efficiency (η_{ith}) = $\dfrac{I.P.}{V_f \times C_v}$

$\eta_{ith} = \dfrac{26.589}{\dfrac{20000}{3600} \times 21}$ = 0.2279 (or 22.79%)

(v) Relative Efficiency (η_r):

$$\text{Air standard efficiency} = \eta_a = 1 - \frac{1}{r^{(\gamma-1)}} = 1 - \frac{1}{6.5^{(1.4-1)}}$$

∴ $\eta_a = 0.527$

∴ $\eta_r = \dfrac{\eta_{ith}}{\eta_a} = \dfrac{0.2279}{0.527}$

η_r = **0.4324 (or 43.24%)** … Ans.

Example 4.24: A two stroke diesel engine was motored when the meter reading was 1.5 kW. Then the test on the engine was carried out for one hour and the following observations were recorded: Brake torque = 120 Nm; Speed = 600 rpm; Fuel used = 2.5 kg; calorific value of fuel = 40.3 MJ/kg; Cooling water used = 818 kg; Rise in temperature of cooling water = 10°C.

Exhaust gas temperature = 345°C. Room temperature = 25°C; A/F = 32 : 1.

Determine: (i) bp, (ii) ip, (iii) Mechanical efficiency, (vi) Indicated thermal efficiency, (v) Draw heat balance sheet on minute basis and also in percentage. **(P.U. Dec. 2006)**

Solution:

(a)
$$B.P. = \frac{2\pi NT}{1000} = 2\pi \times \frac{600}{60} \times \frac{120}{1000} = \textbf{7.54 kW}$$

$$I.P. = B.P. + F.P. = 7.54 + 1.5 = \textbf{9.04 kW}$$

$$\text{Mechanical } \eta = \frac{7.54}{9.04} = 0.834 = \textbf{83.4\%}$$

$$\text{Indicated thermal } \eta = \frac{I.P.}{\text{Heat supplied}}$$

$$= \frac{9.04 \times 3600}{2.5 \times 40.3 \times 10^3} = 0.323 = \textbf{32.3\%}$$

(b) Heat Balance for the Engine:

1. Energy supplied $= \dfrac{2.5 \times 40300}{60} =$ **1680 kJ/min.**

2. Energy Distributed
   (a) Heat in B.P. = 7.54 × 60 = **452.4 kJ/min.**
   (b) Heat in cooling water
   $$= \frac{818}{60} \times 4.2 \times 10 = \textbf{570.8 kJ/min}$$
   (c) Heat in exhaust gases = $m_g\, C_{pg}\, (\Delta T)$
   $$= \frac{33 \times 2.5}{60} \times 1.05\,(345 - 25) = \textbf{462 kJ/min.}$$
   (d) Heat unaccounted (by difference)
   $$= 1680 - (452.4 + 570.8 + 462)\; \boxed{= \textbf{197.8 kJ/min.}}$$

Percentage Heats:

Heat supplied = 1679 kJ/min. = **100%**

(a) Heat in B.P. = $\dfrac{452.4}{1679} \times 100$ = **20.94%**

(b) Heat in cooling water = $\dfrac{462}{1679} \times 100$ = **33.97%**

(c) Heat in exhaust gases = $\dfrac{462}{1679} \times 100$ = **27.51%**

(d) Heat unaccounted = $\dfrac{197.8}{1679} \times 100$ = **11.78%**

Example 4.25: The following observations were recorded in a test of one hour duration on a single cylinder oil engine working on 4-stroke cycle.

Bore = 300 mm; Stroke = 450 mm; Fuel used = 8.8 kg; Calorific value = 41800 kJ/kg; Average speed, N = 200 rpm; Spring constant = 2.9 bar/cm; Area of indicator diagram = 12 cm^2, Length of indicator diagram = 6 cm; Brake friction load = 1860 N, Quantity of cooling water = 650 kg; Temperature rise = 22°C, diameter of brake wheel = 1.22 m; Calculate: (i) Mean effective pressure, (ii) Mechanical efficiency, (iii) Brake thermal efficiency, (iv) Draw heat balance sheet on minute and percentage basis.

Solution:

(i) Mean Effective Pressure (P_m):

$$= \dfrac{\text{Area}}{\text{Length}} \times \text{Spring index}$$

∴ $P_m = \dfrac{12}{6} \times 2.9$ = **5.8 bar**

(ii) Mechanical Efficiency (η_m) = $\dfrac{B.P.}{I.P.}$

Indicated Power = $\dfrac{P_{mep} \times L \times a \times N}{60}$

∴ $n = \dfrac{N}{2}$ for four stroke

$= 5.8 \times 100 \times \dfrac{450}{1000} \times \dfrac{\pi}{2}\left(\dfrac{300}{1000}\right)^2 \times \dfrac{200}{60 \times 2}$

I.P. = $\dfrac{61.49}{2}$ kW

= **30.745 kW**

Breaking torque = Brake friction Load × Radius of brake drum

T = $\dfrac{1860 \times 1.22}{2}$

$$T = 1134.6 \text{ Nm}$$

$$\therefore \quad B.P. = \frac{2\pi NT}{60} = 23.76 \text{ kW}$$

(ii) Mechanical Efficiency ;

$$= \frac{B.P.}{I.P.} = \frac{23.763}{30.745} = \mathbf{77.29\%}$$

(iii) Brake Thermal Efficiency:

$$= \frac{\text{Brake power}}{\text{Heat supplied}} = \frac{2376}{\frac{88}{3600} \times 41800} = 0.2325 = \mathbf{23.25\%}$$

(iv) Heat Balance Sheet – Heat Supplied

$$= m_f \times C_v = \frac{8.8}{60} \times 41800 = \mathbf{6130.6 \text{ kJ/min.}}$$

Heat converted into break power = 1425.36 kJ/min. = **23.25%**

Heat carried by cooling water:

$$= m_w \times Cp_w \cdot (\Delta t) = \frac{650}{60} \times 4.18 \times 22 = 997.30 = \mathbf{16.28\%}$$

Heat by fuel gases and unaccounted

$$= 60.47\% = \mathbf{3707.17 \text{ kJ/min}} \qquad \ldots \text{ Ans.}$$

Example 4.26: A 4-cylinder petrol engine with 70 mm bore and 100 mm stroke length working on 4-stroke principle develops torque 140 Nm at 4000 rpm. The clearance volume per cylinder is 0.065 litres. Fuel consumption is 14 kg/hr. Calculate: (i) bp, (ii) bmep, (iii) Brake thermal efficiency, (iv) Relative efficiency.

Take C_v of fuel = 42500 kJ/kg and γ = 1.4 for air. **(P.U. Dec. 2007)**

Solution:

(i) $\quad B.P. = 2\pi NT$

$$= 2 \times \pi \times \frac{4000}{60} \times 140 \times 10^{-3} = \mathbf{58.65 \text{ kW}}$$

(ii) Brake Thermal Efficiency (η_{bth})

$$\therefore \quad \eta_{bth} = \frac{B.P. \times 3600}{m_f/hr. \times C_v} = \frac{58.65 \times 3600}{14 \times 42500}$$

$$= \mathbf{0.3548 \text{ or } 35.48\%}$$

(iii) Brake Mean Effective Pressure (bmep):

$$bmep = \frac{B.P.}{L \cdot A \cdot N \times \text{Number of cylinders}}$$

$$= \frac{58.65 \times 10^3}{0.1 \times \frac{\pi}{4} \times (0.07)^2 \times \frac{4000}{2 \times 60} \times 4} \times \frac{1}{10^5}$$

$$= \frac{58.65 \times 10^3 \times 4 \times 120}{0.1 \times \pi \times (0.07)^2 \times 4000 \times 4 \times 10^5}$$

= **11.43 bar**

(iv) Relative Efficiency (η_{rel}):

$$\text{Compression ratio} = r = \frac{V}{V_c} = \frac{V_c + V_s}{V_c}$$

$$V_c = 0.065 \text{ lit.} = 0.065 \times 10^{-3} \text{ m}^3$$

$$V_s = \frac{\pi}{4} D^2 \times L = \frac{\pi}{4} \times (0.07)^2 \times 0.1$$

$$= 3.85 \times 10^{-4} \text{ m}^3$$

∴ $$r = \frac{3.85 \times 10^{-4} + 0.065 \times 10^{-3}}{0.065 \times 10^{-3}} = 6.923 = 7$$

$$\eta_{air} \text{ standard} = 1 - \frac{1}{r^{\gamma-1}} = 1 - \frac{1}{7^{1.4-1}}$$

∴ η_{air} standard = 0.541 or 54.1%

∴ $$\eta_{rel} = \frac{\eta_{bth}}{\eta_{air} \text{ standard}}$$

$$= \frac{0.3548}{0.541}$$

= 0.6558 or **65.58%**

∴ Relative efficiency = **65.58%** ... Ans.

Example 4.27: The following observations were recorded during a trial on a 4-stroke diesel engine:

Power absorbed by non-firing engine when driven by an electric motor	= 10 kW
Speed of the engine	= 1750 rpm
Brake torque	= 327.4 Nm
Fuel used	= 15 kg/hr.
Calorific value of fuel	= 42000 kJ/kg
Air supplied	= 4.75 kg/min.
Cooling water circulated	= 16 kg/min.
Outlet temperature of cooling water	= 65.8°C
Temperature of exhaust gas	= 400°C
Room temperature	= 20.8°C
Specific heat of water	= 4.19 kJ/kg·K
Specific heat of exhaust gas	= 1.25 kJ/kg·K

Determine: (i) bp, (ii) Mechanical efficiency, (iii) bsfc, (iv) Draw up heat balance sheet on kW basis.

Solution:

(i) Brake Power (b.p.):

$$\text{b.p.} = 2\pi NT = 2 \times \pi \times \frac{1750}{60} \times 327.4 \times 10^{-3}$$

$$= \textbf{60.01 kW}$$

(ii) Mechanical Efficiency (η_m):

$$\eta_m = \frac{\text{b.p.}}{\text{i.p.}}$$

But, i.p. = b.p. + f.p.
      f.p. = 10 kW

Given that power absorbed by non-firing engine when driven by electric motor. This is frictional power.

This type of testing is done in a motoring test which is used to calculate the frictional power of an engine.

Hence,   f.p. = 10 kW
∴   i.p. = b.p. + f.p.
                 = 60.01 + 10
∴   i.p. = **70.01 kW**

∴ $\eta_m = \dfrac{60.01}{70.01} = 0.8571$

∴ $\eta_m = \textbf{85.71\%}$

(iii) bsfc: Brake Specific Fuel Consumption:

$$\text{bsfc} = \frac{m_f/\text{hr.}}{\text{b.p.}} = \frac{15}{60.01}$$

∴   bsfc = **0.25 kg/kWhr**

(iv) Heat Balance Sheet in kW basis:

(1) Power supplied by fuel = $m_f \times C_v$

$$= \frac{15}{3600} \times 42000$$

$$= \textbf{175 kW}$$

(2)   Brake power = 60.01 kW
(3)   Power to cooling water = $m_w C_{pw} \Delta T$

$$= \frac{16}{60} \times 4.19 \times (T_o - T_{in})$$

T_o = 65.8 + 273 = 338.8 K

T_{in} = 20.8 + 273 = **293.8 K**

Power lost to cooling water = 50.28 kW

(4)   Power to exhaust $= m_E \, C_{P_E} \, \Delta T$

Here, mass of exhaust gases

$$m_E = m_a + m_f$$

$$= \frac{4.75}{60} + \frac{15}{3600}$$

$$= 0.0833 \text{ kg/s}$$

Power lost to exhaust $= 0.0833 \times 1.25 \times (400 - 20.8)$

= **39.48 kW**

Heat Balance Sheet:

	Input (kW)	%	Output	kW	%
01	Power from fuel 175 kW	100%	Brake power	60.01	34.29
			Power lost to cooling water	50.28	28.73
			Power lost to exhaust	39.48	22.56
			Unaccounted power	25.23	14.42
Total	174 kW	100%	Total	175	100%

Example 4.28: A single cylinder engine running at 180 rpm develops a torque of 8 Nm. The indicated power of the engine 1.8 kW. Find the loss due to friction power as the percentage of brake power.

Solution: Given Data: Single cylinder engine

$$\text{Speed of engine} = N = 1800 \text{ rpm}$$

$$\text{Torque} = T = 8 \text{ Nm}$$

$$\text{I.P.} = 1.8 \text{ kW}$$

$$\text{Brake power} = \text{B.P.} = \frac{2\pi NT}{60}$$

$$= \frac{2\pi \times 1800 \times 8}{60}$$

$$= 1507.96 \text{ W}$$

$$= \mathbf{1.50796 \text{ kW}}$$

$$\text{Friction power} = \text{F.P.} = \text{I.P.} - \text{B.P.}$$

$$= 1.8 - 1.50796$$

$$= \mathbf{0.29204 \text{ kW}}$$

Loss due to friction power as the percentage of brake power

$$= \frac{0.29204}{1.50796} \times 100$$

$$= \mathbf{19.37\% \text{ of brake power}} \qquad \text{... Ans.}$$

(B) SUPERCHARGING

4.14 INTRODUCTION (S-10, W-10)

The power output of an engine depends upon:
- (a) The amount of air inducted per unit time,
- (b) The degree of utilization of this air and
- (c) The thermal efficiency of the engine.

The amount of air inducted per unit time can be increased by increasing engine speed or by increasing the density of air at intake.

The increase in engine speed has disadvantages:
- Needs a rigid and robust engine as the inertia loads increase.
- The engine friction and bearing loads also increase and the volumetric efficiency decreases when the speed is increased.

Therefore, the method of increasing the inlet air density, called **supercharging**, is usually employed to increase the power output of the engine. This is done by supplying air at a pressure higher than the pressure at which the engine naturally aspirates air from the atmosphere by using a pressure boosting device called a *supercharger*.

- The power output can also be increased by increasing the thermal efficiency of the engine, say by increasing the compression ratio.
- However, this increases the maximum cylinder pressure.
- The rate of increase of maximum cylinder pressure is less than the rate of increase of brake mean effective pressure in case of a supercharged engine. This means that for a given maximum cylinder pressure more power can be obtained by supercharging as compared to that obtained by increase in compression ratio.
- The rate of increase of maximum temperature is also low in case of supercharging. This results in lower thermal loads.

4.15 OBJECTS OF SUPERCHARGING (W-10)

The increase in the amount of air inducted per unit time by supercharging is obtained mainly to burn a greater amount of fuel in a given engine and thus increase its power output. The objects of supercharging include one or more of the following:

1. To increase the power output for a given weight and bulk of the engine. This is important for aircraft, marine and automotive engines where weight and space are important.
2. To compensate for the loss of power due to altitude. This mainly relates to aircraft engines which loses power at an approximate rate of one per cent 100 metres altitude.
3. To obtain more power from an existing engine.

4.16 THERMODYNAMIC CYCLE WITH SUPERCHARGING (S-10)

Fig. 4.19 shows p-v diagram for an ideal otto-cycle supercharged engine. The pressure P_1 represents the supercharging pressure and P_5 is the exhaust pressure.

- Area 8-6-7-0-1-8 represents the work done by the supercharger (mechanically driven) in supplying air at a pressure P_1 while the area 1-2-3-4-1 is the output of the engine.
- Area 0-1-6-7-0 represents the gain in work during the gas exchange process due to supercharging. Thus, a part of the supercharger work is recovered.
- However, the area 1-6-8-1 cannot be recovered and represents a loss of work. This loss of work causes the ideal thermal efficiency of the supercharged engine to decrease with an increase in supercharging pressure.

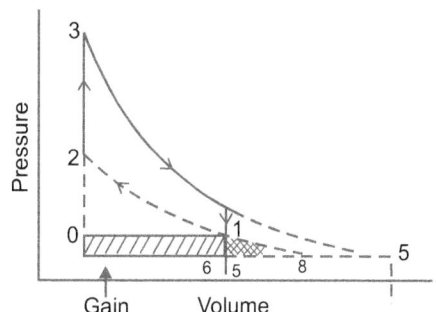

Fig. 4.19: p-v Diagram for an Ideal Otto Cycle Supercharged Engine

Fig. 4.20 shows the difference between the p-v diagram of an unsupercharged and supercharged engines. Two important differences are:
(i) Increase in pressure over the unsupercharged cycle.
(ii) The pumping loop of a supercharged engine is positive instead of negative. Hence, to get the net ip the power represented by pumping loop is to be added instead of being subtracted.

$$I_{mep} = \frac{(\text{Area 1-2-3-4-1} + \text{Area 1-5-6-7}) \times \text{Spring number}}{\text{Length of the indicator diagram}}$$

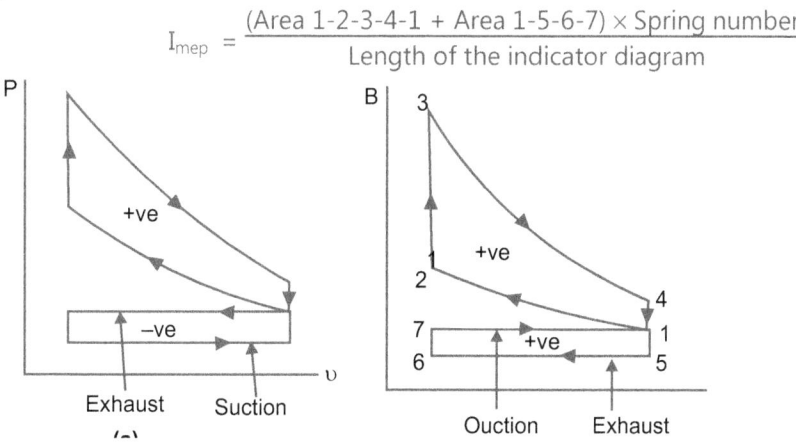

(a) Naturally Aspirated Engine (b) Supercharged Engine

Fig. 4.20: Difference between the p-v Diagrams of Naturally Aspirated and Supercharged Engines

The gain in the output of a supercharged engine is mainly due to increase in the amount of air inducted for the same swept volume. An additional amount of air is also inducted due to compression of residual volume to a higher pressure. Supercharging also results in an increase in mechanical efficiency, and in better gas-exchange process. An engine should be designed from the start as a supercharged engine to obtain optimum performance with the desired life.

4.17 SUPERCHARGING POWER

The power required for driving the supercharger can be calculated by considering the steady flow process.

The power required to drive the supercharger can be derived as,

$$p = \frac{m_a * C_v T_1 \left\{ \left(\frac{p_2}{p_1}\right)^{\frac{\gamma-1}{\gamma}} - 1 \right\}}{\eta_s} \qquad \ldots (4.18)$$

where, m_a is the amount of air supplied by the supercharger.

This power can be supplied by a separate drive for the supercharger, or by connecting the supercharger directly to the engine shaft or to a gas turbine driven by the engine exhaust gases. In all cases the gain in the power output of the engine would be many times the power required to driven the compressor.

4.18 SUPERCHARGING OF SPARK IGNITION ENGINES

As far as spark ignition engines are concerned, supercharging is employed only for aircraft and racing car engines. This is because the increase in supercharging pressure increases the tendency to detonate and pre-ignite.

Supercharging of SI engines results:
    (i)   increasing the volumetric efficiency of the engine,
    (ii) increase in the intake temperature of the engine.

Increased intake pressure and temperature reduces ignition delay and increases flame speed. Both these effects result in a greater tendency to detonate or pre-ignite. *For this reason, the supercharged petrol engines employ lower compression ratios.*

The use of lower compression ratios and increased heat losses due to higher values of specific heats and dissociation losses at higher temperatures results in lower thermal efficiencies for such engines. Thus, supercharged petrol engines have a greater fuel consumption than naturally aspirated engines.

Increased flame make the petrol engine more sensitive to fuel-air ratio and the engine cannot run on weak mixtures without knock. Rich mixtures are used to control detonation (Fig. 4.21). This further increases the specific fuel consumption of the engine.

Fig. 4.21 shows the performance of a supercharged petrol engine for different speeds. Knocking can be controlled in high supercharged engine by injection of water in the combustion chamber. However, large amount of liquid needed for this purpose becomes prohibitive. Another alternative is to use intercooling of the charge before it is fed to the engine.

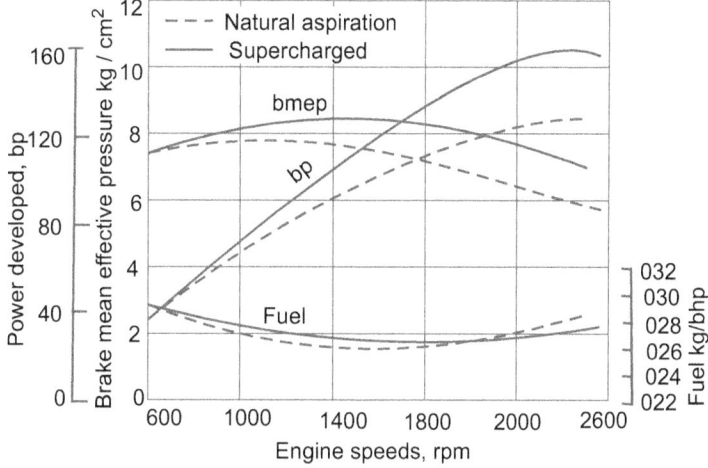

Fig. 4.21: Effect of Supercharging on a Petrol Engine

Because of its poor fuel economy, supercharging of petrol engines is not very popular and is used only when a large amount of power is needed or when more power needed to compensate altitude loss.

4.19 SUPERCHARGING OF CI ENGINES

- Supercharging does result in combustion problem in case of SI engines. Supercharging improves combustion in a diesel engine.
- Increase in pressure and temperature of the intake air reduces ignition delay and hence the rate of pressure rise resulting in a better, quieter and smoother combustion.
- This improvement in combustion allows a poor quality fuel to be used in a diesel engine and it is also not sensitive to the type of fuel used.
- The increase in intake air temperature reduces volumetric and thermal efficiency but the increase in the density due to pressure compensate for this and intercooling is not necessary except for highly supercharged engines.

However, mechanical and thermal loading increases with an increase in supercharging. But this increase in mechanical and thermal loading is only moderate because of the use of lower compression ratios and the effect of cooling due to increased valve overlap of the supercharged engine. It is possible to use lower fuel-air in a supercharged engine as the increase in fuel flow is less than the increase in air flow. This results in lower temperatures over the full engine cycle and reduced smoke from engine. Low fuel-air ratio and high expansion ratio results in lower exhaust temperature. This results in increased life of the exhaust valves.

4.20 EFFECT OF SUPERCHARGING ON PERFORMANCE OF THE ENGINE

The performance parameters like power output, mechanical efficiency, fuel consumption are discussed here.

4.20.1 Power Output

The power output of a supercharged engine is higher than its naturally aspirated counterpart due to the following reasons:
1. The amount of air inducted per cycle for a given swept volume is increased.
2. The mechanical efficiency is slightly improved.
3. During the gas exchange process some of the work done on the supercharge is recovered.
4. Supercharging results in better scavenging and reduced exhaust gas temperatures in the engine. The reduced residual gas fraction helps in better combustion and reduced temperatures improve volumetric efficiency.

The above mentioned effects are common in both petrol and diesel engines. However, in petrol engines supercharging results in tendency to knock. In contrast to this, the diesel engine runs smoother and is able to utilize low fuel-air ratios consumption are some other benefits of supercharging a diesel engine.

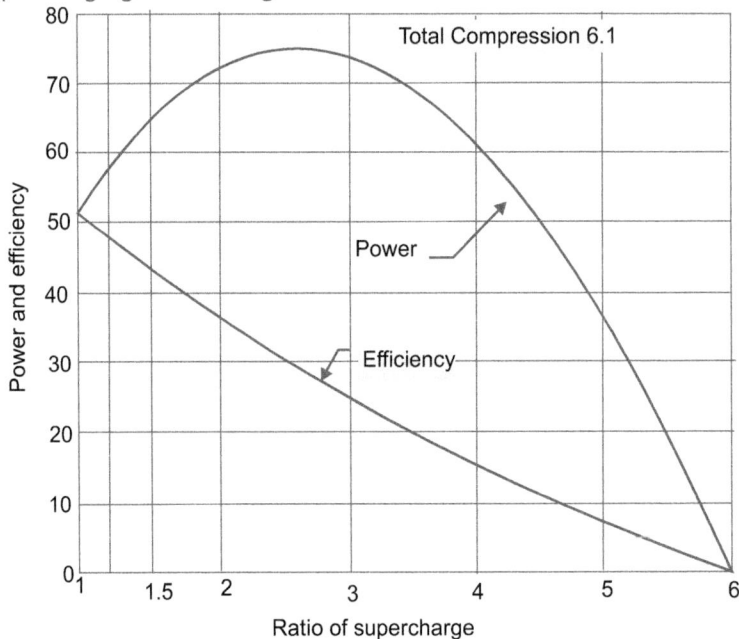

Fig. 4.22: Effect of Supercharging Ratio on Power and Efficiency

Fig. 4.22 shows the effect of supercharging ratio on power output and overall efficiency of an engine.

4.20.2 Mechanical Efficiency

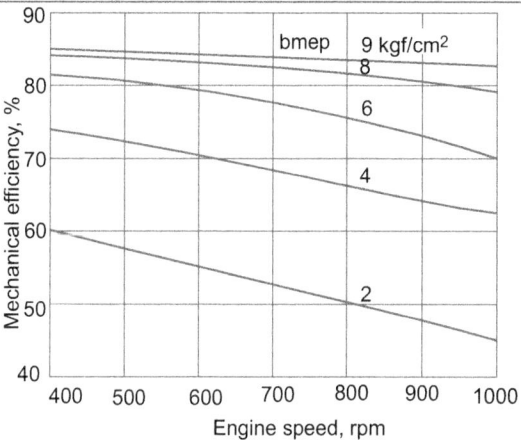

Fig. 4.23: Mechanical Efficiencies of a Supercharged Cummins CI Engine

- An increase in the supercharging pressure increases the gas load and hence large bearing areas and heavier components are needed.
- This increases the frictional forces. However, the increase in bmep is much more than increase in frictional forces.
- Typical values are 11% and 7.5% increase in frictional forces for petrol and diesel engines as compared to 40% increase in bmep for 60% supercharging.
- Thus, the mechanical efficiencies if supercharged engines are slightly better than the naturally aspirated engines.
- **Fig. 4.23** shows the mechanical efficiencies obtained for a six cylinder compression ignition Cummins supercharged engine.

4.20.3 Fuel Consumption

The power required to run the supercharger varies with different arrangements of supercharging.
- If the supercharger is directly driven by the engine some of the power developed by the engine will be used in running the supercharger. Moreover, at part loads the compression of the supercharger is not fully utilized.
- This will result in greater loss, hence the specific fuel consumption for mechanically driven superchargers will be more at part loads.
- In additional to this, the fact that highly supercharged Otto engines use very rich mixtures to avoid knock and pre-ignition will give rise to higher specific fuel consumption.
- Thus, in spite of better mixing and combustion due to reduced delay a mechanically consumption higher than a naturally aspirated engine.

The specific fuel consumption for CI engines is somewhat less than that for naturally aspirated engines due to better combustion and increased mechanical efficiency.

Exhaust driven superchargers do not require any power from the engine. Moreover, a part of the exhaust energy is utilized, thus giving about 5% better thermal efficiency at full load. This increase in efficiency results in improved fuel consumption. All turbocharged engines, if properly designed give a specific fuel consumption lower than the naturally aspirated engines.

4.21 SUPERCHARGING LIMITS

The power output of an engine is basically limited by knock, thermal and mechanical loads. Usually, one of these limits is reached earlier than the other limits depending upon the type of engine and its design of the structure, the cooling arrangements etc. For spark ignition engines knock limit is usually reached first while for diesel engines the thermal and the mechanical load limits are reached first.

4.21.1 Supercharging Limits of SI Engines (S-11)

- The degree of supercharging in SI engines is mainly limited by the knock.
- The increase in pressure and in temperature because of supercharging reduces ignition delay and consequently the engine has a knocking tendency at these pressures.
- The knock limit is dependent upon the type of fuel used, mixture ratio, spark advance and the design features of the engine, of which the valve timing and cooling system are important.

Different fuels have different knocking tendencies. Some are more sensitive to increase in pressures; others to increase in temperature. Fig. 4.24 shows highest useful compression ratio for different fuels used.

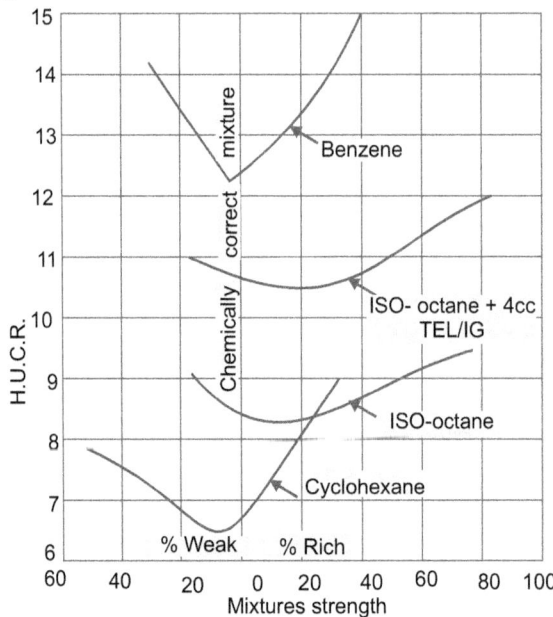

Fig. 4.24: H.U.C.R. vs. Mixture Strength Curves for Different Fuels

- The strongest knocking occurs near chemically correct mixture ratios.
- Very rich and very lean mixtures give non-knocking operation.
- Usually, supercharged engines run on rich mixtures to control knock because the lean limits of non-knocking are narrow and require very accurate control of mixture ratio.
- A slight reduction in lean mixture results in irregular and intermittent engine operation. This can occur with as early as 20% excess air.
- The use of rich mixtures results in a higher specific fuel-consumption for the supercharging engine.

4.22 SUPERCHARGING LIMITS OF CI ENGINES (S-11)

- The limit of supercharging for a CI engine is reached by thermal loading.
- If the temperature of the piston and cylinder is very high results in scuffing of piston rings and heavy liner wear.
- Fig. 4.25 shows the effect of supercharging pressure on compression and firing pressures.

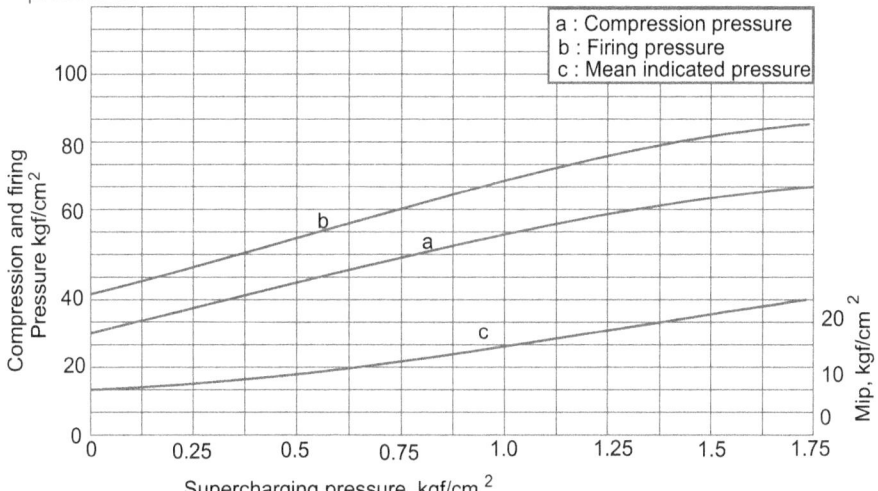

Fig. 4.25: Effect of Supercharging Pressure on Compression and Firing Pressure

- The load on bearings is increased due to increased pressure in the cylinder.
- A maximum cylinder pressure of about 85 kgf/cm^2 limits the supercharge pressure to about 2 atmospheres with a compression ratio of 15: 1 if a copper-lead bearing is used.
- Durability, reliability and fuel economy are the main considerations in limiting the degree of supercharging of a CI engine.
- Increase in maximum pressure in cylinder decreases the reliability of the engine.
- This also increases the rate of heat release and hence the thermal load on the engine is increased.

- For intake pressures greater than 2.5 atmospheres very sturdy and well cooled engines are needed.

Fuel economy is also an important consideration in deciding the degree of supercharging for a CI engine. For intake pressures less than 1.5 atmospheric the cost and complication of the supercharger is not justified.

4.23 MODIFICATION OF AN ENGINE FOR SUPERCHARGING

The power output of a naturally aspirated engine can be increased by supercharging. However, certain modifications will make the engine more suitable to supercharging.

For a diesel engine, injection system must be modified to supply increased amount of fuel; this will require greater nozzle area than the normally aspirated engine. In case of turbocharged engine the exhaust valve opens a bit earlier to supply more energy to the turbocharger. Moreover, the exhaust manifold of such an engine is insulated to reduce heat losses in contrast to the water cooled exhaust manifold of a normally aspirated engine.

4.24 METHODS OF SUPERCHARGING

A supercharger can function in a number of ways. The supercharger may be operated by the engine through gearing. Alternatively an exhaust driven turbine can run the compressor. The main types of arrangements are shown in Fig. 4.26 (a). The compressor is coupled to the engines with a step-up gearing. A part of the engine output is used to run the compressor and the net output increases due to supercharging is obtained by subtracting this power from engine gross output. Fig. 4.26 (a) shows an engine with a compressor.

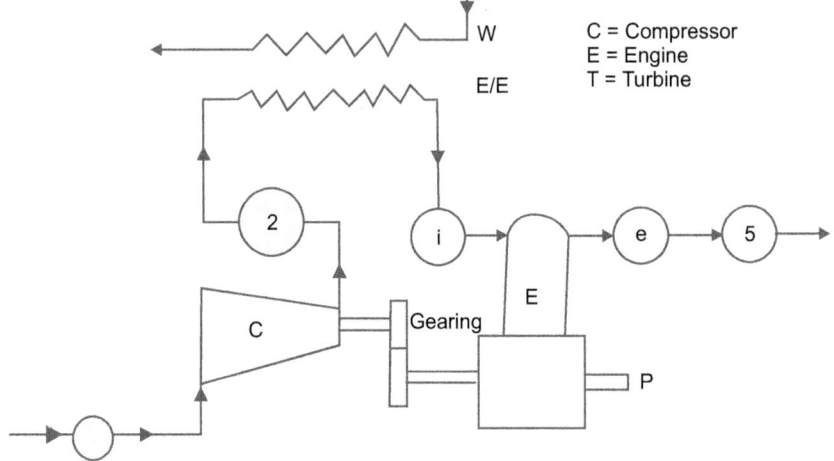

Fig. 4.26 (a)

Fig. 4.26 (b) shows an arrangement in which the exhaust energy of the engine is utilized to drive a turbine to which a compressor is coupled. The compressor turbine used is independent of the engine and has no connection with it except that of the exhaust pipe and the air inlet pipe. The engine output is not used to drive the compressor.

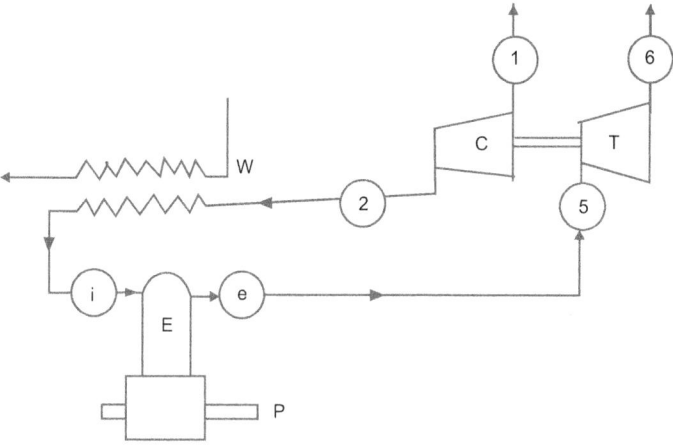

Fig. 4.26 (b)

A third arrangement is shown in Fig. 4.26 (c) in which the engine, turbine and the compressor all are coupled together with gearing.

- If the output of the turbine is not sufficient to run the compressor, this is specially so at part loads, the engine can supply additional power or if the turbine is developing more power than required to compress the air, this can be fed to engine.
- Turbocharged 2-stroke engine requires the assistance of a mechanically driven scavenge blower under part load conditions.
- Therefore, sometimes the turbocharger is coupled to the engine so that is supplies the necessary air at part load, and at full load some of the extra air can be bypassed from the compressor.

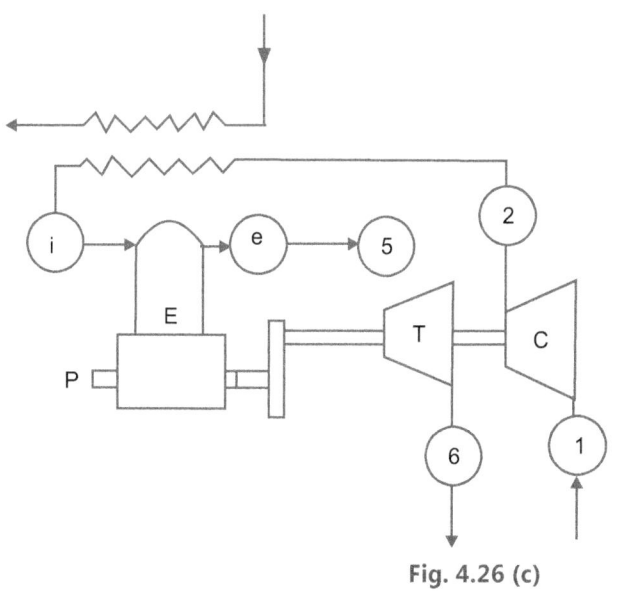

1 : Inlet
2 : Outlet from compressor
5 : Inlet to turbine
6 : Outlet from turbine
C : Compressor
E : Engine
P : Power output
T : Turbine
i : Inlet to engine
e : Exhaust from engine

Fig. 4.26 (c)

Fig 4.26 (d) shows another arrangement for supercharging the arrangement the engine supplies its total power to the compressor and the exhaust gases from the engine drive a turbine to give power output. However, it suffers from one limitation that the thermal efficiency is directly related to boost pressure ratio which reduces at part loads. Moreover, for loads below 25% or so surplus gas has to be blown off because the turbine cannot be run below a certain compressor pressure.

A separately driven compressor from an outside supply source, such as with the help of an electric motor can also be used to supercharge the engine.

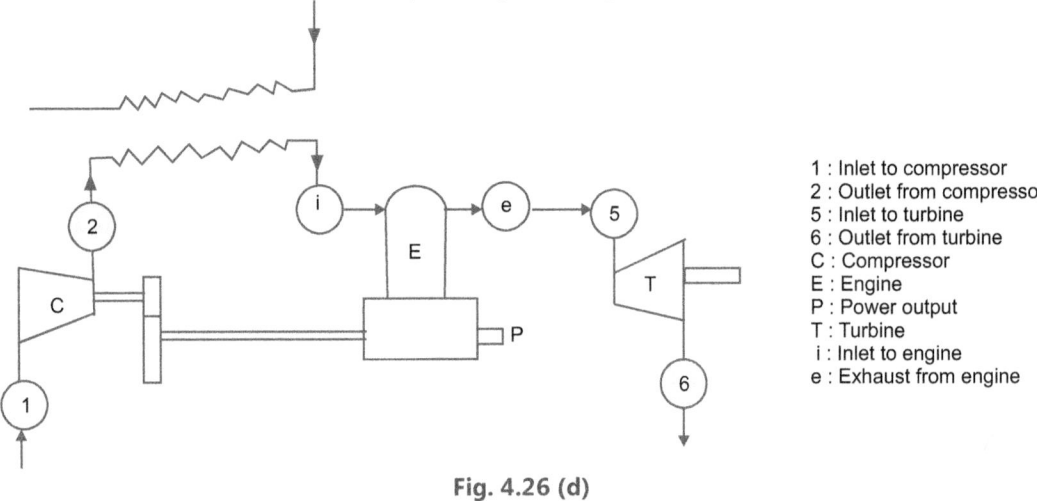

1 : Inlet to compressor
2 : Outlet from compressor
5 : Inlet to turbine
6 : Outlet from turbine
C : Compressor
E : Engine
P : Power output
T : Turbine
i : Inlet to engine
e : Exhaust from engine

Fig. 4.26 (d)

4.25 SUPERCHARGERS

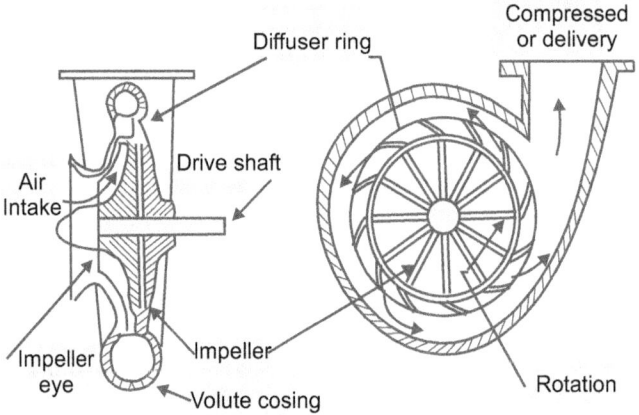

Fig. 4.27: Centrifugal Compressor

Reciprocating compressors, positive displacement type rotary blowers, roots type blower, centrifugal compressor, turbocharger all are used to supercharge engines for various applications. The following is a brief discussion of each type and its main field of application.

4.26 TURBOCHARGERS

Turbochargers are centrifugal compressors (Fig. 4.27) driven by the exhaust gas turbines. These are now-a-days extensively used for supercharging almost all types of two-stroke engines. By utilizing the exhaust energy of the engine it recovers a substantial part of energy which would otherwise go waste. Thus, the turbocharger will not draw upon the engine power.

The concept of turbocharging is very old. As early as 1907, Dr. A. J. Buchi, a Swiss engineer, patented a design for turbo charging. However, it was only in 1930's that this concept developed because the development of high efficiency compressors and turbines was a pre-requisite for successful commercialization of turbocharged engines.

Of the total heat input to an engine about 27 to 38% goes into the exhaust. However, a part of it can be used to run a gas turbine which in turn will supply more air to the engine by driving a compressor. This gas turbine is directly coupled to a centrifugal compressor which supplies extra air to the engine. Such utilization of the exhaust energy boosts engine power and results in better thermal efficiency and fuel consumption.

The power developed by the turbocharger is sufficient to drive the compressor and overcome its frictional resistance. The turbocharger is usually rather independent of the engine in that it is only connected to it by a simple exhaust pipe. The speed of the turbocharger ranges from 20,000 to 50,000 rpm.

Turbochargers are made in all sizes. The power output of turbocharged engine range from 40 kW bp to 20,000 kW bp. Below 50 kW brake power the cost of manufacture of an efficient turbine become excessive.

Methods of Turbocharging:
The turbo charging methods are:
1. Arrangement of exhaust manifolds.
2. Constant pressure turbocharging.
3. Pulse turbocharging.
4. Two stage turbocharging.
5. Miller turbocharging.
6. Hyperbar turbocharging.

Limitations of Turbocharging:
The following are the limitations of turbocharging:
(1) The use of turbocharging requires special exhaust manifolds.
(2) Fuel injection has to be modified to inject more fuel per unit time. This requires either larger pumping elements and/or larger nozzles with the same basic fuel injection equipment. This means overloading of the cams and other components.
(3) A naturally aspirated engine can digest solid particles in the inlet air without undue stress but turbocharged engines pass only the most minute material particle without damage. It can deal with carbon and other combustion products though after a few thousand hours of running blade erosion is common.
(4) The efficiency of the turbine blades is very sensitive to gas velocity so that it is very difficult to obtain good efficiency over a wide range of operation.

The most difficult problem of turbocharging is to obtain satisfactory air charging over the complete operating range of the engine.

MULTIPLE CHOICE QUESTIONS (MCQ'S)

1. The range of mechanical efficiency for automobile is ....
   - (a) 0–30%
   - (b) 30 to 50%
   - **(c) 70–80%**
   - (d) 90–100%

2. The measurement of fractioned power by Willans line is applicable only to ....
   - (a) C.I. engines at a particular speed
   - **(b) SI engines at a particular speed**
   - (c) Any engine at a particular speed only
   - (d) None of the above

3. Morse test is applicable only to ....
   - (a) single cylinder CI engines
   - (b) Single cylinder SI engines
   - **(c) multi cylinder CI engines**
   - (d) Single and multi cylinder SI and CI engines

4. The most accurate method of determining friction power is by ....
   - (a) Willan's line
   - (b) Morse test
   - (c) Motoring test
   - **(d) Measurement of brake and indicated power**

5. In the air base method of measuring air flow, the air base is provided to ....
   - (a) damp out the pulsations
   - (b) have constant temp.
   - **(c) have constant flow.**
   - (d) provide constant velocity of flow

6. The air box/swept volume ratio should be in the range for single-cylinder engine.
   - (a) 10–100%
   - (b) 200–300%
   - **(c) 500–600%**
   - (d) 1000%

7. The best method of measuring speed is by ....
   - **(a) mechanical tachometer**
   - (b) electrical tachometer
   - (c) magnetic pickup
   - (d) none of the above

8. Flame ionization detector is used for measuring ....
   - **(a) HC**
   - (b) CO
   - (c) NOX
   - (d) CO_2

9. Chemilummescence analyzer is used for measuring ....
   - (a) HC
   - (b) CO
   - **(c) NOX**
   - (d) CO_2

10. Non dispersive infrared analyzer is widely accepted instrument for measuring ....
    - (a) Unburned hydrocarbons
    - **(b) Carbone monoxide**
    - (c) Carbone dioxide
    - (d) NOX

11. If n is theorem, number of power strokes per minute in a four stroke engine is ....
    (a) n/2   (b) n
    (c) 2n   (d) 4n
12. If n' is the rpm, number of power strokes per min in a two stroke engine is ....
    (a) n/2   **(b) n**
    (c) 2n   (d) 4n
13. Mechanical efficiency is the ratio of ....
    (a) frictional power to brake power   (b) frictional power to indicated power
    (c) brake power to indicated power (d) indicated power to frictional power
14. Volumetric efficiency is a measure of ....
    (a) power of the engine   (b) speed of the engine
    (c) brathing capacity of the engine (d) pressure rise in the cylinder
15. Thermal efficiency varies ....
    (a) Inversely as specific fuel consumption
    (b) directly as specific fuel consumption
    (c) as square as specific fuel consumption
    (d) as root as specific fuel consumption
16. The spark timing and combustion rate should be such that ....
    (a) one half of the total pressure occurs at TDC
    (b) ignition delay is reduced
    (c) peak pressure occurs at TDC
    (d) none of the above
17. Indicated power is directly proportional to ....
    (a) air consumption   (b) torque
    (c) cylinder peak pressure   (d) none of the above
18. The brake thermal efficiency of SI engines is in the range of ....
    (a) 35% to 60%   **(b) 25% to 35%**
    (c) 60% to 80%   (d) None of the above
19. Performance m_{ep} shows ....
    (a) indicated power vs speed
    (b) both vs speed under various conditions
    (c) b_{emp} vs piston speed under various conditions
    (d) n^{th} vs speed under various conditions ....
20. The boiling point of a four cylinder engine is 30 with all cylinder firing and 20 with one cylinder cut. The mechanical efficiency is ....
    (a) 60%   **(b) 75%**
    (c) 80%   (d) none of the above

21. The base and stroke of a single cylinder four stroke engine are 100 mm and 160 mm respectively. If the brake torque is 50 NM the b_{mep} is ....
    (a) **5 bar** (b) 7-6 bar
    (c) 10 bar (d) 15 bar
22. The volumetric efficiency of a well designed engine is the angle ....
    (a) 30 to 40% (b) 40 to 60%
    (c) 60 to 70% **(d) 75 to 90%**
23. Power produced by the engine is given by $\dfrac{P_m LAN}{60}$ kW where N is ....
    (a) speed of the engine in rpm
    (b) speed of the engine in Hz
    (c) Number of power strokes per minute
    (d) Number of power stroke per second
24. If performance of SI engines of different manufacturer having different capacities sizes and systems are to be compared, the common parameter would be ....
    (a) engine cylinder diameter (b) B.H.P.
    (c) Speed **(d) mean effective pressure**
25. Morse test is conducted on
    (a) single cylinder engine **(b) multi cylinder engine**
    (c) VCC engine (d) horizontal engine
26. Endurance test for IC engines is conducted for
    (a) 100 hrs (b) 200 hrs
    (c) 400 hrs **(d) 500 hrs**
27. Following table shows the observations recorded during laboratory trial of a petrol engine

Observation	A	B	C	D
Fuel supplied kg/mm	0.213	0.221	0.237	0.26
Air supplied kg/min	3.45	3.45	3.46	3.44

28. Fig. shows speed characteristics of a consumption ignition engine in the Fig. what could 'B' stand for ....

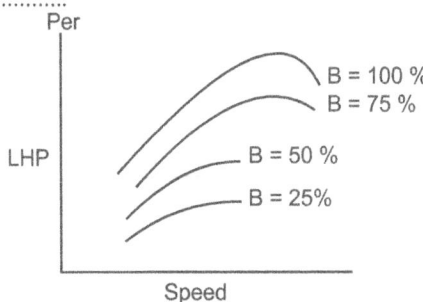

    (a) BHP **(b) fuel for full load operation**
    (c) percentage of fill load on brakes (d) percentage rated speed

29. Which of the following factors will not assist in improving thermal efficiency of a compression ignition engine?
    (a) Fine atomisation and even distribution of fuel
    (b) Minimum heat loss during combustion
    (c) Clear exhaust
    (d) High surface to volume ratio
30. Which statement is incorrect?
    (a) Morse test can be conducted on petrol engines
    (b) Morse test can be conducted on diesel engine
    (c) Morse test can be conducted only on multi cylinder engines
    (d) Morse test can be conducted on CFR engine
31. Rope brake dynamometer falls under the category of ....
    (a) Mechanical friction type dynamometer
    (b) Hydraulic dynamometer
    (c) Transmission type dynamometer
    (d) torsion type dynamometer
32. Prony brakes are used for testing ....
    (a) small engine   (b) Large capacity engines
    (c) slow speed engines   (d) High speed engines
33. Morse test is conducted on ....
    (a) single cylinder engines   (b) slow speed engines
    (c) high speed engines   **(d) multi cylinder engines**
34. Which of the following is preformed for super charging of I.C. engines?
    (a) Roots blower   **(b) Axial flow compressor**
    (c) Sliding vane type compressor (d) Reciprocating compressor
35. From the engine indicator diagram, we obtain ....
    (a) i_{mep}   (b) b_{emp}
    (c) mechanical efficiency   (d) relative efficiency
36. The most accurate dynamometer is ....
    (a) prony brake type   (b) hydraulic type
    (c) swinging field typed (d) eddy current type
37. Most commonly used dynamometer on account of its simplicity of construction is the ....
    (a) brake type   (b) hydraulic type prony
    (c) swinging field type   (d) eddy current type

38. Brake mean effective pressure in an engine depends upon its ....
    (a) speed only
    (b) torque only
    (c) speed and torque
    (d) speed and power

39. Brake thermal efficiency of S.I. engines usually varies between ....
    (a) 25 to 30%
    (b) 30% to 60%
    (c) 60% to 80%
    (d) more than 80%

40. The break power is the ....
    (a) power available at the output shaft
    (b) energy developed inside the cylinder block
    (c) energy lost due to friction
    (d) none of above

41. The total power developed by combustion of fuel is ....
    (a) bp
    (b) ip
    (c) fp
    (d) None of above

42. Mean effective press is the pressure ....
    (a) pressure acting on the crank shaft
    (b) which is acting on the piston throughout the power stroke
    (c) pressure required to inject the fuel in the combustion chamber
    (d) none of the above

43. The mean effective pressure for four stroke engine is ....
    (a) P_{im} ALN
    (b) P_{im} ALN/2
    (c) 2 P_{im} ALN
    (d) 4 P_{im} ALN

44. Fuel air ratio is ....
    (a) mass of fuel to mass of air
    (b) reciprocal of air-fuel ratio
    (c) which affects the combustion phenomenon
    (d) all of the above

45. Specific fuel consumption is ....
    (a) amount of fuel consumed per unit power developed per hour
    (b) amount of fuel consumed per unit indicated power per hour
    (c) amount of fuel consumed per hour
    (d) All of the above

46. Heat balance sheet indicates ....
    (a) amount of heat energy consumed in the combustion chamber
    (b) brake up of the total energy input into different parts
    (c) amount of energy lost through exhaust
    (d) All of above

47. The frictional power is ....
    (a) bp + ip   **(b) bp – ip**
    (c) bp × ip   (d) none of the above
48. Identify the correct statement.
    (a) power friction means less brake power
    (b) lower friction means more brake power
    (c) higher friction means high brake power
    (d) lower friction means power high brake specific fuel consumption
49. Willian's line method is applicable to ....
    (a) compression ignition engines
    (b) spark ignition engines
    (c) compression and spark ignition engines
    (d) none of the above
50. For four cylinder four stroke petrol engine the bore is 11 cm. stroke = 13 cm, engine speed is 2250 rev/min the swept volume/s is ....
    (a) 0.18 m^3/sec   **(b) 0.37 m^3/sec**
    (c) 0.0927 m^3/sec   (d) None of the above
51. A single cylinder four stroke engine having box 18 cm and stroke 36 cm, revolving at 285 rev/min having mean effective pressure 7.2 bar. The indicated power is ....
    (a) 31.4 KW   **(b) 7.85 KW**
    (c) 15.7 KW   (d) None of above
52. The ratio of indicated thermal efficiency to the air standard cycle efficiency is called ....
    (a) net efficiency   (b) efficiency ratio
    (c) relative efficiency   (d) overall efficiency
53. As compared to winter, during summer, volumetric efficiency of IC engine will ....
    (a) increase   **(b) decrease**
    (c) remain same   (d) unpredictable
54. An engine indicator is used to determine the following ....
    (a) BWP and mep   (b) temperature and IHP
    (c) m.e.p. and I.H.P.   (d) BHP and IHP
55. Pick up the wrong statement:
    (a) supercharging reduces knocking in diesel engines
    (b) there can be limited supercharging in petrol engines because of detonation
    (c) supercharging at high altitudes is essential
    (d) supercharging results in fuel economy
56. The ratio of brake power to indicated power of an engine is ....
    (a) thermal efficiency   (b) brake thermal efficiency
    (c) mechanical efficiency   (d) overall efficiency
57. Volumetric efficiency of a supercharged engine is ....
    (a) 1   (b) can't determine
    (c) greater than 1   (d) less than 1

58. The mean effective pressure indicates the ....
    (a) maximum pressure developed
    (b) minimum pressure
    (c) instantaneous pressure at any instant
    (d) average pressure
59. The frictional power (F.P.) is given by ....
    (a) F.P. = B.P. − I.P.   **(b) F.P. = I.P. − B.P.**
    (c) F.P. = B.P./I.P.   (d) F.P. = I.P./B.P.
60. The ratio of the brake mean effective pressure to the indicated mean effective pressure is called ....
    (a) mechanical efficiency   (b) overall efficiency
    (c) indicated thermal efficiency   (d) volumetric efficiency
61. Volumetric efficiency of naturally aspired engine is ....
    (a) less than 1   (b) greater than 1
    (c) 1   (d) 2
62. The power actually developed by the engine cylinder of an I.C. engine is known as ....
    (a) theoretical power   (b) actual power
    (c) indicated power   (d) none of these
63. The ratio of the work obtained at the crankshaft in a given time to the energy supplied during the same time is called ....
    (a) mechanical efficiency   **(b) brake thermal efficiency**
    (c) indicated thermal efficiency   (d) volumetric efficiency
64. The brake power of a diesel engine, keeping other parameters constant, can be increased by ....
    (a) decreasing the density of intake air
    (b) increasing the temperature of intake air
    (c) increasing the pressure of intake air
    (d) decreasing the pressure of intake air
65. The volumetric efficiency of a well designed engine may be ....
    (a) 20%   (b) 40%
    (c) 60 to 70%   (d) 90%
66. Morse test is conducted on IC engine to determine ....
    (a) volumetric efficiency of multi-cylinder engines
    (b) thermal efficiency of two-stroke engines
    (c) mechanical efficiency of multi-cylinder engines
    (d) brake power produced by individual cylinders
67. Motoring test is carried out on an IC engine to determine ....
    (a) BP   (b) IP
    (c) FP   (d) fuel consumption at full load
68. Morse test is conducted on the engine to calculate the mechanical efficiency of ....
    (a) single cylinder SI engine   (b) single cylinder CI engine
    (c) multi-cylinder engines   (d) only on two stroke engines

EXERCISE

(A) Testing and Performance

1. What are the measures of measuring engine speed?
2. How the fuel is measured in an engine test?
3. What are the various methods for measurement of brake power?
4. Describe with sketches how the brake power can be measured by the following methods:
   (a) Prony brake
   (b) Rope brake
   Compare its merits and demerits.
5. Describe with sketches the principle of a hydraulic dynamometers.
6. Describe with a sketch the principle of eddy current dynamometer.
7. What is the difference between absorption dynamometer and transmission dynamometer? Describe with a sketch a transmission dynamometer.
8. What are the various methods of measuring indicated brake power? Briefly compare their relative accuracy.
9. What is Willian's line method? To which type of engine it is applicable? What is the accuracy of this method?
10. Describe the 'Morse Test'. What is the assumption made in this test? What precautions should be taken in performing this test? What is the accuracy of this test?
11. What are the various methods for measuring friction power? Describe the 'motoring' method of measurement of friction power and comment on its accuracy?
12. Sketch a typical variable speed test performance at full throttle of an automotive type SI engine and comment on the nature of curves.
13. Sketch heat balance curves for a SI engine at constant speed and discuss the nature of curves.
14. Sketch heat balance curves for a CI engine at constant speed and discuss the nature of curves.
15. Sketch a typical variable speed test performance at full throttle of an automotive type CI engine and comment on the nature of the curves.
16. What is generalized performance map of IC engines? What is its advantage over conventional performance curves?
17. A single cylinder oil engine has a compression ratio of 10 to 1. The specific fuel consumption is 0.6 kg/kWh. The calorific value of the fuel oil is 44000 kJ/kg. Calculate: (a) The thermal efficiency and (b) The relative efficiency, assuming the engine operates on the constant volume cycle. Take r = 1.4 for air.

[(a) 13.6%, (b) 22.6%]

18. A 4-cylinder, 4-stroke petrol engine has a compression ratio of 6 to 1. A test on its engine gave the following results:

    Net brake load = 20 kg, Effective brake arm = 0.5 m, Indicated mep = 6×10^5 N/m^2, Engine speed = 2400 rpm, Fuel Consumption = 10 kg/h, Calorific value of the fuel = 44000 kJ/kg, Cylinder bore = 86 mm, Engines stroke = 100 mm.

    Calculate: (a) The mechanical efficiency, (b) The brake thermal efficiency, (c) The relative efficiency assuming the engine works on the constant volume cycle and that r = 1.4 for air, and (d) The brake mean effective pressure.

    [(a) 88.4%, (b) 20.2%, (c) 44.8%, (d) 5.35×10^5 N/m^2]

19. A test carried out on a single cylinder, 2-stroke oil engine gave the following data:

    Cylinder bore = 200 mm, Stroke = 250 mm, Engine speed = 300 rpm, Net brake torque = 500 nm, Indicating mean effective pressure = 4.9×10^5 N/m^2, Fuel consumption = 5 kg/min. Temperature rise of cooling water = 55 K, Specific heat capacity of water 4.1868 kJ/kg·K.

    Calculate: (a) The mechanical efficiency, (b) The specific fuel consumption, (c) Draw up an energy balance in kW.

    [(a) 81.6, (b) 0.318 kg/kWh, (c) Q_s = 61.1 kW, bph = 15.7 kW, $Q_{cooling\ water}$ = 15.35 kW, Exhaust etc. = 30.75 kW]

20. The following readings are obtained from a test on the single cylinder oil engine working on the 4-stroke cycle:

    Area of the indicator diagram = 4.1 cm^2, Length of the indicator diagram = 6.25 cm, Indicator spring rating = 0.9 mm, Cylinder bore = 1.5 mm, Engine stroke = 150 mm, Mean diameter of brake wheel = 0.6, Brake load = 18 kg, Spring balance reading = 3 kg, Engine speed = 480 rpm,

    Calculate: (a) Brake power, (b) Indicated power, (c) Mechanical efficiency.

    [(a) 2.23 kW, (b) 3.72 kW, (c) 60%]

(B) Supercharging

21. What are the objectives of supercharging?
22. Draw p-v diagram for an ideal otto cycle supercharged engine.
23. Explain effect of supercharging on power developed by otto engine.
24. Explain the effects of supercharging on the performance of CI engine.
25. Explain supercharging limits of CI engines.
26. Explain methods of supercharging.
27. Explain the limitations of supercharging.

✳✳✳

UNIT V

IC ENGINE SYSTEMS AND IC ENGINE EMISSIONS AND CONTROL

(A) IGNITION SYSTEMS OF S.I. ENGINE

5.1 INTRODUCTION

We know that in case of Internal Combustion (IC) engines, combustion of air and fuel takes place inside the engine cylinder and the products of combustion expand to produce reciprocating motion of the piston. This reciprocating motion of the piston is in turn converted into rotary motion of the crank shaft through connecting rod and crank.

This rotary motion of the crank shaft is in turn used to drive the generators for generating power.

We also know that there are 4-cycles of operations viz.: suction; compression; power generation and exhaust.

These operations are performed either during the 2-strokes of piston or during 4-strokes of the piston and accordingly they are called as 2-stroke cycle engines and 4-stroke cycle engines.

In case of petrol engines during suction operation, charge of air and petrol fuel will be taken in. During compression this charge is compressed by the upward moving piston. And just before the end of compression, the charge of air and petrol fuel will be ignited by means of the spark produced by means of for spark plug. And the ignition system does the function of producing the spark in case of spark ignition engines.

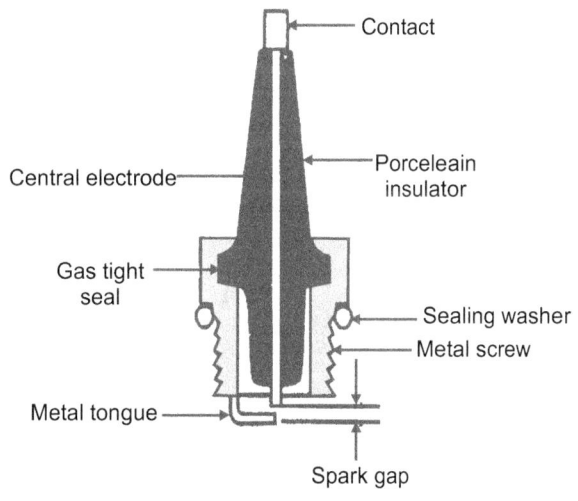

Fig. 5.1: Spark Plug

Fig. 5.1 shows atypical spark plug used with petrol engines. It mainly consists of a central electrode and metal tongue. Central electrode is covered by means of porcelain insulating material. Through the metal screw the spark plug is fitted in the cylinder head plug. When the high tension voltage of the order of 30000 volts is applied across the spark electrodes, current jumps from one electrode to another producing a spark.

Whereas in case of diesel (Compression Ignition-CI) engines only air is taken in during suction operation and in compressed during compression operation and just before the end of compression, when diesel fuel is injected, it gets ignited due to heat of compression of air. Once the charge is ignited, combustion starts and products of combustion expand i.e. they force the piston to move downwards i.e. they produce power and after producing the power the gases are exhausted during exhaust operation.

5.2 IGNITION SYSTEM TYPES

Basically Convectional Ignition systems are of 2 types:
    1.   Battery or Coil Ignition System   2.   Magneto Ignition System

Both these conventional, ignition systems work on mutual electromagnetic induction principle.

Battery ignition system was generally used in 4-wheelers, but now-a-days it is more commonly used in 2-wheelers also (i.e. Button start, 2-wheelers like Pulsar, Kinetic Honda; Honda-Activa, Scooty, Fiero etc.). In this case 6 V or 12 V battery will supply necessary current in the primary winding.

Magneto ignition system is mainly used in 2-wheelers, kick start engines. (Example, Bajaj Scooters, Boxer, Victor, Splendor, Passion etc.).

In this case magneto will produce and supply current to the primary winding. So in magneto ignition system magneto replaces the battery.

5.2.1 Battery or Coil Ignition System   (W-10, S-11, 12)

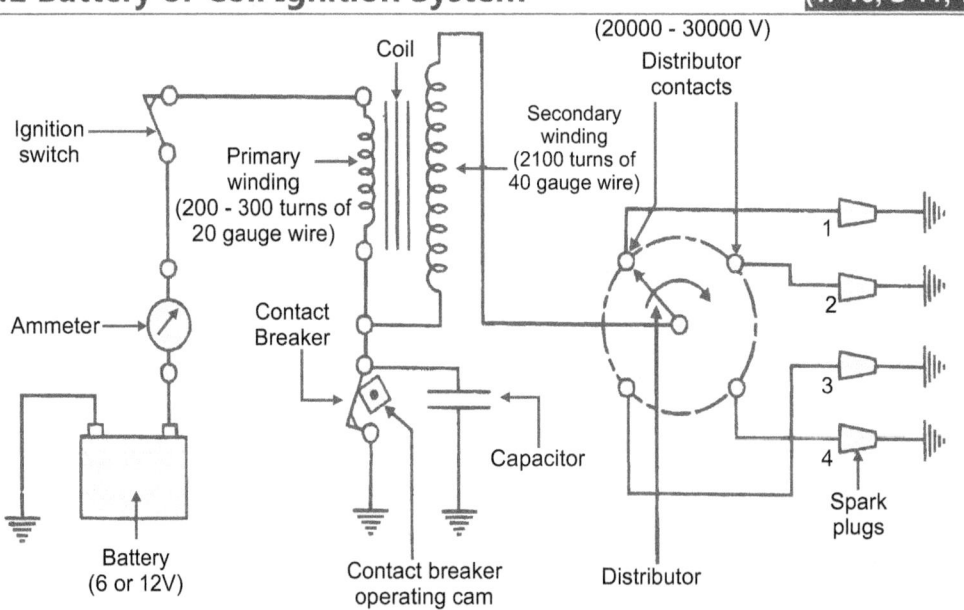

Fig. 5.2: Schematic Diagram of Coil/Battery Ignition System

Fig. 5.2 shows line diagram of battery ignition system for a 4-cylinder petrol engine. It mainly consists of a 6 or 12 volt battery, ammeter, ignition switch, auto-transformer (step up transformer), contact breaker, capacitor, distributor rotor, distributor contact points, spark plugs etc.

Note that the Fig. 5.1 shows the ignition system for 4-cylinder petrol engine, here there are 4-spark plugs and contact breaker cam has 4-corners. (If it is for 6-cylinder engine it will have 6-spark plugs and contact breaker cam will be a perfect hexagon).

The ignition system is divided into 2-circuits.

(i) **Primary circuit:** It consists of 6 or 12 V battery, ammeter, ignition switch, primary winding it has 200-300 turns of 20 SWG (Sharps Wire Gauge) gauge wire, contact breaker, capacitor.

(ii) **Secondary circuit:** It consists of secondary winding. Secondary winding consists of about 21000 turns of 40 (S WG) gauge wire. Bottom end of which is connected to bottom end of primary and top end of secondary winding is connected to centre of distributor rotor. Distributor rotor rotates and makes contacts with contact points and are connected to spark plugs which are fitted in cylinder heads (engine earth).

(iii) **Working:** When the ignition switch is closed and engine in cranked, as soon as the contact breaker closes, a low voltage current will flow through the primary winding. It is also to be noted that the contact beaker cam opens and closes the circuit 4-times (for 4 cylinders) in one revolution. When the contact breaker opens the contact, the magnetic field begins to collapse. Because of this collapsing magnetic field, current will be induced in the secondary winding. And because of more turns (@ 21000 turns) of secondary, voltage goes upto 28000-30000 volts.

This high voltage current is brought to centre of the distributor rotor. Distributor rotor rotates and supplies this high voltage current to proper stark plug depending upon the engine firing order. When the high voltage current jumps the spark plug gap, it produces the spark and the charge is ignited-combustion starts-products of combustion expand and produce power.

Note:

(1) The Function of the capacitor is to reduce arcing at the contact breaker (CB) points. Also when the CB opens the magnetic field in the primary winding begins to collapse. When the magnetic field is collapsing capacitor gets fully charged and then it starts discharging and helps in building up of voltage in secondary winding.

(2) Contact breaker cam and distributor rotor are mounted on the same shaft.

In 2-stroke cycle engines these are motored at the same engine speed. And in 4-stroke cycle engines they are motored at half the engine speed.

5.2.2 Magneto Ignition System

In this case magneto will produce and supply the required current to the primary winding. In this case as shown, we can have rotating magneto with fixed coil or rotating coil with fixed magneto for producing and supplying current to primary, remaining arrangement is same as that of a battery ignition system.

Fig. 5.3 given on next page shows the line diagram of magneto ignition system.

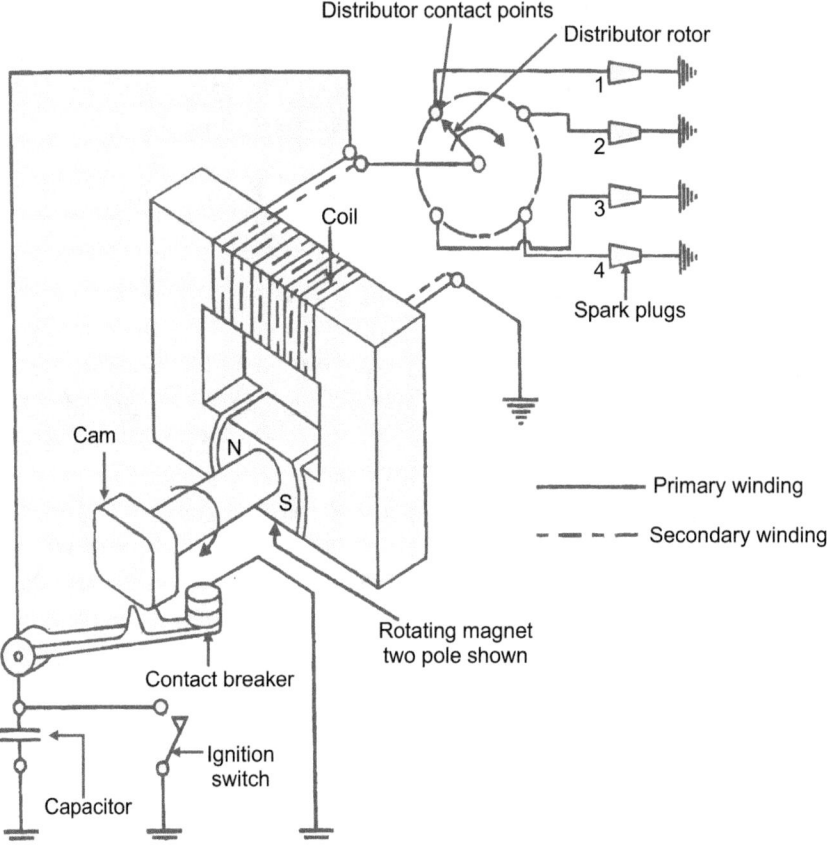

Fig. 5.3: Schematic Diagram of Magneto Ignition System

5.3 COMPARISON BETWEEN BATTERY AND MAGNETO IGNITION SYSTEM

	Battery Ignition		Magneto Ignition
1.	Battery is a must.	1.	No battery needed.
2.	Battery supplies current in primary circuit.	2.	Magneto produces the required current for primary circuit.
3.	A good spark is available at low speed also.	3.	During starting the quality of spark is poor due to slow speed.
4.	Occupies more space.	4.	Very much compact.

Battery Ignition	Magneto Ignition
5. Recharging is a must in case battery gets discharged.	5. No such arrangement required.
6. Mostly employed in car and bus for which it is required to crank the engine.	6. Used on motorcycles, scooters etc.
7. Battery maintenance is required.	7. No battery maintenance problems.

5.4 DRAWBACKS (DISADVANTAGES) OF CONVENTIONAL IGNITION SYSTEMS (W-11, 12)

Following are the drawbacks of conventional ignition systems:
- (i) Because of arcing, pitting of contact breaker point and which will lead to regular maintenance problems.
- (iii) Poor starting: After few thousands of kilometers of running, the timing becomes inaccurate, which results into poor starting (Starting trouble).
- (iii) At very high engine speed, performance is poor because of inertia effects of the moving parts in the system.
- (iv) Some times it is not possible to produce spark properly in fouled spark plugs.

In order to overcome these drawbacks Electronic Ignition system is used.

5.5 ADVANTAGES OF ELECTRONIC IGNITION SYSTEM

Following are the advantages of electronic ignition system
1. Moving parts are absent-so no maintenance.
2. Contact breaker points are absent-so no arcing.
3. Spark plug life increases by 50% and they can be used for about 60000 km without any problem.
4. Better combustion in combustion chamber, about 90-95% of air fuel mixture is burnt compared with 70-75% with conventional ignition system.
5. More power output.
6. More fuel efficiency.

5.6 TYPES OF ELECTRONIC IGNITION SYSTEM

Electronic Ignition System are as follow:
1. Capacitance Discharge Ignition system
2. Transistorised system
3. Piezo-electric Ignition system
4. The Texaco Ignition system

5.6.1 Capacitance Discharge Ignition System

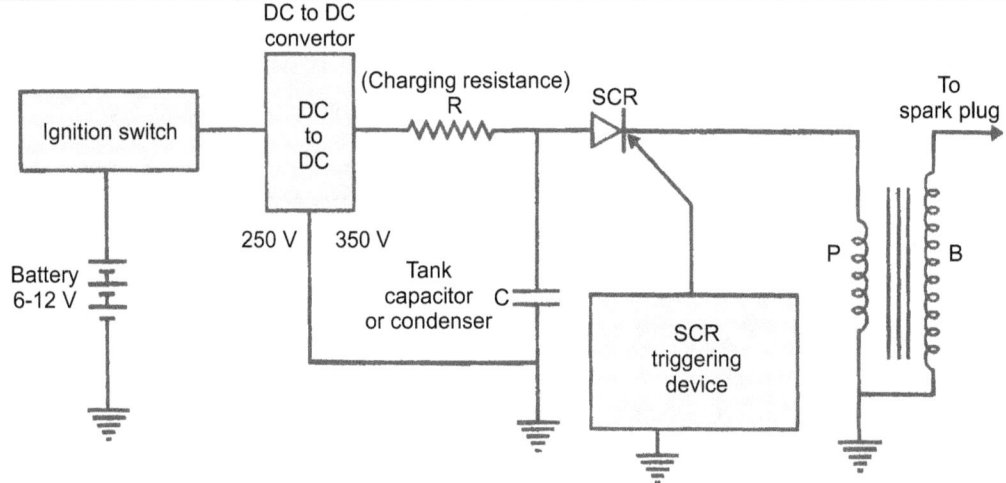

Fig. 5.4: Capacitance Discharge Ignition System

It mainly consists of 6-12 V battery, ignition switch, DC to DC convertor, charging resistance, tank capacitor, Silicon Controlled Rectifier (SCR), SCR-triggering device, step up transformer, spark plugs.

A 6-12 volt battery is connected to DC to DC converter i.e. power circuit through the ignition switch, which is designed to give or increase the voltage to 250-350 volts. This high voltage is used to charge the tank capacitor (or condenser) to this voltage through the charging resistance. The charging resistance is also so designed that it controls the required current in the SCR.

Depending upon the engine firing order, whenever the SCR triggering device, sends a pulse, then the current flowing through the primary winding is stopped. And the magnetic field begins to collapse. This collapsing magnetic field will induce or step up high voltage current in the secondary, which while jumping the spark plug gap produces the spark, and the charge of air fuel mixture is ignited.

5.6.2 Transistorised Assisted Contact (TAC) Ignition System

Fig. 5.5 shows the TAC system.

Advantages:
1. The low breaker-current ensures longer life.
2. The smaller gap and lighter point assembly increase dwell time, minimise contact bouncing and improve repeatability of secondary voltage.
3. The low primary inductance reduces primary inductance reduces primary current drop-off at high speeds.

Disadvantages:
1. As in the conventional system, mechanical breaker points are necessary for timing the spark.
2. The cost of the ignition system is increased.
3. The voltage rise-time at the spark plug is about the same as before.

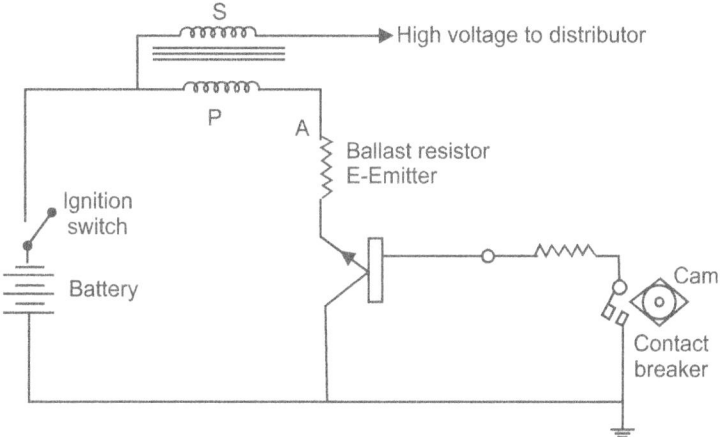

Fig. 5.5: Transistorised Assisted Contact (TAC) Ignition System

5.6.3 Piezo-Electric Ignition System

The development of synthetic piezo-electric materials producing about 22 kV by mechanical loading of a small crystal resulted in some ignition systems for single cylinder engines. But due to difficulties of high mechanical loading need of the order of 500 kg timely control and ability to produce sufficient voltage, these systems have not been able to come up.

5.6.4 The Texaco Ignition System

Due to the increased emphasis on exhaust emission control, there has been a sudden interest in exhaust gas recirculation systems and lean fuel-air mixtures.

To avoid the problems of burning of lean mixtures, the Texaco Ignition system has been developed. It provides a spark of controlled duration which means that the spark duration in crank angle degrees can be made constant at all engine speeds. It is a AC system. This system consists of three basic units: a power unit, a control unit and a distributor sensor.

This system can give stable ignition up to A/F ratios as high as 24 : 1.

5.7 FIRING ORDER

- The order or sequence in which the firing takes place, in different cylinders of a multicylinder engine is called **Firing Order.**
- In case of SI engines the distributor connects the spark plugs of different cylinders according to **Engine Firing Order.**

Advantages:
1. A proper firing order reduces engine vibrations.
2. Maintains engine balancing.
3. Secures an even flow of power.

- Firing order differs from engine-to-engine.
- Probable firing orders for different engines are:
  - 3 cylinder = 1-3-2
  - 4 cylinder engine (inline) = 1-3-4-2
    1-2-4-3
  - 4 cylinder horizontal opposed engine = 1-4-3-2
    (Volkswagen engine)
  - 6-cylinder in line engine = 1-5-3-6-2-4
    (cranks in 3 pairs) 1-4-2-6-3-5
    1-3-2-6-4-5
    1-2-4-6-5-3
  - 8 cylinder in line engine 1-6-2-5-8-3-7-4
    1-4-7-3-8-5-2-6
    8 cylinder V type 1-5-4-8-6-3-7-2
    1-5-4-2-6-3-7-8
    1-6-2-5-8-3-7-4
    1-8-4-3-6-5-7-2

Cylinder 1 is taken from front of inline and front right side in V engines.

(B) LUBRICATION SYSTEMS IN IC ENGINE

5.8 INTRODUCTION

Lubrication of moving parts by means of oil, grease etc. is essential for proper functioning and to reduce friction between the moving parts of automobiles.

5.9 PURPOSE AND FUNCTIONS OF LUBRICATION

Following are the purposes and functions of lubrication:
  (i) To make the moving parts function properly by reducing friction.
  (ii) By reducing friction wear of moving parts will be minimised.
  (iii) Lubricating oil will take up the shocks/vibrations by small extent.
  (iv) Corrosion of parts will be prevented.
  (v) To reduce noise.
  (vi) Because of lubricating oil film between piston rings and cylinder walls, it does not allow any leakage of gases across the rings.

5.10 PROPERTIES OF GOOD LUBRICATING OIL

A good engine lubricating oil must have following properties or characteristics:

1. Viscosity	2. Flash point
3. Fire point	4. Cloud point
5. Pour point	6. Oiliness
7. Corrosion	8. Colour
9. Dilution	10. Emulsification
11. Physical stability	12. Chemical stability
13. Sulphur content	14. Specific gravity
15. Neutralization number	16. Adhesiveness
17. Film strength	18. Cleanliness.

1. **Viscosity:** It is a property which offers resistance to flow.
   - Thick oils have high viscosity.
   - Medium oils have medium viscosity.
   - Thin oils have low viscosity.

   It is inversely proportional to temperature i.e. it decreases as the temperature rises.
   - Lighter oils are recommended for automobile engines.

2. **Flash point:** It is the temperature at which lubricating oil will flash when a small flame is passed across it.
   - It should be sufficiently high to avoid flashing of oil vapours at the temperature occurring in common use.

3. **Fire point:** If the oil is heated after the flash point has been reached, the lowest temperature at which oil will burn continuously.
   - The fire point should be high, so that oil does not burn in service.

4. **Cloud point:** It is the temperature at which oil changes from liquid state to solid state, when subject to low temperatures. In some cases oil starts solidifying which makes it to appear cloudly.
5. **Pour point:** It is the temperature which oil will pour.
   - This property must be considered because of its effect on starting of engines in cold climate.
6. **Oiliness:** An oil is said to be oil when it has oiliness. This property is highly desirable in helping the lubricant to adhere the cylinder walls.
7. **Corrosion:** A lubricant should reduce the corrosion of parts.
8. **Colour:** It is not that important property.
   - It is a test for checking the uniformity of any given grade/brand of oil.
9. **Dilution:** If the piston rings are worn out, then petrol vapour may leak into crank case and dilute the lubricating oil in the crank case.
10. **Emulsification:** A lubricating oil when mixed with water, is emulsified and looses its lubricating property. The emulsification number is an index of an oil to emulsify with water.
11. **Physical stability:** It should be physically stable for a required range of temperature i.e. it should not solidify or vapourise.
12. **Chemically stable:** It should be chemically stable.
13. **Sulphur content:** It must be less otherwise it promotes corrosion.
14. **Specific gravity:** It is a measure of density of oil.
    - It is determined by a hydrometer. The scale used recommended by America Petroleum Institute API° gravity.
15. **Neutralisation number:** Oil may contain alkaline or acid products.
    - Neutralisation number is the weight in milligrams of KOH to neutralize the acid content of one gram of an oil.
16. **Adhesiveness:** It is the property because of which oil particles tick to metal surfaces.
17. **Film strength:** It is the property because of which oil retains a film between two surfaces at high speed and load.
18. **Cleanliness:** It should be clean.

5.11 LUBRICATING SYSTEM

The functions of lubrication system is to provide a sufficient quantity of filtered oil to all moving parts. There are 3 basic types of lubrication systems.

5.11.1 Petrol or Mist System of Lubrication

In this system, lubricating oil will be added to petrol tank only i.e. it is mixed in the petrol in a definite proportion (i.e. generally 30-60 ml/litre e.g. Bajaj scooters, M-80, Luna, Pride etc.). Lubricating oil particles will go to engine cylinder and various parts for lubrication along with air fuel mixture. The various parts to be lubricated are as under.

Parts of IC Engines which requires lubrication are:
- (1) Cylinder
- (2) Piston
- (3) Piston rings
- (4) Gudgeon pin
- (5) Crank pins
- (6) Main bearings
- (7) Cam and camshaft
- (8) Timing gears
- (9) Rocker arms
- (10) Valves etc.

5.11.2 Wet Sump System

These are used in relatively small engines. The bottom of the crankcase contains oil pan (sump) which acts as oil reservoir and oil cooler. Oil supplied to different parts by 2 different methods.

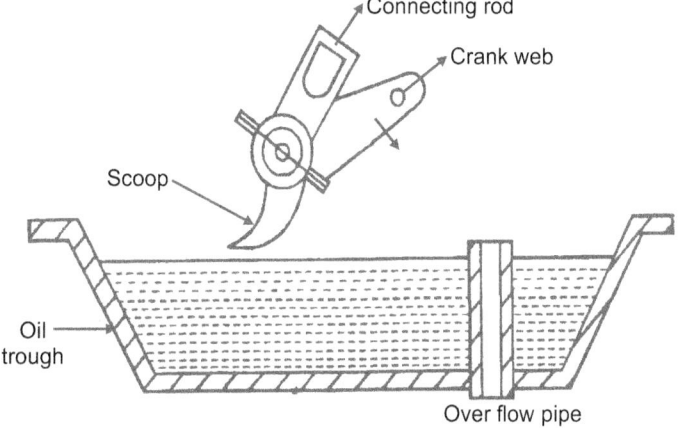

Fig. 5.6: Splash System of Lubrication

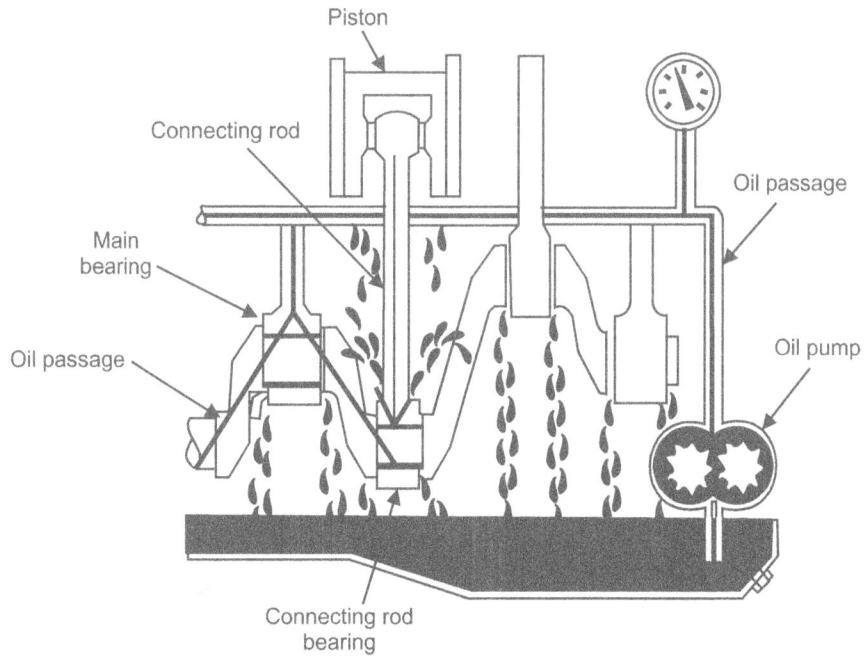

Fig. 5.7: Schematic Diagram of Wet Sump Lubrication System (Pressure Force Feed)

(a) Splash Lubrication: In this type, the oil from the sump is pumped to the oil trough which is located below the crank pins. The extended end of connecting rod known as dipper strikes the oil surface and splashes oil over various parts of engine. The oil returns to sump due to gravity.

(b) Pressure Lubrication: This system mainly consists of a gear pump, oil strainer, oil gallery made up of copper tubing. In this system oil flows to different parts through the drilled passages in the crank shaft and connecting rod.

Oil pump draws filtered oil through the oil strainer and pumps it to the main oil gallery. From where it goes to the main bearings. After lubricating main bearings, lubricating oil will go to crank pin bearings through the drilled holes. And from the crank pin bearings, oil will flow to piston pin bearings through the oil hole drilled through connecting rod web. Small amount of oil is also sprayed on the cylinder walls to lubricate between cylinder walls and piston rings.

Cam shaft, valves mechanisms are lubricated through the separate lines.

5.11.3 Dry Sump System

In this system the oil falling from various parts is removed by a scavenging pump. Oil passes through a filter and goes to the supply tank, oil is again pumped from the supply tank and supplied to various engine parts. Thus oil is prevented from accumulating in this base of engine.

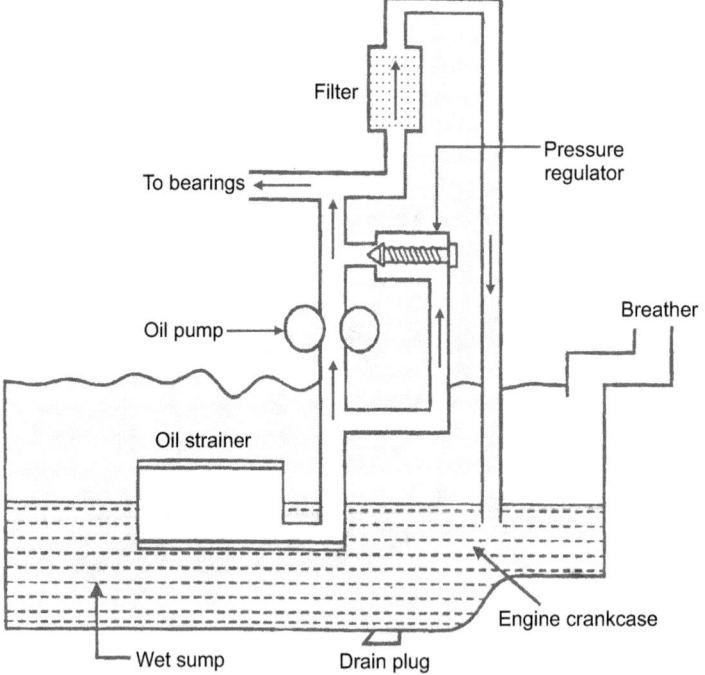

Fig. 5.8: Schematic Diagram of Wet Sump Lubricating System

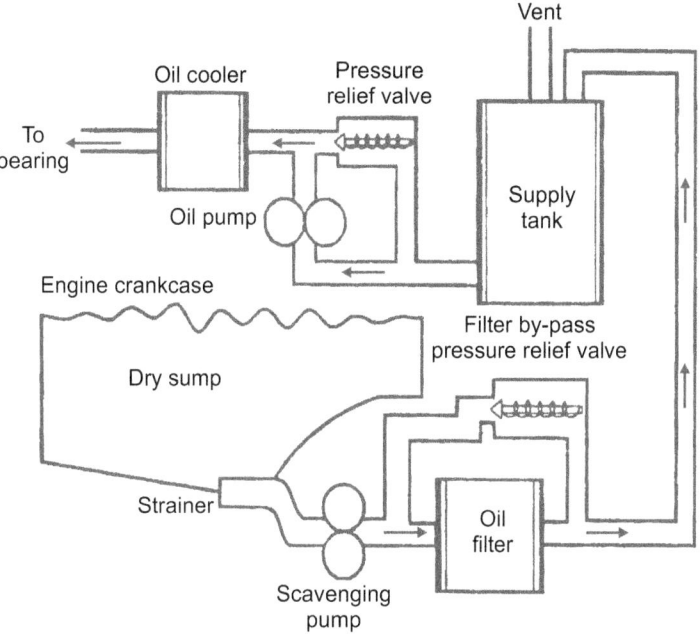

Fig. 5.9: Schematic Diagram of a Dry Sump Lubricating System

This uses only forced (pressure) types feed system. A filter and strainer are used in the oil circuit to remove the foreign materials and impurities. In large, IC engines oil is cooled with the help of cold water to maintain its viscosity in the required range and to prevent it from lubrication.

5.12 IMPORTANT PARTS OF LUBRICATION SYSTEM

Following are the important parts of a lubrication system:

(a) **Oil sump:** It contains lubricating oil and it is the bottom most part of crank case. It is made out of casting.

(b) **Oil pump:** Oil pump is a pump which pumps lubricating oil to various parts to be lubricated. Generally, oil pump will be a gear type pump. It consists of two inter meshing gears in a pump casing. When one of the gears is rotated, other gear will also rotate and the oil will be trapped in the pockets between the pump casing and gear teeth and oil will be pumped.

As shown in Fig. 5.10 it also consists of pressure relief valve to release pressures.

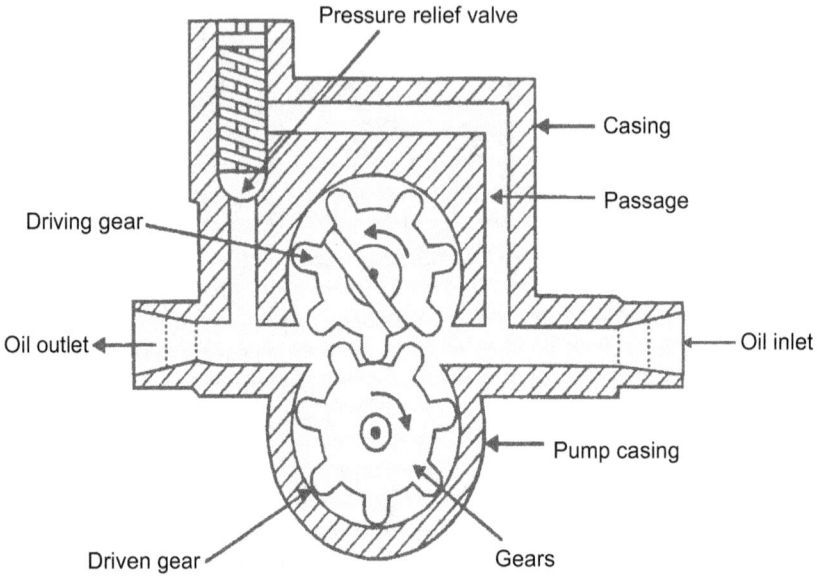

Fig. 5.10: Gear Pump with Pressure Relief Valve

(c) Oil filters: As the name implies oil filters are used in lubricating system to filter out the dirt particles. Various types of oil filters are as under:

(i) Cartridge type, (ii) Edge type, (iii) Centrifugal type

(i) Cartridge type: Fig. 5.11 shows the cartridge type oil filter. It mainly consists of filter element enclosed in a casing as shown. The oil to be filtered enters from top, when it flows down it gets filtered and clean oil will go to main oil gallery, from where it goes to various parts for lubrication.

Filter cartridge element is cleaned oftenly or replaced if required during servicing.

(ii) Edge type oil filter: Fig. 5.12 shows an edge type oil filter. It mainly consists of a central spindle to which a number of discs are attached as shown. Also there is a square rod having alternate discs attached. The clearance between the discs on central spindle and square rod is very very small. When the impure oil enters from oil inlet and flows through the discs to oil outlet, impurities are collected in the clearance between the discs and clean oil comes out from oil outlet.

(iii) Centrifugal type of filter: Fig. 5.13 shows the centrifugal type oil filter. It mainly consists of a central hallows spindle, rotor casing, oil tubes, and stationary casing as shown.

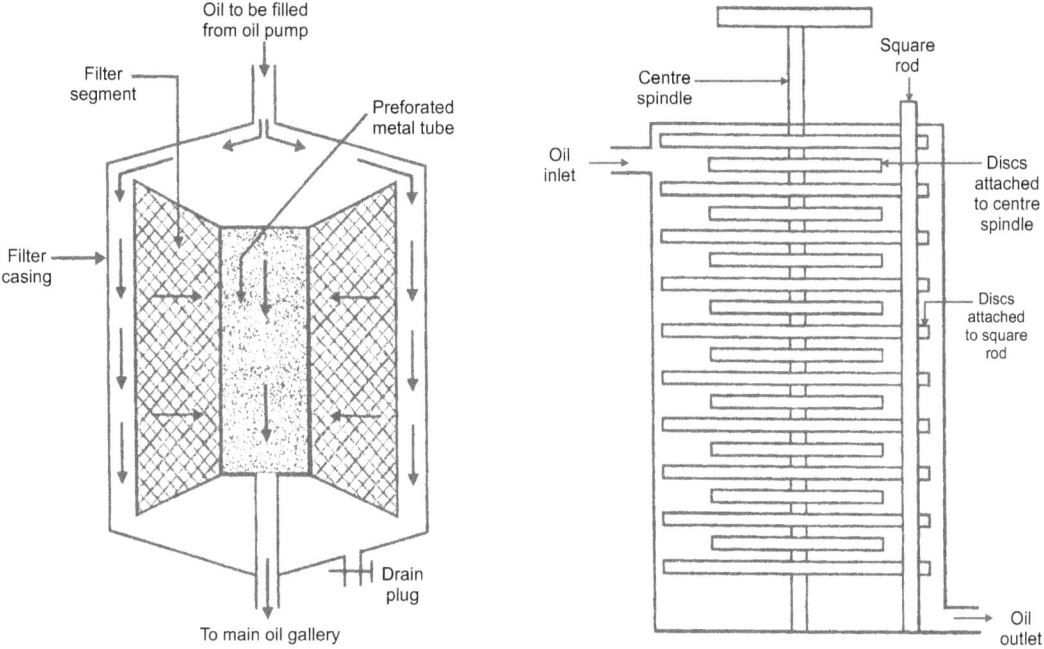

Fig. 5.11: Cartridge Type Oil Filter   Fig. 5.12: Edge Type Oil Filter

Impure oil enters from oil inlet and flows to oil tubes through the spindle holes. From the oil tubes oil jets are issued under pressure. Oil jets when issued it impinges on the walls of stationary casing and rotor starts rotating, pure oil gets separated and comes out from oil outlet.

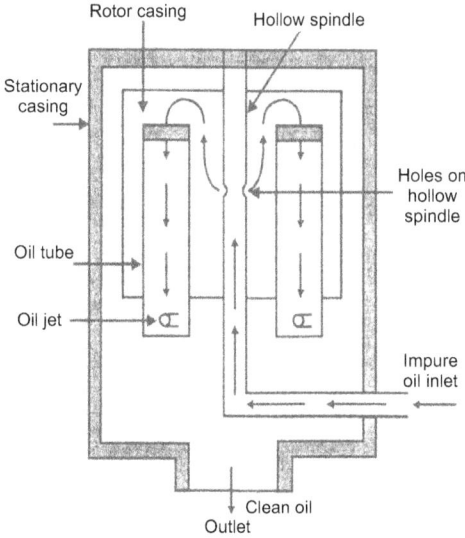

Fig. 5.13: Centrifugal Type Oil Filter

(d) Oil strainers: It consists of a wire mesh. It prevents any impurities from entering the oil pump.

(C) STARTING SYSTEM

5.13 INTRODUCTION

In olden days, auto vehicles were started by manual cranking i.e. (hand cranking ex. Willys Jeep and foot cranking kick start scooters/motor cycles). But now-a-days auto vehicles are started by cranking motors or starting motors. And an arrangement of starting switch, cranking motor, mechanical drive, battery etc. which is used to crank the engine is called starting system.

To start the vehicle – starter switch is turned 'ON' – then current starts flowing to starter motor – starter motor starts rotating – causes the ring gear on FW to rotate – thereby causes the crank to rotate.

Note: In small vehicles 1-3 kgm torque is required and in heavy vehicles 5-15 kgm torque is required.

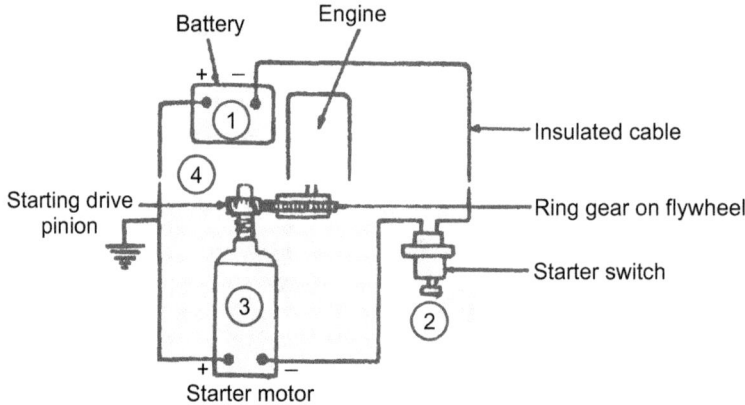

Fig. 5.14: Schematic Arrangement of Starting System Used on Modern 4-Wheelers

1. Battery, 2. Starter switch, 3. Starter motor, 4. Starting drive.

When the crank is rotated, piston is made to reciprocate. So during suction, charge (air or air + petrol fuel) is taken in and compressed, and just before the end of compression, the charge is ignited either by spark or by heat of compression of air for SI and CI engines respectively and the engine starts.

Once the engine starts – starter drive goes out of mesh.

5.14 TYPES OF STARTER MOTORS

Following are the various starter motors:
1. Shunt-wound starter motor.
2. Series-wound starter motor.
3. 2-pole motor.
4. 3-pole motor.
5. 4-pole motor.

5.15 TYPES OF STARTER DRIVE MECHANISMS

For starting purpose following starter drive mechanisms are used:

(A) Bendix Drive Mechanism:
   (i) Bendix drive with torsion spring.
   (ii) Bendix drive with compression spring.
   (iii) Folo-thru drive mechanism.

(B) Over running clutch drive mechanism.

(C) Dyer drive mechanism.

5.16 STARTING DRIVE – STANDARD BENDIX DRIVE HAVING TORSIONAL SPRING

When the starter switch is turned 'ON'. Then current starts flowing to starter motor – the armature shaft rotates – but the pinion mounted on the shaft does not rotate, because of unbalanced weight. It moves towards L.H.S. direction till it is stopped by collar. Then pinion starts rotating to engages with flywheel ring gear to crank the engine. Once the engine starts – starter drives goes out of mesh.

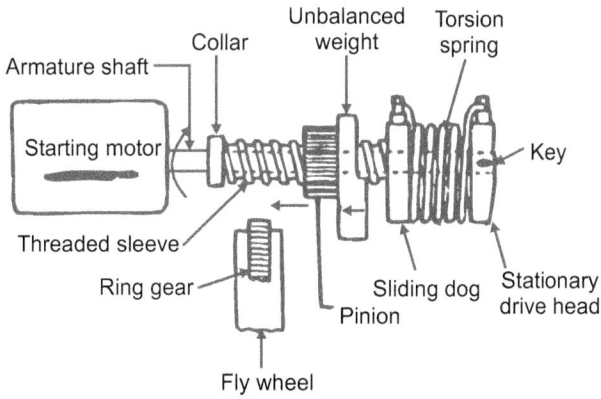

Fig. 5.15: Bendix Drive with Torsioonal Spring

(D) COOLING SYSTEMS IN IC ENGINE

5.17 INTRODUCTION

We know that in case of Internal Combustion engines, combustion of air and fuel takes place inside the engine cylinder and hot gases are generated. The temperature of gases will be around 2300-2500°C. This is a very high temperature and may result into burning of oil film between the moving parts and may result into seizing or welding of the same. So, this temperature must be reduced to about 150-200°C at which the engine will work most efficiently. Too much cooling is also not desirable since it reduces the thermal efficiency. So, the object of cooling system is to keep the engine running at its most efficient operating temperature.

It is to be noted that the engine is quite inefficient when it is cold and hence the cooling system is designed in such a way that it prevents cooling when the engine is warming up and till it attains to maximum efficient operating temperature, then it starts cooling.

It is also to be noted that,
(i) About 20-25% of total heat generated is used for producing brake power (useful work).
(ii) Cooling system is designed to remove 30-35% of total heat.
(iii) Remaining heat is lost in friction and carried away by exhaust gases.

5.18 METHODS OF COOLING

There are mainly 2-types of cooling systems:
(i) Air cooled system
(ii) Water cooled system

(i) Air cooled system: Air cooled system is generally used in small engines say upto 15-20 kW and in aeroplane engines.

In this system fins or extended surfaces are provided on the cylinder walls, cylinder head etc. Heat generated due to combustion in the engine cylinder will be conducted to the fins and when the air flows over the fins, heat will be dissipated to air.

The amount of heat dissipated to air depends upon:
(i) Amount of air flowing through the fins.
(ii) Fin surface area
(iii) Thermal conductivity of metal used for fins.

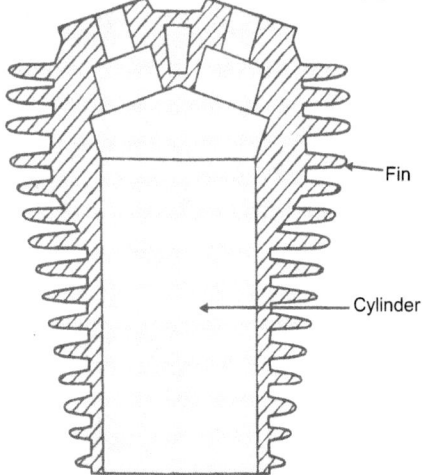

Fig. 5.16: Cylinder with Fins

Advantages of Air Cooled System:
Following are the advantages of air cooled system:
(a) Radiator/pump are absent hence the system is light.
(b) In case of water cooling system there are leakages, but in this case there are no leakages.
(c) Coolant and antifreeze solutions are not required.
(d) This system can be used in cold climates, where if water is used it may freeze.

Disadvantages:
(a) Comparatively it is less efficient.
(b) It is used in aeroplanes and motorcycle engines where the engines are exposed to air directly.

5.19 WATER COOLING SYSTEM

In this method, cooling water jackets are provided around the cylinder, cylinder head, valve seats etc. The water when circulated through the jackets, it absorbs heat of combustion. This hot water will then be cooling in the radiator partially by a fan and partially by the flow developed by the forward motion of the vehicle. The cooled water is again recirulated through the water jackets.

Types of Water Cooling System:

There are two types of water cooling system:

(i) **Thermosiphon System:** In this system the circulation of water is due to difference in temperature (i.e. difference in densities) of water. So in this system pump is not required but water is circulated because of density difference only.

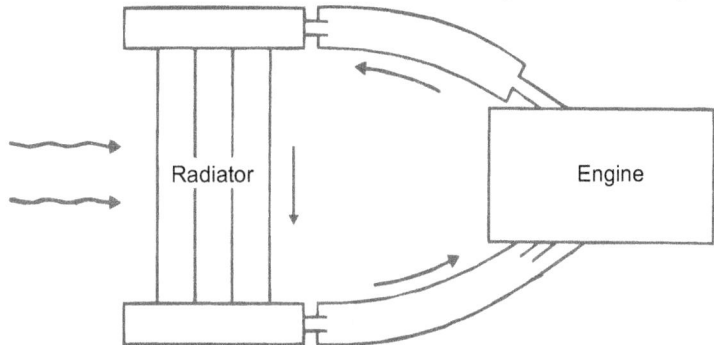

Fig. 5.17: Thermosiphon System of Cooling

(ii) **Pump Circulation System:** In this system circulation of water is obtained by a pump. This pump is driven by means of engine output shaft through V-belts.

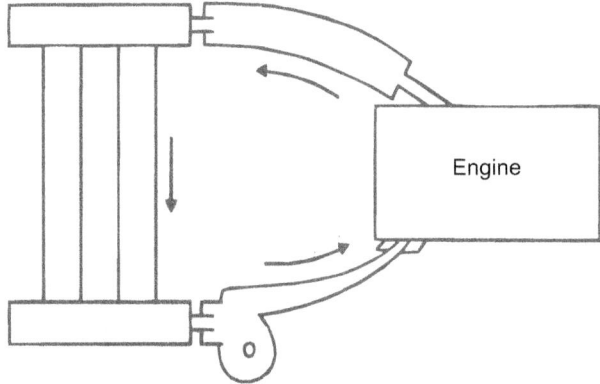

Fig. 5.18: Pump Circulation System

5.20 COMPONENTS OF WATER COOLING SYSTEM

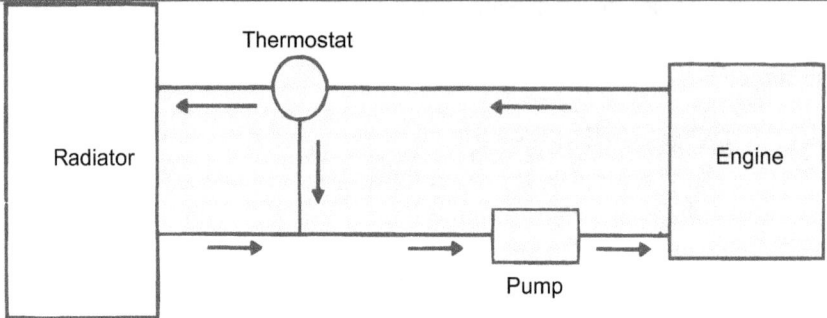

Fig. 5.19: Water Cooling System using Thermostat Valve

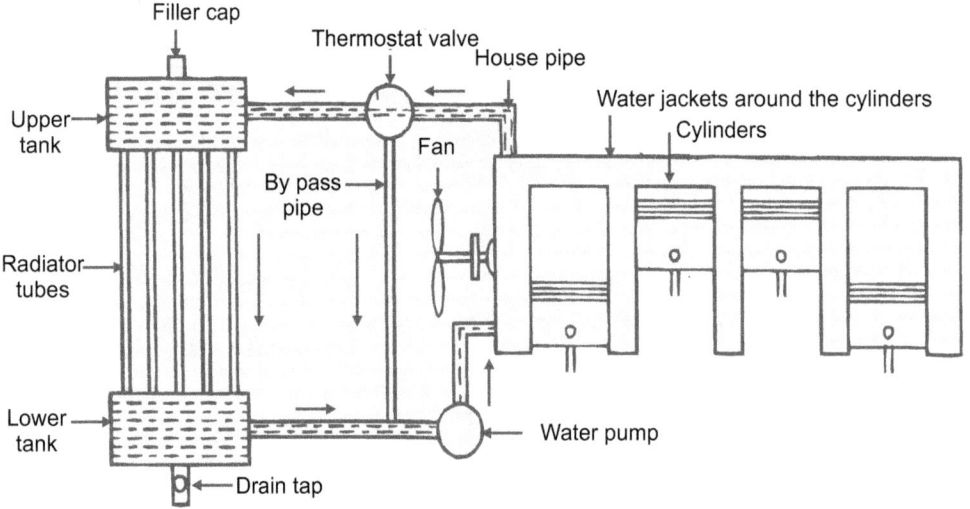

Fig. 5.20: Water Cooling System of a 4-cylinder Engine

Water Cooling system mainly consists of: 1. Radiator, 2. Thermostat valve, 3. Water pump, 4. Fan, 5. Water Jackets, 6. Antifreeze mixtures.

(a) **Radiator (S-09, 10, 11, 13)**: It mainly consists of a upper tank and lower tank and between them is a core. The upper tank is connected to the water outlets from the engines jackets by a hose pipe and the lover tank is connect to the jacket inlet through water pump by means of hose pipes.

There are 2-types of cores: (a) Tubular (b) Cellular as shown.

When the water is flowing down through the radiator core, it is cooled partially by the fan which blows air and partially by the air flow developed by the forward motion of the vehicle. As shown through water passages and air passages, wafer and air will be flowing for cooling purpose.

It is to be noted that radiators are generally made out of copper and brass and their joints are made by soldering.

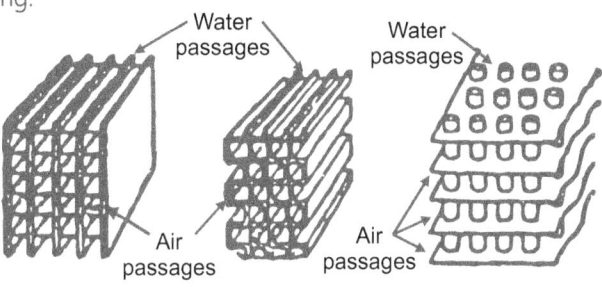

Tubular radiator sections

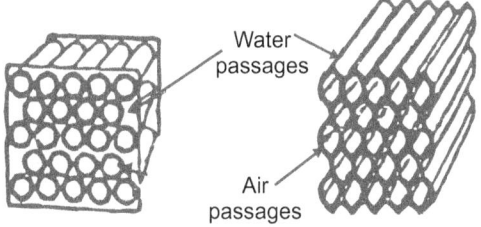

Circullar radiator sections
Fig. 5.21: Radiator Sections

(b) Thermostat Valve: It is a valve which prevents flow of water from the engine to radiator, so that engine readily reaches to its maximum efficient operating temperature. After attaining maximum efficient operating temperature, it automatically begins functioning. Generally, it prevents the water below 70°C.

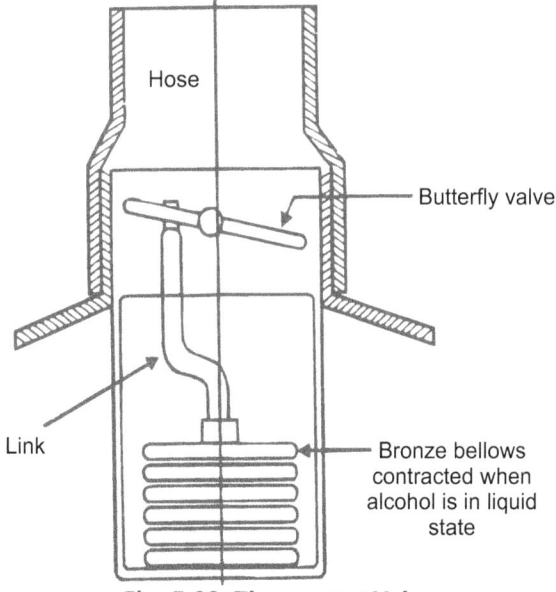

Fig. 5.22: Thermostat Value

Fig. 5.22 shows the Bellow type thermostat valve which is generally used. It contains a bronze bellow containing liquid alcohol. Bellow is connected to the butterfly valve disc through the link.

When the temperature of water increases, the liquid alcohol evapourates and the bellow expands and in turn opens the butterfly valve, and allows hot water to the radiator, where it is cooled.

(c) Water Pump: It is used to pump the circulating water. Impeller type pump will be mounted at the front end.

Pump consists of an impeller mounted on a shaft and enclosed in the pump casing. The pump casing has inlet and outlet openings.

The pump is driven by means of engine output shaft only through belts. When it is driven water will be pumped.

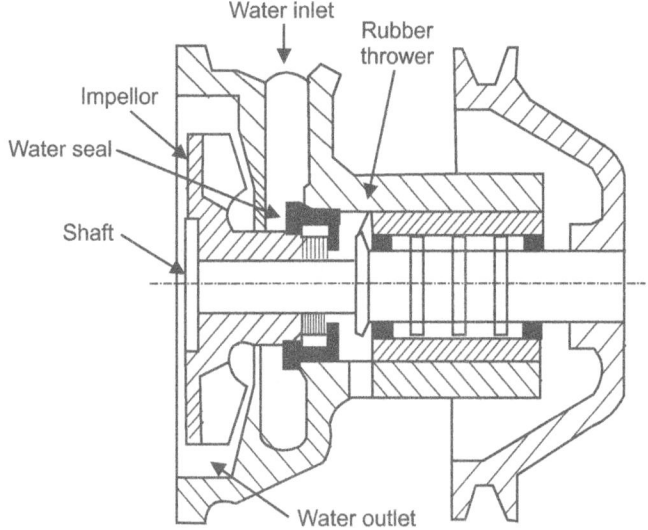

Fig. 5.23: Water Pump

(d) Fan: It is driven by the engine output shaft through same belt that drives the pump. It is provided behind the radiator and it blows air over the radiator for cooling purpose.

(e) Water Jackets: Cooling water jackets are provided around the cylinder, cylinder head, valve seats and any hot parts which are to be cooled. Heat generated in the engine cylinder, conducted through the cylinder walls to the jackets. The water flowing through the jackets absorbs this heat and gets hot. This hot water will then be cooled in the radiator.
(Ref. Fig. 5.24).

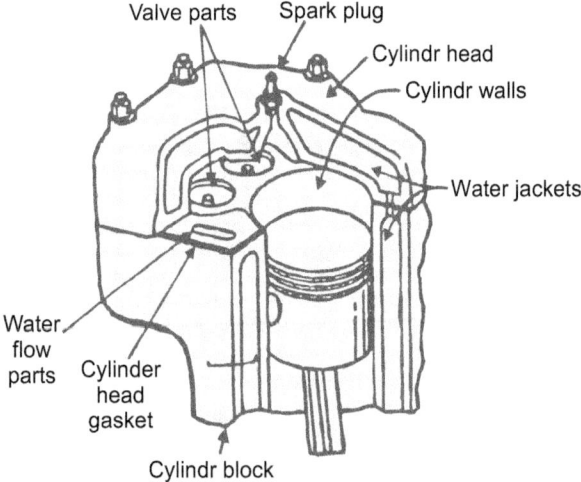

Fig. 5.24: Water Jackets

(f) Antifreeze Mixture: In western countries if the water used in the radiator freezes because of cold climates, then ice formed has more volume and produces cracks in the cylinder blocks, pipes, radiator. So, to prevent freezing antifreeze mixtures or solutions are added in the cooling water.

The ideal antifreeze solutions should have the following properties:
1. It should dissolve in water easily.
2. It should not evapourate.
3. It should not deposit any foreign matter in cooling system.
4. It should not have any harmful effect on any part of cooling system.
5. It should be cheap and easily available.
6. It should not corrode the system.

No single antifreeze satisfies all the requirements. Normally following are used as antifreeze solutions.
(a) Methyl, ethyl and isopropyl alcohols.
(b) A solution of alcohol and water.
(c) Ethylene Glycol.
(d) A solution of water and Ethylene Glycol
(e) Glycerin along with water etc.

5.21 ADVANTAGES OF WATER COOLING SYSTEM
1. Uniform cooling of cylinder, cylinder head and valves.
2. Specific fuel consumption of engine improves by using water cooling system.
3. If we employ water cooling system, then engine need not be provided at the front end of moving vehicle.
4. Engine is less noisy as compared with air cooled engines, as it has water for damping noise.

Disadvantages:
(a) It depends upon the supply of water.
(b) The water pump which circulates water absorbs considerable power.
(c) If the water cooling system fails then it will result in severe damage of engine.
(d) The water cooling system is costlier as it has more number of parts. Also it requires more maintenance and care for its parts.

(E) GOVERNING SYSTEM IN IC ENGINES

5.22 INTRODUCTION

Governor is the mechanism or device used to maintain constant speed irrespective of changes of load on the engine. And the method of maintaining constant speed is called as Governing.

There are three distinct methods adopted for varying the power of the engine in sympathy with the action of governor, these methods will again differ in the mechanical means adopted in regulating the power. In all the cases the ordinary centrifugal governor is used for controlling the mechanical devices.

5.23 METHODS OF GOVERNING (S-10, W-11)

The following is the usual classification adopted for the various methods of governing.

    (a) **Hit and Miss Governing (S-10, W-11):** In this type of governing, the action of the governor causes the fuel inlet valve to remain closed during a cycle so that no fuel is admitted. The engine will thus perform an idle cycle. Or in other words, when the engine speed increases beyond certain limit, the combustion is missed for a few cycles by preventing the charge to enter into the cylinder. So the engine runs idle for few cycles.

It results into the following two disadvantages.

1. Efficiency decreases because of idle cycles along with actual working cycles.
2. Since the combustion is missed during same cycles, it produces very uneven turning movement for the crank shaft.

The hit and miss method of governing is in common use in small gas engines, and is actually quantitative governing.

In small, light oil engines the hit and miss mechanism operates on the exhaust valve and prevents it opening when the speed is too high; the burnt gases are thus retained in the cylinder and are alternately compressed and expanded until the speed is reduced.

In case of gas and diesel engines, if the speed increases certain limit, the combustion inside the cylinder is missed during few cycles by not allowing the fresh charge to the cylinder.

Then the engine will perform idle cycle.

- This method will slightly lower the efficiency by increasing the idle strokes.
- It also has the disadvantages of producing more uneven turning moment on the crank shaft.
- The number of omitted explosions increases with the increase in speed.
- The usual method adopted in case of gas engines is to omit opening of gas valve, by pulling the knife edge projection 'P' towards right.
- And incase of diesel engines – putting the plunger of the pump out of action and during this engine performs idle cycle.

Hit and Miss Governing for Gas Engines:

When the speed is normal, the gas valve is lifted from its seat thus gas is supplied to the engine.
- The lift of valve is obtained with the help of cam 'H' and lever EFG. (End 'E' is lifted once in two revolutions of crank shaft).
- When the load on engine decreases – engine speed increases – flyballs of centrifugal governor fly out due to increased CF forces, sleeve 'A' moves upwards.

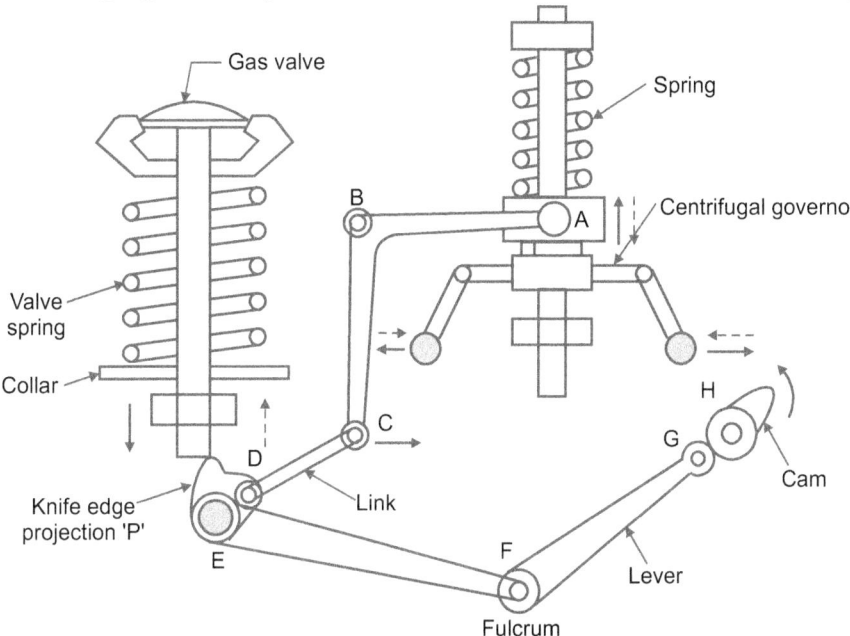

Fig. 5.25: Hit and Miss Governing for Gas Engines

This operates bell crank lever ABC and its end 'C' to move towards RHS.
- So knife edge projection 'P' moves towards RHS direction.
- So it prevents lifting of gas valve and prevents gas supply and the engine performs idle cycle.
- When the engine speed again drops, valve is operated i.e. flyballs move in inwards, sleeve 'A' moves downwards – Lever ABC and 'C' moves left (LHS) and knife edge projection 'P' lifts the valve and gas is supplied.

(b) Quantitative Governing: This method varies the power of the engine by regulating the quantity of mixture (fuel and air) which enters the cylinder. This is sometimes done by throttling the mixture before it enters the cylinder, the movement of the throttle valve being regulated by the lift of the centrifugal governor. Another method of quantitative governing, used in gas engines, is by varying the lift of the inlet valve, and thus reducing the quantity of mixture entering the cylinder.

So, as discussed above, generally centrifugal types of governors are used. Fig. 5.26 shows a centrifugal type of governor used with petrol engine.

Cylindrical part is the air horn and the narrowest cross-section of which is the venturi. Throttle valve is provided to regulate the amount of charge (air + fuel mixture) entering the engine cylinder. Throttle valve is connected to the Governor as shown.

Now when the load on the engine increase, the speed of the engine decreases and because of reduced speed, fly weights move inwards (shown by dotted arrows) and the sleeve moves downwards. Then it opens the throttle valve more and hence more charge enters the engine cylinder to develop more power and to bring engine speed constant.

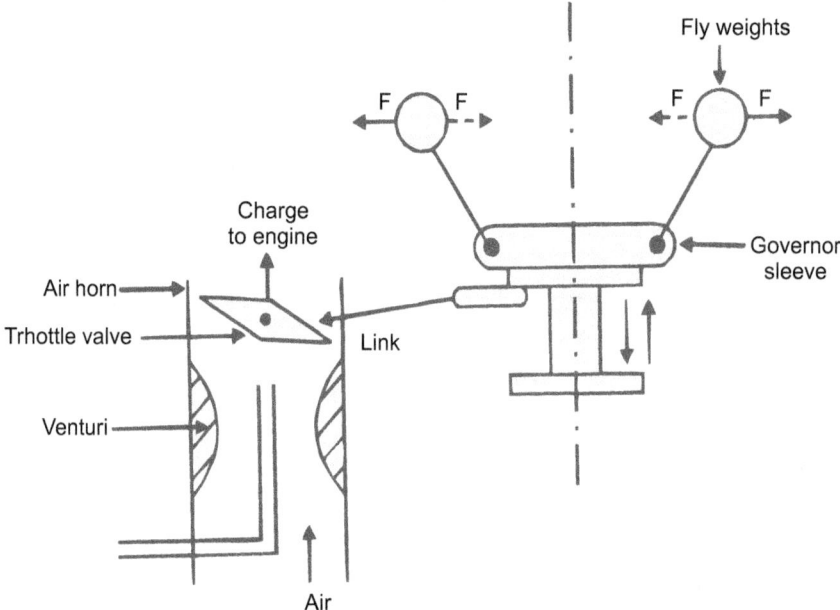

Fig. 5.26: Centrifugal Governor

And when the load on the engine decreases-speed increases-fly weights move outwards (shown by arrow)-close the throttle valve accordingly-reduce the supply of charge. Hence the engine develops required less power and maintain constant speed.

(c) **Qualitative Governing:** In this method of governing the strength of the mixture is altered by the action of the centrifugal governor, thus varying the quality of the mixture. This is done by regulating the amount of fuel entering the cylinder, air supply remaining constant. This method of governing is used in all heavy oil engines using pure air compression.

The amount of fuel entering the cylinder is varied by the action of the governor. It may vary the stroke of the oil pump or it may by pass part of the fuel back to the oil tank or it may delay the closing of the suction valve of the fuel pump. All of these methods will cause a variation in the point of cut-off.

5.24 IMPORTANT TYPES OF CENTRIFUGAL GOVERNORS USED WITH THE ENGINES

Following are the important centrifugal governors.

(i) **Watt Governer (Simple Conical Governer):** It is named after Watt, when the load decreases-speed increases fly weights move outwards as shown by arrows and lift the sleeve. On the other hand when the load increase speed decreases, weight move inwards (shown by dotted arrows) and sleeve moves downwards. (Ref. Fig. 5.27).

(ii) **Porter Governer:** If the central load is provided on the sleeve then watts governor is called its Porter Governor. (Ref. 5.28).

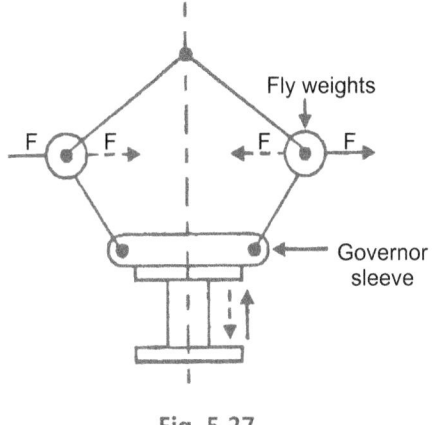

Fig. 5.27

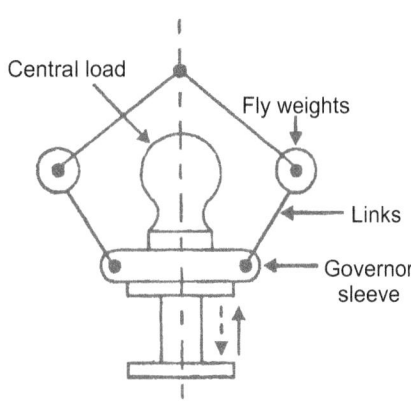

Fig. 5.28

(iii) **Proell Governor:** In this governor fly weights are provided on the extension of lower links as shown and it contains central load. (Ref. Fig. 5.29).

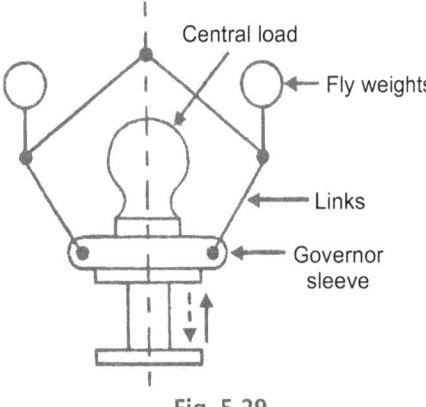

Fig. 5.29

(iv) **Hartnell Governor:** It mainly consists of 2-bell crank levers and compression spring as shown. To the one end of bell crank levers, fly weight are provided and other end rollers. The levers are pivoted at 'O'. When the speed increases fly weight move outwards and the lever which is provided at 'O' lifts the rollers and sleeve against the compression of spring.

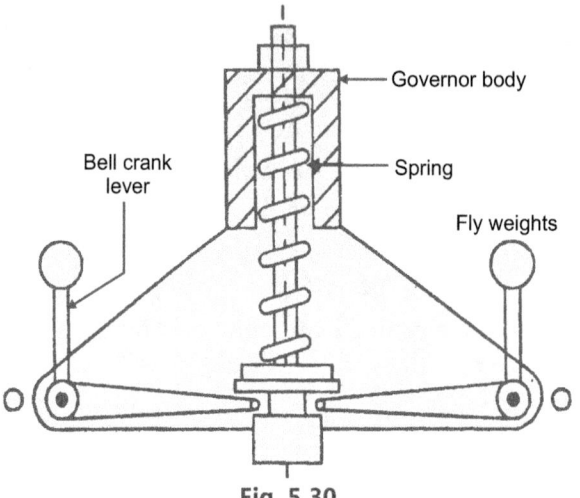

Fig. 5.30

(v) Spring Controlled Governor of Gravity Type (S-09, 13, W-12): Fig. 5.31 shows spring controlled gravity governor. It mainly consists of 2-bell crank levers. They are provided with rollers at one end and fly weights at the other. Rollers will be resting over the cap which forms top end of shaft. Under the cap spring is provided as shown.

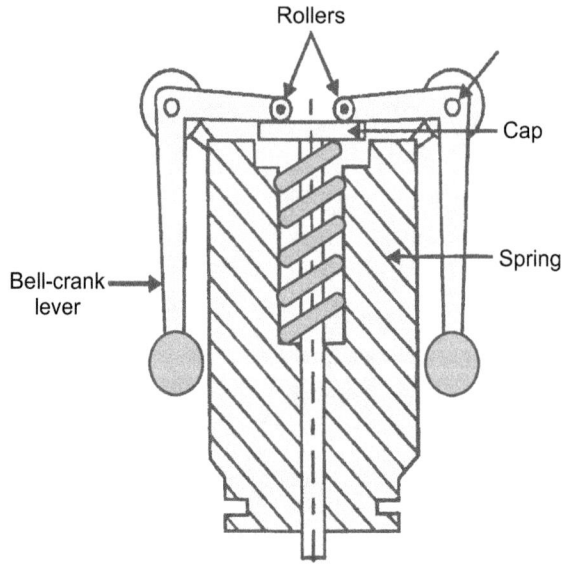

Fig. 5.31

As we know the load decreases, speed increases and fly weight move outwards and the other press cap which in turn compresses the spring.

5.25 APPLICATION OF GOVERNORS

Used in Petrol engines, Diesel engines, Steam engines and Steam turbines etc.

(F) INTAKE AND EXHAUST SYSTEMS

5.26 INTRODUCTION

Fig. 5.32 shows the General Arrangement of intake and exhaust system of an I.C. Engine (particularly SI).

As shown LH side in intake system and RH side carries exhaust system.

As shown intake system has two circuits.

(i) **Fuel circuit:** It contains fuel tank-fuel filter – fuel pump – carburettor – intake manifold to engine cylinder.

(ii) **Air circuit:** It contains air filters to carburettor.

As we know air-fuel mix is produced in carburettor and supplied to cylinder through the engine intake manifold.

Then, this air-fuel mix after combustion produces power and are exhausted through the exhaust manifold – silencer – filter with catalytic converter – Tail pipe. Through this tail pipe gases are exhausted to the atmosphere.

As we know for diesel engines,

(i) Instead of carburettor we have fuel pump and injector.

(ii) Spark plug is absent: Charge gets ignited by the heat of compression of air.

Normally, cylinders have 2-valves, but we can have 4 valves or even 6 valves.

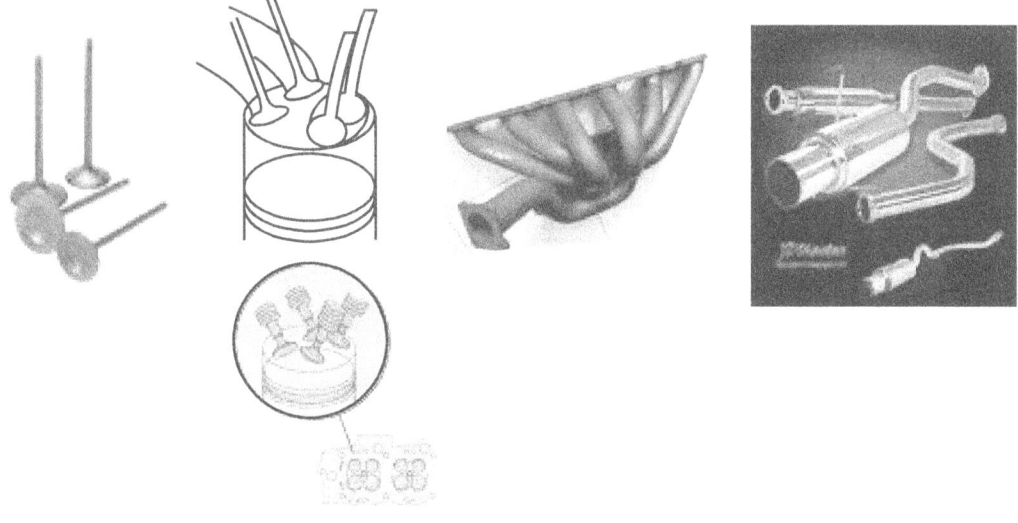

| Valves | Cylinder with 4-valves | Exhaust Manifold for Multicylinder Engine | Silencers |

Fig. 5.32

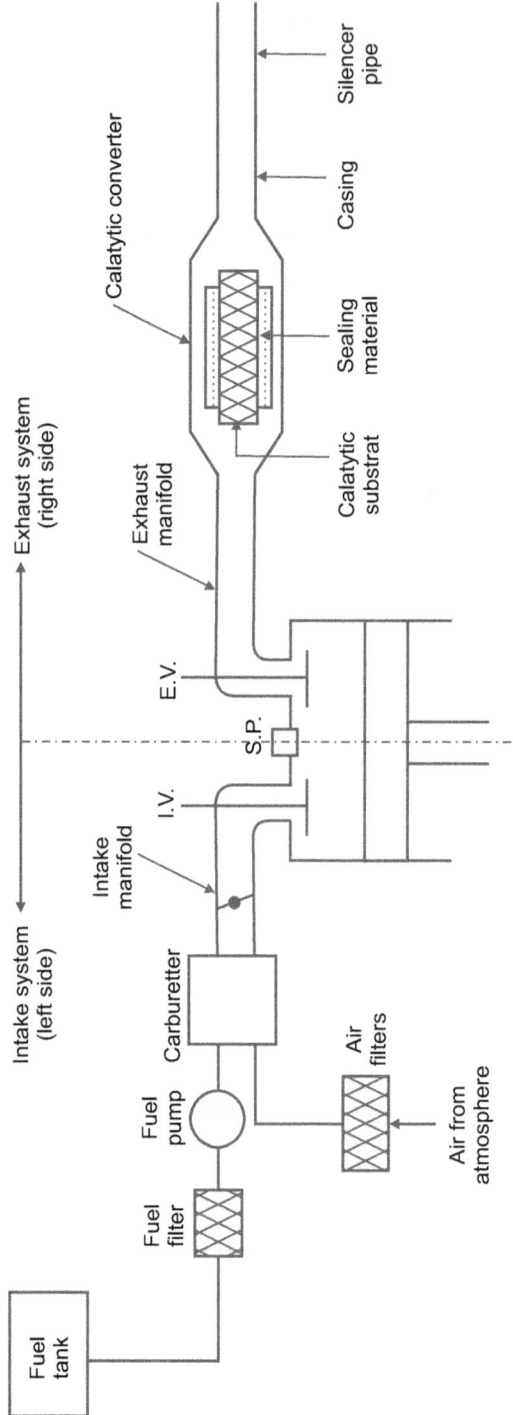

Fig. 5.33: Intake and Exhaust System

5.27 VARIOUS PARTS AND FUNCTIONS OF INTAKE SYSTEM

- Fuel tank   –   Storage of fuel.
- Fuel filter   –   To filter ten fuel and supply clean fuel to the cylinder.
- Fuel pump   –   To suck to fuel from the tank and supply under slight pressure to carburettor.
- Carburettor   –   In a device which produces and supplies correct air-fuel mix to engine cylinder depending upon the load on the engine.
- Air filter   –   To filter the atmospheric air and supply clean air to engine.
- Intake manifold –   It is made out of a casting, through which charge enters engine cylinder.

5.28 VARIOUS PARTS AND THEIR FUNCTIONS OF EXHAUST SYSTEM

1. **Exhaust manifold:**

   It is also made out of casting. Gases after producing power are exhausted through exhaust manifold into the silencer.

2. **Silencer:**

   It is the pipe through which gases are exhausted to atmosphere through its tail end.

3. **Catalytic converter:**

   It is a device which chemically treats the pollutants and converts HC to H_2O and splitting of NO to N_2 and O_2.

Normally, exhaust pollutants.

CO   converted into harmless CO_2.

HC   converted into harmless H_2O.

NO_x converted into harmless N_2 and O_2.

(G) DRIVE TRAIN (CAM SHAFT, VALVES ETC.)

5.29 INTRODUCTION

As we know in case of I.C. engines, combustion of air and fuel takes place inside the engine cylinder and products of combustion expand and produce the reciprocating motion of piston. The reciprocating motion of piston is converted into rotary motion of crank shaft. This rotary motion of crank shaft is used to:

(i) Drive the generators for generating powers.

(ii) Drive the automobile wheels.

Also this rotary motion is used to drive the cam shaft through crank shaft sprocket (1), camshaft sprocket (2) wheel, chain (3).

It is to be noted that cam shaft chain wheel in a 4-stroke engine rotates at half engine speed, so has twice as many teeth as crank shaft sprocket.

As we get the rotary motion of cam shaft (4) depending upon position of cam and (relative opening of valves) cam lifts tappets (5) – push rods (6). Push rods in turn lift rocker arm. Rocker arm is pivoted about rocker shaft (7). Rocker arm front and gets pressed down and valve opens.

Note:

1. **Cam shaft:** It is made out of forged steel or cast iron machined and hardened to give maximum resistance to wear. Cams are provided on cam shaft. Cams are spaced at intervals to match the firing order.

2. Note that to drive cam shaft either chain drive or belt drivers are used as shown in Fig. 5.34.

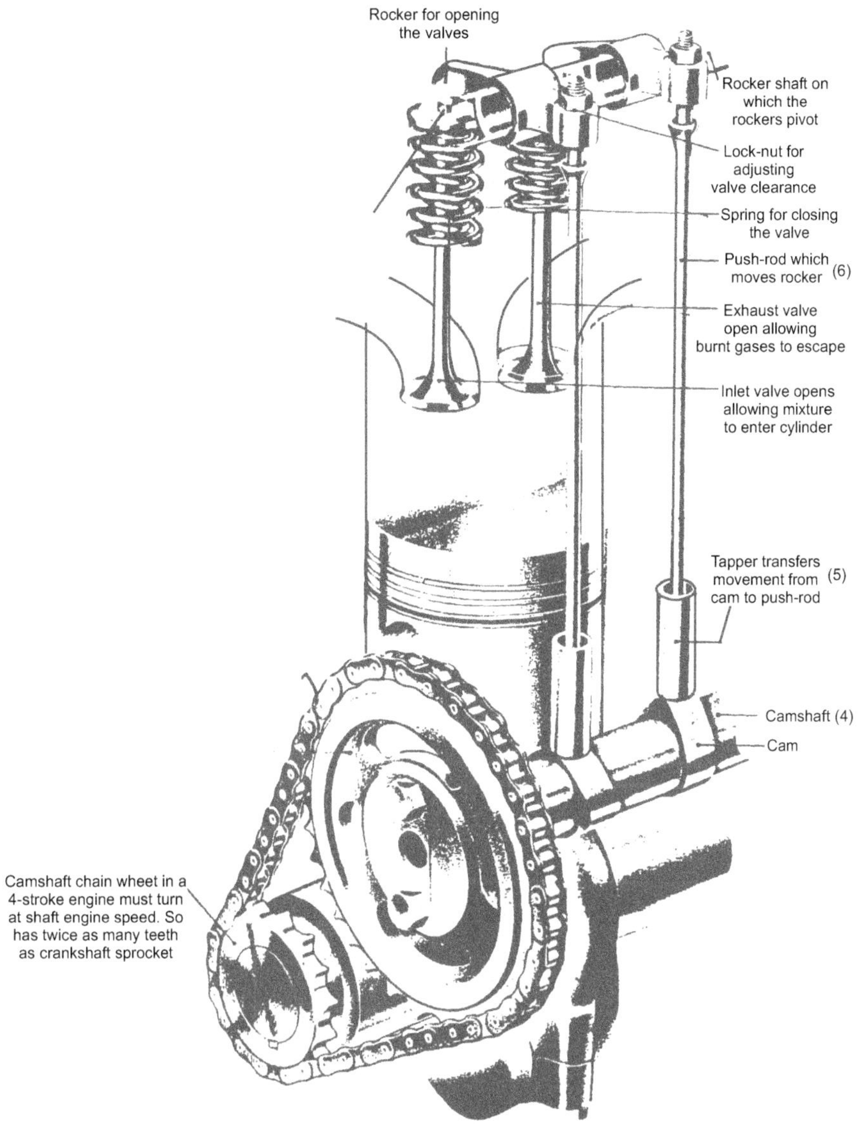

Fig. 5.34: Typical Valve Gear Train Using Push-Rods

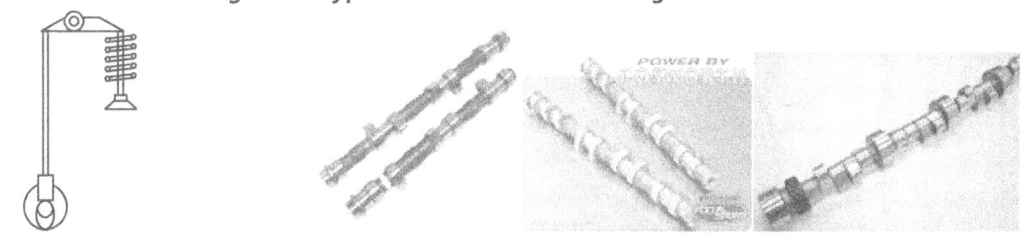

Cam and Valve Mechanism	Cam Shafts

Fig. 5.35

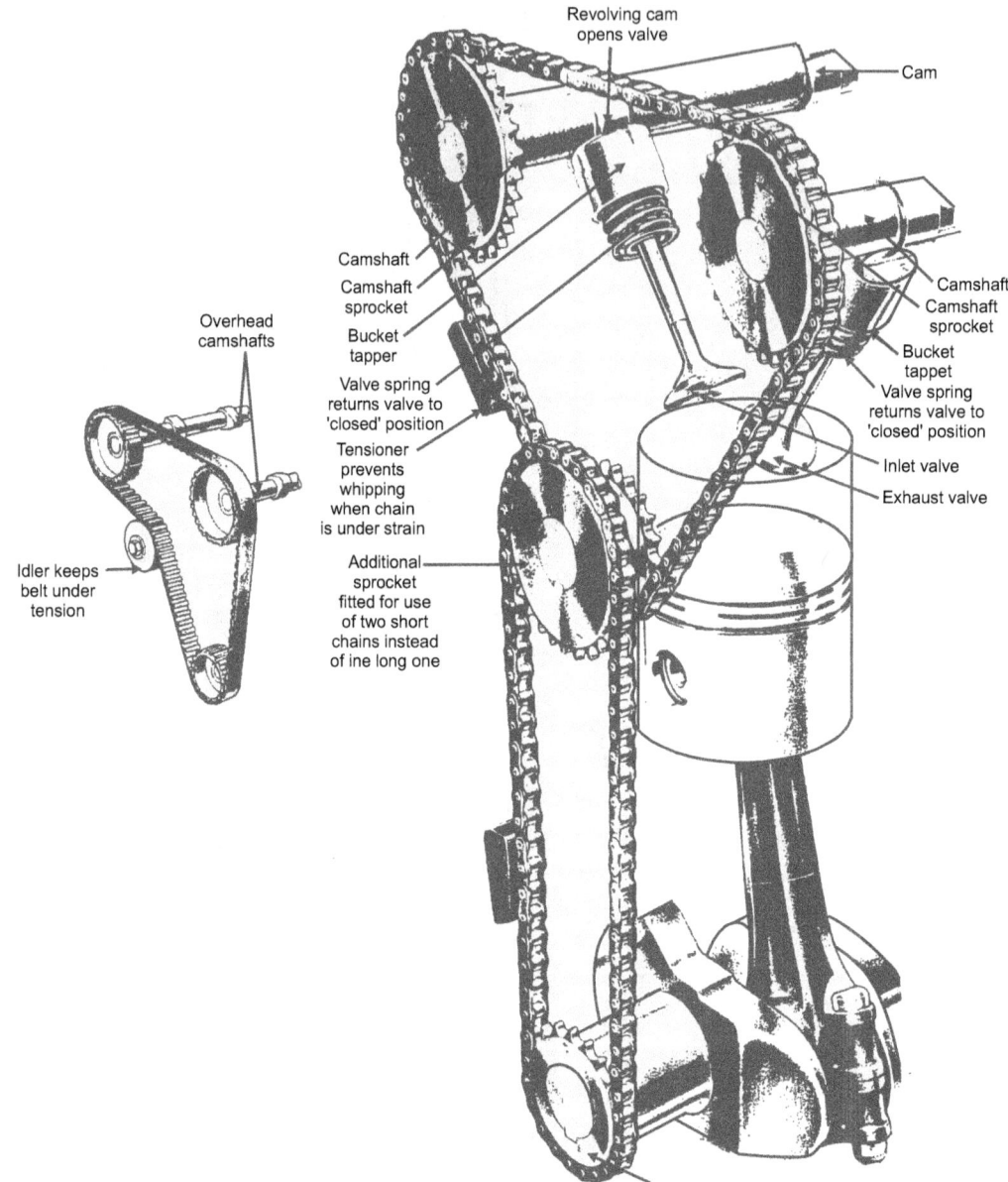

Fig. 5.36: Chain Drive to Overhead Camshafts

(H) EMISSIONS AND POLLUTION CONTROL

5.30 INTRODUCTION

The countries graded as developed and developing country. The mode of transportation in the countries is almost one and the same. The I.C engines are employed for surface transportation. The developed countries have already introduced stringent air pollution norms and are being followed there. The rate of fuel consumption subsequently the exhaust emissions due to high rate of fuel consumption are the issues concern to global warming

The petrol engine has provided a reliable small power unit for personalized transport and has revolutionized the living habits of the people. The passenger car has become both a status of symbol and a necessity not only of the rich people but of the middle class section of the modern society. The diesel engine on the other hand has been a backbone for passengers transport and goods transport systems e.g. passenger buses, trucks, trains, even small vehicles as autorikshaws. Without petrol and or diesel engines, the modern society cannot progress.

Due to rapid progress made by the mankind on the earth, his life has become very fast than earlier. Everyday he has to travel a longer distance than earlier. This all leads to the enhanced use of IC engines on every day basis. The same engines which help to achieve tremendous progress and unprecedented achievements in transportation are now causing air pollution leading to serious adverse effects on the environment. Also it is felt that in India the definite span of three seasons rainy, winter and summer is not observed in a definite span. Exhaust gases emitted from the automobile vehicles are the main sources of atmospheric air pollution. The emissions contain pollutants which are very dangerous to human beings, animals, birds and trees. Therefore, laws are enforced to regulate the quantity of pollutants through exhaust emissions.

Pure air is defined as a mixture of oxygen and nitrogen with traces of rare gases argon, neon, etc.

5.31 AIR POLLUTION

What is addition to our atmosphere of any material which will have a harmful effect on life living beings on earth.
- The main pollutants contributed by automobiles are carbon monoxide (CO), unburned hydrocarbons (UBHC), oxides of nitrogen (NO_X) and lead and other particulate emissions.
- Automobiles are not the only source of air p[pollution, other sources such as electric power generating stations (which mainly emit sulphur oxides, nitrogen oxides, and particulates), industrial and domestic fuel consumption, refuse burning industrial processing, etc. also contribute heavily to contamination of a our environment.

- The various harmful effect of air pollution include :
- The constituents like tar, soot, ash, and sulphur dioxide of coal smoke can cause eye and throat irritation and may lead to serious respiratory ailments.
- Sulphur dioxide is oxidized by sun rays to sulphur trioxide which is hygroscopic. It absorbs moisture to form sulphuric acid.

Term 'smog' was given to mixture of fog and coal smoke.

Another major cause of 'smog' formation was internal combustion engine. The IC engine emissions consist of carbon dioxide, carbon monoxide, nitrogen oxide, unburnt hydrocarbons and particulates. It is believed that particular mixtures of hydrocarbons and nitrogen oxides react photochemically (i.e. with the help of sunrays) to form variety of undesired products including irritant ozone. The substances usually photochemical smog are ozone, aldehydes and some nameless radicals X.

Automotive or photochemical smog occurs on hot, dry summer days, with high ozone concentration and moderate decrease in visibility. This second type of smog is our primary interest.

The CO_2 in the engine emissions cause yet another detrimental effect on atmosphere of the entire earth. CO_2 readily transmits "energy" from sun to earth (high temperature short wavelength radiation) but absorbs radiation in the infrared region (low temperature long wavelength radiation). Consequently, heat rejected from earth to space is *reduced* with increase in CO_2. This increases average temperature of the atmosphere. This is called *the green house effect* which leads to the phenomenon of global warming.

5.32 SOURCES OF S.I. ENGINE EMISSIONS

The S.I. engine emissions are divided into three types namely evaporative emissions, Crankcase Emissions and Exhaust Pipe Emissions shown in **Fig. 5.37**.

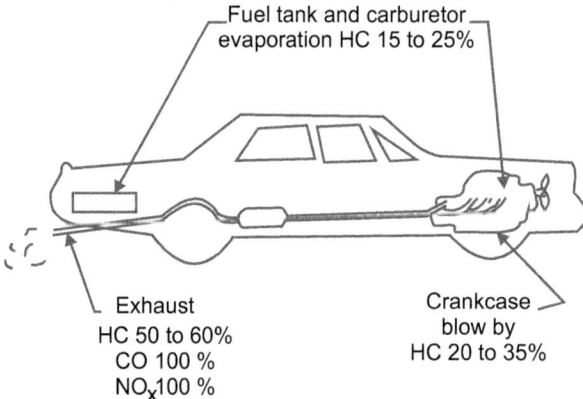

Exhaust
HC 50 to 60%
CO 100 %
NO_x 100 %

Fuel tank and carburetor evaporation HC 15 to 25%

Crankcase blow by
HC 20 to 35%

Fig. 5.37: Distribution of Emissions by Source (Petrol Engine Powered Vehicle)

5.32.1 Evaporate Emissions

There are two main sources of evaporative emissions, the fuel tank and the carburetor.

Fuel Tank Losses: Fuel tank losses occur by displacement of vapour during filling of petrol tank, or by vaporization of fuel in the tank, forcing the vapour through a breather vent to the atmosphere. Where the temperature goes high it 'breathes out' air loaded with petrol vapour. Fuel tank losses occur because the tank temperature is increased during the vehicle operation which causes an increase in the vapour pressure and thermal expansion of tank vapour.

The evaporation from the tank is affected by a large number of variables of which the ambient and fuel tank temperature, the mode of vehicle operation, the amount of fuel in the tank and the volatility of the fuel are important. Other significant factors are the capacity, design and location of the fuel tank with respect to the exhaust system and the flow pattern of the heated air underneath the vehicle. Insulated fuel tank and vapor collection system have been in use to reduce tank emissions.

Carburetor Emissions can be divided into two categories as *running losses* and *parking losses*. Heat produced by the engine causes some evaporation of the gasoline from float chamber. The evaporation of the gasoline constitutes the main reason for the loss of gasoline from the carburetor in running condition; whereas due to atmospheric temperature, some gasoline gets evaporated at parking condition also, which is known as parking loss.

Approximately, 10% of the total hydro carbon emission of the engine into atmosphere is in the form of evaporative emission.

5.32.2 Crankcase Breather or Crankcase Emissions

Blow-by is the phenomenon of leakage past the piston and piston rings from the cylinder into the crankcase. Gases enter past the piston rings into the crankcase during the compression and the power stroke. It consists of the engine blow-by gases and crankcase lubricant fumes. The blow-by is the phenomenon of leakage past the piston from the cylinder to the crankcase because of pressure difference. The blow of hydrocarbon emissions are about 20% of total hydrocarbon emissions from the engine. This is further increased to 30% if piston rings are worn.

5.32.3 Exhaust Pipe Emissions (S-09, 10, 12, 13, W-11)

Tail pipe exhaust emissions are the major source of automotive emissions. Petrol consists of a mixture of various hydrocarbons and if we could **get perfect combustion** then the exhaust would consists only of **carbon dioxide and water vapours plus air that did not enter into the combustion process.** However, for several reasons combustion is incomplete and hence we also get carbon monoxide, a deadly poisonous gas, and Unburnt hydrocarbons (UBHC) in exhaust. Hydrocarbons play an active part in the formation of smog.

In addition to CO and HC, the third main pollutant is oxides of nitrogen (NO_x). The air supplied for combustion contains about 77 percent of nitrogen. At lower temperature the nitrogen is inert but at temperatures higher than $1100°C$ nitrogen in the fuel-air mixture, due to the high temperatures in the combustion chamber, combines with oxygen to form various oxides of nitrogen. Some of the oxides of nitrogen are very toxic and harmful. The different oxides of nitrogen are referred by the chemical symbol NO_x with x standing for the varying amount of oxygen.

5.33 S.I. ENGINE EMISSIONS

The exhaust gas of the S.I. engines may contain one or more of the following emissions :

1. Oxides of nitrogen
2. Carbon Monoxide
3. Unburnt hydrocarbons
4. Aldehydes and oxygenates
5. Particulates
6. Smoke.

5.33.1 Carbon Monoxide

Carbon monoxide is an exhaust gas emission. **Formation of CO is an indication of incomplete combustion of carbon in fuel.** The incomplete combustion of carbon is due to :

- Reduced oxygen availability
- Poor mixing of fuel and air.
- Insufficient time available for complete combustion.

Carbon monoxide is a fuel and can be burned to CO_2,

$$CO + \frac{1}{2}O_2 \rightarrow CO_2 + Heat \uparrow$$

Thus, emission of CO represents loss of thermal energy of the fuel.

Generation of CO decreases as air-fuel ration increases (decrease in richness of mixture) as shown in Fig. 5.38 Formation of CO can be theoretically eliminated if lean mixtures are used but practically total elimination of CO is not possible and presence of 0.5% CO is allowed.

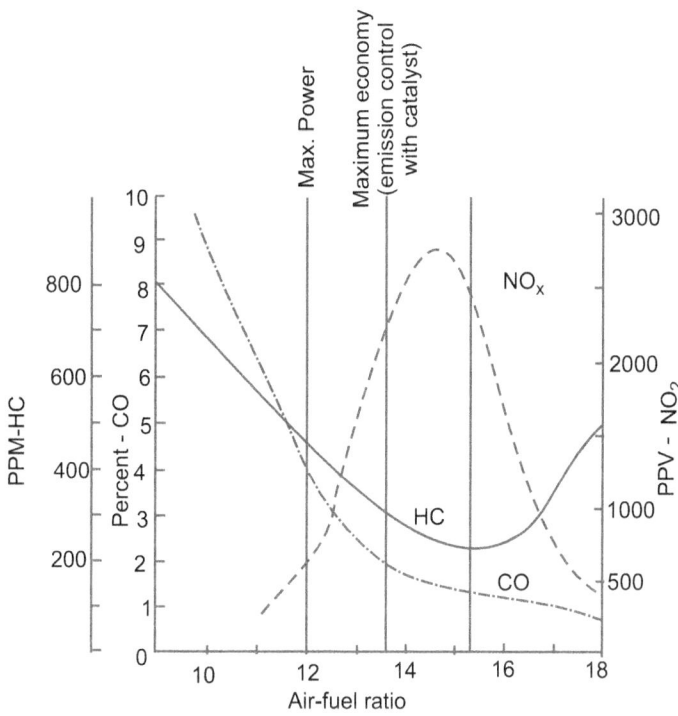

Fig. 5.38: Exhaust Emissions Vs. Air-fuel Ratio for a Petrol Engine

During idling as well as when the vehicle is decelerating, the throttle valve is closed. This reduces the oxygen supply and leads to the production of CO. In fact this is the main cause of CO formation; which is minimum during acceleration and cruising when throttle valve is wide open.

'CO' is colorless, odorless and highly poisonous gas. It attacks the red blood cells which carry oxygen. Inhalation of CO can cause death. Hence, its presence in the atmosphere should be kept to a minimum. The SI engines operate often, close to stoichiometric at part load and fuel rich at full load. Carbon monoxide (CO) emissions are therefore, significant and must be controlled.

5.33.2 Unburned Hydrocarbons (HC)

The unburned hydrocarbon emissions have several sources. (Refer Fig. 5.39).

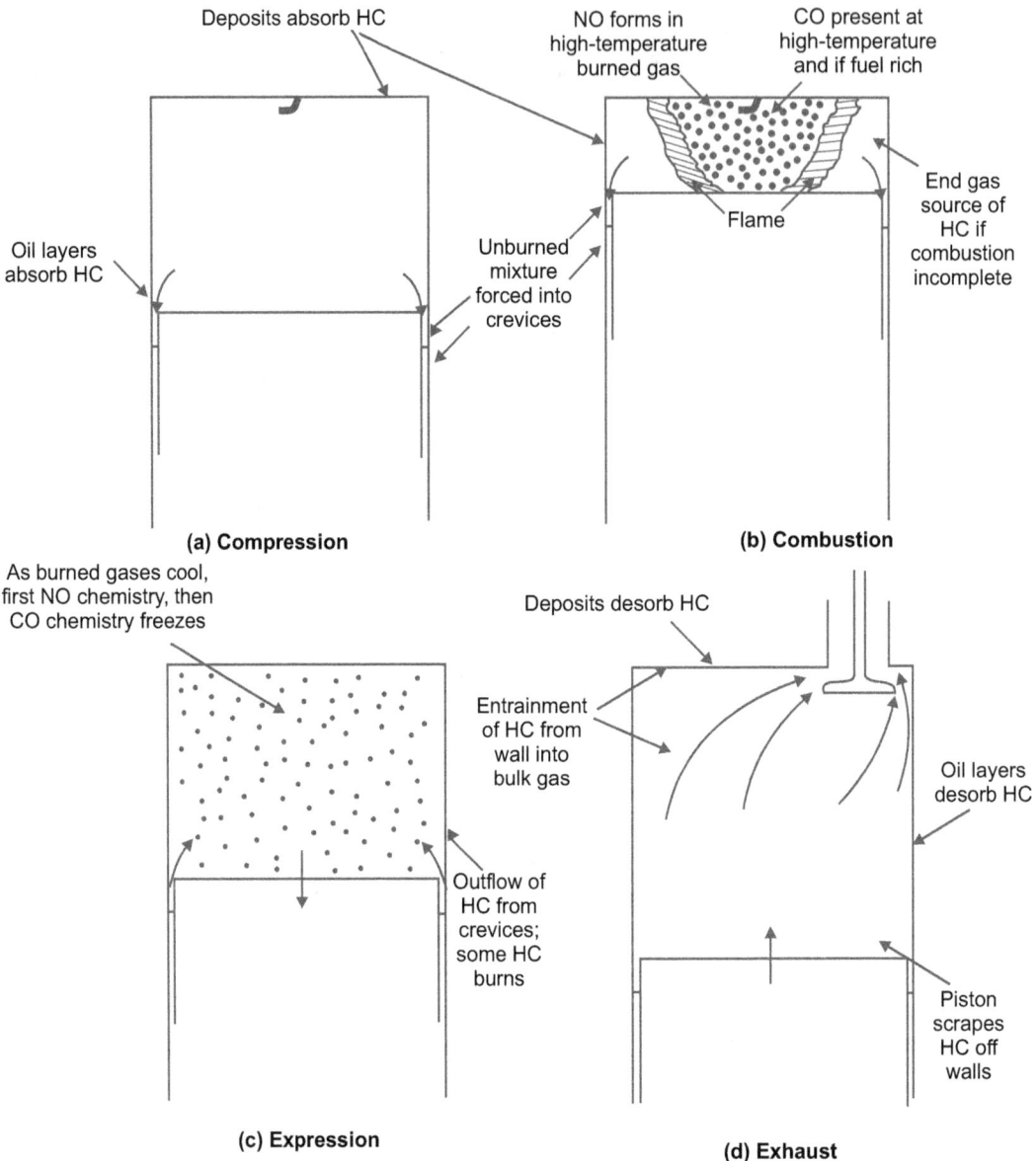

Fig. 5.39: Summary of HC, CO and No Pollutant Formation Mechanisms in a Spark-ignition Engine

- During compression and combustion, the high cylinder pressure forces some of the gas into the cavities i.e. a space between piston, piston rings and the cylinder wall. The flame cannot reach this space. The Unburnt mixture which leaves these cavities during expansion and exhaust is one source of HC emissions.

- The relatively cold cylinder walls retain a quench layer of burned and unburned fuel-air mixture when the flame is extinguished as it approaches the cylinder wall. The unburned fuel is a source of the HC emissions.
- A thin layer of oil is present on the cylinder wall, piston or cylinder head. This oil layer absorbs the fuel hydrocarbons before combustion and desorbs them after combustion. Thus, some fuel escapes the primary combustion process and remains Unburnt.
- Finally, incomplete combustion of fuel in the cylinder leads to HC emissions. The causes of incomplete combustion are presence of fuel rich mixtures, inadequate mixing of fuel and air and high speed operation.
- Hydrocarbon emissions are high at rich fuel-air mixtures and are lowest at equivalent A/F ratio of 0.13.

Presence of hydrocarbon in the engine exhaust is the chief cause of the formation of photochemical smog. Ethylene, benzene, aldehydes, olefins and diolefins are highly reactive in the smog producing chemistry. Some hydrocarbons species are carcinogenic (which cause cancer). The smog in atmosphere impairs visibility and causes throat and eye irritations as well as respiratory ailments.

The engine exhaust also contains compounds called oxygenates. They are carbonyl (like aldehydes and ketones), phenols and non-carbonyls like methanol, ethanol etc. They are irritants and odorants (have bad odor).

5.33.3 Oxides of Nitrogen

S.I. engine emissions contain 500 to 1000ppm of NO_x or 20 kg/kg of fuel. They are mainly Nitrogen oxide (NO) and nitrogen dioxide (NO_2) with small amounts of nitrogen trioxide (N_2O_3), nitrogen pentoxide (N_2O_5), nitrous oxide (N_2O). **The unknown mixture of these oxides is known as NO_x.** NO_x is formed at high temperatures. At low temperatures, NO_x are not formed. Thus, they form near the spark plug during actual combustion.

The maximum flame temperatures occur at stoichiometric air-fuel ratio(equivalent ratio $\phi=1$). But NO_x formation is maximum at ϕ = 0.95 i.e. at slightly leaner mixture. One can refer Fig. 5.38.

The NO_x concentration in exhaust is affected by engine design and the mode of vehicle operation. Air-fuel ratio and the spark advances are the two important factors which significantly affect NO_x emissions.

The NO_x concentration of the exhaust gas from a S.I. engine is primarily a function of *temperature* and *composition* (and secondarily *time*) and is *decreased*.
1. By decreasing the combustion temperature :
   (a) by retarding spark, a design parameter
   (b) by decreasing speed
   (c) by decreasing compression ratio, which is a design parameter
   (d) by exhaust gas recirculation

2. By decreasing the oxygen available in the flame front:
   (a) by using rich mixtures
   (b) by decreasing homogeneity of the mixtures

Photochemical Smog:

The formation of photochemical smog is routed through numerous complex reactions. The general reactions may be given as:

$$NO + O_2 \rightarrow NO_2$$
$$NO_2 + \text{Light energy} \rightarrow NO + O$$

The atomic oxygen is highly reactive and causes the formation of ozone.

$$O + O_2 \rightarrow O_3$$

This ozone will form smog. A typical reaction is

$$O_3 + HC \rightarrow \text{Aldehyde radicals} + \text{Oxyacil radicals} \rightarrow \text{Smog}$$

The mechanism of smog formation is shown in Fig. 5.40.

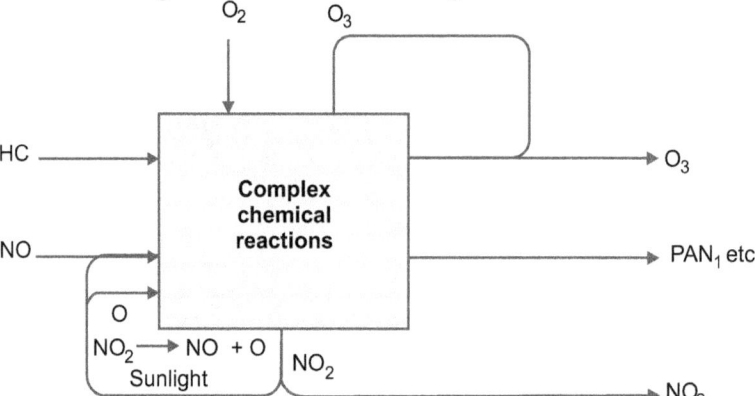

Fig. 5.40: Mechanisms of Photochemical Smog Formation

Ozone at the earth surface is harmful to the living beings. It causes lung irritation and damage to tissues. It is harmful for plant life. The smog produced also causes irritation to eye and throat.

- Nitrogen oxide is a major air pollutant. It forms photochemical smog with unburned hydrocarbons in the presence of sunlight.
- The photochemical smog causes eye and throat irritation, impairs visibility, deteriorates rubber products and is harmful for plant life.

5.33.4 Particulate Matter and Partial Oxidation Products

1. Organic and inorganic compounds of higher molecular weights and lead compounds resulting from the use of TEL (Tetra-ethyl lead) are exhausted in the form of very tiny particles of the order of 0.02 to 0.06μ. About 75% of the lead burnt in the engine is exhausted into atmosphere in this form and rest is deposited on engine parts.

2. Some traces of products of partial oxidation are also present in the exhaust gas of which formaldehyde and acetaldehyde are important. Other constituents are phenols, acids, ketones, ethers etc. are due to incomplete combustion.

5.34 C.I. ENGINE EMISSIONS

In CI engines, fuel distribution is non-uniform. The pollutant formation depends on the fuel distribution. Diesel engine emissions can be summarized as follows:
1. Hydrocarbons
2. Nitrogen oxides
3. Soot
4. Aldehydes

Diesel engines or CI engines however always operate on the lean side of stoichiometric; CO emissions in Diesels are therefore, low enough and are not very important.

The emission levels of different engines at full load and rated speed are given in the Table 5.1.

Table 5.1: Emission levels for different engines

Sr. No.	Emission or Exhaust constituents	Engine		
		Four stroke turbo charged	Four stroke naturally aspirated Medium speed	Four stroke naturally aspirated high speed
1	Co, %	0.03	0.26	0.14
2	CO_2	7.68	7.14	7.79
3	Unburned HC, ppm	250	370	1000
4	NO_x ppm	2550	800	790
5	Smoke	8	60	60
6	Odour, DI units, Turk	3.4	3.3	3.5
7	Air : Fuel ratio	25	25	25

5.34.1 Hydrocarbon Emissions

CI engines contain hydrocarbon compounds with higher boiling points and hence higher molecular weights. Pyrolysis of fuel occurs during combustion. The mixture composition is complex. The HC emissions of diesels therefore range from methane to the heaviest hydrocarbons which remain in vapour phase.

Fuel in diesel engine can escape primary combustion process by two paths:
1. The fuel-air mixture becomes too lean to auto-ignite at a local point.
2. The fuel-air mixture too rich to ignite or support a flame.

Thus HC remains unconsumed due to incomplete mixing or quenching of flame due to excess fuel.

5.34.2 Particulates

Diesel particulates consist principally of soot on which some organic compounds have been absorbed.

Most particulate material results from incomplete combustion of fuel hydrocarbons and or lubricating oil. The emissions are 0.2 to 0.6 g/km. for light duty diesels and 0.5-1.5 g/brake kWh for large DI engines. Above 500°C, the particulates are clusters of spheres of carbon. The individual sphere diameter is **15 to 30 nm**. Below 500°C, the particles become coated with absorbed and condensed compounds like unburned hydrocarbons and oxygenated hydrocarbons (ketones, ethers etc.).

5.34.3 Odour

Diesel engines are famous for the odour it produces. The main constituents responsible for this odour are alkyl benzenes and aldehydes. The products of partial oxidation of fuel components are the main cause of diesel odour. These products are formed because of quenching effect especially in the second phase of diesel combustion.

The factors affecting odour are:
- Fuel-air ratio: Odour is more when lean mixtures are burnt in the engine.
- Engine operation mode: Maximum odour occurs when acceleration from idle mode. The odour is minimum when engine runs at medium speed i.e. on part load.

5.35 EFFECT OF DIFFERENT POLLUTANTS ON HUMAN LIFE

The major air pollutants emitted by a petrol or a diesel engine are CO_2, CO, HC, NO_X, SO_2 ozone, smoke (soot) and lead odour. They are very harmful to the living beings and plant life if their concentration in the air exceeds a particular limit.

All pollutants in general lead to lung and heart deteriorations. They also cause throat and eye irritations. There is no "threshold limit" to these harmful effects. A young and healthy person may not be affected by these pollutants. But old age, serious illness, drop in resistance power due to illness or major operations suddenly make a person very prone to the ill effects of these pollutants.

The harmful effects of the pollutants can be summarized as follows:

(a) **Carbon monoxide (CO):** It is a poisonous gas and can kill a person by suffocation. It affects nerves and heart by reducing the oxygen carrying capacity of blood by attacking the red blood cells.

(b) **Carbon dioxide (CO_2):** Effects are same as that of Carbon monoxide. But CO_2 is not as poisonous gas as CO.
(c) **NO_X:** Causes throat and eye irritations. It affects respiratory systems and genes of all living creatures and so may lead to unpredictable mutations. NO_X form smog with HC and sunlight.
(d) **Hydrocarbons (HC):** Forms smog with NO_X and sunlight. The smog impairs visibility and causes respiratory track problems. Some hydrocarbons are carcinogenic (cause cancer). Hydrocarbon emissions also cause eye and throat irritations.
(e) **Ozone:** It is toxic. It is a byproduct of NO_X reactions. On ground level, it causes irritation of lungs and throat.
(f) **(Sulphur dioxide) SO_2:** It is toxic and corrosive gas. It oxidizes to SO_3 which combines with water to form sulphuric acid aerosols. Sulphuric acid is corrosive and can harm human respiratory truck of animals, plants and crops.
(g) **Soot:** Carbon particles suspended in air are harmful if inhaled. Soot blackens the surfaces of things on which it settles. It may cause lung and throat ailments.
(h) **Odour:** Diesel emissions which contain harmful aromatic. Hydrocarbons may cause intense irritation because of its bad odour. The exhaust fumes can eye irritation and sore eyes.

5.36 DIESEL SMOKE AND CONTROL

Exhaust smoke from diesel engine is a visible product and is due to poor combustion. The amount of soot formed depends upon local fuel-air ratio, type of fuel and pressure. The size of the soot particles affects the appearance of smoke. Bigger the size, darken will be the smoke.

Generally smoke from CI engine will be two types:
- Blue-white smoke
- Black smoke

Blue-white smoke: The blue white smoke is caused by liquid droplets of lubricating oil or fuel oil while starting from cold.

Black smoke: Black smoke is carbon particles suspended in the exhaust gas. It largely depends upon air-fuel ratio and increases rapidly as the load is increased and the available air is depleted.

Causes of Smoke:
(a) **The Injection System:** The injection system characteristics which affect smoke levels include inadequate or excess penetration, unsuitable droplet sizes, excessive duration of injection, improper atomization.

(b) **Maintenance:** The engine condition plays an important role to decide the smoke level in the exhaust.

(c) **Fuel:** The quality of fuel affects the white smoke production in an engine. In general, more volatile fuels give less smoke than heavier fuels of similar cetane number. The cetane number has no effect on black smoke.

(d) **Load:** A rich fuel-air mixture results in higher smoke because the amount of oxygen available is less. Hence any over loading of the engine will result in a very black smoke.

(e) **Engine type and speed:** Naturally aspirated engines have higher smoke level at higher loads than turbocharged engines because the latter have sufficient oxygen even at full lad. The smoke is worse at low and high speeds.

(f) **Fuel-air ratio:** Fig 5.41 shows the effect of fuel-air ratio on smoking tendency of diesel engine. The smoke increases with increasing fuel-air ratio.

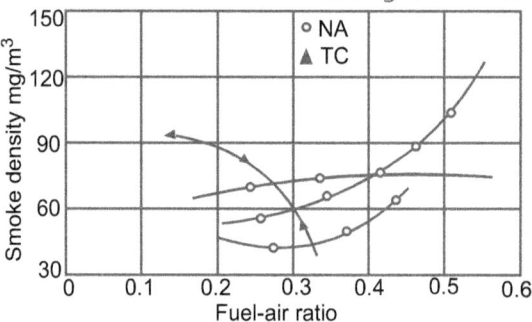

Fig. 5.41: Variation of Smoke Intensity with Fuel-Air Ratio

5.37 EXHAUST GAS TREATMENT/EMISSION CONTROL

The harmful engine emissions can be reduced by removing pollutants from the engine exhaust system. The methods used are,

(a) **Thermal reactors:** For HC and CO.

(b) **Catalytic converters :** Oxidising catalysts for HC and CO, reducing catalysts for NO_x and three way catalysts for all three pollutants.

(c) Traps or filters for particulates.

5.37.1 Thermal Reactor

Thermal reactor is a chamber connected to exhaust pipe. It provides sufficient time to allow appreciable homogeneous oxidation of CO and HC to occur. Secondary air is supplied in the thermal reactor which promotes rapid mixing of the same with the exhaust gases and allows the mixture to remain inside for sufficient time. The high temperature and oxygen oxidizes HC and CO.

The schematic lay out of system is shown in Fig. 5.42. The engine exhaust is connected to the reactor where a secondary is supplied. This assures the sufficient oxygen in the reactor. Therefore CO and HC let out from the engine burn completely here. About 10 to 15% exhaust gas is passed through the intercooler and is recalculated to the engine. Rest is let out the atmosphere before it enters the intercooler. The temperature range of the oxidation process is 600-700°C. The exhaust gas temperatures of conventional engines are not sufficient for oxidation. The thermal reactors must be designed to reduce heat losses and increase the residence time of the exhaust gases.

The reactor is made of thin steel liner which acts as a core, and a cast iron outer casing. A heat shield helps to thermally isolate the liner. The paths are so arranged as to keep the heat losses to minimum and increase the retention time.

The limitations of thermal reactors are as following:
1. Reactors are costly due to complex design and size.
2. Reactor efficiency depends upon proper mixing of secondary air with exhaust gases.

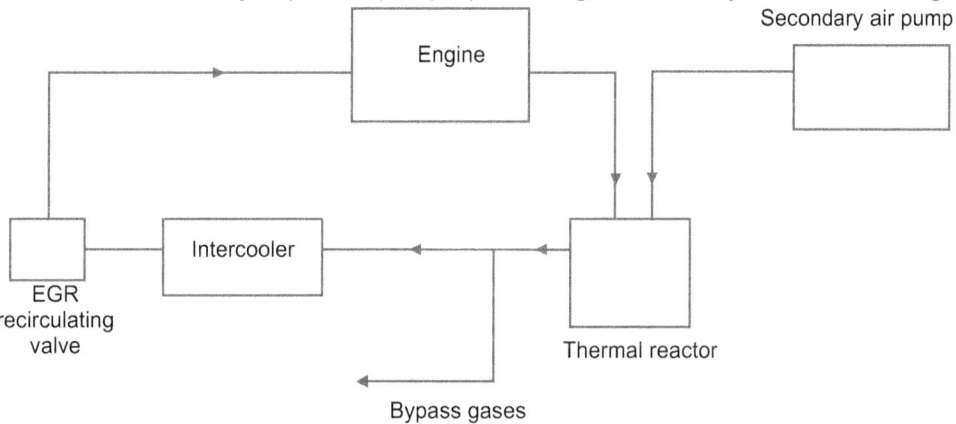

Fig. 5.42: Thermal Reactor Package

5.37.2 Catalytic Converters

The principle of catalytic converter is to control the emission level of HC, CO and NO_X from the engine emissions by changing the chemical characteristics of the exhaust gases.

The engine exhaust contains oxygen. The oxidation of HC without catalyst requires temperatures in excess of 600°C and a residence time of gas in the exhaust pipe of 50 ms or more. In oxidized CO, temperatures in excess of 700°C are required.

Catalytic oxidation of HC and CO can be achieved at temperatures as low as 250°C. For removal of NO, the method used is catalytic process.

The catalytic converters for SI engine consist of a metal casing in which active catalytic material is kept. The catalysts used are generally noble metals like Platinum, Palladium or Rhodium. They are formed in the shape of a mesh to increase its surface area.

Fig. 5.43 shows the configuration of catalytic converter. Converters for HC and CO and NO_x are arranged as in the diagram. The NO_x catalyst is the first element I the gas flow path and does not cause any heat release. The HC/CO catalyst is the next and its heat release is so great that there is a risk of overheating and burning of the element. This requires air injection and hence a secondary air pump. Experiments have shown that axial flow form is superior than radial type. The reactor should provide largest possible surface to gas flow and provide sufficient reaction rate without increasing the back pressure.

The converter design uses a bed of spherical ceramic pellets. This provides a large surface area in contact with the flow. The catalyst material is impregnated into a highly porous surface of alumina sphere (about 3 mm in diameter) to a depth of about 250 µm. The pellet material chosen has good crush and abrasion resistance after exposure to temperatures of the order of 1000°C. The gas flow over the pellets is turbulent which results in high mass-transfer rates.

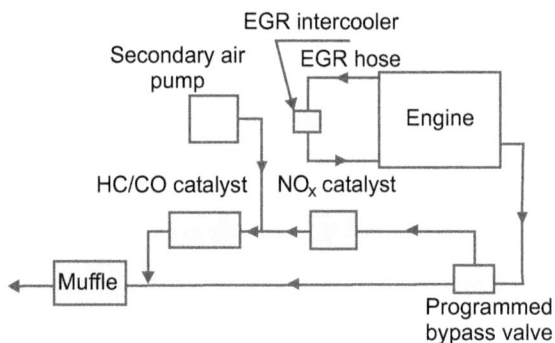

Fig. 5.43: Catalytic Converter Package

5.37.3 Oxidation Catalyst

These catalysts oxidize CO and hydrocarbons in the exhaust gases to CO_2 and water. A typical exhaust gas contains about 12% CO_2 and H_2O, 100 to 2000 ppm NO, 20 ppm SO_2, 1 to 5% O_2, 0.2 to 5% CO and 1000 to 6000 ppm carbon in HC with small amounts of lead and phosphorus. About half the hydrocarbons emitted by the SI engine are unburned fuel compounds. Sufficient oxygen must be present to oxidize CO and HC. This may be supplied either by the engine running on lean mixtures or by a pump that introduces air into the exhaust ports just downstream of the valve.

'NO' Catalysis or Two Way Catalyst

This catalyst not only oxidizes HC and CO but also reduces 'NO' to CO_2, N_2, NH_3, N_2O by using CO, HC and H_2 in the exhaust gases. The reactions are :

$$NO + CO \rightarrow \frac{1}{2} N_2 + CO_2$$

$$NO + H_2 \rightarrow \frac{1}{2} N_2 + H_2O$$

$$2 NO + 5H_2 \rightarrow 2 NH_3 + 2H_2O$$

The catalyst is used for reduction. The 'NO' reduction stage is followed by oxidation catalyst to oxidize HC and CO.

Three Way Catalytic Converter

This converter removes all the three pollutants i.e. NO, HC and CO simultaneously. However, to achieve a high conversion efficiency of say about 80 [percent, the air-fuel ratio has to be controlled within a very narrow range of 0.1 air-fuel ratio.

A close loop control of equivalence ratio is therefore essential. An oxygen sensor placed in the exhaust indicates whether engine is operating on lean or rich side of stoichiometric. An appropriate signal is then given to achieve a desired air-fuel mixture.

Limitations of Catalytic Converters

1. Since lead destroys catalytic activity, the engine cannot use leaded patrol.
2. Exhaust systems are hotter than normal as a result of exothermic reactions in the catalyst bed.
3. The emission of SO_3 increases if fuel contains sulphur.
4. The use of equipment adds to the cost.

5.37.4 Particulate Traps

These are called Trap Oxidizers. A filter which can sustain high temperatures is used to remove the particulate material from the diesel engine exhaust. The particulates are then 'oxidized' by burning them-off in the filter itself. This is done by raising the temperature inside the filter to about 500-600°C. The oxygen in exhaust gas then supports the combustion. Use of catalysts can reduce the temperatures of the oxidation by about 200°C.

The types of filters used include ceramic monolith filters, alumina coated wire mesh filters, ceramic foam filters, ceramic fibre mat filters etc.

This technology, however is difficult to implement because of the following reasons:

1. The filter, even when clean, increases the pressure of the exhaust system.
2. This pressure goes on increasing as the pressure of the exhaust system.
3. The collected particulates do not ignite and oxidise under normal engine operating conditions.
4. The ignition and oxidation processes must be controlled carefully to avoid excess temperature and destruction of the trap.

5.38 EXHAUST EMISSION STANDARDS AND NORMS

As stated earlier, the exhaust gases emitted from IC engines to the atmosphere contain hydrocarbon (HC), carbon monoxide (CO) and nitrogen oxide (NO_X), which are responsible for air pollution. These pollutions are known to cause serious health problems. Hence, there are laws on emission standards, which limit the amount of each pollutant in the exhaust gas emitted by an automobile engine.

Emission norms prescribe carbon monoxide (CO), hydrogen (HC) and nitrous oxides (NO_X) levels, set by the government, which a vehicle would emit when running on road. All the IC engine as well as automobile manufactures need to implement the same from the date of implementation.

5.38.1 Euro Norms

Euro norms refer to the permissible exhaust emission levels from both petrol and diesel vehicles which have been implemented in Europe.

Euro I, Euro II, Euro III and Euro IV norms to be implemented by the automobile manufactures so as to reduce the exhaust emissions and protect our environment. To reduce the emissions, some technical changes in their vehicle and engine may be required.

5.38.2 Emission Norms in India

- The first Indian IC engine (automobile) emission regulations were idle emission limits and became effective in 1989.
- These idle emission regulations were soon replaced by mass emission limits for both gasoline (1991) and diesel (1992) vehicles.
- Since the year 2000. India started adopting European emission and fuel regulations for four-wheeled light-duty and for heavy-duty vehicles.
- Indian own emission regulations still apply to two-and-three-wheeled vehicles.

On 6th October, 2003, the National Auto Fuel Policy has been announced, which envisages a phased program for introducing Euro-II-IV emission and fuel regulations by 2010.

The implementation schedule of EU emission standards in India is summarized in **Table 5.2**.

Table 5.2: Indian Emission Standards (4-wheel vehicles)

Standard	Reference	Date	Region
India 2000	Euro II	2000	Nationwide
Bharat Stage II	Euro II	2001	NCR[*], Mumbai, Kolkata, Chennai
		2003-04	NCR[*], 10 Cities[+]
		2005-04	Nationwide
Bharat Stage III	Euro III	2005-04	NCR[*], 10 Cities[+]
		2010-04	Nationwide
Bharat Stage IV	Euro IV	2010-04	NCR[*], 10 Cities[+]
[*] National Capital Region (Delhi) [+] Mumbai, Kolkata, Chennai, Bengaluru, Hyderabad, Ahmedabad, Pune, Surat, Kanpur and Agra.			

The previous standards apply to all the new 4-wheel vehicles sold and registered in the respective regions. In addition, the National Auto Fuel Policy introduces certain emission requirements for interstate buses with routes originating or terminating in Delhi or the other 10 cities.

For 2 – and 3- wheelers, Bharat Stage II (Euro 2) are applicable from April 1, 2008, but not later than April 1, 2010.

5.38.3 Emissions from Tracks and Buses

Emission standards for new heavy-duty diesel engines-applicable to vehicles of weight more than 3,500 kg are listed in Table 5.3. Emissions are tested over the ECE R 49 13 – mode test (through the Euro II stage).

Table 5.3: Emission Standards for Diesel Truck and Bus Engines, g/kWh

Year	Reference	CO	HC	NO_X	PM
1992	----	17.3 – 32.6	2.7 – 3.7	----	----
1996	----	11.20	2.40	14.4	----
2000	Euro I	4.5	1.1	8.0	0.36*
2005+	Euro II	4.0	1.1	7.0	0.15
2010+	Euro III	2.1	0.66	5.0	0.10

* 0.612 for engines below 85 kW
+ Earlier introduction in selected regions, see Table 6.1

5.38.4 Emissions from Light Duty Diesel Vehicles

Emission standards for light-duty diesel vehicles (Gross Vehicle Weight ≤ 3,500 kg) are summarized in **Table 5.4**. Ranges of emission limits refer to different classes (by reference mass) of light commercial vehicles : compare the EU light-duty vehicle emission standards page for details on the Euro I and later standards. The lowest limit in each range applies to passengers cars (Gross Vehicle Weight ≤ 2,500 kg : up to 6 seats).

Table 5.4: Emission Standards for Light-Duty Diesel Vehicles, g/km

Year	Reference standard	CO	HC	HC + NO_X	PM
1992	-----	173.32.6	2.7 – 3.7	-----	----
1996	-----	5.0 – 9.0	-----	2.0 – 4.0	----
2000	Euro I	2.72 – 6.90	-----	0.97 – 1.70	0.14 – 0.25
2005+	Euro II	1.0 – 1.5	-----	0.7 – 1.2	0.08 – 0.17

+ earlier introduction in selected regions, see Table 13.1.

The test cycle has been the ECE + EUDC for low power vehicles (with maximum speed limited to 90 km/h). Before 2000, emissions were measured over an Indian test cycle

Engine for use in light – duty vehicles can be also emission tested using an engine dynamometer. The respective emission standards are listed in Table 5.5.

Table 5.5: Emission Standards for Light – Duty Diesel Engines, g/kWh

Year	Reference	CO	HC	NO_x	PM
1992	----	14.0	3.5	18.0	---
1996	----	11.20	2.40	14.4	---
2000	Euro I	4.5	1.1	8.0	0.36*
2005	Euro II	4.0	1.1	7.0	0.15

* 0.612 for engines below 85 kW
+ Earlier introduction in selected regions, see Table 13.1

5.39 LIGHT DUTY GASOLINE VEHICLES

Four-Wheel Vehicles : Emission standards for gasoline/petrol vehicles (Gross Vehicle Weight ≤ 3,500 kg) are summarized in Table 5.6. Range of emission limits refer to different classes of light commercial vehicles (compare the EU light-duty vehicle emission standards page). The lowest limit in each applies to passengers cars (Gross Weight ≤ 2,500 kg : upto 6 seats).

Table 5.6: Emission Standards for Gasoline Vehicles (GVW ≤ 3,500 kg), g/km

Year	Reference	CO	HC	HC + NO_x
1991	----	14.3 – 27.1	2.0 – 2.9	----
1996	----	8.68 – 12.4	----	3.00 – 4.36
1998*	----	4.34 – 6.20	----	1.50 – 2.18
2000	Euro I	2.72 – 6.90	----	0.97 – 1.70
2005+	Euro II	2.2 – 5.0	----	0.5 – 0.7

* For catalytic converter fitted vehicles
+ Earlier introduction in selected regions, see Table 13.1.

Gasoline vehicles must also meet an evaporative (SHED) limit of 2 g/test (effective 2000).

5.40 THREE AND TWO-WHEEL VEHICLES

Emission standards for 3-and 2-wheel gasoline vehicles are listed in the following tables 5.7 through 5.12.

Table 5.7: Emission Standards for 3 – Wheel Gasoline Vehicles, g/km

Year	CO	HC	HC + NO_x
1991	12 – 30	8 – 12	----
1996	6.75	----	5.40
2000	4.00	----	2.00

Table 5.8: Emission Standards for 2 – Wheel Gasoline Vehicles, g/km

Year	CO	HC	HC + NO_x
1991	12 – 30	8 – 12	----
1996	4.50	----	3.60
2000	2.00	----	2.00

Table 5.9: Specifications of Indian Gasoline for the year 2000

Characteristics	Leaded	Unleaded
Colour, Visual	Orange	Colorless
Density @ 15°C, kg/cubic m	710 – 770	710 – 770
Distillation :		
Recovery upto 70°C, vol.-%, min	10 – 45	10 – 45
Recovery upto 100°C, vol. - %, min	40 – 70	40 – 70
Recovery upto 180°C, vol. - %, min	90	90
Final Boiling Point, °C, max.	215	215
Residue, vol. - % max.	2	2
Anti – knock index, min	84	84
Existent gum, g/cubic m., max.	40	40
Sulphur content, wt., max.	0.20	0.10
Lead content, g/1, max.	0.15	0.013
Reid Vapour Pressure @ 38°C kPa.	35 – 60	35 – 60
Vapour Lock Index (VLI), max.		
All months	950	950
Benzene content, vol. - % max.	5.0	5.0

Table 5.10: Indian Specifications for High Speed Diesel for year 2000

Characteristics	Requirements
Ash, % wt., max.	0.01
Carbon residue, wt., max.	0.30
Cetane no., min.	48
Distillation	
85% vol., recovery @ °C, max.	350

Characteristics	Requirements
95% vol., recovery @ °C, max.	370
Flash point, min.	35
Kinematic viscosity, cSt, @ 40 °C	1 to 5
Density @ 15°C, kg/cubic m	820 to 860
Total sulphur, wt. %, max.	0.25
Total sediments, mg. per 100 ml, max.	1.6

Table 5.11: Proposed changes in gasoline for year 2005

Characteristics	Requirements
R.V.P., kPa	35 – 50
Benzene, vol. %, max.	1-2
Oxygen, wt. %, max.	2.3-2.7
Sulphur, wt. %, max.	0.03 – 0.05
Aromatics, vol. %, max.	40-50
Olefins, vol. %, max.	20-25
Distillation, vol. %, min	
@ 100°C	45
@ 150°C	75
Final boiling point, max.	0.005-0.013
Lead content, g/1, max.	730-770
Anti-knock index, (RON + MON)/2, min.	87 -90

Deposit control additives are also required, meeting the specified performance test.

Table 5.12: Proposed Changes in High Speed Diesel for Year 2005

Characteristics	Requirements
Sulphur, wt. %, max	0.035 – 0.05
Cetane No.	50-51
Polycyclic aromatics, wt, %	10-12
Max.	820-845
Density @ 15°C	360-365
95% vol.distilled °C, max.	370-375
Final boiling point, °C, max.	

5.41 CONTROL OF ENGINE EMISSIONS

The present steps towards reducing air pollutants can be divided into the following classification.
- Modifications of engine, its components and fuels to reduce pollution from sources which are known (or suspected) for many years.
- Design of new components to reduce evaporative emissions from the fuel system.
- Design of new components to reduce undesirable exhaust emissions.

5.41.1 Engine Components and Fuel Modifications

(a) **Reduction of compression ratio (CR) : The reduction in CR** from the high 10+ to more desirables values of 8 to 8.5 Reduction in CR reduces combustion temperatures subsequently reduces NO_x and increases exhaust temperatures and hence less HC. Reduction in CR is possible only through engine modification.

(b) **Positive Crankcases Ventilation (PCV) :** Earlier the crankcase ventilation was obtained by a draft which discharges the blow by into the atmosphere.

Filtered air is drawn from air cleaner and passes into the crankcase. The air and blowby gases pass through a flow calibrated (spring loaded valve) (PCV valve) and then to the inlet manifold. component modification is Desirable. The system gives two benefits :

    (i) Atmospheric pollution by blowby becomes negligible.
    (ii) With improved crankcases ventilation, formation of oil sludge and oil contamination is reduced.

(c) **Fuel Modifications :** The lead additives added are reduced, or totally eliminated to eliminate lead compounds in the exhaust. Certain reactive compounds of hydrocarbons. For example, olefins, aromatics have been reduced or eliminated.

(d) **Increase of Idle Speed :** Idle speeds in the past were low viz. 400-500 rpm. They demand very reach mixtures with high HC and CO emissions. The idle speeds used now are 500-700 rpm with accompanying leaner mixture and greater spark retard. These conditions require greater throttle opening with more air flow (more combustion). This reduces HC and CO emissions.

5.41.2 Evaporative Emission Control

Evaporative losses of fuel arise from the breather pipe of the petrol tank (say 5 percent of total car emissions) and from the fuel bowl of the carburetor, especially when it is hot (1-6 percent depending on temperatures). Fuel loss also arises from refueling evaporation and spillage.

Evaporative losses can be reduced by:
1. Sealing the petrol filling pipe on the fuel tank with a pressure cap and vent the vapour emissions into carburetion system.
2. Providing the carburetor with heat shields and venting the carburetor bowl into air cleaner cover.

5.42 METHODS TO CONTROL OXIDES OF NITROGEN

The following are the methods which have been used to control oxides of nitrogen.
    (a) Exhaust gas recirculation   (b) Water injection   (c) Catalyst

(a) **Exhaust Gas Recirculation (EGR) System:** This is shown in Fig. 5.44. A portion of the exhaust gas is re-circulated to the cylinder intake charge. This reduces maximum combustion temperatures, since the inert gas serves as a heat sink. This also reduces the quantity of oxygen available for combustion.

The exhaust gas re-circulated is regulated and supplied to the intake manifold of the engine as shown in Fig. 5.44.

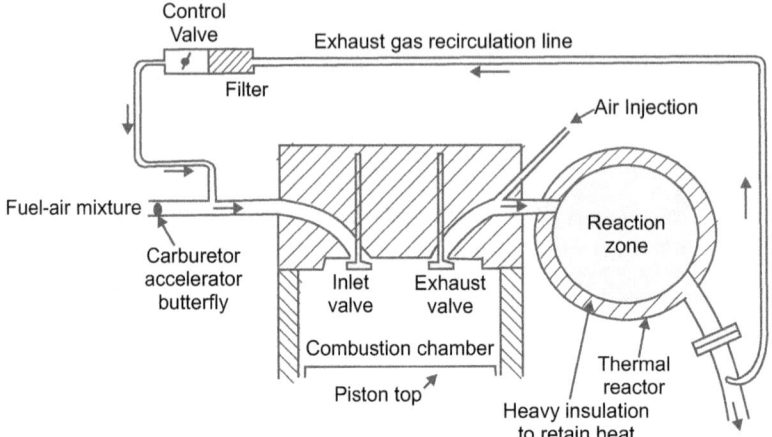

Fig. 5.44: Exhaust Gas Recirculation Device (EGR) for Control of NO_x Emission

The effect of exhaust gas recirculation on the missions is shown in Fig. 5.45 for various Air-fuel ratios. From the figure it is clear that NO_x emissions occur during lean mixture limits where exhaust gas recirculation is least effective.

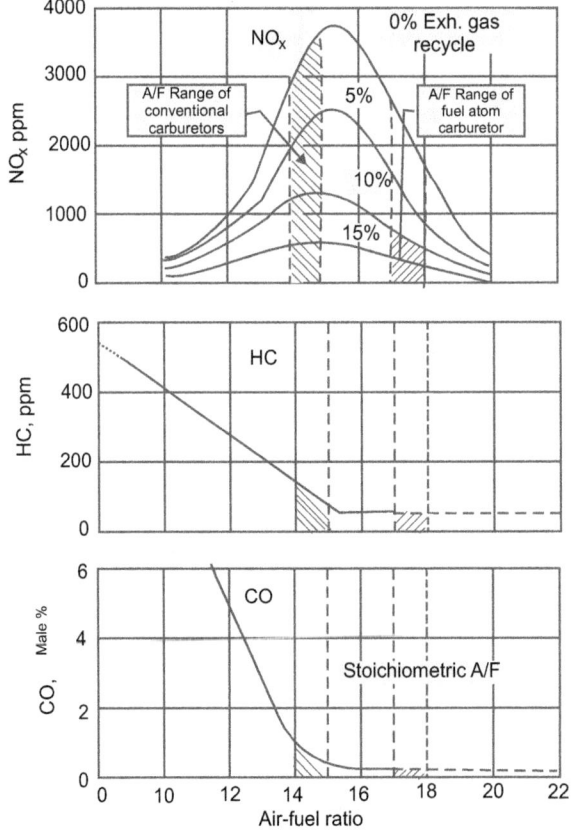

Fig. 5.45: Effect of Recycling of Gas on NO_x Concentration

(b) Water Injection

Fig. 5.46 shows oxides of nitrogen reduction as a function of water injection rate. The water injection reduces the temperature in the combustion chamer hence the NO_x formation.

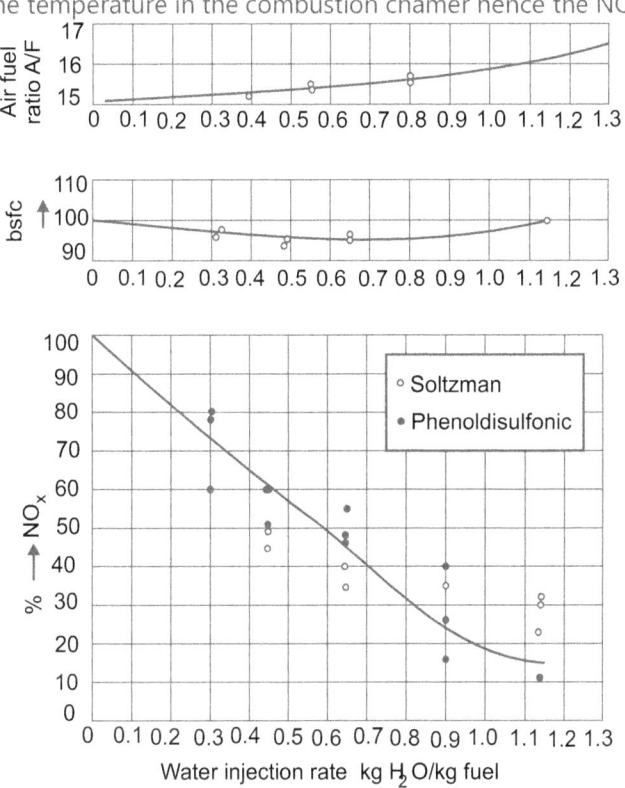

Fig. 5.46: Effect of Water Injection on NO_x Concentration

(c) Catalyst:

A few types of catalysts have been tested to reduce the NO_x emission. A copper catalyst is used in the presence of CO for this purpose.

5.43 HYBRID VEHICLES

A hybrid vehicle combines two or more sources of power. In fact many people have probably owned a hybrid vehicle at some point. For example, a mo-ped (a motorized pedal bike) is a type of hybrid vehicle because it combines the power of a gasoline engine with the pedal power of its rider.

In application we are having various types of hybrid vehicles. Many locomotives are diesel-electric hybrids. Giant mining trucks are often diesel-electric hybrids. Submarines are also hybrid vehicles, some are nuclear-electric and some are diesel-electric.

Any vehicle that combines two or more sources of power that can be directly or indirectly propulsion power is hybrid.

The gasoline-electric hybrid car is just that a cross between a gasoline-powered car and an electric car.

5.43.1 Hybrid Electric-Vehicle (HEVs)

Hybrid electric vehicles (HEVs) available today combine an internal combustion engine with a battery and electric motor. The practical benefits of HEVs include improved fuel economy and lower emissions compared to conventional vehicles. The inherent flexibility of HEVs allows them to be used in a wide range of applications, from personal transportation to commercial transport.

- Many configurations are possible for HEVs. Essentially, a hybrid combines an energy storage system, a power unit such as a spark ignition engine, and a vehicle propulsion system.
- The primary options for energy storage include batteries, ultra capacitors, and flywheels. Although batteries are by far the most common energy storage choice, research is still being done in other energy storage areas.
- Propulstion can come entirely from an electric motor, such as in a series configuration, or the engine might provide direct mechanical input to the vehicle propulstion system in a parallel configuration system.
- A hybrid's efficiency and emissions depend on the particular combination of subsystems, how these subsystems are integrated into a complete system, and the control strategy that integrates the subsystems.
- Gasoline-electric hybrids have a gasoline engine as their main power source but also use an electric motor for additional power when needed.
- Hybrid vehicles can capture the energy which is normally lost during breaking and store it as electricity in a special battery.
- Unlike all-electric vehicles, hybrids run on regular unleaded gasoline and never need to be "plugged in" to an electrical outlet.
- What's more, hybrids don't waste energy idling. The gasoline engine shuts-off when the car comes to a stop (e.g. at a red light), to be started instantly by the electric motor when needed again.

5.43.2 Components of the Hybrid Electric Vehicles

(a) **Gasoline Engine:** The hybrid car has a *gasoline engine* much like the one you will find on most cars. However, the engine on a hybrid is smaller and uses advanced technologies to reduce emissions and increase efficiency.

(b) **Fuel Tank:** The *fuel-tank* in a hybrid is the energy storage device for the gasoline engine. Gasoline has a much higher energy density than batteries do. For example, it takes about 500 kg of batteries to store as much energy as 3.5 kg of gasoline.

(c) **Electric motor:** The *electric motor* on a hybrid car is very sophisticated. *Advanced electronics allow it to act as a motor as well as a generator.* For example, when it needs to, it can draw energy from the batteries to accelerate the car. But acting as a generator, it can slow the car down and return energy to the batteries.

(d) **Generator:** The *generator* is similar to an electric motor, but it acts only to produce electrical power. It is used mostly on series hybrids.

(e) **Batteries:** The *batteries* in a hybrid car are the energy storage device for the electric motor. Unlike the gasoline in the fuel tank, which can only power the gasoline engine, the electric motor on a hybrid car can put energy into the batteries as well as draw energy from them.

(f) **Transmission:** The *transmission* on hybrid car performs the same basic function as the transmission on a conventional car.

5.43.3 Types of Configuration

HEVs can have a parallel design, a series design, or a combination of the two.

(a) **Series Type:** Here engine, batteries and electric motor are connected in series. The primary engine is connected to a generator that produces electricity. The electricity charges the batteries, which drives an electric motor that powers the wheels. Series HEVs have the mechanical connection between the hybrid power unit and the wheels. This means that all motive power is transferred from chemical energy to mechanical energy to electrical energy and back to mechanical energy to drive the wheels. Here are some benefits of a series configuration:

1. Idling of engine never happens, which reduces vehicle emissions.
2. The engine drives a generator to run at optimum performance.
3. The design allows for a variety of options, when mounting the engine and vehicle components.
4. Some series hybrid vehicles don't need a transmission.

The downside is that series HEVs require large and therefore, heavier battery packs than parallel vehicles. In addition, the engine works hard to maintain battery charge, because the system is not operating in parallel.

(b) **Parallel Type:** In a parallel design, the energy conversion unit and electric propulsion system are connected directly to the vehicle's wheels. The primary engine is used for highway driving. The electric motor provides added power during hill climbs, acceleration, and other periods of high demand. HEVs can also be built to use the series configuration at low speeds and the parallel configuration for high way driving and acceleration. Some benefits of parallel configurations:

(a) The vehicle gets more power because both the engine and the motor supply power simultaneously.
(b) Most of the parallel vehicles do not need a separate generator because the motor regenerates the batteries.

5.43.4 Benefits of Hybrid Vehicle

(a) I conventional vehicle, energy lost due to application of brakes is not recovered. The brakes of a car remove this energy and dissipate it in the form of heat. A hybrid car recollects some of this energy and stores it in the battery to use later. It does this by using "regenerative braking". That is, instead of just using the brakes to stop the car, the electric motor that drives the hybrid can also slow the car. In this mode, the electric motor acts as a generator and charges the batteries while the car is slowing down.

(b) Because of extra power that electric motor provides, gasoline engines in hybrids can be made smaller in size without compromising the vehicle's performance. By allowing the engine to operate more efficiently, engine downsizing increases the environmental performance of hybrids and their fuel economy.

(c) There is a provision to stop the engine, when vehicle stops. This reduces emissions, because during idling maximum emissions would take place, and improves fuel efficiency. Idling off makes hybrid a particular efficient option in city, stop and go traffic.

(d) Some hybrids have electric drive only powering the car with the battery alone at speeds up to 10 to 15 miles/hour. This provides significant fuel savings and emission reductions because combustion engines operate least efficiently at low speeds.

5.43.5 The Future of Hybrid Vehicles

- Today, all major automakers are working on producing HEVs and fuel cell vehicles.
- Auto manufactures are looking to create various versions of hybrids.
- Some using diesel engines and a battery pack, others with a "mild hybrid" system where the battery pack gently assists the conventional engine, and still others where fuel cells would be integrated into the hybrid system.
- There are many ways to configure an HEV and many different approaches to fueling the vehicles as well.
- HEVs are now at the forefront of transportation technology development. Hybrids have the potential to allow continued growth in the automotive sector, while also reducing critical resource consumption, dependence on foreign oil, air pollution, and traffic congestion.
- Hybrids are a hot subject today and they are beginning to show up on the roads and highways across the world.

5.44 ENGINE REQUIREMENTS FOR AUTOMOTIVE APPLICATIONS

Internal combustion engines are extensively used in automotive applications. Automotive applications are mainly in the form of passenger transports and the goods transport. For passenger engines, we are in need of moderate power with high speed whereas for goods transport, large power at moderate speed is required.

For a particular application, engine should require to fulfil the following requirements:

- (a) **Capacity of Engine:** Capacity of the engine is nothing but the power and torque developed by the engine. Engine develops power with required torque as per its capacity. So as to fulfil the various requirements in a particular automotive application.
- (b) **Specific Fuel Consumption (bsfc):** bsfc of the engine should be as less a possible so that the power developed by the engine per kg fuel supply is more, which increases the efficiency of the engine.
- (c) **Weight to Power Ratio:** Weight to power ratio should be sufficiently less, so that the overall engine weight on the chassis is less, so as to develop the low weight vehicles which are more efficient for passenger transport.
- (d) **Specific Engine Output:** Specific engine output (power per kg fuel) should be as large as possible so as to get better efficient vehicle.
- (e) **Starting System of the Engine:** Starting system of the engine is to be provided in such a way that engine can be easily started at all conditions as like in cold starting in winter seasons a swell as in rainy seasons.
- (f) **Cooling System of the Engine:** Cooling system of the engine is to be appropriately designed so as to keep the engine cool at its operating temperature. The system should be easy to maintain so as to avoid the unexpected overheating problems as well as cold starting problems.
- (g) **Lubrication System:** Proper lubrication system is to be provided to the engine so as to avoid the unexpected wear and tear of the engine as well as to increase the efficiency by reducing the various friction losses.
- (h) **Fuel Supply System:** There is to be proper fuel system that provides the sufficient amount of fuel at required time so as to get the proper combustion of fuel, which increases efficiency of the engine.
- (i) **Emission Control:** Engine has to fulfil the all emission control norms as per the emission standard requirement laid down by the government to control the air pollution.
- (j) **Engine Compactness:** Engine is to be as compact as possible so as to mount it on chassis in small space.
- (k) **Mounting of Engine on Chassis:** Engine has to be provided with the proper locators so as to much it at required place on the chassis.

5.45 SELECTION OF ENGINE FOR AUTOMOTIVE APPLICATIONS

Selection of the engine for automotive applications is made based on following points. :

(a) Number of Strokes:

Two-stroke engine and four-stroke engine.

Two stroke engines have a power stroke for every rotation of the crank shaft. It produces almost 1.5 times the power that is produced by the 4-stroke engine for identical conditions. Two stroke engines produce more pollution than that of 4-stroke engine. Two stroke engines have high power to weight ratio and are used for marine applications.

4 stroke engines produce less pollution hence are used in the vehicles for surface transportation.

(b) Fuel Used:
Petrol, Diesel, LPG.
- In the petrol engine, fuel ignition takes place due to spark provided by spark ignition system. So the compression ratio is less (9 to 10). So engine is light. So these types of engines are used for scooters, motorcycles and passenger cars.
- In the diesel engine, fuel ignition takes place due to the compression of air. The air is heavily compressed with high compression ratio (14 to 15) due to which the pressure in the engine is sufficiently large. So the engine is comparatively heavy. So diesel engines are used in trucks, buses and cars.
- LPG consists of butane and propane, which are condensed to liquid state by compression and cooling. They are stored in the sealed pressure tank or cylinder. This LPG so used as fuel for engines, as at atmospheric condition it is vaporized state these can be easily used in the petrol engine cylinders. But the storage cylinder acquires sufficiently large space. So these types of engines are used for passengers cars, buses, trucks etc.

(c) Cooling System:
Air-cooled or water-cooed engines.

In air cooled engines fins are provided on the cylinder and cylinder head. Normally air cooling is preferred for small capacity engines. This type of cylinder is sued in motorcycle, scooters, motorcycles and autorickshawa. In deserts, a sufficient amount of water is not available for cooling. Therefore, air-cooling is preferred in deserts for cooling the engine. In very cold countries, water would freeze in the cooling jacket, therefore, there too, air cooling is preferred for an automobile engine.

For water cooled engines, water jacket is provided around the combustion chamber in the cylinder block to keep the temperature of eth engine in operating range. Water cooled engines are generally used in passenger cars, buses, trucks etc.

(d) Speed of Engine:
Low, medium and high speed engines.
- Spark ignition engines used for passenger cars and motorcycles are having the speed of 4500-7500 r.p.m., whereas Wankel engines with spark ignition run with a speed of 6000-8000 r.p.m.
- Medium passed engines are used for engines in trucks, buses etc. which operate in the speed range of 3600-5000 rpm in spark ignition engines and in 21004000 rpm in compression engines.

- Large gas engines, with spark ignition, have speed in the range of 300-900 r.p.m. Locomotive diesel engines have speeds between 425-1800 r.p.m. Large diesel engines run within the speed range of 110-440 r.p.m.

(e) Number of Cylinders: *Single cylinder engines*:

These engines are used in scooters, mopeds, motorcycles and autorickshaws.
- *Three cylinder engines*: This type of engine is well balanced engine with light weight, many times used in small passenger cars, buses.
- *Four cylinder engines*: In this type of engines, the torque produced is uniform so four cylinder engines are most popular for cars of medium size.
- *Six cylinder engines*: These types of engines are popular in trucks and buses.

As the load carrying capacity of each vehicle increases, which is for the large power requirement, eight cylinder, twelve cylinder and sixteen cylinder engines are used.

(f) Compact Integral Engines:

To make the small, compact and comfortable cars, the compact integrated engines are considered. These are of two types:
- Three cylinder inline, transverse front engine with front wheel drive, which is having the advantage of reduced weight, reduced length and improved fuel consumption besides being dynamically balanced. These engines are used for small cars as like Maruti 800 and utility vehicle like Omoni.
- Four cylinder inline, transverse front engine with front wheel drive, the engine is compact. The torque obtained in these engines is more uniform and fuel efficiency is too highly improved. These types of engines are used in the medium size cars as like ford icon, Hyundai Accent etc.

These points are generally considered at the time of selection of the engine for the application.

5.46 SPECIFICATIONS OF AUTOMOTIVE ENGINES

The automotive engine specifications consist of following points:
1. Type of engine. (number of cylinder, number of strokes and type of cooling system used).
2. Appearance and Layout.
3. Injection/Ignition system.
4. Engine sizes (Bore and stroke).
5. Capacity in terms of cubic centimeter of swept volume.
6. Compression ratio.
7. Power generation at rated condition as well maximum power.
8. Torque generation at rated condition as well maximum torque.
9. The Maximum and minimum speed.
10. Power to weight ratio.
11. Fuel used
12. Power/litre.

5.47 ZERO EMISSION VEHICLES

(a) Battery Vehicles

Electric cars, powered by an electric motor and batteries, provide drivers with another alternative. To recharge the batteries, operators plug the car into a 120-volt or 240-volt outlet. A typical electric car averages 60 to 200 km (40 to 100 mi) per charge.

- Usually we use the Nickel Cadmium batteries which require more space and give very less efficiency.
- In next few years we will start to use Lithium ion batteries or the batteries will be of a nano composite V205 or of nickel metal hydrides which will be of smaller size and larger capacities.

(b) Compressed Air Vehicle

The compressed air vehicle was first built in 1828; as it could not give good output the research in compressed air vehicle has stopped.

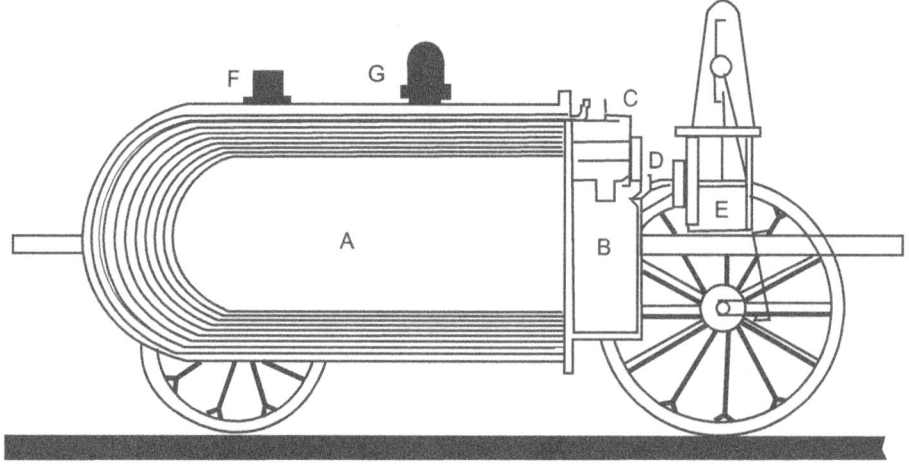

Fig. 5.47: Parsey's Compressed-Air Engine

The reservoir A was filled with air "compressed to as great an extent as was compatible with safety" which fed chamber B, kept at engine pressure by automatic reducing valve C. Pipe D fed the double-acting engine E. At F is the air recharge valve, and G is the safety valve. The locomotive was intended for coal-mine work, but again it is not clear if it was actually built.

(c) Solar Vehicle

Solar vehicles usually work on solar cells which are Photovoltaic cells. Solar cells called photovoltaic made from thin slices of crystalline silicon, gallium arsenide, or other semiconductor materials convert solar radiation directly into electricity. Cells with conversion efficiencies greater than 30 percent are now available. By connecting large numbers of these cells into modules, the cost of photovoltaic electricity has been reduced to 20 to 30 cents per kilowatt-hour. Americans currently pay 6 to 7 cents per kilowatt-hour for conventionally generated electricity. Many solar race cars have complex data acquisition systems that monitor the whole electrical system while even the most basic cars have systems that provide information on battery voltage and current to the driver. Solar cars usually use the batteries like lead acid batteries, Nickel metal hydride batteries (NiMH), Nickel-Cadmium batteries (NiCD), Lithium ion batteries and Lithium polymer batteries.

(d) Hydrogen Vehicle

In a hydrogen fuel cell, hydrogen is supplied to the fuel cell's anode, and an oxidant, commonly the oxygen present in air, is supplied to the cathode. The fuel cell strips electrons from the hydrogen atoms. These electrons move from the anode through the electric circuit to the cathode, creating an electric current that can be tapped to provide power. The electron-deficient hydrogen atoms meanwhile pass through the electrolyte to the cathode. There the electrons that passed through the circuit recombine with the electron-deficient hydrogen atoms. Oxygen (from the air) reacts with this reformed hydrogen, producing water. Water produced at the cathode has to be removed continuously to avoid flooding the cell.

(e) Hybrid Vehicles

The hybrid electric vehicle (HEV) uses both an electric motor or motors and a gasoline or diesel engine to extend the car's range and often to provide additional power. A conventional HEV, such as the Toyota Prius, uses battery power up to certain speeds and the gasoline engine for higher speeds, and can draw on both power sources if needed. The batteries are recharged by the gasoline engine, which acts as a generator and in most models by the energy generated from braking.

ARE HYBRID CARS REALLY THE WAVE OF THE FUTURE?

Really the hybrid cars are becoming the wave of the future because:
- The cars run about 220 kms in a single charge.
- For the faster speeds it uses the fuel.
- It save a lot of fuel.
- It also helps the green environment.

Advantages:
- Freedom from highly discomforting noise and vibrations so common in diesel vehicles.
- Recurring savings of petrol or diesel.
- Ideal vehicle to keep environment clean.
- Ideally suited as public transport in congested areas, factories, wild life sanctuaries, airport, schools and places of historic Importance.
- No engine related maintenance expenses and much lesser maintenance.

5.48 ALTERNATIVE FUELS FOR I.C. ENGINES

List of alternative fuels for S.I. and CI engines are as given below.
1. Alternative fuels for SI engines.
   (a) Liquefied Petroleum Gas (LPG).
   (b) Compressed Natural Gas (CNG).
   (c) Alcohol (Methanol and Ethanol).
   (d) Hydrogen.
2. Alternative fuels for CI engines :
   (a) Compressed Natural Gas (CNG).
   (b) Methanol-Diesel Fuel Blends.
   (c) Vegetable Oils : Jatrofa ande Karanja Oil.

5.49 DEFINITION OF CARBON CREDITS

One carbon credit is equivalent to one tonne of CO_2 and it is called a CO_{2c}. In view of the above discussion, the carbon credit has become a new currency which can be traded in the international market.

Based on Kyoto Protocol, each country can set 'quotas' on the emission of installations run by local business houses and other organizations. These are termed as "Operators".

According to Kyoto Protocol, any country short fall of 1 lakh tonne of CO_2, it must purchase carbon credits from another country that has been planting trees or using efficient and green energy technologies to reduce emissions. Cost of each carbon credit ranges between 10-40 US dollars.

Long term plans to reduce CO_2 emissions.
1. Reduce the fuel consumption by adopting efficient technologies.
2. Forests are to be untouched, as trees absorb CO_2.
3. Go for new plantation of trees.
4. Uses of latest technology so as to reduce the CO_2 emissions.
5. Power generation may be through wind mills, nuclear power, thermal power using natural gas, i.e. power generation with no emissions or less emissions.
6. Use of alternate energy sources.
7. Preserving weed and vegetation.

5.50 GLOBAL WARMING POTENTIAL (GWP)

Global warming potential is a number that refers to the amount of global warming caused by a substance. GWP is the ratio of the warming caused by a substance to the warming caused by a similar mass of carbon dioxide (CO_2). Thus, the GWP of CO_2 is one. The GWP of some other substances (refrigerants) are given in the Table 5.13.

Table 5.13: GWP of Refrigerants

Substance	GWP per kg
CO_2	1.0
R_{12}	3639
R_{22}	560
Water	0
R502	5244
R134a	388

Other green house gases include CO, NO_x, methane and HFC's (say R22).
(The thermal conductivity of these gases is of the order of 0.007 W/mK).
These gases namely CO, NO_x, CO_2 etc. are emitted into atmosphere from the industries like power, steel, cement, textile and fertilizer industries. They rise to the stratospheric level and form an insulating layer. This layer allows the solar radiations to enter into the atmosphere to reach earth. During the return journey of reflected solar radiations back to the space the green house gases offer resistance, and this lead to delay of radiations back to space. Subsequently, leading to global warming effect.

In last one hundred years, the rise in earth's temperature is of the order of 1°C. If this rise in temperature higher than 4.4°C may lead to no life on earth. With increase in global warming, ice caps at the northern and southern poles may melt and cover up some of the earth's surface.
The concept of carbon credits came into existence as a result of increasing awareness of the need for controlling emissions of green house gases and save the earth from global warming.

In 1997, in Kyoto, Japan around 170 countries initiated an agreement to reduce emanation of green house gases. This agreement is known as Kyoto protocol. According to this agreement, the 'quota' of maximum amount of green house gases were fixed for developed and developing countries. India and China stayed out of Kyoto Protocol for the reasons of unequality of quota based on 450 parts per million (ppm) by volume between the developed and developing countries.
In the world, USA is a maximum contributor of green house gases amongst all the countries in the world. India and China are not the significant contributors.
Kyoto meeting decided that each country producing CO_2 must contain CO_2 by tree plantation or other processes that can absorb CO_2 reduce CO_2 emission. If a country produces more CO_2 that it can absorb, it must purchase an "absorption ability" from other countries.

Kyoto's Flexible Mechanisms:
A credit can be an emissions allowance which was originally allocated or auctioned by the national administrators of a cap-and-trade program, or it can be an offset of emissions. Such offsetting and mitigating activities can occur in any developing country which has ratified the

Kyoto Protocol, and has a national agreement in place to validate its carbon project through one of the UNFCCC's approved mechanisms. Once approved, these units are termed Certified Emission Reductions, or CERs. The Protocol allows these projects to be constructed and credited in advance of the Kyoto trading period.

The Kyoto Protocol provides for three mechanisms that enable countries or operators in developed countries to acquire greenhouse gas reduction credits.

- Under Joint Implementation (JI) a developed country with relatively high costs of domestic greenhouse reduction would set up a project in another developed country.
- Under the Clean Development Mechanism (CDM) a developed country can 'sponsor' a greenhouse gas reduction project in a developing country where the cost of greenhouse gas reduction project activities is usually much lower, but the atmospheric effect is globally equivalent. The developed country would be given credits for meeting its emission reduction targets, while the developing country would receive the capital investment and clean technology or beneficial change in land use. However, geologists from Cass Business School are sceptical on this program, arguing that the introduction of carbon credits does little to encourage companies to reduce emissions and instead allows the existence of 'carbon cowboys'.
- Under International Emissions Trading (IET) countries can trade in the international carbon credit mar'-let to cover their shortfall in allowances. Countries with surplus credits can sell them to countries with capped emission commitments under the Kyoto Protocol.

These carbon projects can be created by a national government or by an operator within the country. In reality, most of the transactions are not performed by national governments directly, but by operators who have been set quotas by their country.

Emission Markets:
- For trading purposes, one allowance or CER is considered equivalent to one metric tonne of CO_2 emissions.
- These allowances can be sold privately or in the international market at the prevailing market price.
- These trade and settle internationally and hence allow allowances to be transferred between countries.
- Each international transfer is validated by the UNFCCC. Each transfer of ownership within the European Union is additionally validated by the European Commission.
- Climate exchanges have been established to provide a spot market in allowances, as well as futures and options market to help discover a market price and maintain liquidity.
- Carbon prices are normally quoted in Euros per tonne of carbon dioxide or its equivalent (CO_2e). Other greenhouse gasses can also be traded, but are quoted as standard multiples of carbon dioxide with respect to their global warming, potential.

Currently there are five exchanges trading in carbon allowances: the Chicago Climate Exchange, European Climate Exchange, Nord Pool, PowerNext and the European Energy Exchange. Recently, NordPool listed a contract to trade offsets generated by a CDM carbon project called Certified Emission Reductions (CERs).

How buying carbon credits can reduce emissions

Carbon credits create a market for reducing greenhouse emissions by giving a monetary value to the cost of polluting the air. Emissions become an internal cost of doing business and are visible on the balance sheet alongside raw materials and other liabilities or assets.

For example, consider a business that owns a factory putting out 100,000 tonnes of greenhouse gas emissions in a year. Its government is an Annex I country that enacts a law to limit the emissions that the business can produce. So the factory is given a quota of say 80,000 tonnes per year. The factory either reduces its emissions to 80,000 tonnes or is required to purchase carbon credits to offset the excess. After costing up alternatives the business may decide that it is uneconomical or infeasible to invest in new machinery for that year. Instead it may choose to buy carbon credits on the open market from organizations that have been approved as being able to sell legitimate carbon credits.

We should consider the impact of manufacturing alternative energy sources. For example, the energy consumed and the Carbon emitted in the manufacture and transportation of a large wind turbine would prohibit a credit being issued for a predetermined period of time.

- One seller might be a company that will offer to offset emissions through a project in the developing world, such as recovering methane from a swine farm to feed a power station that previously would use fossil fuel. So although the factory continues to emit gases, it would pay another group to reduce the equivalent of 20,000 tonnes of carbon dioxide emissions from the atmosphere for that year.
- Another seller may have already invested in new low-emission machinery and have a surplus of allowances as a result. The factory could make up for its emissions by buying 20,000 tonnes of allowances from them. The cost of the seller's new machinery would be subsidized by the sale of allowances. Both the buyer and the seller would submit accounts for their emissions to prove that their allowances were met correctly.

EXERCISE

1. Explain battery ignition system with a neat sketch.
2. Explain magneto ignition system with a neat sketch.
3. Drawbacks of conventional ignition system?
4. Explain any one type of electronic ignition system.
5. Write a note on engine firing order.
6. What are the functions of lubrication system?
7. Write a note on properties of lubricating oil.
8. Explain with neat sketches:
   (i) Splash lubrication system
   (ii) Pressure system of lubrication
   (iii) Dry sump system of lubrication
9. Write a note on oil filters.
10. Write a note on starting system.

11. Explain water cooling system used in a 4-wheeler. Also explain various parts with neat sketches.
12. What is governing of I.C. engines? Explain: (i) Hit and miss governing, (ii) Quality governing, (iii) Quantity governing.
13. What do you mean by intake and exhaust systems? Explain with sketches various parts of intake and exhaust systems in brief.
14. What do you mean by drive train mechanism. Explain with sketches.
15. What are the different kinds of fuels used in IC engines ?
16. Briefly explain the chemical structure of petroleum.
17. Give the general chemical formula of the following fuels :
    (i) Paraffin, (ii) Olefin, (iii) Diolefin, (iv) Naphthene, (v) Aromatic.
    Also state their molecular arrangements and mention whether they are saturated or unsaturated.
18. Briefly describe the rating of CI engine fuels.
19. Briefly explain the petroleum refining process.
20. How are SI engine fuels rated ?
21. Discuss the significance of distillation curve.
22. Discuss the important qualities of an SI engine fuel.
23. Describe the important qualities of a CI engine fuel.
24. What is the effect of high sulphur content on the performance of SI and CI engines?
25. What is air pollution ? Explain the contributers to air pollution and their bad effects on human beings.
26. What are the sources of emissions from S.I. engine ?
27. Explain the effect of air-fuel ratio on the emissions of CO, HC and NO_x for petrol engines.
28. What are the sources of hydrocarbons ?
29. Explain the mechanism of smog formation.
30. What are the C.I. engine emissions ?
31. Explain diesel smoke and causes of smoke.
32. Explain exhaust gas treatment methods.
33. Explain with a neat sketch "Thermal reactor package".
34. Explain "catalytic converter package".
35. What are Euro norms ? Are they different from Bharat norms.
36. Enlist emission norms for trucks and buses.
37. What are Bharat emission norms for light duty gasoline vehicles.
38. Explain the methods to control oxides of nitrogen.
39. Explain the working of hybrid vehicles and also discuss the function of its components.
40. What are the engine requirements for automotive applications ?
41. Give specifications of automotive engines.
42. Explain zero emission vehicles.

✱✱✱

UNIT VI

POSITIVE DISPLACEMENT COMPRESSOR

A. RECIPROCATING COMPRESSORS

6.1 INTRODUCTION

An air compressor is a machine to compress the air and to raise its pressure. The air compressor sucks the air from the atmosphere, compresses it and then delivers the high pressure air to a storage vessel. From the storage vessel, it may be conveyed by the pipe line to a place where the supply of compressed air is required. Since process of compressing the air requires some work to be done on it, therefore, compressor must be driven by some prime mover.

The general arrangement of the compressor and prime mover used to run the compressor is shown in Fig. 6.1.

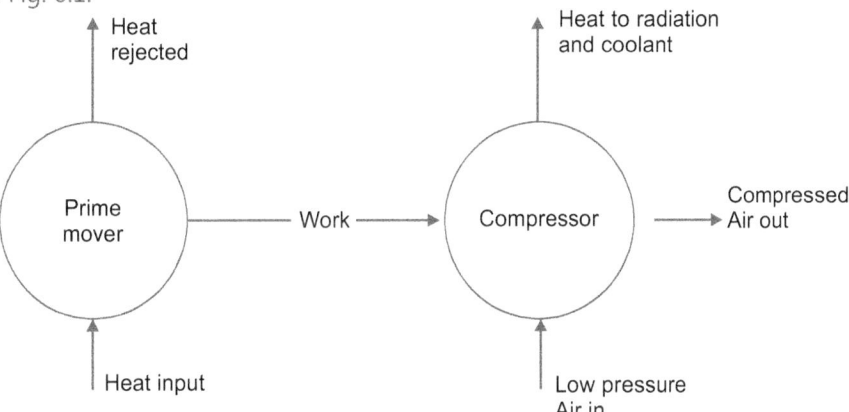

Fig. 6.1: General Arrangement of Prime Mover and Compressor

Part of the heat supplied to the prime mover (I.C. engine, steam engine is converted into work to drive the compressor. Some part of the work supplied to the compressor is lost in friction, heat radiation and to the coolant used to cool the compressor and the remaining is used to increase the pressure of the air. The compressor must be designed to use the maximum work supplied to increase the pressure of the air.

Uses of Compressed Air:

The compressed air has wide applications in industry as well as in commercial equipments, as listed below:
- In industry, it is used to blast sand and to clean the jobs in foundry.
- To operate revetting tools in aircraft industry,
- Spray painting,

- For starting and supercharging of I.C. engines, in gas turbine plants, jet engines and air motors,
- For driving pneumatic tools and air-operated controlling equipments, etc.
- Chemical industries like fertilizer plant,
- In refrigeration systems, air conditioning, drying and ventilation fields.

6.2 CLASSIFICATION OF AIR COMPRESSORS

1. Positive Displacement Air Compressors:

In positive displacement air compressors, the air is trapped in specified boundaries and delivered at regular interval to the receiver after compression.

(a) **Reciprocating Air Compressors:** In reciprocating air compressors, the air pressure is increased by means of variation in the cylinder volume with the help of moving piston.

(b) **Rotary Air Compressors:** In these compressors, the air is entrapped between two sets of engaging surfaces, and pressure rise is either by back flow of air (roots blower) or by both squeezing action and back flow of air (vane type).

2. Dynamic Compressors:

These are also known as steady-flow or non-positive displacement compressors. In these compressors, air flows continuously and steadily. The energy from the impeller is transferred to the air as the air flows through the system and increases pressure mainly due to dynamic effects.

6.3 DIFFERENCE BETWEEN RECIPROCATING AND ROTARY COMPRESSORS

Reciprocating Compressor	Rotary Compressor
1. These compressors are suitable for high pressure with low volume.	1. These compressors are suitable for low pressure with large volume.
2. Receiver is required because of intermittent delivery.	2. No need of receiver delivering air at uniform rate.
3. For the same flow rate, size of compressor is large and weight is more.	3. For the same flow rate, size of compressor is small and it is light weight.
4. They are subjected to heavy vibrations.	4. Comparatively, these face low vibrations.
5. Maintenance cost is more.	5. Maintenance cost is less.
6. Leakage problem is more.	6. Comparatively low leakage.

6.4 DIFFERENCE BETWEEN COMPRESSOR AND BLOWER

Compressor	Blower
1. Compressor is a device for compressing air or gas at high pressure.	1. Blower is a device for blowing air or gas. They relatively operate at low pressure.
2. Compressor compresses gases and increases their pressure or internal energy.	2. Blower is capable of providing kinetic energy to the gases.
3. It may be reciprocating or rotary type.	3. It is rotary type with axial flow or radial flow.
4. Some types of compressors need cooling arrangement.	4. Cooling arrangement is not required for blowers.
5. Compressors are used to supply compressed air for various applications such as rock drills, machine tools, etc.	5. Blowers are used for low-pressure applications such as agitation, pneumatic conveying or combustion air.
6. They consume more power.	6. They consume less power.

6.5 SINGLE-STAGE RECIPROCATING COMPRESSOR

6.5.1 Working of Single-stage Reciprocating Compressor

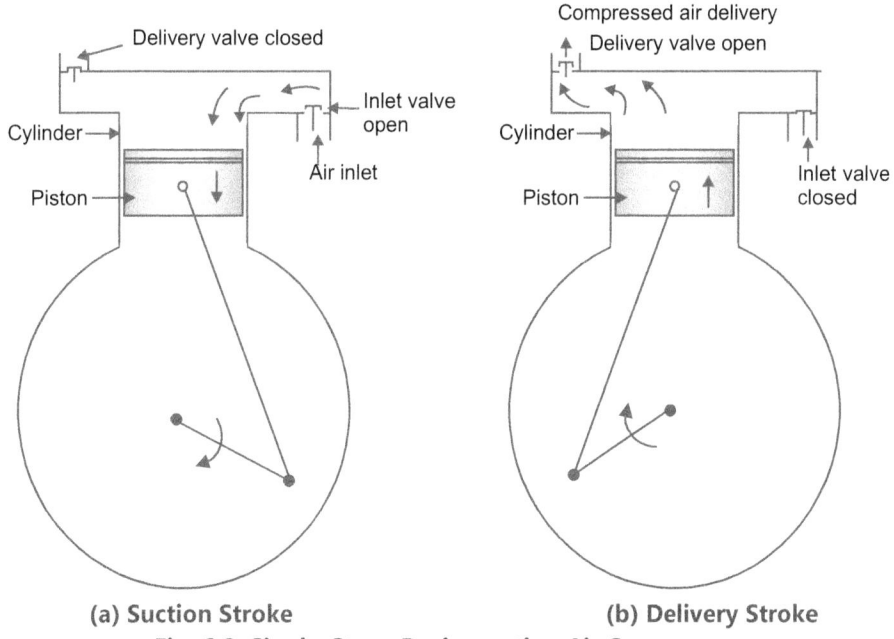

(a) Suction Stroke   (b) Delivery Stroke
Fig. 6.2: Single-Stage Reciprocating Air Compressor

- The single-stage reciprocating air compressor consists of a piston which reciprocates in a cylinder, driven through a connecting rod and crank mounted in a crank case.
- There are inlet and delivery valves mounted in the head of the cylinder. These valves are usually of the pressure differential type, operates as a result of the pressure difference across the valve.
- As shown in Fig. 6.2 (a), the downward movement of piston in the cylinder causes pressure drop in the cylinder below the atmospheric pressure. The inlet valve is opened due to pressure difference. The air is taken into the cylinder until the piston reaches bottom dead centre position.
- As shown in Fig. 6.2 (b), the piston is now moving upwards. A slight increase in cylinder pressure will close the inlet valve. The pressure starts increasing continuously until the pressure inside the cylinder is above the pressure of the delivery side which is connected to the receiver. Then the delivery valve opens and compressed air is delivered during the remaining upward motion of the piston to the receiver.
- At the end of delivery stroke, small volume of high pressure air is left in the clearance space. This air expands as the piston starts moving downwards and pressure of the air falls until it is just below the atmospheric pressure. This causes opening of inlet valve and entry of atmospheric air in the cylinder and the cycle is repeated. The suction, compression and delivery of the air take place within two strokes of the piston or one revolution of the crank.
- There is intermittent flow of air in a reciprocating air compressor.

6.5.2 Computation of Work Done (Neglecting Clearance)

Fig. 6.3 shows a theoretical p-V diagram for a single-stage reciprocating compressor neglecting clearance.

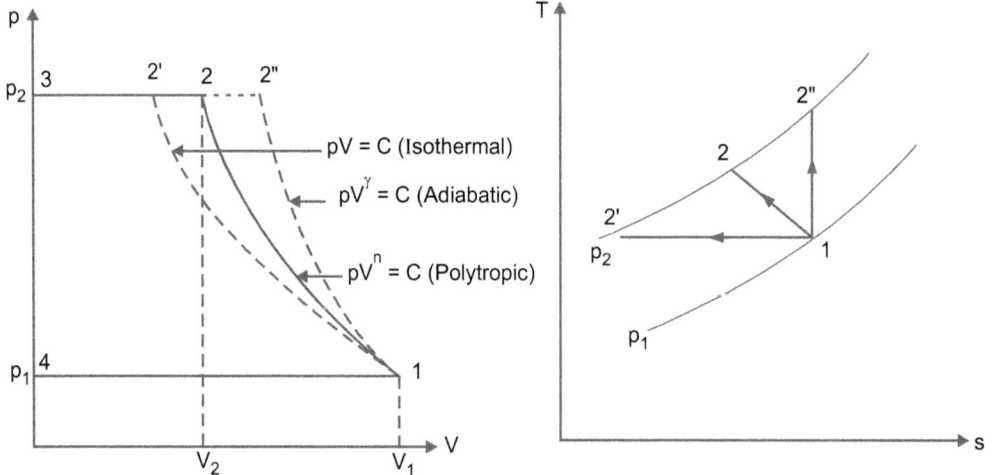

Fig. 6.3: Theoretical p-V and T-s diagrams for a single-stage reciprocating air compressor

Three different operations of the compressors viz. suction, compression and delivery, are shown in Fig. 6.3.

4-1 (Suction) : Air of volume V_1 enters into compressor at pressure p_1 and temperature T_1.

1-2 (Compression) : Air compressed according to the law $pV^n = C$, from pressure p_1 to p_2. Volume decreases from V_1 to V_2. Temperature increases from T_1 to T_2.

2-3 (Delivery) : Compressed air of volume V_2 delivered from compressor at pressure p_2 and temperature T_2.

1. **Work Done during polytropic compression ($pV^n = C$):**

The area 4-1-2-3-4 represents the work done per cycle,

$$W = p_2V_2 + \frac{p_2V_2 - p_1V_1}{n - 1} - p_1V_1$$

$$= (p_2V_2 - p_1V_1) + \frac{p_2V_2 - p_1V_1}{n - 1}$$

$$= (p_2V_2 - p_1V_1)\left[1 + \frac{1}{n - 1}\right]$$

$$= \frac{n}{n - 1}(p_2V_2 - p_1V_1) \qquad \ldots (6.1)$$

$$= \frac{n}{n - 1}p_1V_1\left[\frac{p_2V_2}{p_1V_1} - 1\right] \qquad \ldots (6.2)$$

But, $\quad p_1V_1^n = p_2V_2$

$$\therefore \quad \frac{V_2}{V_1} = \left(\frac{p_1}{p_2}\right)^{\frac{1}{n}} = \left(\frac{p_2}{p_1}\right)^{-\frac{1}{n}}$$

Substituting this in equation (6.2), we have,

$$W = \frac{n}{n - 1}p_1V_1\left[\frac{p_2}{p_1} \cdot \left(\frac{p_2}{p_1}\right)^{-\frac{1}{n}} - 1\right]$$

$$= \frac{n}{n - 1}p_1V_1\left[\left(\frac{p_2}{p_1}\right)^{1 - \frac{1}{n}} - 1\right]$$

$$W = \frac{n}{n - 1}p_1V_1\left[\left(\frac{p_2}{p_1}\right)^{\frac{n-1}{n}} - 1\right] \qquad \ldots(6.3)$$

$$= \frac{n}{n - 1}mRT_1\left[\left(\frac{p_2}{p_1}\right)^{\frac{n-1}{n}} - 1\right] \quad (\because p_1V_1 = mRT_1) \ldots (6.4)$$

Work done per kg of air delivered = $\dfrac{n}{n-1} RT_1 \left[\left(\dfrac{p_2}{p_1}\right)^{\frac{n-1}{n}} - 1 \right]$ ... (6.5)

The air delivery temperature T_2 can be obtained by using equation,

$$\dfrac{T_2}{T_1} = \left(\dfrac{p_2}{p_1}\right)^{\frac{n-1}{n}}$$

2. **Work done during isothermal compression (pV = C):**

   The area 4-1-2'-3-4 represents work done per cycle if compression process is isothermal,

   $$W' = p_2 V_2' + p_1 V_1 \ln\left(\dfrac{V_1}{V_2'}\right) - p_1 V_1$$

   But, $\quad p_1 V_1 = p_2 V_2'$ is the required condition for isothermal process

   $\therefore \quad W' = p_1 V_1 \ln\left(\dfrac{V_1}{V_2'}\right) = p_1 V_1 \ln\left(\dfrac{p_2}{p_1}\right) = p_1 V_1 \ln r \left(r = \dfrac{p_2}{p_1}\right)$ ... (6.6)

   $\qquad\qquad = mRT_1 \ln\left(\dfrac{p_2}{p_1}\right)$

3. **Work done during isentropic (Adiabatic) compression ($pV^\gamma = C$):**

   The area 4-1-2"-3-4 represents work done per cycle when compression is isentropic.

   $$W'' = \dfrac{\gamma}{\gamma - 1} p_1 V_1 \left[\left(\dfrac{p_2}{p_1}\right)^{\frac{\gamma - 1}{\gamma}} - 1 \right] \qquad \text{... (6.7)}$$

6.6 ISOTHERMAL EFFICIENCY (S-09, 13, W-09, 11)

- Inspection of p-V diagram (Fig. 6.3 (a)) shows that, the work required to run the compressor becomes minimum if the compression follows isothermal process (minimum area under isothermal process) than actual compression ($pV^n = C$).
- Isothermal compression cannot be achieved in practice but an attempt is made to approach the isothermal case by cooling the compressor either by addition of cooling fins or a water jacket to a compressor cylinder.
- For a reciprocating compressor, a comparison between the actual work done during compression and ideal isothermal work done is made by means of the isothermal efficiency.

This is defined as,

$$\text{Isothermal efficiency} = \dfrac{\text{Isothermal work done}}{\text{Actual work done}}$$

Thus, higher the isothermal efficiency, the more nearly has the actual compression approached the ideal isothermal compression (when point 2 moves towards 2', the area under the curve i.e. actual work done decreases and isothermal efficiency increases).

$$\eta_i = \frac{W'}{W}$$

Substituting W and W' from equations (6.3) and (6.6), above equations becomes,

$$\eta_i = \frac{p_1 V_1 \ln\left(\frac{p_2}{p_1}\right)}{\frac{n}{n-1} p_1 V_1 \left[\left(\frac{p_2}{p_1}\right)^{\frac{n-1}{n}} - 1\right]} \quad \ldots (6.8)$$

6.6.1 Methods for Improving Isothermal Efficiency (S-10, 11, 13)

The following practical methods are used to achieve nearly isothermal compression (n little above one) for high speed compressors. The object of all these methods is to reduce the final temperature T_2 during compression so that actual work approaches more closely to the isothermal compression. These methods are as follows:

1. External Fins:
Effective cooling can be achieved for small capacity air compressor with the use of fins on the external surface of the compressor.

2. Spray Injection:
The water supply injection into compressor cylinder towards the end of compression stroke used some years ago, has following disadvantages.
    (a) Needs special gear for injection.
    (b) Injected water mixes with cylinder lubrication and attacks cylinder walls and valves.
    (c) The water mixed with air should be separated before using air.

3. Water Jacketing:
In this method, the water is circulated around the cylinder through the water jacket which helps to cool the air during compression. Now-a-days, this is commonly used method.

4. Inter-cooling:
Water jacketing is not much effective when the speed of compressor is high and pressure ratio required is also high with single-stage compression. Inter-cooling is used in addition to water jacketing by dividing the compression process into two or more stages. The air compressed in first stage is cooled in a heat exchanger known as inter-cooler to its original temperature before it is taken to the second stage.

5. By a suitable choice of cylinder proportions:
By providing short stroke and a large bore in conjunction with sleeve valves, a much greater surface is available for cooling, and the surface of the cylinder head is far more effective in this respect than the surface of the barrel. Because the periodic motion of the piston does not allow the barrel to be exposed to the air for a sufficient time for heat to flow away. Moreover the air is compressed against the cylinder cover.

6.7 SINGLE-STAGE COMPRESSORS WITH CLEARANCE VOLUME

- The clearance volume is the volume within the cylinder between cylinder head and piston, at the end of inward stroke.
- The effect of clearance volume is to reduce the volume actually aspirated. Therefore, clearance volume should be as small as possible.
- It is not possible to reduce clearance volume to zero, for mechanical reason. Moreover, it is not desirable to allow the piston head to come in contact with the cylinder head.
- In addition to this, the passage leading to the inlet and outlet valves always contribute to clearance volume.

As shown in Fig. 6.4, at point 1, the cylinder is full of intake air, volume V_1 and the piston is about to start its compression stroke. The air is compressed polytropically (pV^n = C) to delivery pressure p_2 and volume V_2. At point 2, delivery valve theoretically opens and compressed air is delivered till the piston reaches at 3. At this stage, there will be some air (equal to clearance volume) left in the clearance space of the cylinder at pressure p_2. Then the piston begins intake stroke and the expansion of residual air takes place polytropically to the pressure p_1 and volume V_4. At point 4, inlet valve opens to take fresh air charge in. For remainder of intake stroke (4 to 1) fresh charge is taken into the cylinder. This volume ($V_1 - V_4$) is the effective swept volume.

Work done per cycle,

$$W = \text{Net area 1-2-3-4-1}$$
$$= \text{Area 1-2-6-5-1} - \text{Area 3-4-5-6-3}$$

Assuming polytropic compression and clearance expansion,

$$W = \frac{n}{n-1} p_1 V_1 \left[\left(\frac{p_2}{p_1}\right)^{\frac{n-1}{n}} - 1\right] - \frac{n}{n-1} p_4 V_4 \left[\left(\frac{p_3}{p_4}\right)^{\frac{n-1}{n}} - 1\right] \quad \ldots (6.9)$$

But $p_4 = p_1$ and $p_3 = p_2$, then equation (6.9) becomes,

$$W = \frac{n}{n-1} p_1 V_1 \left[\left(\frac{p_2}{p_1}\right)^{\frac{n-1}{n}} - 1\right] - \frac{n}{n-1} p_1 V_4 \left[\left(\frac{p_2}{p_1}\right)^{\frac{n-1}{n}} - 1\right]$$

$$= \frac{n}{n-1} p_1 (V_1 - V_4) \left[\left(\frac{p_2}{p_1}\right)^{\frac{n-1}{n}} - 1\right] \quad \ldots (6.10)$$

$$= \frac{n}{n-1} p_1 V_a \left[\left(\frac{p_2}{p_1}\right)^{\frac{n-1}{n}} - 1\right] \quad \ldots (6.11)$$

where $V_a = V_1 - V_4$ is the actual volume of free air delivered per cycle.

$$W = \frac{n}{n-1} m_1 RT_1 \left[\left(\frac{p_2}{p_1}\right)^{\frac{n-1}{n}} - 1\right] \quad \ldots (6.12)$$

where m_1 is the actual mass of the air delivered per cycle.

∴ Work done per kg of air delivered

$$= \frac{n}{n-1} RT_1 \left[\left(\frac{p_2}{p_1}\right)^{\frac{n-1}{n}} - 1\right] \quad \ldots (6.13)$$

From equations (6.5) and (6.13), it is clear that, the clearance volume does not affect the work of compression per kg of air.

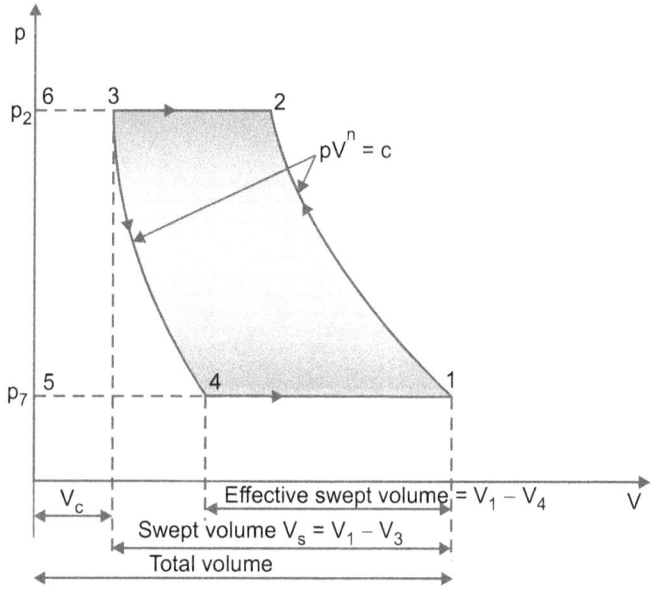

Fig. 6.4: p-V diagram for single stage-compressor with clearance volume

- The clearance volume of the compressor is given as a percentage of the stroke volume.

6.8 VOLUMETRIC EFFICIENCY

- The volumetric efficiency of a compressor is the ratio of free air delivered to the displacement of compressor. It is also expressed as the ratio of effective stroke volume to the stroke volume.

$$\text{Volumetric efficiency} = \frac{\text{Effective stroke volume}}{\text{Stroke volume}}$$

$$\eta_{vol} = \frac{V_1 - V_4}{V_1 - V_3} \quad \ldots (6.14)$$

- Because of the presence of clearance volume, volumetric efficiency is always less than unity. As a percentage, it usually varies from 60% to 85%.
- Volumetric efficiency can be expressed in terms of clearance ratio C and pressure ratio (p_2/p_1).

The clearance ratio,

$$C = \frac{\text{Clearance volume}}{\text{Stroke volume}} = \frac{V_3}{V_1 - V_3} = \frac{V_c}{V_s} \quad \ldots (6.15)$$

The C is expressed as percentage of stroke volume and in general it is between 4% and 10% of the stroke volume.

From equation (6.15),

$$V_3 = (V_1 - V_3) \cdot C \quad \ldots (6.16)$$

From relation $p_3 V_3^n = p_4 V_4^n$

$$V_4 = V_3 \cdot \left(\frac{p_3}{p_4}\right)^{\frac{1}{n}}$$

Substituting V_3 from equation (6.16), we get,

$$V_4 = C \cdot (V_1 - V_3) \left(\frac{p_3}{p_4}\right)^{\frac{1}{n}}$$

Also, $p_1 = p_4$ and $p_3 = p_2$

$$\therefore \quad V_4 = C (V_1 - V_3) \left(\frac{p_2}{p_1}\right)^{\frac{1}{n}}$$

$$= C \cdot V_s \cdot \left(\frac{p_2}{p_1}\right)^{\frac{1}{n}}$$

Now,

$$\eta_{vol} = \frac{V_1 - V_4}{V_1 - V_3} = \frac{V_1 - V_4}{V_s}$$

But,

$$V_1 = V_c + V_s = C \cdot V_s + V_s$$

$$\therefore \quad \eta_{vol} = \frac{C \cdot V_s + V_s - C \cdot V_s \left(\frac{p_2}{p_1}\right)^{\frac{1}{n}}}{V_s}$$

$$\therefore \quad \eta_{vol} = 1 + C - C \left(\frac{p_2}{p_1}\right)^{\frac{1}{n}}$$

$$= 1 - C \left[\left(\frac{p_2}{p_1}\right)^{\frac{1}{n}} - 1\right] \quad \ldots (6.17)$$

Fig. 6.5 is the plot of equation (6.17).

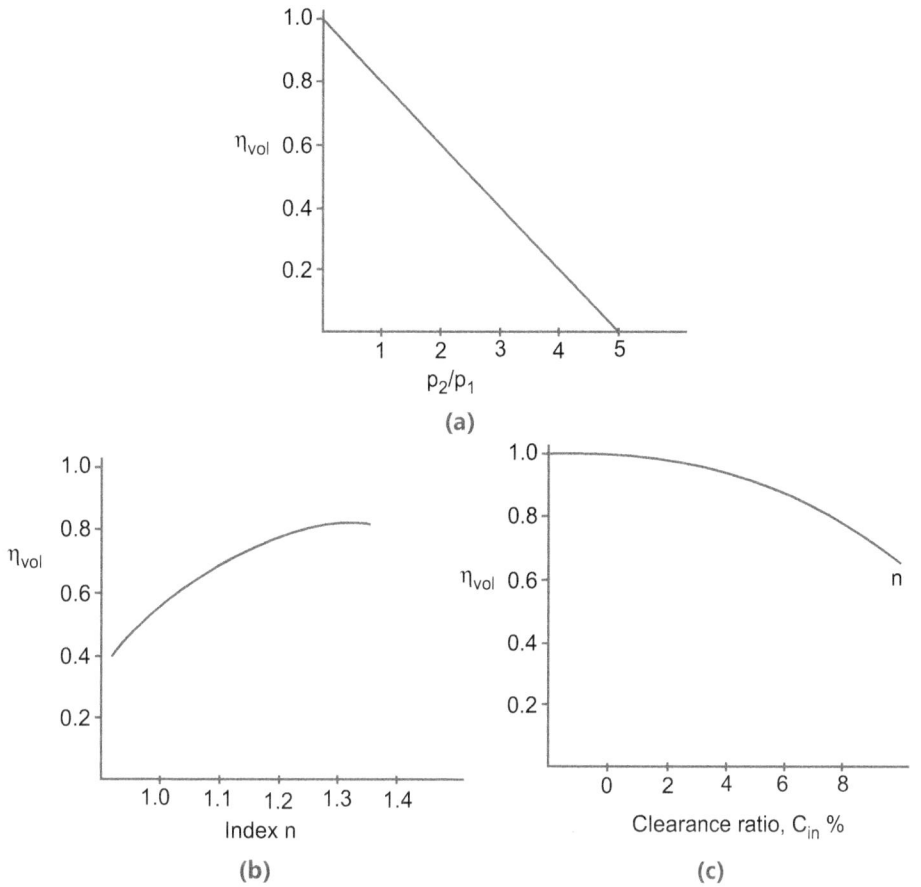

Fig. 6.5: Effect of Clearance Ratio, Pressure Ratio and Index n on Volumetric Efficiency

From the plot, it is observed that,

For $p_2 = p_1$, there is no compression and η_{vol} = 100%.

Volumetric efficiency decreases with increase in delivery pressure p_2 and clearance ratio C.
Volumetric efficiency increases with increase in index n.
The volumetric efficiency is lowered by any one of the following conditions:
  (i)   Very high speed.
  (ii) Leakage past the piston.
  (iii) Obstruction at inlet valves.
  (iv) Overheating of air by contact with hot cylinder walls.
  (v)   Inertia effect of air in suction pipe.

By paying careful attention in the design of the compressor to these causes of loss, an improvement in volumetric efficiency can be obtained.

6.9 POWER OF A SINGLE-STAGE COMPRESSOR

The power required to drive the compressor can be obtained from the relation,

$$p = \frac{W \cdot N_w}{60} \text{ watts}$$

If N is the speed of the compressor in r.p.m., then number of working strokes per minute (N_w),

$$N_w = N \quad \text{... (For single-acting compressor)}$$
$$= 2N \quad \text{... (For double-acting compressor)}$$

Since the compression takes place in three different ways, therefore, power obtained from different work done will be different and given as,

$$\text{Isothermal power} = \frac{W' N_w}{60} \text{ watts}$$

$$\text{Indicated power} = \frac{W N_w}{60} \text{ watts}$$

$$\text{Isentropic/Adiabatic power} = \frac{W'' N_w}{60} \text{ watts}$$

where, W', W, W'' = Isothermal, Polytropic, Isentropic work done respectively

6.10 MECHANICAL EFFICIENCY

The mechanical efficiency of the compressor is the ratio of indicated power to the brake power (shaft power).

$$\eta_{mech} = \frac{\text{Indicated power}}{\text{Brake power}}$$

6.11 MEAN EFFECTIVE PRESSURE

In practice, air pressure on the compressor piston keeps on changing with movement of piston in the cylinder. The mean effective pressure (p_m) of the compressor can be determined mathematically by dividing the work done per cycle to the stroke volume.

$$p_m = \frac{\text{Work done}}{\text{Stroke volume}}$$

Work done per cycle,

$$W = \frac{n}{n-1} p_1 (V_1 - V_4) \left[\left(\frac{p_2}{p_1}\right)^{\frac{n-1}{n}} - 1 \right]$$

$$\therefore \quad p_m V_s = \frac{n}{n-1} p_1 \cdot V_a \left[\left(\frac{p_2}{p_1}\right)^{\frac{n-1}{n}} - 1 \right] \quad \left(\because p_m = \frac{W}{V_s}\right)$$

$$\therefore \quad p_m = \frac{n}{n-1} p_1 \frac{V_a}{V_s}\left[\left(\frac{p_2}{p_1}\right)^{\frac{n-1}{n}} - 1\right]$$

$$\therefore \quad p_m = \frac{n}{n-1} p_1 \cdot \eta_{vol}\left[\left(\frac{p_2}{p_1}\right)^{\frac{n-1}{n}} - 1\right] \qquad \left(\because \eta_{vol} = \frac{V_a}{V_s}\right)$$

6.12 FREE AIR DELIVERY

The Free Air Delivered (F.A.D) is the actual volume delivered at the stated pressure reduced to intake temperature and pressure. It is expressed in m³/min. The displacement is actual volume in m³/min swept out.

The free air delivered per minute is less than the displacement of the compressor because of the following reasons:

1. The fluid resistance through the air intake, and valves prevents the cylinder being fully charged with air at atmospheric conditions.
2. On entering the hot cylinder, the air expands, so that the mass of the air present (compared with that at atmospheric temperature) is reduced.
3. The high pressure air tapped in the clearance space, must expand to a pressure below atmospheric before the automatic suction valves can open; a portion of the suction stroke is therefore wasted in effecting this expansion.
4. A certain loss is caused by the leakage.

6.13 ACTUAL p-V (INDICATOR) DIAGRAM FOR SINGLE-STAGE COMPRESSOR (S-09, W-09, 11)

The actual p-V diagram for a single-stage compressor is shown in Fig. 6.6.

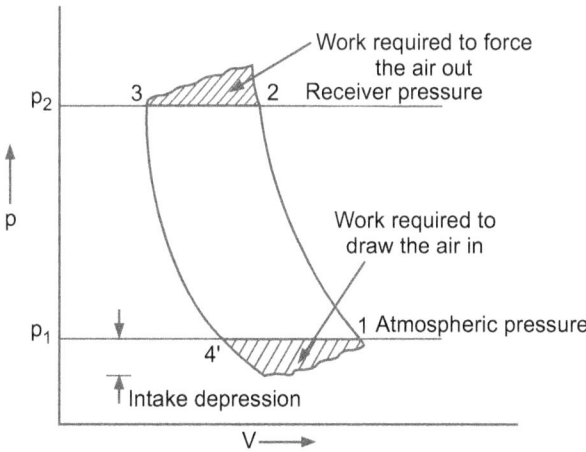

Fig. 6.6: Actual p-V (Indicator) Diagram for a Single-Stage Compressor

APPLIED THERMODYNAMICS — POSITIVE DISPLACEMENT COMPRESSOR

The actual diagram differs from the theoretical as there are intake and discharge losses. The intake losses include:
- the friction loss in pipe,
- friction loss in inlet valve
- valve inertia loss.

- Theoretically, the inlet valve should open at 4, but in actual practice it will not open. This is because of inlet valve inertia and pressure difference required to open the valve. Thus, the pressure drops below atmospheric pressure until the valve is closed (i.e. point 1). The oscillating part of the curve indicates valve bounce or valve flutter due to vibration of valve. This negative pressure is known as intake depression.
- Similar situation occurs on the delivery side also. Theoretically, discharge valve should open at 2, but actually it opens afterwards at pressure more than delivery pressure with bounce or flutter.
- The effect of these added shaded areas is to increase the work required per kg of air delivered to the receiver. Therefore, the actual work required to compress the air will be greater than the theoretical work.

SOLVED PROBLEMS ON SINGLE-STAGE COMPRESSOR

Problem 6.1:
A single-stage, single-acting air compressor delivers 15 m³/min of free air from 1 bar to 8 bar at 300 r.p.m. The clearance volume is 6.25% of the stroke volume and compression and expansion follow the law $pV^{1.3}$ = C. Find the diameter and stroke of the compressor. Take L/D = 1.5. The temperature and pressure of air at suction are same as that of free air. Also determine indicated power of the compressor.

Solution: Given: F.A.D. = 15 m³/min, p_1 = 1 bar, p_2 = 8 bar, N = 300 r.p.m., n = 1.3, C = 0.0625, L/D = 1.5.

Diameter and Stroke:

$$\text{Free air delivery per cycle} = V_a = \frac{\text{F.A.D/min}}{N} = \frac{15}{300}$$

$$V_a = 0.05 \text{ m}^3/\text{cycle}$$

Volumetric efficiency is given by,

$$\eta_{vol} = 1 - C\left[\left(\frac{p_2}{p_1}\right)^{\frac{1}{n}} - 1\right]$$

$$= 1 - 0.0625\left[\left(\frac{8}{1}\right)^{\frac{1}{1.3}} - 1\right]$$

$$= 0.753 = \mathbf{75.306\%}$$

Volumetric efficiency is also written as,

$$\eta_{vol} = \frac{V_a}{V_s}$$

∴ Stroke volume, $V_s = \dfrac{V_a}{\eta_{vol}}$

$$= \frac{0.05}{0.753}$$

$$= 0.06639 \text{ m}^3$$

But, $V_s = \dfrac{\pi}{4} D^2 \cdot L = \mathbf{0.06639}$

∴ $\dfrac{\pi}{4} D^2 \times 1.5\, D = \mathbf{0.06639}$

$$D^3 = \frac{0.06639 \times 4}{1.5\,\pi} = 0.05635$$

∴ D = 0.383 m = 383 mm

and L = 1.5 × D = 1.5 × 0.383 = 0.575 m = **575 mm**

Indicated power:

The work done per cycle,

$$W = \frac{n}{n-1} p_1 V_a \left[\left(\frac{p_2}{p_1}\right)^{\frac{n-1}{n}} - 1\right]$$

$$= \frac{1.3}{1.3-1} \times 1 \times 10^5 \times 0.05 \left[\left(\frac{8}{1}\right)^{\frac{1.3-1}{1.3}} - 1\right]$$

$$= 13344 \text{ J/cycle} = 13.344 \text{ kJ/cycle}$$

Indicated power,

$$P = \frac{W \cdot N_w}{60}$$

$$= \frac{13344 \times 300}{60 \times 1000}$$

$$= \mathbf{66.72 \text{ kW}}$$

Problem 6.2:

A single-stage, single-acting reciprocating air compressor takes in air at 1 bar, 27°C and delivers at 7 bar, volume of air entering the compressor is 5 m³/min. Air is compressed according to $pV^{1.3}$ = C. Calculate isothermal efficiency, power required to drive the compressor, neglecting clearance volume. **(P.U. December 2005)**

Solution: Given: p_1 = 1 bar, T_1 = 27°C, p_2 = 7 bar, V_1 = 5 m³/min, n = 1.3.

Isothermal efficiency:

$$\eta_i = \frac{W'}{W} = \frac{p_1 V_1 \ln\left(\frac{p_2}{p_1}\right)}{\frac{n}{n-1} p_1 V_1 \left[\left(\frac{p_2}{p_1}\right)^{\frac{n-1}{n}} - 1\right]}$$

$$= \frac{\ln\left(\frac{7}{1}\right)}{\frac{1.3}{0.3}\left[(7)^{\frac{0.3}{1.3}} - 1\right]}$$

$$\eta_i = 0.7922$$

Isothermal efficiency, η_i = **79.22%**

Power:

Power required to drive the compressor is nothing but work done per second.

Work done per cycle is given by,

$$W = \frac{n}{n-1} p_1 V_1 \left[\left(\frac{p_2}{p_1}\right)^{\frac{n-1}{n}} - 1\right] \qquad (V_1 \text{ in } m^3)$$

In above equation, V_1 is in m^3. When V_1 is taken as m^3/sec, we get power required to drive the compressor.

$$\therefore \text{Power} = \frac{n}{n-1} p_1 V_1 \left[\left(\frac{p_2}{p_1}\right)^{\frac{n-1}{n}} - 1\right] \qquad \left(V_1 \text{ in } \frac{m^3}{sec}\right)$$

$$= \frac{1.3}{0.3} \times 1 \times 10^5 \times \frac{5}{60} \times \left[(7)^{\frac{0.3}{1.3}} - 1\right]$$

$$= 20468.86 \text{ W}$$

$$= \mathbf{20.468 \text{ kW}}$$

Power required to drive the compressor neglecting clearance volume = 20.468 kW.

Problem 6.3:

A single-stage, single-acting air compressor works between 01 bar and 16 bar by the compression law $pV^{1.3}$ = C at 350 mm. Piston speed is 200 m/min. Indicated power is 30 kW. Determine cylinder dimensions, if the volumetric efficiency of the compressor is 85%.

Solution: Given: p_1 = 1 bar, p_2 = 16 bar, n = 1.3, N = 350 r.p.m., Piston speed = 200 m/min, p_{ind} = 30 kW, η_{vol} = 0.85.

Power of single-stage compressor,

$$p = \frac{W \cdot N}{60} \text{ watts}$$

$$30 \times 10^3 = \frac{W \times 350}{60}$$

∴ W = 5142.857 N·m/cycle

Work done per cycle,

$$W = \frac{n}{n-1} p_1 V_a \left[\left(\frac{p_2}{p_1}\right)^{\frac{n-1}{n}} - 1 \right]$$

$$5142.857 = \frac{1.3}{0.3} \times 1 \times 10^5 \times V_a \times \left[\left(\frac{16}{1}\right)^{\frac{0.3}{1.3}} - 1 \right]$$

V_a = **0.01324 m³**

Volumetric efficiency,

$$\eta_{vol} = \frac{V_a}{V_s}$$

∴ $$V_s = \frac{V_a}{\eta_{vol}}$$

$$= \frac{0.01324}{0.85}$$

V_s = **0.01558 m³**

Piston speed/min = 2 LN

200 = 2L × 350

$$L = \frac{200}{2 \times 350}$$

= **0.2857 m**

Stroke volume, $V_s = \frac{\pi}{4} \times D^2 \times L$

$$0.01558 = \frac{\pi}{4} \times D^2 \times 0.2857$$

D = 0.2635 m

Length of piston stroke = **285 mm**
Diameter of cylinder = **264 mm**

Problem 6.4:

A single-acting air compressor has a cylinder bore of 15 cm and piston stroke of 25 cm. The crankshaft is rotating at 600 r.p.m. Air is taken from atmosphere at pressure 1.013 bar and 27°C and delivered at 11 bar. Assume compression takes place polytropically by law $pV^{1.25}$ = C. The clearance volume is 5% of the stroke volume. Mechanical efficiency of the compressor is 80%. **(P.U. May 2005)**

Determine:
(i) Power required to drive the compressor,
(ii) Volumetric efficiency,

(iii) Delivery temperature,
(iv) Time required to deliver air of volume 1 m³.

Solution: Given: D = 0.15 m, L = 0.25 m, N = 600 r.p.m. p_1 = 1.013 bar, T_1 = 27°C = 27 + 273 = 300 K, p_2 = 11 bar, n = 1.25, C = 0.05, η_{mech} = 0.8.

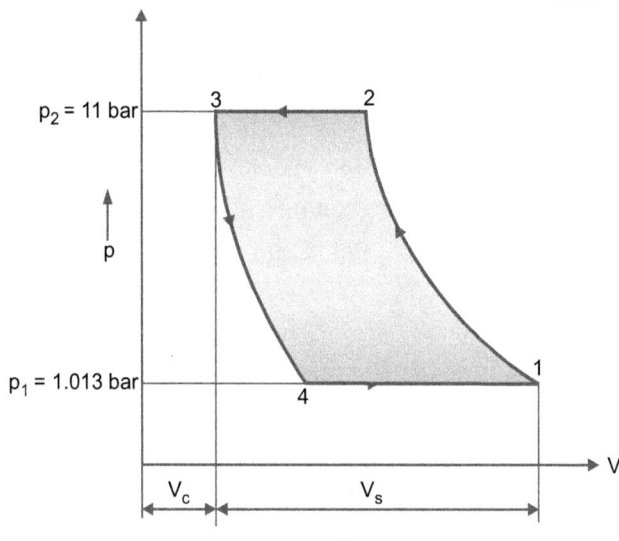

Fig. 6.7

$$\text{Stroke volume} = \frac{\pi}{4}D^2L = \frac{\pi}{4} \times 0.15^2 \times 0.25$$

$$V_s = 4.417 \times 10^{-3} \text{ m}^3$$

$$\text{Clearance volume, } V_c = C \times V_s = 0.05 \times 4.417 \times 10^{-3}$$

$$= \mathbf{2.21 \times 10^{-4} \text{ m}^3}$$

$$\text{Volume, } V_1 = V_c + V_s$$

$$= 2.21 \times 10^{-4} + 4.42 \times 10^{-3}$$

$$= \mathbf{4.64 \times 10^{-3} \text{ m}^3}$$

For expansion process (3-4),

$$p_3 V_3^{1.25} = p_4 V_4^{1.25}$$

$$V_4 = V_3 \left(\frac{p_3}{p_1}\right)^{\frac{1}{n}} = 2.21 \times 10^{-4} \times \left(\frac{11}{1.013}\right)^{\frac{1}{1.25}}$$

$$= \mathbf{1.489 \times 10^{-3} \text{ m}^3}$$

$$V_a = (V_1 - V_4) = (4.64 - 1.489) \times 10^{-3}$$

$$= \mathbf{3.151 \times 10^{-3} \text{ m}^3}$$

(i) Power required to drive the compressor:

Indicated work done per cycle,

$$W = \frac{n}{n-1} p_1 V_a \left[\left(\frac{p_2}{p_1}\right)^{\frac{n-1}{n}} - 1 \right]$$

$$= \frac{1.25}{0.25} \times 1.013 \times 10^5 \times 3.151 \times 10^{-3} \times \left[\left(\frac{11}{1.013}\right)^{\frac{0.25}{1.25}} - 1 \right]$$

$$= \mathbf{975.5 \ J/cycle}$$

Indicated power,

$$p = \frac{W N_w}{60}$$

$$= \frac{975.5 \times 600}{60}$$

$$= 9755.06 \ W$$

$$= \mathbf{9.755 \ kW}$$

Power required to drive the compressor

$$= \frac{\text{Indicated power}}{\text{Mechanical efficiency}}$$

$$= \frac{9.76}{0.8} = \mathbf{12.20 \ kW}$$

(ii) Volumetric efficiency:

$$\eta_{vol} = 1 - C \left[\left(\frac{p_2}{p_1}\right)^{\frac{1}{n}} - 1 \right]$$

$$= 1 - 0.05 \left[\left(\frac{11}{1.013}\right)^{\frac{1}{1.25}} - 1 \right]$$

$$= 0.713$$

$$= \mathbf{71.30\%}$$

(iii) Delivery temperature:

$$T_2 = T_1 \left(\frac{p_2}{p_1}\right)^{\frac{n-1}{n}}$$

$$= 300 \times \left(\frac{11}{1.013}\right)^{\frac{0.25}{1.25}}$$

$$= \mathbf{483.38 \ K}$$

(iv) Time required to deliver 1 m³ air:

$$p_2 V_2 = m_2 R T_2$$

Mass delivered,

$$m_2 = \frac{p_2 V_2}{R T_2} = \frac{11 \times 10^5 \times 1}{287 \times 483.37}$$

$$= 7.929 \text{ kg}$$

Mass per cycle $= \dfrac{p_1 (V_1 - V_4)}{R T_1} \times N$

$$= \frac{1.013 \times 10^5 \times 3.151 \times 10^{-3}}{287 \times 300} \times 600$$

$$= 2.232 \text{ kg/min}$$

Time required to deliver 1 m³ volume

$$= \frac{\text{Mass delivered}}{\text{Mass per minute}}$$

$$= \frac{7.929}{2.232}$$

$$= \textbf{3.55 minutes}$$

Problem 6.5:

Following data relate to a performance test of a single-acting 14 cm × 10 cm reciprocating compressor.

Suction and delivery pressure = 1 bar and 6 bar.

Suction and delivery temperature = 20°C and 180°C

Mass of delivered = 1.7 kg/min

Compressor speed = 1200 r.p.m.

Shaft power = 6.25 kW

Find volumetric efficiency, indicated power, isothermal efficiency and mechanical efficiency.

Solution: Given: p_1 = 1 bar, p_2 = 6 bar, T_1 = 20 + 273 = 293 K, T_2 = 180 + 273 = 453 K, N = 1200 r.p.m., m_a = 1.7 kg/min, p_{shaft} = 6.25 kW, D = 0.14 m, L = 0.1 m.

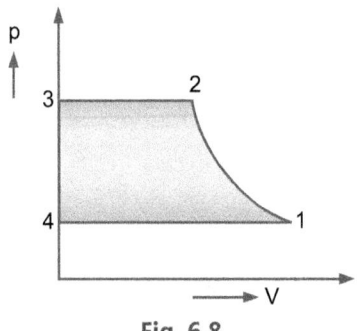

Fig. 6.8

(i) Volumetric efficiency:

$$\text{Stroke volume, } V_s = \frac{\pi}{4} D^2 LN$$

$$= \frac{\pi}{4} \times (0.14)^2 \times 0.1 \times 1200$$

$$= 1.8473 \text{ m}^3/\text{min}^*$$

We know, $\quad p_1 V_1 = mRT_1$

$$V_1 = \frac{mRT_1}{p_1} = \frac{1.7 \times 287 \times 293}{1 \times 10^5}$$

$$= 1.4295 \text{ m}^3/\text{min}$$

$$\eta_{vol} = \frac{V_1}{V_s} = \frac{1.4295}{1.8473} = 0.7738$$

$$= \mathbf{77.38\%}$$

(ii) Indicated power:

We know,

$$\frac{T_2}{T_1} = \left(\frac{p_2}{p_1}\right)^{\frac{n-1}{n}}$$

$$\ln\left(\frac{T_2}{T_1}\right) = \frac{n-1}{n} \ln\left(\frac{p_2}{p_1}\right)$$

$$\frac{n-1}{n} = \frac{\ln(T_2/T_1)}{\ln(p_2/p_1)} = \frac{\ln(453/293)}{\ln(6/1)} = 0.2432$$

$$n - 1 = 0.2432\, n$$

$$0.7568\, n = 1$$

$$\therefore \quad n = 1.32$$

Work done per cycle is given by,

$$W = \frac{n}{n-1} p_1 V_1 \left[\left(\frac{p_2}{p_1}\right)^{\frac{n-1}{n}} - 1\right] \qquad (V_1 \text{ in m}^3)$$

Work done per unit time gives power. If V_1 is taken in m³/sec, the power is given as,

$$\text{Indicated power} = \frac{n}{n-1} p_1 V_1 \left[\left(\frac{p_2}{p_1}\right)^{\frac{n-1}{n}} - 1\right] \qquad (V_1 \text{ in m}^3/\text{sec})$$

$$= \frac{1.32}{0.32} \times 1 \times 10^5 \times \frac{1.4295}{60} \times \left[\left(\frac{6}{1}\right)^{\frac{0.32}{1.32}} - 1\right]$$

$$= 5339.59 \text{ W}$$

$$= \mathbf{5.34 \text{ kW}}$$

---

*__Note :__ Unit of V_1 is m³/min because mass is taken in kg/min.

(iii) Isothermal efficiency:

$$\text{Isothermal power} = p_1 V_1 \ln\left(\frac{p_2}{p_1}\right) = 1 \times 10^5 \times \frac{1.4295}{60} \ln\left(\frac{6}{1}\right) = \textbf{4269 W}$$

$$\eta_{iso} = \frac{\text{Isothermal power}}{\text{Indicated power}}$$

$$= \frac{4269}{5339} = 0.7995 = \textbf{79.95\%}$$

(iv) Mechanical efficiency:

$$\eta_{mech} = \frac{\text{Indicated power}}{\text{Shaft power}}$$

$$= \frac{5.34}{6.25} = 0.8544 = \textbf{85.44\%}$$

6.14 NEED OF MULTISTAGE COMPRESSION

- We have seen that the volumetric efficiency of a reciprocating compressor is a function of clearance ratio C, pressure ratio (p_2/p_1) and index of compression/ expansion.
- If clearance volume is fixed, the volumetric efficiency of a compressor decreases with an increase in pressure ratio.
- A stage may be reached when the volumetric efficiency becomes zero as can be seen from Fig. 6.9.

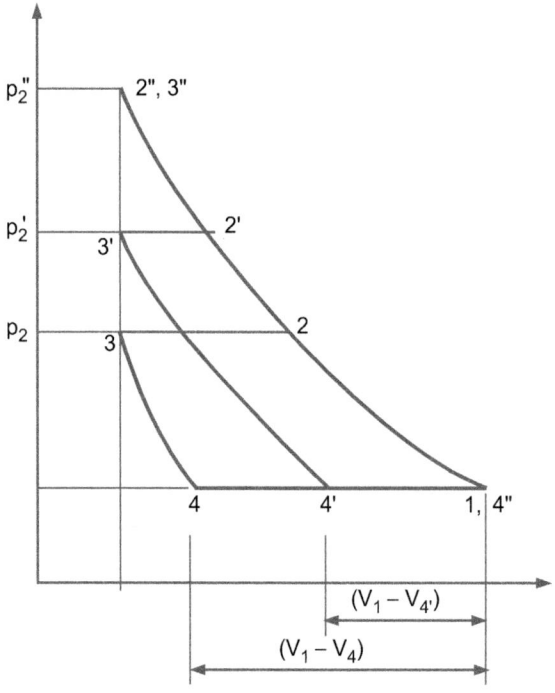

Fig. 6.9: Effect of increased pressure on actual air delivered by a compressor at fixed clearance

- From Fig. 6.9, it is observed that the volume of air admitted in the compressor decreases with increase in delivery pressure for the same clearance volume and fixed intake pressure. At a stage of delivery pressure (p_2''), volume of intake air becomes zero ($V_1 - V_4'' = 0$) and also the volume of air delivered becomes zero ($V_2'' - V_3'' = 0$). The attempt made to deliver the air at a high pressure p_2'' would result in compression and re-expansion of same air again and again without any delivery of high pressure air.
- Therefore, the maximum pressure ratio attainable with a single-stage reciprocating compressor is limited by the clearance volume.

In addition to above, it has been observed that, use of single-stage compression for producing high pressure air (8 bar and above) delivers following drawbacks:

- The size of the cylinder and piston will be too large. This will increase the balancing problem and high torque fluctuation will require a heavier flywheel.
- There is rise in temperature of delivery air.

To overcome above mentioned difficulties, multistage compression with two or more cylinders in series with intercooler is used effectively.

The p-V diagram for two-stage air compression without intercooler is shown in Fig. 6.10.

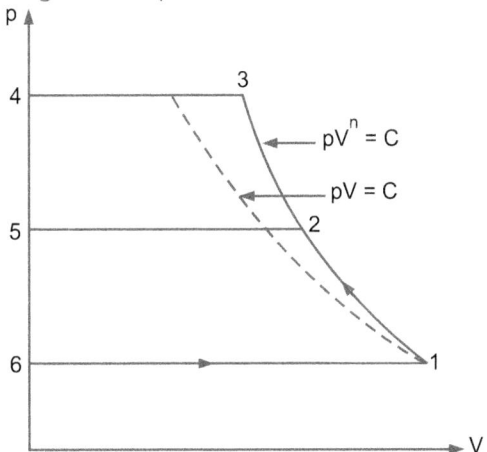

Fig. 6.10: Two-Stage Compression

6.15 TWO-STAGE RECIPROCATING AIR COMPRESSOR WITH INTERCOOLER

In multistage compression, air cooling after leaving each stage is possible. A two-stage reciprocating air compressor with intercooler is shown in Fig. 6.11. Both the cylinders are mounted on the same shaft and driven by a prime mover.

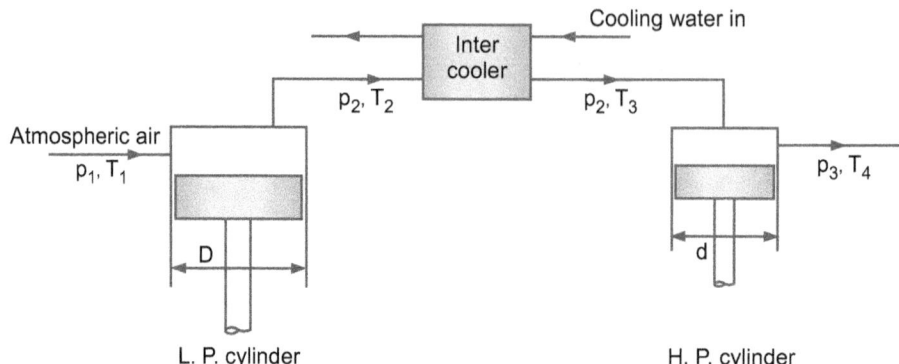

Fig. 6.11: Two-Stage Air Compressor with Intercooler

- In two-stage air compressor, first of all, the fresh air from atmosphere is taken into low pressure (L.P.) cylinder at pressure p_1 and temperature T_1. In low pressure cylinder air is compressed (first stage). Then it is delivered to intercooler at pressure p_2 and temperature T_2. Now the air is cooled in intercooler at constant pressure p_2, from temperature T_2 to T_3 ($T_3 < T_2$). Further, air is compressed in high pressure (H.P.) cylinder (second stage) to give pressure p_3 and temperature T_4 and discharged to the receiver.
- The work saved by introducing the intercooler is shown in Fig. 6.12 (a) by the area 2-3-4-6-2. Sometimes a cooler is used to cool the air before passing to the receiver known as after cooler. This reduces size of the receiver and not the work done.
- If the temperature of air leaving the intercooler (i.e. T_3) is more than the atmospheric air temperature (i.e. T_1) as shown in Fig. 6.12 (b), then the intercooling is known as incomplete or imperfect intercooling. Here, point 3 lies on right side of the isothermal curve.

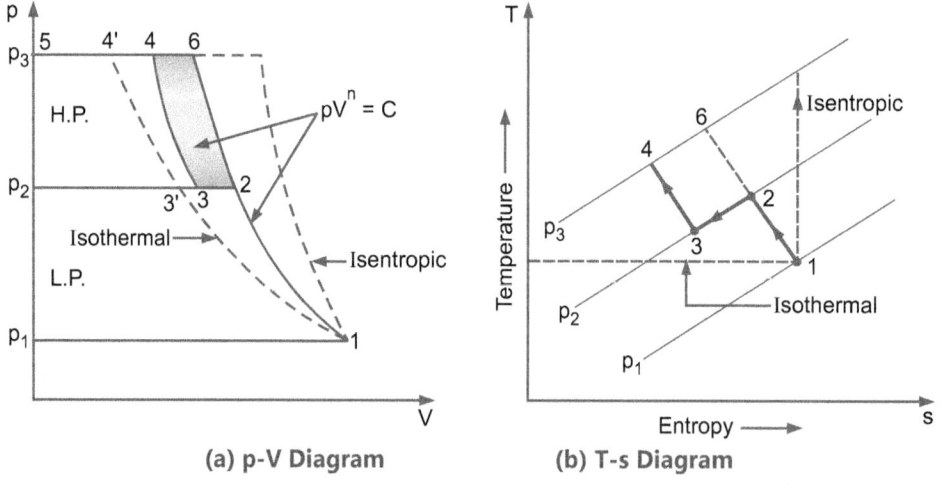

(a) p-V Diagram   (b) T-s Diagram

Fig. 6.12: Two-Stage Compression with Imperfect Intercooling

Work done for a two-stage reciprocating air compressor with intercooler: For a two-stage reciprocating air compressor with intercooler, air is compressed in L.P. and H.P. cylinders. So total work done is the addition of the work done per cycle in L.P. and work done per cycle in H.P. cylinder.

∴ $\quad W = W_{L.P.} + W_{H.P.}$

$$= \frac{n}{n-1} p_1 V_1 \left[\left(\frac{p_2}{p_1}\right)^{\frac{n-1}{n}} - 1\right] + \frac{n}{n-1} p_2 V_3 \left[\left(\frac{p_2}{p_1}\right)^{\frac{n-1}{n}} - 1\right] \quad \ldots (6.18)$$

6.16 CONDITION FOR MINIMUM WORK OF COMPRESSION OR MAXIMUM EFFICIENCY (PERFECT INTERCOOLING)

Fig. 6.12 shows p-V and T-s diagram for two-stage compressor with imperfect cooling and equation (6.18) gives the work done for the same. In this, temperature $T_3 > T_1$.

When the temperature of air leaving the intercooler (T_3) is equal to the atmospheric air temperature (T_1), then the intercooling is known as complete or perfect intercooling and $p_1 V_1 = p_2 V_3 = mRT_1$.

p-V and T-s diagrams for perfect intercooling are shown in Fig. 6.13.

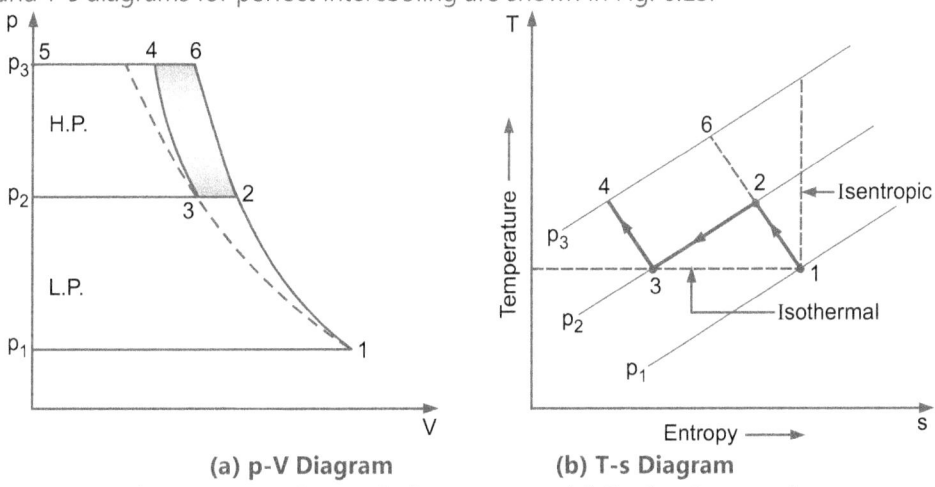

(a) p-V Diagram (b) T-s Diagram
Fig. 6.13: Two-Stage Air Compressor with Perfect Intercooler

The work done for two-stage air compressor with perfect cooling (i.e. $p_1 V_1 = p_2 V_3 = mRT_1$) is given by,

$$W = \frac{n}{n-1} mRT_1 \left[\left(\frac{p_2}{p_1}\right)^{\frac{n-1}{n}} - 1\right] + \frac{n}{n-1} mRT_1 \left[\left(\frac{p_3}{p_2}\right)^{\frac{n-1}{n}} - 1\right] \quad \ldots (6.19)$$

$$= \frac{n}{n-1} mRT_1 \left[\left(\frac{p_2}{p_1}\right)^{\frac{n-1}{n}} + \left(\frac{p_3}{p_2}\right)^{\frac{n-1}{n}} - 2\right]$$

$$= a \cdot mRT_1 \left[\left(\frac{p_2}{p_1}\right)^a + \left(\frac{p_3}{p_2}\right)^a - 2 \right] \qquad \left(\because \frac{n-1}{n} = a\right)$$

If the intake pressure p_1 and the delivery pressure p_3 are fixed, then the intermediate pressure p_2 for the minimum work done to drive the compressor is determined by,

$$\frac{dW}{dp_2} = 0$$

$$\therefore \frac{d}{dp_2}\left(a \cdot mRT_1 \left[\frac{p_2^a}{p_1^a} + \frac{p_3^a}{p_2^a} - 2\right]\right) = 0$$

$$\frac{d}{dp_2}\left(a \cdot mRT_1 \left[\frac{p_2^a}{p_1^a} + p_3^a \cdot p_2^{-a} - 2\right]\right) = 0$$

$$\therefore a \cdot mRT_1 \left[\frac{a \cdot p_2^{a-1}}{p_1^a} + p_3^a(-a)\cdot p_2^{-a-1}\right] = 0 \qquad (\because p_1 \text{ and } p_3 \text{ are fixed})$$

$$\therefore \frac{a \cdot p_2^{a-1}}{p_1^a} - \frac{ap_3^a}{p_2^{a+1}} = 0$$

$$\therefore \frac{p_2^{a-1}}{p_1^a} = \frac{p_3^a}{p_2^{a+1}}$$

$$p_2^{(a-1+a+1)} = p_1^a \, p_3^a$$

$$p_2^{2a} = p_1^a \cdot p_3^a$$

$$p_2^2 = p_1 \cdot p_3$$

$$\therefore p_2 = \sqrt{p_1 \cdot p_3}$$

or $\qquad \dfrac{p_2}{p_1} = \dfrac{p_3}{p_2} \qquad \ldots (6.20)$

Above relation shows that for minimum work required or for maximum efficiency, the intermediate pressure is the geometric mean of initial and final pressure ($p_2^2 = p_1 p_3$) or pressure ratio in each stage is same $\left(\dfrac{p_2}{p_1} = \dfrac{p_3}{p_2}\right)$.

6.16.1 Work Done

Now, substituting $\dfrac{p_3}{p_2} = \dfrac{p_2}{p_1}$ in equation (6.18), we have minimum work required for two-stage reciprocating air compressor.

$$W = \frac{n}{n-1} p_1 V_1 \left[\left(\frac{p_2}{p_1}\right)^{\frac{n-1}{n}} + \left(\frac{p_2}{p_1}\right)^{\frac{n-1}{n}} - 2\right]$$

$$= \frac{n}{n-1} p_1 V_1 \left[2 \cdot \left(\frac{p_2}{p_1}\right)^{\frac{n-1}{n}} - 2 \right]$$

$$= 2 \times \frac{n}{n-1} p_1 V_1 \left[\left(\frac{p_2}{p_1}\right)^{\frac{n-1}{n}} - 1 \right]$$

$= 2 \times$ Work required for each stage

and minimum work required for X-stage compressor,

$$W = X \cdot \frac{n}{n-1} \cdot p_1 V_1 \left[\left(\frac{p_2}{p_1}\right)^{\frac{n-1}{n}} - 1 \right] \qquad \ldots (6.21)$$

or

$$W = X \frac{n}{n-1} p_1 V_1 \left[\left(\frac{pX+1}{p_1}\right)^{\frac{n-1}{Xn}} - 1 \right] \qquad \ldots (6.21\,(a))$$

Similarly, we can write for pressure ratio,

$$\frac{p_2}{p_1} = \frac{p_3}{p_2} = \frac{p_4}{p_3} = \ldots \frac{p(X+1)}{p(X)} \qquad \ldots \text{(For X-stage compression)}$$

6.17 HEAT REJECTED PER KG OF AIR

If the air is cooled to its initial temperature ($T_3 = T_1$), all the work done is rejected to the cooling medium (partly during the compression process and the remaining after compression), and there is no change in internal energy. (i.e. $\Delta u = 0$). Then, we have,

Heat rejected per kg of air = Work done per kg of air

$Q = W$

$\therefore \qquad Q = \dfrac{n}{n-1} RT_1 \left[\left(\dfrac{p_2}{p_1}\right)^{\frac{n-1}{n}} - 1 \right] \qquad (\because m = 1 \text{ kg})$

$= \dfrac{n}{n-1} RT_1 \left[\dfrac{T_2}{T_1} - 1 \right] \qquad \left(\because \left(\dfrac{p_2}{p_1}\right)^{\frac{n-1}{n}} = \dfrac{T_2}{T_1} \right)$

$= \dfrac{n}{n-1} R (T_2 - T_1)$

$= \dfrac{n}{n-1} (c_p - c_v)(T_2 - T_1) \qquad (\because R = c_p - c_v)$

$= \left[c_p + c_v \left(\dfrac{\gamma - n}{n-1}\right) \right] (T_2 - T_1)$ per kg of air $\qquad \ldots (6.22)$

$\left[\text{Note} : \dfrac{n}{n-1}(c_p - c_v) = c_p + c_v \left(\dfrac{\gamma - n}{n-1}\right) \right]$

$Q = c_p (T_2 - T_1) + \dfrac{c_v (\gamma - n)}{n-1} (T_2 - T_1)$

Heat rejected per kg of air = Heat rejected to the coolant in the intercooler + Heat rejected to the coolant during compression process

In a single-stage compression, no cooling is done after compression, so first term will disappear.

6.18 CAPACITY CONTROL OF COMPRESSORS

Compressors are not running at their maximum rated capacity at all the time. To run them depending on demand, the controlling arrangement is required to balance demand and supply. Following are the common methods to control the compressors:

(i) Throttle Control:

Fig. 6.14 shows typical arrangement for throttle control. When the demand for high pressure air is less, pressure in the receiver increases and pushes spring loaded piston in downward direction. Thus, closes partly the suction valve and air intake is partly throttled. The reverse valve movement takes place to meet increase in demand of high pressure air.

In throttle control, fresh air flow from atmosphere to low pressure cylinder is controlled as per demand. Air taken through separate connection from receiver is used for valve movement.

(ii) Blowing Air to Atmosphere:

When the excessive pressure built up in the receiver due to decrease in demand, the air from last stage cylinder is directly blown off to the atmosphere. Fig. 6.15 shows the arrangement for blowing air directly to atmosphere. High pressure air from receiver operates the relay piston against dead weight, and opens the port at B. High pressure air flows from B to C, and pushes piston at C in downward side. This causes opening of blows off valve at D, and air from high pressure cylinder is directly released to the atmosphere instead of supplying air to receiver.

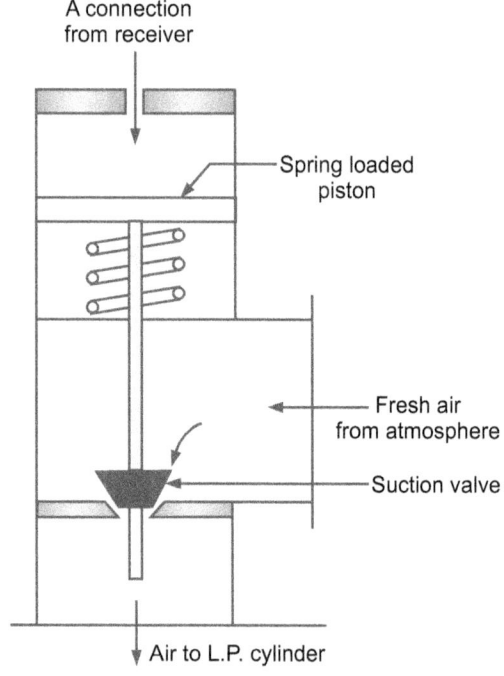

Fig. 6.14: Throttle Control Arrangement

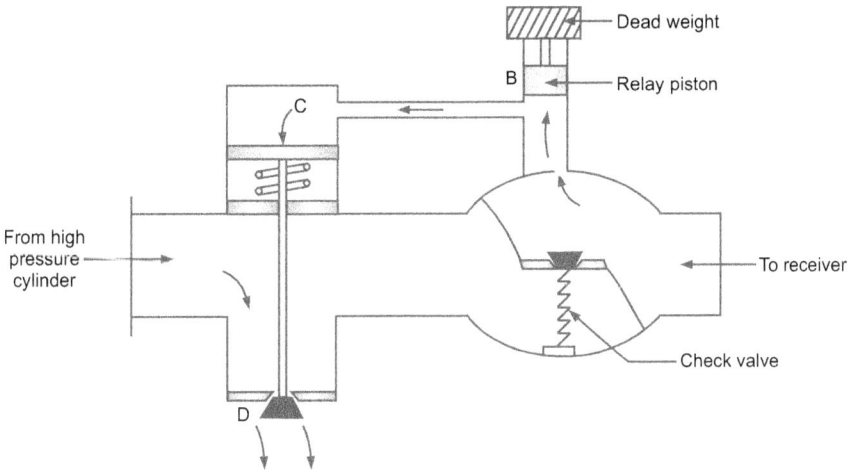

Fig. 6.15: Blowing off air to atmosphere

(iii) **Clearance Control:**

In this method, the volumetric efficiency is changed in proper proportion to control the output. This is achieved by having air pockets (clearance pocket) adjacent to the cylinder which is brought into communication with the cylinder by automatically operated valves.

6.19 DIFFERENCE BETWEEN INTERCOOLER AND AFTERCOOLER

Intercooler	Aftercooler
1. The cooler which is placed in between stages is called as intercooler. L.P Cylinder → Inter-cooler → H.P. Cylinder	1. The cooler fitted between last stage and receiver is called as aftercooler. H.P. Cylinder → After-cooler → Receiver
2. It reduces work done required for compression in next stage.	2. Aftercooler reduces size of the receiver and not the work done.

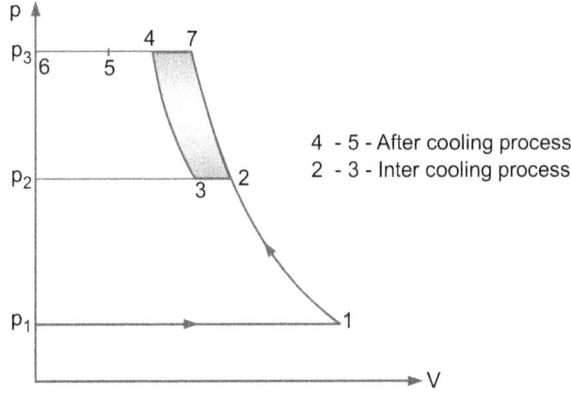

4 - 5 - After cooling process
2 - 3 - Inter cooling process

Fig. 6.16: Intercooling and Aftercooling on p-V Diagram

6.20 THEORETICAL AND ACTUAL p-V (INDICATOR) DIAGRAM FOR TWO-STAGE COMPRESSORS

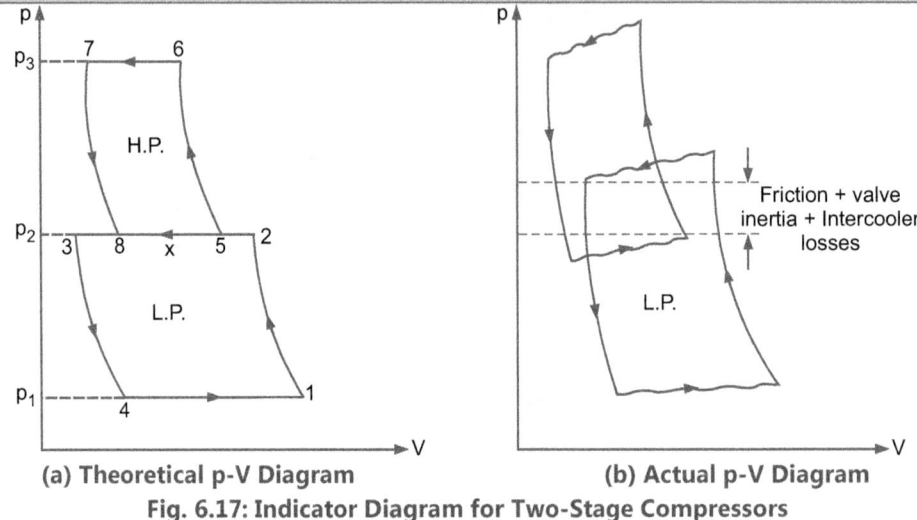

(a) Theoretical p-V Diagram   (b) Actual p-V Diagram

Fig. 6.17: Indicator Diagram for Two-Stage Compressors

6.21 CYLINDER DIMENSIONS OF MULTISTAGE COMPRESSORS FOR PERFECT INTERCOOLING

$V_{s1} \cdot \eta_{V_1} \cdot p_1 = V_{s2} \cdot \eta_{V_s} \cdot p_2 = V_{s3} \cdot p_3 = \ldots\ldots$

η_v, V_s = Volumetric efficiency and stroke volume respectively.

6.22 ADVANTAGES OF MULTISTAGE COMPRESSORS

The advantages of multistage compressor with intercooling between stages are listed below:
1. The work done per kg of air is reduced by using an intercooler between two stages compared with single-stage compressor for the same delivery pressure.
2. Low pressure and temperature range in each stage results in
   (a) Reduced losses due to air leakage.
   (b) Effective lubrication due to lower temperature range.
   (c) The low pressure cylinder is designed to withstand low pressure and high pressure cylinder is designed for high pressure. This reduces cost of the compressor.
   (d) Improved volumetric efficiency.
3. Multistage machines have better mechanical balance, gives smooth torque diagram.

Disadvantages:

A multistage compressor with intercooler is more costly in initial cost than a single-stage compressor of the same capacity.

SOLVED PROBLEMS ON MULTISTAGE COMPRESSORS

Problem 6.6:

A single-acting, two-stage air compressor with perfect intercooling delivers 15 kg/min of air at 25 bar pressure. The air from atmosphere is sucked in compressor at 1 bar and 15°C. The compression follows the law $pV^{1.25} = C$. Calculate:

(i) Indicated power
(ii) F.A.D.
(iii) The isothermal efficiency.

Solution: Given: $X = 2$ (two stages), $n = 1.25$, $m = 15$ kg/min, $p_3 = 25$ bar, $p_1 = 1$ bar, $T_1 = 15°C = 15 + 273 = 288$ K, $n = 1.25$.

For perfect intercooling,

Intermediate pressure, $p_2 = \sqrt{p_1 \times p_3} = \sqrt{1 \times 25} = 5$ bar

(i) Indicated power:

$$I.P. = X \cdot \frac{n}{n-1} \cdot mRT_1 \left[\left(\frac{p_2}{p_1}\right)^{\frac{n-1}{n}} - 1 \right]$$

$$= 2 \times \frac{1.125}{0.25} \times \frac{15}{60} \times 287 \times 288 \times \left[\left(\frac{5}{1}\right)^{\frac{0.25}{1.25}} - 1 \right]$$

$$= 78467.34 \text{ kW}$$

$$= \mathbf{78.467 \text{ kW}}$$

(ii) Isothermal efficiency:

$$\text{Isothermal power} = mRT_1 \ln\left(\frac{p_3}{p_1}\right)$$

$$= \frac{15}{60} \times 287 \times 288 \times \ln\left(\frac{25}{1}\right)$$

$$= 66514.85 \text{ W}$$

$$= \mathbf{66.515 \text{ kW}}$$

$$\eta_{iso} = \frac{\text{Isothermal power}}{\text{Indicated power}}$$

$$= \frac{66.515}{78.467} = 0.8476$$

$$= \mathbf{84.76\%}$$

(iii) Free Air Delivered (F.A.D.):

$$p_1 V_1 = mRT_1$$

$$1 \times 10^5 \times V_1 = 15 \times 287 \times 288$$

Free air delivered,
$$V_1 = \frac{15 \times 287 \times 288}{1 \times 10^5}$$
$$= 12.398 \text{ m}^3/\text{min}$$

Problem 6.7:

A two-stage, single-acting reciprocating air compressor draws in air at 1 bar and 300 K. The delivery pressure is 12 bar. The intermediate pressure is ideal for minimum work and the intercooling is perfect. The index of compression is 1.3. Flow rate of air through the compressor is 0.15 kg/sec. Determine:

  (i) Power required to drive the compressor,
  (ii) Saving in power compared to single stage,
  (iii) Isothermal efficiency for multistage and single stage,
  (iv) Heat rejected in intercooler if c_p = 1 kJ/kg·K and R = 0.287 kJ/kg·K.

Solution: Given: X = 2 (two stages), p_1 = 1 bar, T_1 = 300 K, p_3 = 12 bar, n = 1.3, m = 0.15 kg/sec, c_p = 1 kJ/kg·K, R = 0.287 kJ/kg·K.

For minimum work and perfect intercooling,

Intermediate pressure, $p_2 = \sqrt{p_1 \times p_3} = \sqrt{1 \times 12}$ = 3.4641 bar

(i) Power required to drive the compressor (multistage):

$$\text{Indicated power} = X \frac{n}{n-1} mRT_1 \left[\left(\frac{p_2}{p_1}\right)^{\frac{n-1}{n}} - 1\right]$$

$$= 2 \times \frac{1.3}{0.3} \times 0.15 \times 0.287 \times 300 \times \left[\left(\frac{3.4641}{1}\right)^{\frac{0.3}{1.3}} - 1\right]$$

$$= 37.166 \text{ kW}$$

(ii) Saving in power compared to single stage:

$$\text{I.P. (single stage)} = \frac{n}{n-1} mRT_1 \left[\left(\frac{p_3}{p_1}\right)^{\frac{0.3}{1.3}} - 1\right]$$

$$= \frac{1.3}{0.3} \times 0.15 \times 0.287 \times 300 \times \left[\left(\frac{12}{1}\right)^{\frac{0.3}{1.3}} - 1\right]$$

$$= 43.34 \text{ kW}$$

Power saving = I.P. (single stage) − I.P. (multistage)
= 43.34 − 37.166
= **6.17 kW**

(iii) Isothermal efficiency:

$$\text{Isothermal power} = mRT_1 \ln\left(\frac{p_3}{p_1}\right)$$

$$= 0.15 \times 0.287 \times 300 \times \ln\left(\frac{12}{1}\right)$$

$$= \mathbf{32.09 \text{ kW}}$$

For multistage,

$$\eta_{iso} = \frac{\text{Isothermal power}}{\text{Indicated power}}$$

$$= \frac{32.09}{37.166} = \mathbf{0.8635}$$

$$= \mathbf{86.35\% \text{ (multistage)}}$$

$$\eta_{iso} = \frac{32.09}{43.34} = 0.7404$$

$$= \mathbf{74.04\% \text{ (single stage)}}$$

(iv) Heat rejected in intercooler:

Temperature after first stage,

$$T_2 = T_1 \left(\frac{p_2}{p_1}\right)^{\frac{n-1}{n}} = 300 \times \left(\frac{3.4641}{1}\right)^{\frac{0.3}{1.3}} = 399.62 \text{ K}$$

Heat rejected in intercooler,

$$Q = mc_p (T_2 - T_1) = 0.15 \times 1 \times (399.62 - 300)$$

$$= \mathbf{14.94 \text{ kJ/sec}}$$

Problem 6.8:

A four stage compressor works between limits of 1 bar and 115 bar. The index of compression in each stage is 1.28. The temperature at the start of compression in each stage is 35°C and intermediate pressure are so chosen that the work is divided equally amongst stages. Neglecting clearance, calculate:
  (i)   Pressures p_2, p_3 and p_4.
  (ii) Isothermal efficiency.
  (iii) Delivery temperature in each stage.

Solution: Given: X = 4, p_1 = 1 bar, p_5 = 115 bar, n = 1.28, T_1 = 35°C = 35 + 273 = 308 K.

Here, inlet temperature for each stage is 35°C, so cooling is perfect cooling.

(i) Pressures p_2, p_3 and p_4:

For perfect intercooling,

$$\frac{p_2}{p_1} = \frac{p_3}{p_2} = \frac{p_4}{p_3} = \frac{p_5}{p_4} = k$$

$$p_2 = kp_1$$

$$p_3 = kp_2 = k^2 p_1$$

Similarly,
$$p_5 = k^4 p_1$$
$$\therefore \quad 115 = k^4 \times 1$$
$$\therefore \quad k = 3.27$$
$p_2 = 3.27$ bar, $p_3 = 10.69$ bar, $p_4 = 34.96$ bar.

(ii) Isothermal efficiency:
Indicated power,
$$I.P. = X \cdot \frac{n}{n-1} mRT_1 \left[\left(\frac{p_2}{p_1}\right)^{\frac{n-1}{n}} - 1 \right]$$
$$= 4 \times \frac{1.28}{0.28} \times 1 \times 0.287 \times 308 \times \left[\left(\frac{3.27}{1}\right)^{\frac{0.28}{1.28}} - 1 \right]$$
$$= 478.22 \text{ kJ/kg}$$

Isothermal power $= mRT_1 \ln\left(\frac{p_5}{p_1}\right)$
$$= 1 \times 0.287 \times 308 \times \ln\left(\frac{115}{1}\right)$$
$$= 419.43 \text{ kJ/kg}$$

Isothermal efficiency,
$$\eta_{iso} = \frac{\text{Isothermal power}}{\text{Indicated power}} = \frac{419.43}{478.22} = 0.877$$
$$= 87.7\%$$

(**Note:** Here mass flow rate is considered as 1 kg/sec and indicated power and isothermal power are calculated. If mass is taken as 1 kg then, we get, work done per cycle. Ratio of work done will give same isothermal efficiency.)

(iii) Delivery temperature in each stage:
Temperature at suction and work done for each stage is equal, so delivery temperature in each stage is same. It is given by,
$$\frac{T_2}{T_1} = \left(\frac{p_2}{p_1}\right)^{\frac{n-1}{n}}$$
$$\therefore \quad T_2 = \left(\frac{3.27}{1}\right)^{\frac{0.28}{1.28}} \times 308$$
$$= 399.2 \text{ K}$$

Problem 6.9:
A two-stage compressor running at 210 r.p.m. delivers free air at 2.2 m³/min. The pressure and temperature of air at the suction are 1 bar and 298 K respectively. The delivery pressure is 55 bar. Clearance for both the cylinders is 5% of the stroke. Strokes of both cylinders are equal to the diameter of the L.P. cylinder. The index of compression and re-expansion is 1.3.

Determine:
   (i) Minimum power required to run the compressor when intercooling is perfect,
   (ii) Stroke and diameters of cylinders,
   (iii) Ratio of cylinder volumes.

Solution: Given: $X = 2$, F.A.D. (V_1) = 2.2 m³/min, N = 210 r.p.m., p_1 = 1 bar, T_1 = 298 K, p_3 = 55 bar, C = 0.5% = 0.05, n = 1.3, $L_{L.P.} = L_{H.P.} = D_{L.P.}$

$$p_1 V_1 = mRT_1$$
$$1 \times 10^5 \times 2.2 = m \times 287 \times 298$$
$$\therefore \quad m = 2.57 \text{ kg/min}$$

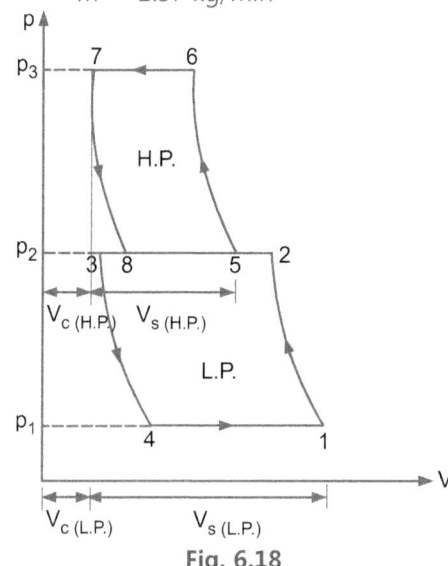

Fig. 6.18

For perfect intercooling,
Intermediate pressure,
$$p_2 = \sqrt{p_1 \times p_3} = \sqrt{1 \times 55} = 7.42 \text{ bar}$$

(i) **Minimum power required to run the compressor:**

$$\text{I.P.} = X \cdot \frac{n}{n-1} mRT_1 \left[\left(\frac{p_2}{p_1}\right)^{\frac{n-1}{n}} - 1 \right]$$

$$= 2 \times \frac{1.3}{0.3} \times \frac{2.57}{60} \times 0.287 \times 298 \times \left[\left(\frac{7.42}{1}\right)^{\frac{0.3}{1.3}} - 1 \right]$$

$$= \mathbf{18.67 \text{ kW}}$$

(ii) **Stroke and diameters of cylinders:**
The volumetric efficiency of L.P. cylinder is given by,

$$\eta_{vol\,(L.P.)} = 1 + C - C \left(\frac{p_2}{p_1}\right)^{\frac{1}{n}}$$

APPLIED THERMODYNAMICS — POSITIVE DISPLACEMENT COMPRESSOR

$$= 1 + 0.05 - 0.05 \left(\frac{7.42}{1}\right)^{\frac{1}{1.3}}$$

$$= 0.8164$$

$$= \mathbf{81.64\%}$$

Also, volumetric efficiency is given by,

$$\eta_{vol\,(L.P.)} = \frac{V_{a\,(L.P.)}}{V_{s\,(L.P.)}}$$

$$V_{s\,(L.P.)} = \frac{2.2}{0.8164} = \mathbf{2.6947\ m^3/min}$$

$$V_{s\,(L.P.)} = \frac{2.6947}{N} = \frac{2.6947}{210} = \mathbf{0.0128\ m^3}$$

$$V_{s\,(L.P.)} = \frac{\pi}{4} D_{L.P.}^2\, L_{L.P.} \qquad (\because L_{L.P.} = D_{L.P.})$$

$$= \frac{\pi}{4} D_{L.P.}^3$$

$$\therefore \quad D_{L.P.}^3 = V_{s\,(L.P.)} \times \frac{4}{\pi}$$

$$= 0.0128 \times \frac{4}{\pi}$$

$$\therefore \quad D_{L.P.} = 0.2538\ m = \mathbf{25.38\ cm}$$

$$L_{L.P.} = 0.2538\ m = \mathbf{25.38\ cm}$$

The volumetric efficiency of both cylinders is same because $\dfrac{p_2}{p_1} = \dfrac{p_3}{p_2}$ and clearance is same.

$$\eta_{vol\,(L.P.)} = \eta_{vol\,(H.P.)}$$

$$\therefore \quad D_{L.P.}^2\, p_1 = D_{H.P.}^2 \cdot p_2$$

$$\therefore \quad D_{H.P.}^2 = \frac{D_{L.P.}^2 \cdot p_1}{p_2}$$

$$= \frac{0.2538^2 \times 1}{7.42}$$

$$D_{H.P.} = 0.0932\ m = \mathbf{9.32\ cm}$$

(iii) Ratio of cylinder volumes:

Points 1 and 5 are on isothermal line, we have,

$$p_1 V_1 = p_5 V_5 \qquad (\because V_1\ \text{and}\ V_5\ \text{cylinder volumes of L.P. and H.P.})$$

$$\therefore \quad \frac{V_1}{V_5} = \frac{p_5}{p_1} = \frac{7.42}{1} = \mathbf{7.42}$$

Problem 6.10:

A single-acting, two-stage compressor with complete intercooling delivers 6 kg/min of air at 16 bar. Intake air conditions are 1 bar and 15°C. Compression and expansion follows law $pV^{1.3} = C$.

Calculate:
  (i) Power required to run the compressor at 420 r.p.m.,
  (ii) Isothermal efficiency,
  (iii) Free air delivered per second,
  (iv) Swept volume for each cylinder if volumetric efficiency of both cylinders is 90%,
  (v) Net heat transferred in L.P. and H.P. cylinders during compression and also in intercooler.

Assume R = 0.287 kJ/kg·K, C_v = 0.71 kg/kg·K.

Solution: Given: X = 2, m = 6 kg/min, p_3 = 16 bar, p_1 = 1 bar, T_1 = 15°C = 15 + 273 = 288 K, n = 1.3, N = 420 r.p.m., η_{vol} = 90%, R = 0.287 kJ/kg·K, c_v = 0.71 kJ/kg·K

Intermediate pressure, $p_2 = \sqrt{p_1 \cdot p_3}$
$= \sqrt{1 \times 16} = 4$ bar.

(i) Power required to run the compressor:

$$\text{Indicated power} = X \cdot \frac{n}{n-1} mRT_1 \left[\left(\frac{p_2}{p_1}\right)^{\frac{n-1}{n}} - 1 \right]$$

$$= 2 \times \frac{1.3}{0.3} \times \frac{6}{60} \times 0.287 \times 288 \times \left[\left(\frac{4}{1}\right)^{\frac{0.3}{1.3}} - 1 \right]$$

$$= \mathbf{27\ kW}$$

(ii) Isothermal efficiency:

$$\text{Isothermal power} = mRT_1 \ln\left(\frac{p_3}{p_1}\right)$$

$$= \frac{6}{60} \times 0.287 \times 288 \times \ln\left(\frac{16}{1}\right)$$

$$= 22.92\ kW$$

$$\text{Isothermal efficiency, } \eta_{iso} = \frac{\text{Isothermal power}}{\text{Indicated power}} = \frac{22.92}{27} = 0.8489$$

$$= \mathbf{84.89\%}$$

(iii) Free air delivered:

$$p_1 V_1 = mRT_1$$

$$V_1 = \frac{6}{60} \times \frac{287 \times 288}{1 \times 10^5}$$

$$= \mathbf{0.08265\ m^3/sec}$$

(iv) Swept volume:

$$\text{Swept volume}_{(L.P.)} = \frac{F.A.D}{N \times \eta_{vol}}$$

$$= \frac{0.08265}{\frac{420}{60} \times 0.90}$$

$$= 0.01312 \text{ m}^3$$

But,
$$V_{s\,(L.P.)} \cdot \eta_{vol\,(L.P.)} \cdot p_1 = V_{s\,(H.P.)} \cdot \eta_{vol\,(H.P.)} \cdot p_2$$
$$\eta_{vol\,(H.P.)} = \eta_{vol.\,(H.P.)}$$

∴
$$\text{Swept volume}_{(H.P.)} = \frac{V_{s\,(L.P.)} \times p_1}{p_2}$$

$$= \frac{0.01312 \times 1}{4}$$

$$= \mathbf{0.00328 \text{ m}^3}$$

(v) Heat transferred:

Temperature T_2 is given by,

$$\frac{T_2}{T_1} = \left(\frac{p_2}{p_1}\right)^{\frac{n-1}{n}}$$

∴
$$T_2 = \left(\frac{4}{1}\right)^{\frac{0.3}{1.3}} \times 288 = 396.58 \text{ K}$$

and
$$c_p = c_v + R = 0.71 + 0.287 = 0.997 \text{ kg/kg·K}$$

alsom
$$\gamma = \frac{c_p}{c_v} = \frac{0.997}{0.71} = 1.404$$

Heat transferred in L.P. cylinder

$$= m \cdot c_v \frac{\gamma - n}{n - 1}(T_2 - T_1)$$

$$= \frac{6}{60} \times 0.71 \times \frac{1.404 - 1.3}{1.3 - 1} \times (396.58 - 288)$$

$$= \mathbf{2.6725 \text{ kJ/sec}}$$

Heat transferred in H.P. cylinder
$$= \text{Heat transferred in L.P. cylinder}$$
$$= \mathbf{2.6725 \text{ kJ/sec}}$$

Heat transferred in intercooler $= m \cdot C_p (T_2 - T_1) = \frac{6}{60} \times 0.997 \times (396.58 - 288)$

$$= \mathbf{10.825 \text{ kJ/sec.}}$$

APPLIED THERMODYNAMICS — POSITIVE DISPLACEMENT COMPRESSOR

Problem 6.11:
A two-stage, double-acting air compressor, operating at 220 r.p.m. takes in air at 1.0 bar and 27°C. The size of the L.P. cylinder is 360 × 400 mm. The stroke of H.P. cylinder is the same as that of L.P. cylinder and the clearance of both the cylinders is 4%. The L.P. cylinder discharges the air at a pressure of 4.0 bar. The air passes through the intercooler so that it enters the H.P. cylinder at 27°C and 3.8 bar, finally it is discharged from the compressor at 15.2 bar. The value of n in both the cylinders is 1.3, c_p = 1.0035 kJ/kg·K and R = 0.287 kJ/kg·K.
Calculate:
  (i)   Heat rejected in the intercooler,
  (ii) Diameter of H.P. cylinder,
  (iii) Power required to drive the H.P. cylinder.

Solution: Given: X = 2, Double acting, N = 220 r.p.m., p_1 = 1 bar, T_1 = 27°C, $D_{L.P.}$ = 360 mm = 0.36 m, $L_{L.P.}$ = 0.4 m, $L_{H.P.}$ = 0.4 m, p_2 = 4.0 bar, C = 0.04, p_5 = 3.8 bar, T_5 = 27°C = 27 + 273 = 300 K, p_7 = 15.2 bar, n = 1.3, c_p = 1.0035 kJ/kg·K, R = 0.287 kJ/kg·K.

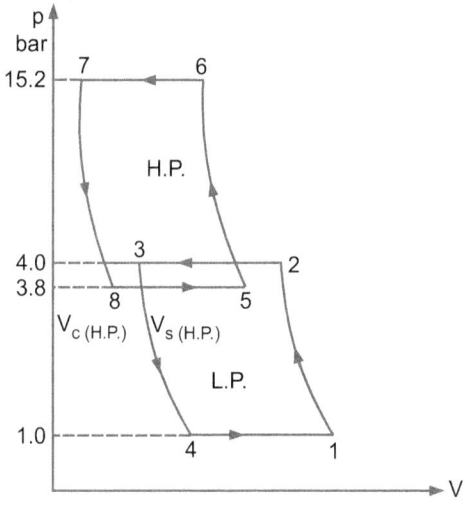

Fig. 6.19

Swept volume of L.P. cylinder = $\dfrac{\pi}{4} D_{L.P.}^2 \times L_{L.P.} = \dfrac{\pi}{4} \times 0.36^2 \times 0.4$

$$= 0.04071 \text{ m}^3$$

Volumetric efficiency of L.P. cylinder,

$$\eta_{vol\,(L.P.)} = 1 + C - C\left(\dfrac{p_2}{p_1}\right)^{\frac{1}{n}} = 1 + 0.04 - 0.04 \times \left(\dfrac{4}{1}\right)^{\frac{1}{1.3}}$$

$$= 0.9238 = 92.38\%$$

Chp 6 | 6.39

Also, $\eta_{vol\,(L.P.)} = \dfrac{V_1}{V_s}$

∴ $V_1 = V_s \cdot \eta_{vol\,(L.P.)} = 0.04071 \times 0.9238$

$= 0.03761 \text{ m}^3$

$V_1/\text{min} = V_1 \times 2 \times 220$ (2 for double acting)

$= 16.54 \text{ m}^3/\text{min}$

Also, $p_1 V_1 = mRT_1$

$m = \dfrac{p_1 V_1}{RT}$

$= \dfrac{1 \times 10^5 \times 16.54}{287 \times 300}$

$= 19.22 \text{ kg/min}$

(i) Heat rejected in the intercooler:

$$\dfrac{T_1}{T_2} = \left(\dfrac{p_2}{p_1}\right)^{\frac{n-1}{n}}$$

∴ $T_2 = T_1 \times \left(\dfrac{p_2}{p_1}\right)^{\frac{n-1}{n}} = 300 \times \left(\dfrac{4}{1}\right)^{\frac{0.3}{1.3}} = 413 \text{ K}$

$Q_{intercooler} = m\, c_p\, (T_2 - T_5) = \dfrac{19.22}{60} \times 1.0035 \times (413 - 300)$

$= 36.37 \text{ kJ/sec}$

(ii) Diameter of H.P. cylinder:

Volume of air drawn in H.P. cylinder per minute,

$V_{5\,(H.P.)}/\text{min} = \dfrac{mRT_5}{p_5} = \dfrac{19.22 \times 287 \times 300}{3.8 \times 10^5}$

$= 4.355 \text{ m}^3/\text{min}$

$\dfrac{p_2}{p_1} = 4,\quad \dfrac{p_6}{p_5} = \dfrac{15.2}{3.8} = 4$

i.e. $\dfrac{p_2}{p_1} = \dfrac{p_6}{p_5}$

and $C_{L.P.} = C_{H.P.} = 0.4$

∴ $\eta_{vol\ (H.P.)} = \eta_{vol\ (H.P.)} = 0.9238 = 92.38\%$

∴ $V_{5\ (H.P.)} = \dfrac{V_5}{\eta_{vol\ (H.P.)}} =$ **0.0107 m³**

$$V_{5\ (H.P.)} = \dfrac{\pi}{4} D_{H.P.}^2 \times L_{H.P.}$$

$$0.0107 = \dfrac{\pi}{4} \times D_{H.P.}^2 \times 0.4$$

$$D_{H.P.} = 0.1847 \text{ m}$$

$$= \textbf{18.47 cm}$$

(iii) Power required to drive the H.P. cylinder:

$T_6 = T_2$ and $T_5 = T_1$

∴ Power required to drive the H.P. cylinder,

$$= \dfrac{n}{n-1} mR (T_6 - T_5)$$

$$= \dfrac{1.3}{0.3} \times \dfrac{19.12}{60} \times 0.287 \times (413 - 300)$$

$$= \textbf{45 kW}$$

6.23 ROOTS BLOWER COMPRESSORS

- A roots blower compressor consists of two lobe rotors in an air-tight casing as shown in Fig. 6.20. For higher pressure ratio, three or four versions are used.
- The lobes of rotor are of involute, epicycloid or hypocycloid profile to ensure correct meeting.

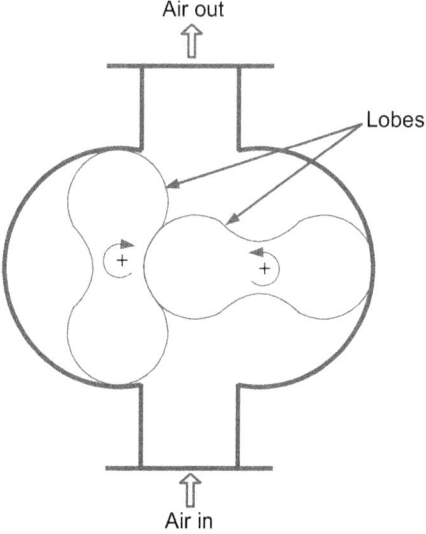

Fig. 6.20: Roots Blower Compressor

- One of the rotors is connected to the drive and the second rotor is gear driven from the first.
- As the rotors rotate, the air at atmospheric pressure, is trapped in pockets formed between the lobes and casing.
- The rotary motion of the lobe delivers the entrapped air to the receiver.
- Thus, more and more flow of air into the receiver increases its pressure.
- Finally the air at higher pressure is delivered from the receiver.
- When the rotating lobe uncovers the outlet port, some air from the receiver flows back into the compressor pocket. This is termed as backflow process. The back flow air is mixed with entrapped air in the pocket. The back flow stops when pressure in the pocket and receiver becomes equal. Thus the pressure of the air entrapped in the pocket is increased at constant volume entirely by the back flow of the air.
- There is clearance between casings and lobes to reduce wear. But this clearance causes leakage. This leakage affects efficiency of compressors with increase in pressure ratio.

The p-V diagram for roots blower is shown in Fig. 6.21.

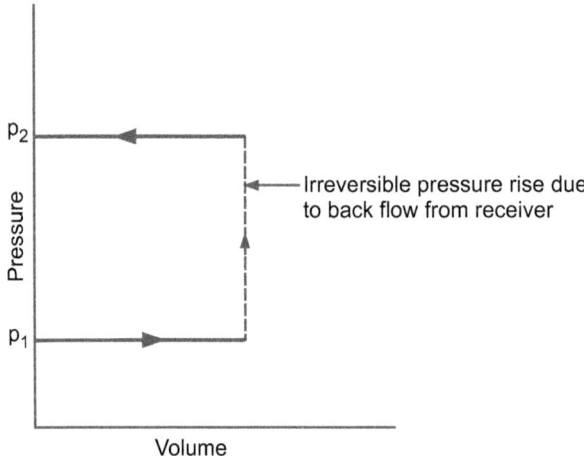

Fig. 6.21: p-V Diagram for Roots Blower Compressor

Let, p_1, p_2 = Intake and discharge pressure of air

γ = Isentropic index for air, and

V_1 = Volume of compressed air

Theoretical work done in compressing air is,

$$W_t = \frac{\gamma}{\gamma - 1} \times p_1 V_1 \left[\left(\frac{p_2}{p_1}\right)^{\frac{\gamma - 1}{\gamma}} - 1 \right]$$

and actual work done, $W_a = V_1 (p_2 - p_1)$

Efficiency of roots blower is given by,

$$\eta = \frac{W_t}{W_a}$$

$$\eta = \frac{\frac{\gamma}{\gamma-1} \times p_1 V_1 \left[\left(\frac{p_2}{p_1}\right)^{\frac{\gamma-1}{\gamma}} - 1\right]}{V_1 (p_2 - p_1)}$$

$$= \frac{\gamma}{\gamma-1} \times \frac{\left[(r)^{\frac{\gamma-1}{\gamma}} - 1\right]}{(r-1)} \qquad \text{where, } r = p_2/p_1 \text{ pressure ratio}$$

Also, $\quad \dfrac{\gamma}{\gamma-1} = \dfrac{c_p}{R}$

$$\therefore \quad \eta = \frac{c_p}{R} \times \frac{\left[(r)^{\frac{\gamma-1}{\gamma}} - 1\right]}{(r-1)}$$

From above equation it can be seen that efficiency of roots blower decreases with increase in pressure ratio. For high pressure, two or more roots blowers are arranged in series and intercoolers are used at each stage.

This compressor has number of demerits but it is suitable for scavenging and supercharging of internal combustion engines.

6.24 VANE BLOWER COMPRESSORS

- A vane blower compressor consists of a rotor mounted eccentrically in an air-tight casing as shown in Fig. 6.22.

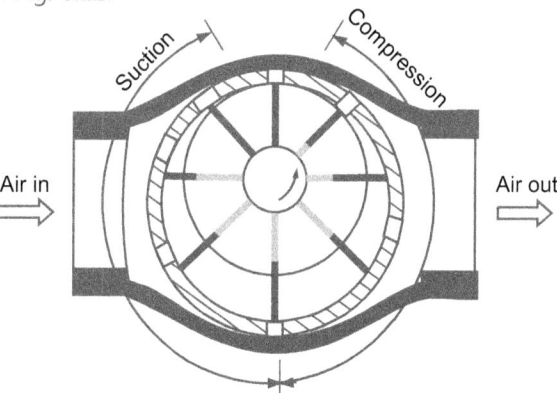

Fig. 6.22: Vane Blower Compressor

- The rotor has number of slots containing vanes.
- When the rotor rotates vanes are pressed against the casing and forms air-tight passage. The air is trapped in the passage formed between the vanes and the casing.

- When the rotating vanes uncover the exist port, some air under high pressure flows back into the passage. The backflow air mixed with entrapped air in this passage.
- The back flow stops when pressure in the passage and receiver becomes equal.
- Thus, the pressure of the air entrapped in the pocket is increased first by decreasing the volume and then by the back flow of the air. The p-V diagram for vane blower is shown in Fig. 6.23.

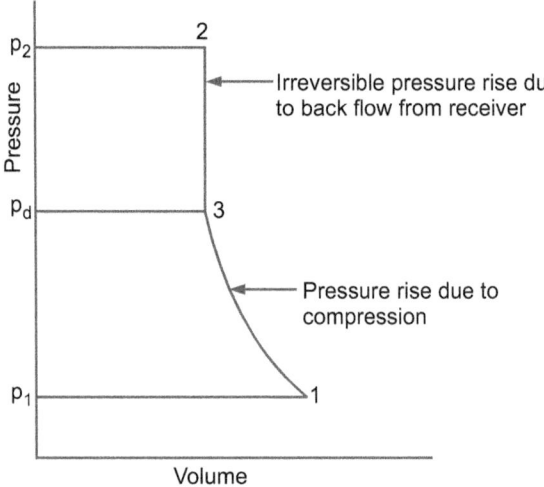

Fig. 6.23: p-V diagram of Vane Blower Compressor

Theoretical work done due to compression (1-3)

$$W_1 = \frac{\gamma}{\gamma - 1} \times p_1 V_1 \left[\left(\frac{p_2}{p_1}\right)^{\frac{\gamma-1}{\gamma}} - 1 \right]$$

and actual work done due to backflow (3-2)

$$W_2 = V_2 (p_2 - p_d)$$

Total work done, $W = W_1 + W_2$

Efficiency of roots blower is given by,

$$\eta = \frac{W_2}{W_1 + W_2}$$

6.25 ROTARY SCREW COMPRESSORS

- Rotary screw compressors consist of two rotors within a casing where the rotors compress the air internally. There are no valves. These units are basically oil cooled (with air cooled or water cooled oil coolers) where the oil seals the internal clearances.
- Since the cooling takes place right inside the compressor, the working parts never experience extreme operating temperatures. The rotary compressor, therefore, is a continuous duty, air cooled or water cooled compressor package.

- Rotary screw air compressors are easy to maintain and operate. Capacity control for these compressors is accomplished by variable speed and variable compressor displacement.
- For the latter control technique, a slide valve is positioned in the casing. As the compressor capacity is reduced, the slide valve opens, bypassing a portion of the compressed air back to the suction. Advantages of the rotary screw compressor include smooth, pulse-free air output in a compact size with high output volume over a long life.
- The oil-free rotary screw air compressor utilizes specially designed air ends to compress air without oil in the compression chamber yielding true oil-free air. Oil-free rotary screw air compressors may be air cooled and water cooled and provides the same flexibility as oil flooded rotaries when oil-free air is required.

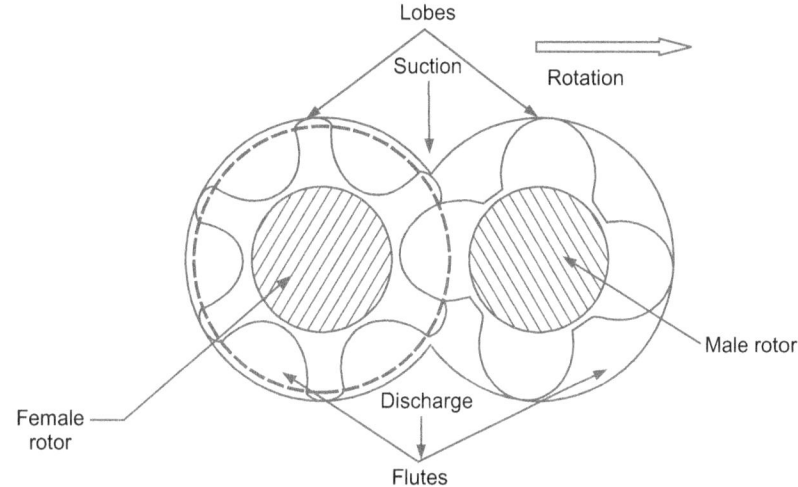

Fig. 6.24: Rotary Screw Compressor

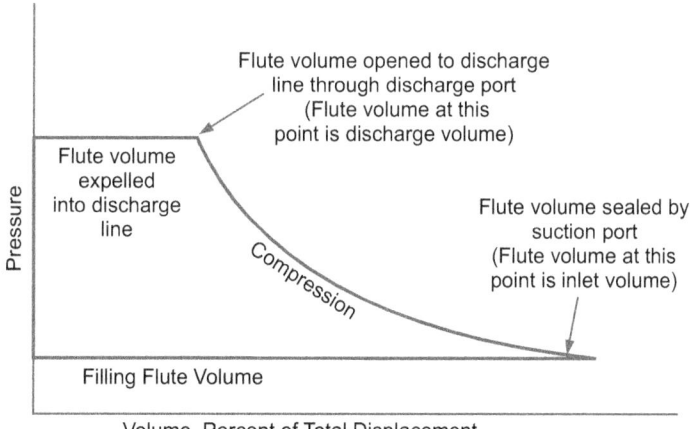

Fig. 6.25: p-V Diagram of Rotary Screw Compressor

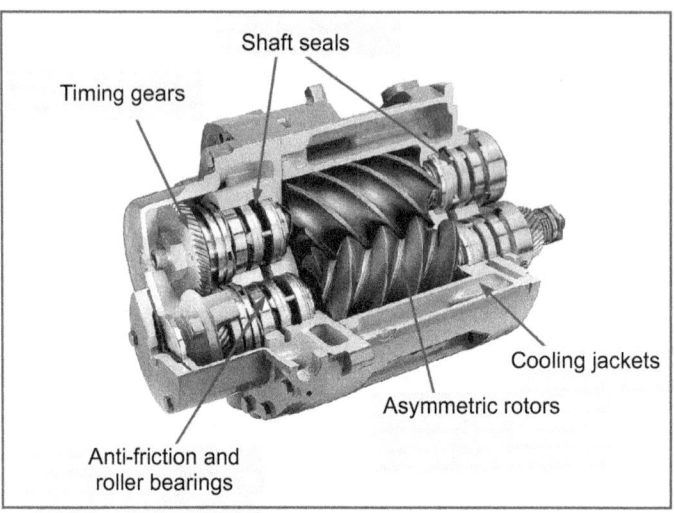

Fig. 6.26: Rotary Screw Compressor

A rotary screw compressor has no clearance, so there is no clearance expansion at the end of the discharge event. Theoretically, a rotary screw compressor would have 100% volumetric efficiency, but there is not a gas-tight seal between the rotors and between the rotors and the housing. This causes leakage between flutes and lowers the volumetric efficiency. Leakage is a function of compressor tip speed and pressure difference, and will decrease the inlet volume to about 90% of displacement.

SOLVED PROBLEMS

Problem 6.12: A roots blower compressor compresses 0.08 m³ of air from 1.0 bar to 1.5 bar per revolution. Determine the compressor efficiency.

Solution: Given : $V_1 = 0.08$ m³, $p_1 = 1.0$ bar, $p_2 = 1.5$ bar

We know theoretical work done in compressing air is,

$$W_t = \frac{\gamma}{\gamma - 1} \times p_1 V_1 \left[\left(\frac{p_2}{p_1}\right)^{\frac{\gamma-1}{\gamma}} - 1\right]$$

$$= \frac{1.4}{1.4 - 1} \times 1 \times 10^5 \times 0.08 \times \left[\left(\frac{1.5}{1.0}\right)^{\frac{1.4-1}{1.4}} - 1\right]$$

$$= \mathbf{3438.89 \text{ N-m}}$$

and actual work done

$$W_a = V_1 (p_2 - p_1)$$

$$= 0.08 \times (1.5 \times 10^{-5}) = \mathbf{4000 \text{ N-m}}$$

Efficiency of roots blower is given by,

$$\eta = \frac{W_t}{W_a} = \frac{3438.89}{4000.00} \times 100$$

$$= \mathbf{85.97\%}$$

Problem 6.13: A roots blower and a vane compressor having same induced volume of 0.03 m³ per revolution. The inlet and outlet pressures are 1.013 bar and 1.52 bar respectively. For vane type compressor internal compression takes place through half the pressure range. Compare the work input required for these compressors.

Solution: Given : $V_1 = 0.03$ m³, $p_1 = 1.013$ bar, $p_2 = 1.52$ bar

1. Roots Blower:

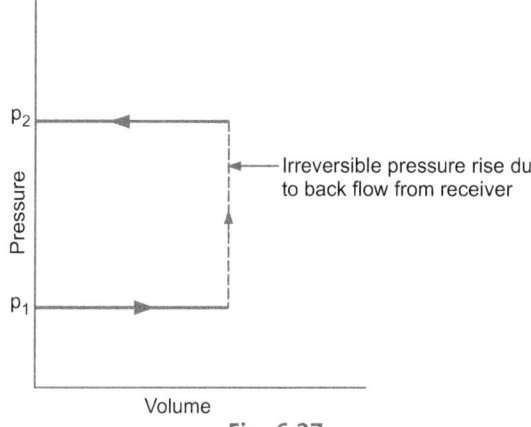

Fig. 6.27

For roots blower, actual work done

$$W_a = V_1 (p_2 - p_1)$$
$$= 0.03 \times (1.52 \times 10^5 - 1.013 \times 10^5) = \mathbf{1.52 \text{ kJ}}$$

2. Vane Blower:

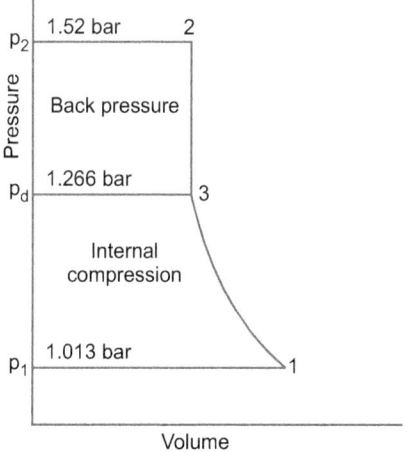

Fig. 6.28

The pressure, $$p_d = \frac{1.52 + 1.013}{2} = \mathbf{1.266 \text{ bar}}$$

Theoretical work done due to compression (1-3)

$$W_t = \frac{\gamma}{\gamma - 1} \times p_1 V_1 \left[\left(\frac{p_d}{p_1}\right)^{\frac{\gamma-1}{\gamma}} - 1 \right]$$

$$= \frac{1.4}{1.4 - 1} \times 1 \times 10^5 \times 0.03 \times \left[\left(\frac{1.266}{1.013}\right)^{\frac{1.4-1}{1.4}} - 1 \right] \text{ kJ/rev}$$

$$= 0.702 \text{ kJ/rev}$$

The volume, $$V_2 = V_1 \times \left(\frac{p_1}{p_d}\right)^{1/\gamma} = 0.03 \times \left(\frac{1.013}{1.266}\right)^{1/\gamma} = 0.0256 \text{ m}^3$$

and actual work done due to back flow (3.2),

$$W_2 = V_2 (p_2 - p_d)$$
$$= 0.0256 \times (1.52 \times 10^5 - 1.266 \times 10^5) = 0.65 \text{ kJ/rev}$$

The total work done = 0.702 + 0.65
= **1.352 kJ/rev**

Comparison:

Sr. No.	Compressor type	Work input required
1.	Roots blower	1.52 kJ / rev
2.	Vane blower	1.352 kJ / rev

EXERCISE

1. Describe the working of a single-stage reciprocating air compressor.
2. Derive the expression for work in case of single acting single-stage air compressor.
3. Derive an expression for volumetric efficiency of a reciprocating air compressor in terms of clearance ratio, pressure ratio and compression index.
4. Define 'clearance ratio' in air compressor. What is its effect on work and volumetric efficiency? Also comment on effect of pressure ratio and compression index on volumetric efficiency.
5. Explain the methods to improve isothermal efficiency of an air compressor.
6. Derive expression for compression ratio to give maximum compressor efficiency
7. Explain in brief:
    (a) Isothermal efficiency
    (b) Volumetric efficiency
    (c) Mechanical efficiency
    (d) Free air delivery
    (e) Mean effective pressure

8. What are disadvantages of compressing air in single stage compressor through large ratio? Explain with the help of p-V diagram. How are they overcome in multi-staging?

9. Prove that, for multistage reciprocating air compression, the intermediate pressure, with perfect intercooling and for minimum work output, is geometric mean of its neighboring pressures.

10. Explain throttle control of compressor.

11. How actual indicator diagram for a single stage compressor differs from theoretical indicator diagram?

12. What is the difference between rotary and reciprocating compressors?

13. Derive an expression for efficiency of a roots blower in terms of pressure ratio and ratio of specific heat.

14. Derive an expression for efficiency of a vane type compressor.

15. How compressors are classified?

16. How you will differentiate compressors with blowers?

17. Explain working of following rotary compressors with neat sketches. Also draw p-V diagrams for them.
    (i) Roots blower   (ii) Vane type compressor   (iii) Rotary screw compressor

PROBLEMS FOR PRACTICE

1. A single-stage reciprocating air compressor is required to compress 60 m^3 of air from 1 bar to 8 bar at 22°C. Find work done by the compressor, if the compression of air is:
   (a) Isothermal **(Ans.** 12.5 MJ**)**
   (b) Isentropic with isentropic index as 1.4 **(Ans.** 17 MJ**)**
   (c) Polytropic with polytropic index as 1.25 **(Ans.** 15.5 MJ**)**

2. A single-stage, double acting reciprocating air compressor compress air from 1bar to 7 bar according to law $pV^{1.2}$ = C. Indicated power is 11 kW. The average piston speed is 150 m/s. L/D = 1.5. Neglecting clearance volume, determine cylinder dimensions.

   (Ans. 156 mm, 234 mm**)**

3. A single acting, single-stage reciprocating air compressor compress air from 1bar at 20°C to 5.5 bar according to law $pV^{1.2}$ = C and clearance volume is 5% of the stroke

volume. The bore and stroke of compressor are 200 mm and 300 mm respectively. Determine

    (a) Mean effective pressure   **(Ans.** 1.807 bar)

    (b) Power required to drive the compressor at 500 r. p.m.   **(Ans.** 14.19 kW)

4. A single acting, two stage reciprocating air compressor compress air from 0.1 MPa at 16°C to 0.7 MPa. The air is taken in at the rate of 0.2 m³/s. The intermediate pressure is ideal and intercooling is perfect. The compression index in both stages is 1.25 and the compressor runs at 600 r. p. m. Neglect effect of clearance.

   Determine:

- The intermediate pressure,   **(Ans.** 0.2646 MPa)
- The total volume of each cylinder,   **(Ans.** 0.02 m³, 0.0076 m³)
- The power required to drive the compressor, and   **(Ans.** 42.97 kW)
- Rate of heat rejection in the intercooler   **(Ans.** 15 kJ/s)

5. A vane compressor compresses 4.5 m³ of air per minute from 1.0 bar to 2.0 bar when running at 450 r.p.m. Find the power required to drive the compressor when :
   (i)   If there is no internal compression, and
   (ii) There is 50% increase in pressure because of internal compression.
                                                                          (Ans. (i) 7.5 kW, (ii) 6.03 kW)

6. A roots blower compressor compresses 0.06 m³ of air from 1.0 bar to 1.45 bar per revolution. Determine the compressor efficiency.   **(Ans.** 87.11%)